D1405442

Windows® XP MVP

Comcast. Net

Sclal section

m A h s plus

8d80 7967

Registration

eBay Membership

silds 8730

Confirmation Code - 55313

Windows® XP MVP

**John Barnett, Curt Simmons,
Alan Simpson and David Dalan**

WILEY

Wiley Publishing, Inc.

Windows® XP MVP

Published by
Wiley Publishing, Inc.
111 River Street
Hoboken, N.J. 07030-5774
www.wiley.com

Copyright © 2005 by Wiley Publishing, Inc., Indianapolis, Indiana

Published simultaneously in Canada

ISBN-13: 978-0-7645-9786-2

ISBN-10: 0-7645-9786-8

Manufactured in the United States of America

10 9 8 7 6 5 4 3 2 1

1B/RS/QZ/QV/IN

No part of this publication may be reproduced, stored in a retrieval system or transmitted in any form or by any means, electronic, mechanical, photocopying, recording, scanning or otherwise, except as permitted under Sections 107 or 108 of the 1976 United States Copyright Act, without either the prior written permission of the Publisher, or authorization through payment of the appropriate per-copy fee to the Copyright Clearance Center, 222 Rosewood Drive, Danvers, MA 01923, (978) 750-8400, fax (978) 646-8600. Requests to the Publisher for permission should be addressed to the Legal Department, Wiley Publishing, Inc., 10475 Crosspoint Blvd., Indianapolis, IN 46256, (317) 572-3447, fax (317) 572-4355, or online at www.wiley.com/go/permissions.

LIMIT OF LIABILITY/DISCLAIMER OF WARRANTY: THE PUBLISHER AND THE AUTHOR MAKE NO REPRESENTATIONS OR WARRANTIES WITH RESPECT TO THE ACCURACY OR COMPLETENESS OF THE CONTENTS OF THIS WORK AND SPECIFICALLY DISCLAIM ALL WARRANTIES, INCLUDING WITHOUT LIMITATION WARRANTIES OF FITNESS FOR A PARTICULAR PURPOSE. NO WARRANTY MAY BE CREATED OR EXTENDED BY SALES OR PROMOTIONAL MATERIALS. THE ADVICE AND STRATEGIES CONTAINED HEREIN MAY NOT BE SUITABLE FOR EVERY SITUATION. THIS WORK IS SOLD WITH THE UNDERSTANDING THAT THE PUBLISHER IS NOT ENGAGED IN RENDERING LEGAL, ACCOUNTING, OR OTHER PROFESSIONAL SERVICES. IF PROFESSIONAL ASSISTANCE IS REQUIRED, THE SERVICES OF A COMPETENT PROFESSIONAL PERSON SHOULD BE SOUGHT. NEITHER THE PUBLISHER NOR THE AUTHOR SHALL BE LIABLE FOR DAMAGES ARISING HEREFROM. THE FACT THAT AN ORGANIZATION OR WEB SITE IS REFERRED TO IN THIS WORK AS A CITATION AND/OR A POTENTIAL SOURCE OF FURTHER INFORMATION DOES NOT MEAN THAT THE AUTHOR OR THE PUBLISHER ENDORSES THE INFORMATION THE ORGANIZATION OF WEB SITE MAY PROVIDE OR RECOMMENDATIONS IT MAY MAKE. FURTHER, READERS SHOULD BE AWARE THAT INTERNET WEB SITES LISTED IN THIS WORK MAY HAVE CHANGED OR DISAPPEARED BETWEEN WHEN THIS WORK WAS WRITTEN AND WHEN IT IS READ.

For general information on our other products and services or to obtain technical support, please contact our Customer Care Department within the U.S. at (800) 762-2974, outside the U.S. at (317) 572-3993 or fax (317) 572-4002.

Wiley also publishes its books in a variety of electronic formats. Some content that appears in print may not be available in electronic books.

Library of Congress Control Number: 2005927628

Trademarks: Wiley and the Wiley Publishing logo are trademarks or registered trademarks of John Wiley and Sons, Inc. and/or its affiliates. Windows XP is a registered trademark of Microsoft Corporation. All other trademarks are the property of their respective owners. Wiley Publishing, Inc. is not associated with any product or vendor mentioned in this book.

WILEY

About the Authors

John Barnett has been a Microsoft MVP since 2000, with a specialty in XP Help and Support. He contributes to Window XP Trial and the Windows Expertzone newsgroups often, and usually can be found in the General/Basic/New user/Customizing Your Computer and Performance and Maintenance sections of the Expertzone. He is also an IT journalist who contributes to numerous magazines. John's Web site is http://xphelpandsupport.mvps.org.

Curt Simmons (MCP, MCSE, MCSA) is an author, trainer, and courseware developer who was awarded an MVP in 2004. The author of more than 50 general computing books on a wide variety of topics, he most often writes about operating systems and Microsoft products. You can reach Curt at www.curtsimmons.com.

Alan Simpson is an award-winning computer book author with some 90 published books to his credit. His books are published in many languages throughout the world and have sold millions of copies. Alan has taught introductory and advanced computer programming courses at San Diego State University and University of California, San Diego Extension. He has also worked as a freelance programmer and computer consultant for the U.S. Navy and Air Force, as well as for private business.

David Dalan spends his professional time deploying software in the Caribbean, and playing network fireman and desktop architect for a municipal government when he is not writing about technologies that excite him. He currently enjoys working on wireless networking strategies for a wide range of users, from Web-surfing "teleworkers," to law enforcement personnel.

Credits

Acquisitions Editor
Michael Roney

Project Editor
Maureen Spears

Technical Editor
Steven Wright

Copy Editor
Marylouise Wiack

Editorial Manager
Robyn Siesky

Vice President & Group Executive Publisher
Richard Swadley

Vice President & Publisher
Barry Pruett

Project Coordinator
Maridee Ennis

Graphics and Production Specialists
Carrie Foster
Denny Hager
Heather Ryan
Ron Terry

Quality Control Technician
John Greenough

Proofreading and Indexing
TECHBOOKS Production Services

Preface

I f you cruise your favorite bookstore, you'll find many Windows XP titles. So, why another book about Windows XP and what makes the book you're holding so different? We've had the privilege of helping people use Windows XP, and there's one thing we have found to be true: Most people need help from time to time with Windows XP, and when they need help, they need it right now! After all, the main thing you really want with Windows XP is for it to do what you want it to do — not to become a computer expert.

That's where this book comes in. It was designed to be your own personal team of tech support experts. You can think of Windows XP MVP as your "most valuable professional" resource — like having MVP's sitting in your home or small office. We have been working with Windows XP since the very first beta (pre-release) software was available. It's been a bumpy road, but we've also enjoyed it. In addition, we have been active in the user community and have experimented with virtually every feature Windows XP provides. We teamed up with the best-selling author Alan Simpson, who brings years of experience to the table, and networking expert David Dalan. What you're holding is a book written by a very diverse and well-rounded group of authors — and you should find that refreshing from a computer book's point of view.

Although this book is a not a troubleshooting book per se, it focuses on configurations and issues that you are likely to use and possibly find problematic. In this book, you'll find short introductions and plenty of steps. It focuses how to do things rather than spending endless pages explaining how they work. In the following pages, you'll find most everything you need to make Windows XP do what you want it to. You'll see how to perform network configurations, but we'll explore fun stuff, such as digital media. We hope you enjoy the book, and hope it makes your work and play with Windows XP much more enjoyable.

John Barnett and Curt Simmons

Acknowledgments

Thanks to everyone at Wiley for the opportunity to write this book. A special thanks to Mike Roney and Maureen Spears for getting things started and keeping things moving in the right direction. Also, a special thanks to Steve Wright and Marylouise Wiack for their attention to detail. A special thanks to the contributors, Alan Simpson and David Dalan. Also thanks to Margot Hutchison for working out the details.

Contents at a Glance

Contents

Introduction

Windows XP is a great operating system that is full of features and possibilities. Of course, you have never had any problems with it, and you are never confused by its many windows, dialog boxes, and services. Right?

Have you ever felt like you needed a Windows XP professional sitting by your desktop, helping you wade through this very complex operating system? If that's how you feel, then look no further. Windows XP MVP is written with you in mind. It is designed for the smart home user or the small office user, and in these pages, you can find solutions, steps, and information that will make your work and play with Windows XP more productive and enjoyable.

This book is written to cover practically everything that you may need to know. You will see how to perform standard configurations, get a network up and running, and manage features and problems. You will also learn how to manage files, digital media, Internet options, and how to keep your computer safe. Divided into five sections, or solutions, this book is designed to be the definitive guide to all aspects of using and maintaining Windows XP. In short, it is like having a Windows XP professional sitting right beside you as you work. This book is designed to be your Windows XP professional that sits beside you when you work with Windows XP.

We have kept this book concise by not rambling on with boring explanations and discussions. This book is action-oriented and is designed to show you what to do. Its modular and task based format offers a wealth of good, sound, professional advice, lightly interspersed with personal tips, notes and how-to examples. This book addresses many of the problems the end user is likely to encounter. In order to make the book easier to use, there are a few important features that you should know about. These include three icons:

 This icon contains important information that we have discovered as we have worked with Windows XP. You should always read every MVP icon that you see because they contain helpful and important information.

 These icons are designed to provide a helpful piece of information about a process. Always read them.

These icons are designed to give you some extra information that will help you to better understand or use the technology that is being discussed.

In addition, you may encounter different sidebars as you read through the book. These give you more insight and information into the inner workings of Windows XP:

+ **Expert's Notebook:** These sidebars tell you important information from an expert's point of view. They may also contain configuration information or steps. Always check out these sidebars because they can be very helpful as you work with Windows XP.

+ **FYI:** These sidebars provide additional information about a technology or process. They are not required reading, but they can help you to understand a subject in more detail.

+ **Troubleshooting:** These sidebars point out troubleshooting tips or tactics that you should keep in mind.

This book is not written in a linear format, so feel free to skip around and find the specific topic that you are interested in. You can find plenty of screen shots and steps to help you along the way. We hope you enjoy using this book as much as we have enjoyed writing it. Welcome to Windows XP MVP!

Configuring and Personalizing Windows XP

I

Windows XP comes your way with a "default" interface. The default is all you'll need, but if you're like most of us, you may prefer to configure and personalize Windows XP in a way that meets your needs and personal taste. No problem — you have many different configuration and personalization options you can put to work.

In this part, you find out how to configure the XP interface, manage programs, install and manage hardware, manage power options, start-up and shutdown, customize and manage folders and files, and how to manage user accounts. You also see some additional options and features to help you configure and personalize Windows XP.

Configuring the Windows XP Interface

1

T he desktop is the basic part of the interface that allows you to maneuver around Windows XP and get to what you need. In the past, the desktop was full of icons, but under the default Windows XP Desktop, you're likely to see only the Recycle Bin. The purpose of the desktop is to make your work and play with Windows XP easier. As such, you have many options that enable you to reconfigure the desktop in a variety of ways.

This chapter focuses on customizing and personalizing the desktop and the basic Windows XP interface. You'll see how to change the configuration of Windows XP so that it looks the way you want.

Customizing the XP Desktop

Windows XP is essentially a theme. This means that the desktop, icon appearance, colors, fonts, and desktop wallpaper are all determined by some preconfigured settings under Windows XP. That's fine, and if you like the desktop the way it is, you can leave things as they are. However, if you are curious and prefer to change things to match your personal taste, the desktop area is most likely the place you'll start. Fortunately, you can easily make a number of apparent and not-so-apparent changes to the desktop to customize it. The following sections explore the customization features that you'll find in Windows XP.

Choosing the Classic Theme

The default appearance of Windows XP is a basic theme that is preconfigured when you buy your computer. However, if you are nostalgic for the earlier days of Windows, then you can easily change the default look of Windows XP so that it looks like an earlier version of Windows, such as Windows 98. Changing the theme, however, doesn't actually change the functionality of your Windows XP computer — it just changes the desktop appearance.

To change the Windows XP desktop theme, follow these steps:

1. **Click Start ➪ Control Panel.**

2. **Double-click the Display icon.** This opens the Display Properties dialog box (Figure 1-1).

   You can also right-click an empty area of the desktop and click Properties to open the Display Properties dialog box.

3. **On the Themes tab, shown in Figure 1-1, click the Theme drop-down menu and click Windows Classic.** If you have a Windows XP Plus Pack installed on your computer, you may see additional themes that you can choose as well.

4. **Click OK**. The Windows Classic theme is applied to your computer.

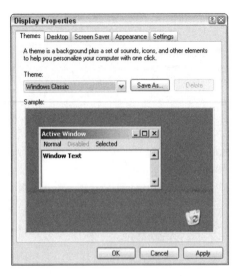

Figure 1-1: Choose the Windows Classic theme option.

Expert's Notebook: Saving a Custom Theme

Themes use default configuration options. However, you can select a theme, and then make changes to your desktop configuration. Once you do that, the theme name appears with "modified" notation attached to the name. You can click the Save As button on the Themes tab and rename your modified theme to something else. This allows you to create custom themes between which you can toggle by simply choosing the assigned theme name on the Themes tab. When you choose the Save As option, you see a standard Save As dialog box. You can then give your new theme a name, and save it in the My Documents folder with a .theme file extension. *Curt Simmon*

Note

In the Theme drop-down menu, look for the More themes online option. This option takes you to Microsoft.com where you can purchase the Microsoft Plus! SuperPack for Windows XP. This gives you four additional themes. You can also directly visit the SuperPack page at www.microsoft.com/windows/plus/screensavers.asp.

Changing the Desktop Wallpaper

Wallpaper is a term used to describe what you see as the background on the desktop. You can use the default theme wallpaper, choose from a list of wallpapers, use your own picture as wallpaper, or simply pick a color. Windows makes it easy for you to make the desktop look however you want with minimal fuss.

1. **Click Start ⇨ Control Panel.**

2. **Double-click the Display properties icon.** This opens the Display Properties dialog box.

3. **Click the Desktop tab.** On the Desktop tab, you have the following options:

   • **Selecting a Desktop Color:** Choose the None option in the Background section, and then click the Color drop-down menu and choose a desktop color, as shown in Figure 1-2. This action gives your desktop the selected color with no additional graphics or pictures.

   • **Selecting a Desktop Pattern:** Choose a desktop picture or pattern from the available options in the Background section of the dialog box, as shown in Figure 1-3. The options that you see here vary, depending on whether you have any PlusPacks installed.

   • **Select your own picture.** Click the Browse button and locate a desired photo file in a standard format, such as a JPEG, BMP, and so on. Select the photo and click Open. The photo appears in the Background selection options and is selected. You can use the Position drop-down menu to Center, Tile, or Stretch the photo, if necessary.

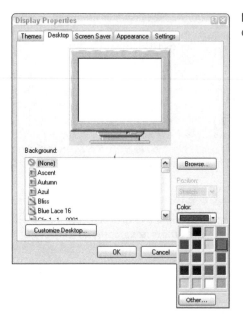

Figure 1-2: You can choose a desktop color from the drop-down menu.

Figure 1-3: Choose a desktop wallpaper option.

Note

You can select most standard photo file formats, such as JPEG, BMP, PNG, and so on. You can use HTML files as well. However, program-specific files do not work. For example, you can create a Photoshop file and save it as a PSD file. However, Windows XP does not recognize the file as a standard photo file. To work around this problem, re-open the file in Photoshop and save it as a JPEG.

4. Click OK when you're done. The desktop wallpaper changes.

Adding Desktop Icons

By default, the Windows XP theme only places the Recycle Bin on the desktop. The idea is to give you a cleaner desktop without a bunch of icons crowding up the space. However, you can place My Documents, My Computer, My Network Places, or Internet Explorer directly on the desktop. You can create a shortcut to any Start menu item or folder on your computer and place it on the desktop as well.

To place My Documents, My Computer, My Network Places, or Internet Explorer on the desktop, follow these steps:

1. **Click Start ➪ Control Panel.**

2. **Double-click the Display properties icon and click the Desktop tab.**

3. **Click the Customize Desktop button.**

4. **On the Desktop Items dialog box, select the General tab.** Click the desired check boxes for the standard desktop icons that you want to place on the desktop, as shown in Figure 1-4.

5. **Click OK.**

Figure 1-4: Select the desktop icons that you want to use.

To add other icons to the desktop, you can click the Start menu and simply drag any icon to the desktop. This creates a shortcut on the desktop. You can also create a shortcut for any application or folder and place it on the desktop as well. You can learn more about creating and managing shortcuts later in this chapter.

Changing the Appearance of a Desktop Icon

Like previous versions of Windows, Windows XP has a default appearance for standard desktop icons, such as My Computer and My Documents. However, you can change the appearance of those icons and even create an icon with a graphics program, such as Paint, Adobe Photoshop, or Jasc Paint Shop Pro. You can then use the icon that you have created as a default icon. Follow these steps:

1. **Click Start ➪ Control Panel.**

2. **Double-click the Display properties icon and click the Desktop tab.**

3. **Click the Customize Desktop button.** On the General tab of the Desktop Items dialog box, notice the default icon appearance for My Computer, My Documents, and so on (see Figure 1-5).

4. **To change an icon, select it and click the Change Icon button.**

5. **On the Change Icon dialog box, shown in Figure 1-5, select the icon that you want to use, or click the Browse button to select an alternate *.ico file.**

6. **Click OK when you're done.** The icons appear.

Figure 1-5: Windows XP has various icon options for you to choose.

Note   **When you use the Change Icon option, it changes the appearance of the icon in all places that the icon appears on your computer, including the Start menu.**

Expert's Notebook: Automatic Desktop Cleanup

Windows XP has an automated feature called Desktop Cleanup. The Desktop Cleanup wizard attempts to remove older icons from your desktop that you have not used for more than 60 days by placing the old icons in an Unused Desktop Shortcuts folder. Although by default, the tool runs every 60 days, you can manually start it by clicking the Clean Desktop Now button on the Desktop Items dialog box. You may find this tool helpful if you use a lot of desktop icons, yet, in my experience, the Desktop Cleanup wizard has a tendency to move things around that you may not want moved. If you want to maintain better control of what is on your desktop, you can disable the feature by unchecking the "Run Desktop Cleanup Wizard every 60 days" check box on the General tab of Desktop Items. *Curt Simmons*

Using HTML Content on the Desktop

Like previous versions of Windows, Windows XP allows you to place active HTML content and even complete Web pages on your desktop. You can configure these desktop Web pages to update periodically so that you always see fresh content. Since its inception, this feature has not been very popular, because a Web page on your desktop tends to clutter things up, and you can just as easily configure Internet Explorer to use your favorite Web site as a start page (see Chapter 13). However, if you want to keep track of a particular Web site and see it on the desktop, you can easily do so. Follow these steps:

1. **Click Start ⇨ Control Panel.**

2. **Double-click the Display properties icon and click the Desktop tab.**

3. **Click the Customize Desktop button and click the Web tab on the Desktop Items dialog box**.

4. **On the Web tab, click the New button.** This opens the New Desktop Item wizard, as shown in Figure 1-6. You can click Visit Gallery to see the downloadable desktop options that are available at Microsoft.com. You can also enter the URL of the Web page that you want to use on the desktop, or click Browse to add a picture or HTML document.

 Note

Like using HTML content on the desktop, the Internet Explorer Gallery is one of those features that never really took off. The gallery contains some active desktop content that you can download and use, but the stuff you find there isn't too exciting. Fee l free to check it out, though.

5. **Click OK.** The Web page will now appear as an option on the Web tab, as shown in Figure 1-7. You can click the Synchronize button to update the Web site. A connection to the Internet is required.

Figure 1-6: Enter the desired URL, or choose to visit the gallery.

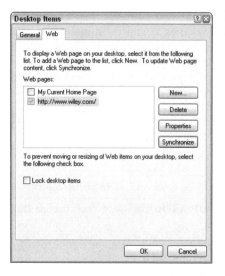

Figure 1-7: The Web tab of the Desktop Items dialog box

6. **Click OK on the Web tab when you're done.** The Web page will now appear on your desktop.

Configuring Desktop Appearance Options

If you open the Display Properties dialog box and click the Appearance tab, a number of options allow you to configure how everything looks on Windows XP. This includes Window and button styles, color schemes, font styles, and a number of advanced features. These are all easy to configure, and they enable you to fine-tune the appearance of Windows XP. Follow these steps:

1. **Click Start ➪ Control Panel.**

2. **Double-click the Display properties icon to open the Display Properties dialog box.**

3. **On the Appearance tab, shown in Figure 1-8, you can choose either Windows XP style or Windows Classic appearance for windows and buttons.** Under Color scheme, you can choose a standard color scheme that will govern the appearance of windows. You can choose between the default blue, olive green, or silver schemes when the Windows XP scheme is used. If you're using the Classic scheme, you'll see additional options. You can also adjust the font size used on windows to normal, large fonts, or extra-large fonts.

Figure 1-8: The Appearance tab lets you choose your desktop scheme.

4. **Click the Advanced button**. On the Advanced Appearance dialog box, you can choose a desktop feature using the Item drop-down menu, as shown in Figure 1-9. You can then adjust the size and colors, as well as the font size and colors to use for that particular item. For example, the settings shown in Figure 1-9 govern the appearance and size of the Active Title Bar. You can work through the list in the Item drop-down menu and fine-tune exactly how each item appears. Make any desired changes and click OK.

5. **On the Appearance tab, click the Effects button.** The Effects dialog box appears, shown in Figure 1-10. Notice that you can adjust the appearance of transition effects, screen fonts, shadow options, drag behavior, and underlined letters. Most of these options are selected by default if you are using the Windows XP theme, but you can change them, if desired. Click OK when you're done.

6. **Click OK on the Appearance tab.** Your changes are applied.

Figure 1-9: The Advanced Appearance dialog box offers several options.

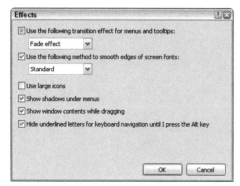

Figure 1-10: The Effects dialog box and its options

Using a Screen Saver

In the early days of computing, screen savers were little programs that kept a screen active when you were idle. This was a necessary feature because screens at that time could suffer from "screen burn." When the computer was idle for too long, the current data on the screen could actually burn itself onto the monitor tubes so that you would always see this burned screen as a ghost in the background, no matter what else you might be doing.

Monitors today are not susceptible to screen burn, so the screen saver is just a leftover novelty item that is available to you as a security features as well as entertainment. You can configure your screen saver to require a password when it is resumed.   You have a basic set of screen savers available on Windows XP (and even more if you have a PlusPack installed).

Tip

If you love screen savers, be sure to check out www.jumbo.com and www. screensaverdirectory.com. You can find some free and inexpensive screen savers for Windows XP at these Web sites. You may run into some screen savers that are not appropriate for children, however, so parents beware.

Standard Screen Savers

To configure a screen saver, follow these steps:

1. **Open the Display Properties dialog box and click the Screen Saver tab.**

2. **In the Screen saver drop-down menu, choose a screen saver**. This is shown in Figure 1-11.

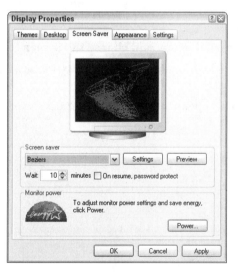

Figure 1-11: The Screen Saver tab on the Display Properties dialog box

3. **Click OK on the Appearance tab.**

4. **Click the Settings button**. In the dialog box that appears, adjust any available settings that determine how the screen saver will behave.

5. **Choose a Wait time.** This is idle time that passes before the screen saver starts. Also, you may want to choose the On resume, password protect option. This option causes your computer to go to the Welcome screen when you move the mouse. This setting provides you some protection if you are away from your computer so that others cannot access it. Of course, your user account must be configured with a password for this setting to help (see Chapter 10 for help with passwords).

6. **Click OK when you're done.** Your changes are applied.

Screen savers are fun, but they can zap battery power if you're using a laptop. For example, the 3D screen saver options (FlowerBox, Flying Objects, etc.) use a lot of processor power, which puts a drain on batteries. Avoid these screen savers if you are running on batteries.

My Pictures Slideshow

If you love personal digital photos (and most of us do), you can use a fun screen saver called My Pictures Slideshow. This screen saver displays a folder of photos using random transition effects. It's fun and works well, and it's a great way to day-dream about that Caribbean vacation you took last year when you're stuck at the office. Do this:

1. **Open the Display Properties dialog box and choose the Screen Saver tab.**

2. **Using the Screen Saver drop-down menu, choose the My Pictures Slideshow option.**

3. **Click the Settings button.** This opens the My Pictures Screen Saver Options dialog box, as shown in Figure 1-12.

Figure 1-12: My Pictures Screen Saver Options

4. **Click the Browse button and locate the folder that holds the photos that you want to use in the screen saver.**

5. **Adjust the other settings on the My Pictures Screen Saver Options dialog box.** Notice that you can determine how often the pictures change, how big the pictures should be, and whether or not to stretch small pictures. You can also determine whether to show file names, use transition effects between pictures, and allow scrolling through pictures with the keyboard. Make your selections and click OK.

6. **Click OK again on the Screen Saver tab.**

Configuring the Start Menu and Taskbar

The Start menu and taskbar are standard elements of the Windows interface, and so you may tend to ignore them. However, there are many ways that you can customize the Start menu and taskbar so that they are tailored to meet your needs. Check out the following sections for information about customizing these features.

Customizing the Windows XP Start Menu

You can easily make some changes to the appearance and behavior of the Windows XP Start menu. Follow these steps:

1. **Right-click the Start Menu button and click Properties.** The Taskbar and Start Menu Properties dialog box appears.

2. **On the Start Menu tab, shown in Figure 1-13, click the Customize text button that is available next to the Start Menu feature.**

3. **On the General tab of the Customize Start Menu dialog box, select the options that you want.** You have the following options, shown in Figure 1-14:

   • **Icon size:** You can choose large or small icons for the Start menu. Small icons are more difficult to see, but enable to you to put more items on the Start menu.

   • **Programs:** Windows XP places shortcuts to programs that you use most often on the Start menu for easier access. By default, the six most commonly used programs appear, but you can change the default setting to allow more (up to 30) or fewer shortcuts. You can also click the Clear List button to clear the current list of icons found on the Start menu.

   • **Show on Start menu:** You can choose to show a browser and e-mail client on the Start menu. By default, Internet Explorer and Outlook Express appear, but you can click the drop-down menus and choose different options, depending on what programs you use.

Figure 1-13: Click the Customize button

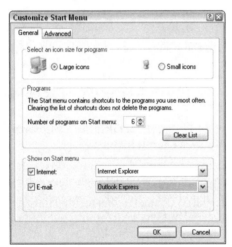

Figure 1-14: You can make basic changes to the Start menu.

4. **Click the Advanced tab, shown in Figure 1-15.** You have the following options:

  • **Start menu settings.** By default, submenus open when you point to them, and newly installed programs are highlighted. You can choose to leave these options enabled or disabled.

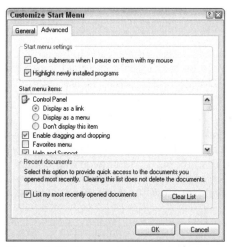

Figure 1-15: Choose advanced customization options

 The "Highlight newly installed programs" option is a feature that reminds a user that a new program has been installed. If you don't need help remembering that you installed a new program, you can safely deselect this feature.

- **Start menu items.** Use this list to control what items appear by default on the Start menu, and how they are displayed (as a link, menu, or not at all). For example, by default, the My Music folder appears on the Start menu. However, if you rarely use My Music, then locate it in the list here and click the "Don't Display this item" radio button. You can also adjust other behavioral options, such as enabling dragging and dropping, help and support, the manufacturer's link, and so on.

- **Recent documents:** You can choose to list the most recently opened documents on the Start menu (enabled by default), and you can click the Clear List button to clear the current list.

5. **When you're done making changes, just click OK twice.**

 You can quickly alphabetize items on the All Programs menu, or in any All Programs submenu. Just right-click any item on the menu and choose Sort By Name. You can also drag items up and down on the menu. But to do so, you need to choose the Enable Dragging and Dropping option under the Start menu items section on the Advanced tab of the Customize Start Menu dialog box.

Expert's Notebook: Get the Most from the Start Menu

The left side of the Start menu is a great place for storing icons to frequently used programs, folders, and files. This is because no matter how crowded your desktop, the Start menu is always one click away. Unfortunately, when you're using large icons, there isn't a lot of room on the left side of the Start menu.

If you don't mind using smaller icons, you can put many more icons on the left side of the Start menu. To use small icons, right-click the Start button, choose Properties, and then click the Customize button. Choose Small Icons from the General tab. You can now increase the "Number of programs on Start menu" to 10 or even higher (depending on your screen resolution). Click OK in each of the open dialog boxes, and when you click the Start button, you'll see that you have a lot more room for icons. *Alan Simpson*

Pinning a Shortcut to the Start Menu

The right side of the Start menu gives you access to common Windows elements and folders, such as My Computer, Printers and Faxes, Control Panel, and so on. By default, the left side of the Start menu gives you access to your browser and e-mail client. Notice that on the left-side column, a faint line separates your browser and e-mail from other program icons (see Figure 1-16). The programs that appear under the faint line are all commonly used programs. The programs that you see here change, depending on how you are using Windows XP (and you can determine how many are displayed, as explained in the previous section). However, you can also pin any program to the Start menu so that it always appears there, even if you haven't used it lately. This feature keeps the desired program icon from rotating off as other programs are used more commonly. Follow these steps:

1. **Click Start.**

2. **Locate the program that you want to pin in the program list on the left side of the Start menu.**

3. **Right-click the program icon and choose Pin to Start menu, as shown in Figure 1-16**. The program icon now appears with the browser and e-mail icons above the faint line. You can repeat this process to pin other icons to the Start menu, as well.

Using the Classic Start Menu

By default, your computer uses the Windows XP Start menu. The XP Start menu gives you quicker and easier access to the items that you want, rather than having a desktop full of stuff. However, you can also make the Start menu look like the Windows Classic Start menu if you prefer. Follow these steps:

1. **Right-click the Start button and click Properties.** The Taskbar and Start Menu Properties dialog box appears.

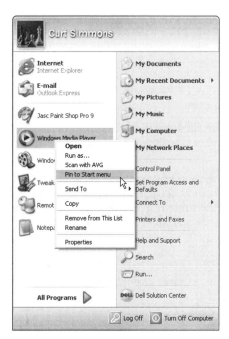

Figure 1-16: To keep a program from rotating off the Start menu, use the Pin to Start menu option.

2. **On the Start Menu tab, shown in Figure 1-17, choose the Classic Start menu radio button.**

3. **Click OK.** The Start menu will now look like the Windows Start menu found in previous versions of Windows.

Figure 1-17: Choose the Classic Start menu radio button.

Customizing the Classic Start Menu

If you choose to use the Classic Start menu, you have a few customization options to consider. Follow these steps:

1. **Right-click the Start button and click Properties.** The Taskbar and Start Menu Properties dialog box appears.

2. **On the Start Menu tab, click the Customize button next to the Classic Start menu option.** The Customize Classic Start Menu dialog box, shown in Figure 1-18, appears.

3. **You can choose to add, remove, or sort items that appear on the Classic Start menu**. The Add button allows you to create a shortcut to any program or folder and include it on the Start menu. You can also click the Clear button to remove records of recently accessed documents, programs, and Web sites.

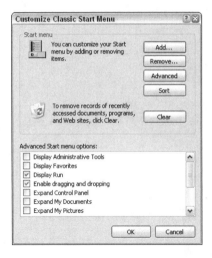

Figure 1-18: Choose the desired options to customize the Start menu.

4. **Select Advanced Start menu options.** Under Advanced Start menu options, notice that you see a series of check box options that enable certain features of the Start menu. These items are self-explanatory, so look through the list and enable any item you want by clicking the check box next to it.

5. **When you're done, click OK twice.**

Customizing the Taskbar

The taskbar also contains a few customization options that you may find useful. The taskbar, for the most part, doesn't need a lot of attention from you, but there are a few things that you can customize. Follow these steps:

1. **Right-click the Start button or any empty area of the taskbar and click Properties.** The Taskbar and Start Menu Properties dialog box appears.

2. **Click the Taskbar tab.**

3. **Select taskbar appearance options.** The Taskbar tab displays check box options, shown in Figure 1-19, that allow you to manage the appearance of the taskbar. You can enable or disable any of these features by clicking the check box options:

Figure 1-19: Choose customization options on the taskbar.

- **Lock the taskbar:** This option keeps the taskbar at the current position. Normally, you can drag the taskbar around so that it is located in another area, such as the top or sides of the desktop, rather than the bottom. However, if you select the Lock-the-taskbar feature, the taskbar cannot be moved. You can also lock or unlock the taskbar at any time by simply right clicking the taskbar and choosing to lock or unlock the taskbar from the contextual menu that appears.

- **Keep the taskbar on top of other windows:** This option, enabled by default, keeps other windows from covering up the taskbar.

- **Group similar taskbar buttons**: This option, enabled by default, groups similar items together. For example, if you open several Internet Explorer pages, you can group them together and collapse them into a single button if you open too many. This feature enables you to open many items and see them on the taskbar in an organized way.

- **Show Quick Launch.** The Quick Launch bar can be displayed on the taskbar, but this feature is not enabled by default. Quick Launch has been around for several iterations of Windows, but has fallen out of favor among many people. You can use Quick Launch to show programs on the taskbar, but because the Start menu now works so well for this purpose, the Quick Launch feature isn't particularly helpful and takes up taskbar space.

4. **Click OK when you're done.**

Managing Notification Area Items

The Notification area appears at the right side of the taskbar and contains the clock and a number of other icons, depending on what is installed on your computer. By default, the Notification area items that are inactive are hidden from view (you can see them all by clicking the arrow button on the Notification area). You can manage how these notifications behave by following these steps:

1. **Right-click the Start button or the taskbar, and then click Properties.** The Taskbar and Start Menu Properties dialog box appears.

2. **Click the Taskbar tab.** On the Taskbar tab, notice that you can choose to show the clock in the Notification area and to hide inactive icons. Both of these options are selected by default, but you can change them if you like.

3. **Click the Customize button.** The Customize Notifications dialog box appears, as shown in Figure 1-20. When you click the Behavior option for the desired item, a drop-down menu appears. You can choose Hide when inactive, Always hide, or Always show. By default, most icons are listed as "Hide when inactive." This is typically the best setting because it will keep your Notification Area from looking so cluttered.

4. **When you're done, click OK twice.**

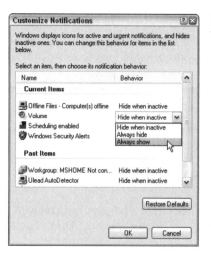

Figure 1-20: You can adjust the behavior of the notification area items.

Troubleshooting: A Shortcut Doesn't Access the Desired Item

Think of a shortcut as a link. Let's say that you create a shortcut to a folder on your computer. The shortcut contains a link to the folder, such as C:\Documents and Settings\Curt\Transfer. When you double-click the shortcut, the folder opens. However, what if you move the folder to another location on your computer? The link is no longer valid because it points to a folder that is not in the original place. In such cases, you need to update the link by finding the target folder. To do this, right-click the shortcut and click Properties. On the Shortcut tab, manually change the path in the Target dialog box or click the Find Target button to browse for the folder on your computer. Once you have corrected the link, click OK and your shortcut will work. *Curt Simmons*

Creating Shortcuts

Shortcuts make your computer easier to use and give you fast access to commonly used items. A shortcut is an icon that contains a pointer to something else on your computer. When you double-click the shortcut, the pointer opens the desired program or folder. Essentially, icons such as My Computer, My Documents, and other similar Start menu items are shortcuts to those items. For example, the My Computer folder doesn't actually reside on your Start menu, but the icon is a shortcut to it.

Expert's Notebook: Customizing Shortcut Icons

You can customize any shortcut icon to make it visually stand out from other icons. This is especially useful for shortcuts to folders and files which all tend to look the same. If you want to make a shortcut icon stand out by giving it a unique icon, just right-click the shortcut icon and choose Properties. Then, on the Shortcut tab, click the Change Icon button. Once the Change Icon dialog box is open, you can choose the icon that you want. You can also click the Browse button to choose from among other icons on your hard drive. For example, if you have a folder of icons (.ico files), use the Browse button to navigate to that folder and choose any icon you like.

By default, all shortcut icons show the little black arrow icon. If you want to change, or get rid of, that little arrow, you can use the Tweak UI tool, which is available from www.microsoft.com/windowsxp/downloads/powertoys/xppowertoys.mspx at the time of this writing. If the URL changes by the time you read this, then go to search.microsoft.com and search for "Windows XP PowerToys". *Alan Simpson*

You can create shortcuts for any program, folder, or file on your computer. You can then put those shortcuts on your Start menu or desktop so that you can easily access these particular items. To create a shortcut, follow these steps:

1. **Right-click any desired program icon, folder, or document file.** You can directly access program icons on Start ⇨ All Programs.

2. **Choose Create Shortcut from the context menu that appears.** The shortcut appears (it is indicated by a small arrow on the icon).

3. **You can now drag the shortcut to the Start menu or any other location you want.**

Managing Programs

2

Naturally, the major focus of your computing is using programs. In fact, even the operating system itself is made up of a bunch of different programs and code that you use, and you will certainly install your own programs and applications. Program management under Windows XP is easier than ever, and if a program is written for Windows XP, you are not likely to have many problems. However, it is important for you to manage your programs and solve problems when they occur.

In this chapter, you explore the management of programs. You learn how to install, remove, and manage programs as you use Windows XP.

In This Chapter

Installing and Removing Programs

Working with Older Programs

Programs and Users

Managing Programs

Installing New Programs

We don't need to spend a lot of time talking about installing new programs or applications because the process is so straight-forward. Typically, you install a new program from an installation CD, or if you have downloaded the program from the Web, you double-click the downloaded icon that unpacks the installation files and begin the installation process. All you need do is follow the setup program's steps and answer any questions it may ask of you.

You can also use Add/Remove Programs in Control Panel, shown in Figure 2-1, to install a program. If you click the Add New Programs button, it asks you to choose to install from a CD or Floppy, or check Windows Updates for new programs. There's nothing exciting here, and actually, using Add or Remove Programs really just creates an additional step that you don't need. Still, if you are having problems installing something new, you can try Add or Remove Programs.

If you install a program from a CD and nothing seems to happen, open My Computer and then open the CD-ROM drive. Look for a setup.exe icon and double-click it to start the installation.

Figure 2-1: You can use Add or Remove Programs to install a new program

Removing a Program

There are two basic ways to remove a program from your computer. First, some programs come with their own uninstall option, which you typically see on programs you download from the Internet. If you click Start ➪ All Programs, locate the program's folder and then you can see if there is an Uninstall option in the folder. If not, the best way to remove the program is to simply use Add/Remove Programs.

1. **Open Add or Remove Programs in the Control Panel.** You can open the Control Panel by clicking Start ➪ Settings ➪ Control Panel.

Troubleshooting: When You Can't Remove a Program

From time to time, you'll end up with a program that seems to really like you and you can't get rid of it. There is no uninstall option and the program doesn't even show up in Add or Remove Programs. This often happens with older programs or poorly written utilities you have downloaded from the Internet. If you can't seem to remove a program, open C:\Program Files and locate the application's folder. Right-click it and click delete. This deletes the program, but it leaves registry entries for it, which may cause some error messages. You may want to run a registry cleaner tool, such as RegClean from Microsoft, after doing this. Deleting the program's folder is a last-ditch effort, so be sure and try to remove it through Add or Remove Programs first.

Also, if you download a program that seems to cause your system some problems, remember that Windows XP has a great System Restore feature just for such occurrences. You can find out more about the System Restore feature in Chapter 34. *Curt Simmons*

2. **Select the Change or Remove Programs button as shown in Figure 2-2.**

3. **Select the program you want to remove and click the Remove button.** Follow any steps that appear.

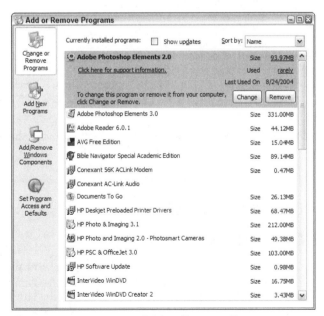

Figure 2-2: You can use Add or Remove Programs to remove any programs you don't want.

Troubleshooting: Removing Orphaned Program Entries in Add or Remove Programs

Occasionally, when you remove a program from Add or Remove Programs, the entry for the program still appears in the list, even when you have uninstalled the actual program. When this happens, you can remove the orphaned program entry in two ways. First, you can use the TweakUI utility that can be downloaded from www.microsoft.com. You can also fix the problem by editing the registry (see the Appendix) for a registry editing primer). Follow these steps to edit the registry:

1. **Click Start ➪ Run.** Type **regedit** in the dialog box and press Enter.

2. **Navigate to locate and click the following registry key:** HKEY_LOCAL_MACHINE\ Software\Microsoft\Windows\CurrentVersion\Uninstall. Each key under Uninstall represents a program that appears in Add/Remove Programs.

3. **To determine which program that each key represents, click the key, and then view the values.** The values tell you the display name in Add/Remove Programs.

4. **Once you have located the desired key that represents the orphaned program listing, right-click the key, and then click Delete.**

5. **After you delete the key, open Add/Remove Programs and verify that the program has been deleted from the list.**

Note   Some program listings in Add or Remove Programs give you both a Change and a Remove button while some only give you Change/Remove. If you have programs that you can update with additional software, you'll likely see the Change button in addition to remove. If not, the program is simply listed with a Change/Remove button.

Cross-Reference   If you want to find and get rid of spyware, malware, and adware, be sure to see Chapter 13.

Making an Older Program Work with Windows XP

Yes, I know. You have some older programs that came from the days of Windows 9x that you really want to use with Windows XP. Perhaps it is a favorite game or maybe even a custom application developed specifically for your business. The problem is Windows XP is a very different operating system than the old Windows 9x systems, so compatibility problems with older applications are likely to give you some grief.

But wait! Windows XP provides a feature that lets you run older programs on Windows XP. Called the Program Compatibility Wizard, this feature essentially helps you use older programs by making Windows XP act like previous versions of Windows. It doesn't work perfectly and it doesn't work with every application or program, but in many cases, you can use the Program Compatibility Wizard with some success.

Caution   **The Program Compatibility Wizard is not designed to work with older anti-virus software, backup programs or system programs. Only use this program with applications and general programs for your PC.**

If you want to use an older program with Windows XP, you can use the Program Compatibility Mode Wizard to help you setup a compatibility mode for your program. Follow these steps:

1. **Click Start ⇨ All Programs ⇨ Accessories ⇨ Program Compatibility Wizard.** The Program Compatibility wizard appears, as shown in Figure 2-3.

2. **Click Next on this screen.**

3. **Select how you want to locate the program.** Choose the desired radio button to locate the program, shown in Figure 2-4, and click Next. If you select a program from your computer or CD, the next window gives you a selection option.

FYI: How Compatibility Mode Works

The Compatibility Mode feature allows certain portions of the Windows XP kernel and operating procedures to act like previous versions of Windows, from Windows 95 up to Windows 2000. Windows XP's compatibility functions use application database files that interact with programs that you install. Because programs are outside of the operating system kernel, the application database file acts as a translator between the program and the operating system. These fixes that are made, which are also called "shims," are held in this database file. Essentially, a compatibility mode enables XP to use the identified shims for that category and hopefully fix the application compatibility problems the program has with Windows XP. Shims emulate the operating system that the program needs. For example, if an application is written for Windows 95, the shims can emulate the structure of the Windows 95 registry, the location of certain system and user folders, file paths, and related changes in the operating system so that the program can function normally. The compatibility modes and shims provided with Windows XP support around 100 of the most popular programs so they can work with Windows XP. Although your particular program or custom application may not be directly supported, you can still try to use one of these applications with compatibility mode to fix some problems. Be sure to use Windows XP's dynamic update and Windows update from time to time to ensure that your XP system has all of the available shims in its database. *Curt Simmons*

Figure 2-3: Click Next to start the Program Compatibility Wizard.

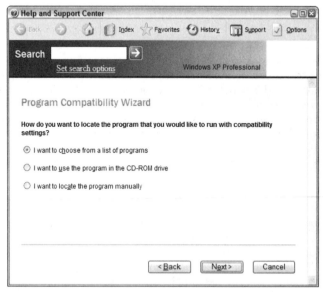

Figure 2-4: Choose your program location selection.

4. **Locate the program, select it, and click Next.**

5. **Choose the operating system that you want to emulate.** For example, you can choose Windows 95, NT 4.0, Windows 98 /Me, or Windows 2000, as shown in Figure 2-5.

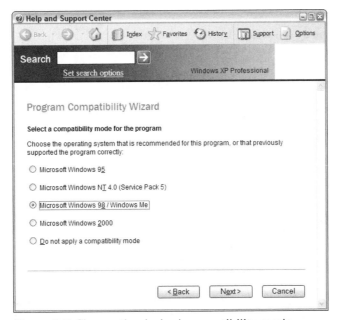

Figure 2-5: Choose the desired compatibility mode.

6. **Select your display setting for the program.** In the next window, you can choose the screen resolution that the program works best under, or you can choose to disable Windows visual themes, which can interfere with some older programs, shown in Figure 2-6. However, the settings here typically apply to games and educational programs that use a lot of graphics. If you do not want to use any of the settings, simply click Next without selecting any items.

7. **In the next window, click Next to test the compatibility settings with the program.** The program opens and runs.

8. **Use the program for a few minutes to see if the program works correctly.** Then, close the program to return to the wizard. The wizard asks you if the program works correctly. If so, click Yes to continue, or No to try different compatibility settings.

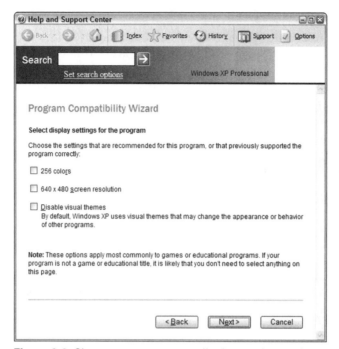

Figure 2-6: Choose any necessary display setting options.

9. **Click Next.** The Program Compatibility Wizard collects information about your program and provides you a dialog box so that you can send compatibility information to Microsoft.

10. **Click Yes or No and click Next.**

11. **Click Finish**. To change settings at a later time, simply rerun the wizard. You can now open the program and use it normally.

If you dislike using wizards, there is a work-around where you can apply the Compatibility setting you want without the wizard (as you might have imagined). To manually apply a compatibility setting, just do this:

1. **Right-click the program's executable file and click Properties.** You can find the executable file in Start ➪ All Programs. You see a Compatibility tab, shown in Figure 2-7.

2. **Simply choose to run the program in compatibility mode, choose an operating system to emulate, and apply any display settings as needed.**

3. **Click OK to finish applying the settings.**

Troubleshooting: Slow Running Programs

You may install a new program and think, "Geez, this thing is slow." That's happened to me plenty of times. In some cases, the slow program is the program's fault. In others, it is issues with system resources and Windows XP. Still, sometimes slow programs are not really the programs at all, but signs of spyware and other junk your system has collected. How do you sort all of this out? There are several different tactics you can put to work, and you can find out about them in Chapter 33. *Curt Simmons*

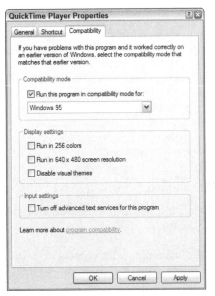

Figure 2-7: Choose to run the program in Compatibility Mode.

Running 16-bit and MS-DOS Programs

Older 16-bit applications and MS-DOS applications can typically run under Windows XP without too much fuss. Of course, it is important to remember that these programs were written for the 386 processor family and not for the 32-bit environment of Windows XP. The new programs you buy are 32-bit applications because 16-bit programs are no longer sold, although you may still be able to download an old 16-bit or MS-DOS application from the Internet.

The general rule to follow is this: Update your software and get something new. You'll be much happier with the results. Yet, you may have older applications that you love or some custom 16-bit applications that were designed for your business that you still want to use under Windows XP. That's no crime, and you can certainly have some success with these older programs.

When you run a 16-bit or MS-DOS program, Windows XP starts a virtual machine, which is a subsystem that mimics the Windows 3.x environment. The virtual machine runs the program in its own memory space so that it does not interfere with other programs already running. Virtual machines consume more memory and more system resources than running typical 32-bit applications. They also run more slowly, so it is prudent to try and avoid using 16-bit and MS-DOS applications if at all possible because of performance issues.

Tip

If you are not sure if an application is a 16-bit or 32-bit, start the application and open Windows Task Manager (just press CTRL+ALT+DEL). Click the Processes tab and look for NTVDM.exe and the Wowexec.exe processes. If you see them, you know you're running a virtual machine.

If you need to run several 16-bit applications, keep in mind that Windows XP places all of them in the same virtual memory space. That means if one application crashes, all of the applications will crash (ah, remember those old Windows days!). To avoid this, you can choose to run each program in its own memory space to protect other 16-bit programs from crashing should one crash. However, multiple virtual machines place a drain on your system resources. So, you need to decide which is more important to you. If you want to use multiple virtual machines, do this:

1. **Create a shortcut to the program if necessary, and then right-click the shortcut icon and click Properties.**

2. **Click the Advanced button on the Shortcut tab.**

3. **In the Advanced Properties dialog box, click the Run in separate memory space check box and click OK and OK again.**

If you are running a full-screen MS-DOS program, you can press Alt+Enter to toggle between the full screen and window view. If that doesn't work, try Alt+Tab or Ctrl+Esc to gain control.

Managing Programs and Users

Windows XP is a multi-user operating system. Typically, you have a default user account and several other Limited accounts, although you can create more Administrator accounts if necessary. The Administrator account(s) have the ability to install programs, but limited users are not allowed to do so. This is a security feature of Windows XP that prevents multiple users in the same office (or even multiple users in the same family) from having free reign over the PC, and one of the Limited account functions is installing new programs.

In terms of the accounts, the Administrator account has system-wide power to make any changes and install or remove programs. Limited accounts cannot make changes to hardware or system configuration, which includes removing and installing programs. As a general rule, this approach to Windows is a good security feature. Give one or at the most two people Administrative powers and do not let the others make changes to Windows, including changes in the programs list. Naturally, if you use your computer in a home setting, you may want everyone to have Administrator privileges, and that's fine, but think carefully before doing so.

One final issue concerning programs and Limited users: If you are trying to install and run 16-bit and MS-DOS programs, you can expect some problems and even odd behavior if you are using a Limited user account. These older programs do not know how to handle the security structure and nature of a multi-user environment, so it is always best to work with these programs using an Administrator account.

If you really need to keep control of Limited users and you do not want them to even consider trying to install or remove a new program, one thing you can do is simply remove the Add or Remove Programs Control Panel applet. Logged on with the Administrator account, you can use local Group Policy to invoke this setting on all other users. This is just one of many setting changes you can enforce using local Group Policy. Follow these steps:

1. **Log on with a local administrator account.**

2. **Click Start ⇨ Run. Type MMC and click OK.**

3. **In the MMC window, click File ⇨ Add/Remove Snap-in.**

4. **In the Snap-in window, click Add.**

5. **In the Snap-in dialog box, select Group Policy and click Add, shown in Figure 2-8.** A window appears with local group policy as the selected option by default, shown in Figure 2-9.

Note   **Group Policy is only available in Windows XP Professional. It is not available in Windows XP Home. You can only enter Group Policies by clicking Start ⇨ Run and then typing gpedit.msc and clicking OK.**

Figure 2-8: Select the Group Policy option.

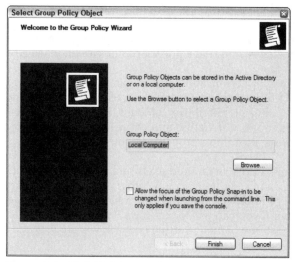

Figure 2-9: Click Finish

6. **Click Finish and click Close on the Add Snapin window.** Next, click OK on the remaining window.

7. **The Group Policy console is now available, shown in Figure 2-10.**

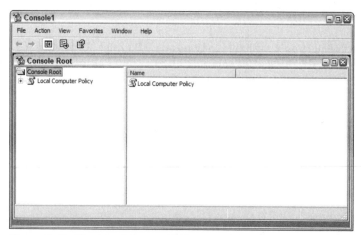

Figure 2-10: The Local Group Policy console

8. **Expand the folders to locate Add or Remove Programs.** Click User Configuration, Administrative Templates, Control Panel, and then Add/Remove Programs. Open the Remove Add or Remove Programs policy in the right windowpane and enable it, as shown in Figure 2-11.

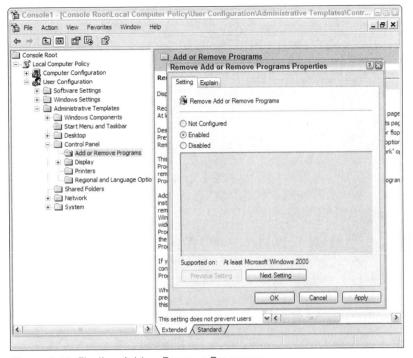

Figure 2-11: Finding Add or Remove Programs

9. **Click OK and close the Group Policy console.**

Managing Programs with Task Manager

The Task Manager is an older Windows tool that's been around since the days of Windows 9x. If you were into computing in those days, you probably used Task Manager a lot to kill hung applications. The good news is you're not as likely to have to do that under Windows XP (thank goodness), but that doesn't mean that problems with applications can't crop up. If they do, or if you just want more information about what's going on with programs, the Task Manager remains the best tool to use. The following steps show you how to use the Task Manager for program management.

1. **To use Task Manager, press Ctrl+Alt+Delete.** You'll see the Windows Task Manager, shown in Figure 2-12. On the Applications tab, you see all applications that are currently open and their status (running, failed, etc.).

2. **To stop an application from running, simply select the application in the list and click End Task.**

Figure 2-12: Windows Task Manager

3. **You can also use the Processes tab, found in Task Manager, to end application processes or set application priority.** If you click the Processes tab, you can right-click an executable that is running and point to Set Priority, and then select a different priority for the application, shown in Figure 2-13. The priorities available are:

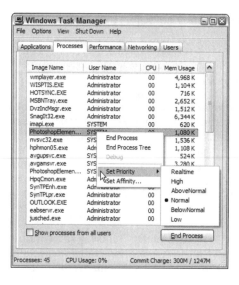

Figure 2-13: You can change the priority setting of an application.

- **Realtime:** The realtime priority allows an application to have total control over all system resources. This can make the process run much faster, but it has the potential to crash your system, so as a general rule, avoid this setting.

- **High:** The High priority gives the processes priority over all other applications. This may make the process run faster, but it may interfere with other processes running on your computer. Use this setting with caution.

- **AboveNormal:** This option gives a process slightly more priority than other processes. This can help speed up an application, but it can slow other applications down.

- **Normal:** This is the default setting.

- **BelowNormal:** This setting allows other tasks to have precedence. Use this setting for tasks that should never get priority over other applications.

- **Low:** This option gives other processes more priority than this process.

Windows XP does a good job of managing application priority, but if you have several applications running and you want to make one run a bit faster than the other, try giving the application an AboveNormal priority to see if this helps performance. You'll need to experiment a bit to see if you gain any performance, but be careful with these settings — as a general rule, Windows XP does a good job of managing them without any help.

Managing Automatic Updates

Automatic Updates is a feature of Windows XP that has become more important over time. In fact, you probably downloaded and installed Service Pack 2 through automatic updates. Frankly, I think this feature is great. It is safe and easy to use and it is the perfect way to get necessary updates to Windows XP without taking up any of your time. The suggested configuration is to turn on Automatic Updates and let it automatically download updates as they are available. You can set the time when Windows XP checks for and downloads updates with a broadband connection (mine is set for 3 a.m. so that I am never interrupted by them). In fact, Microsoft thinks Automatic Updates are so important that the Windows Security Center will warn you if Automatic Updates is not configured to work automatically. As such, the automatic function is best. However, you have a few other options available to you. If you want to choose a different option, you can do so by accessing System Properties in Control (or right-click My Computer and click Properties). You can see the options on the Automatic Updates tab, shown in Figure 2-14.

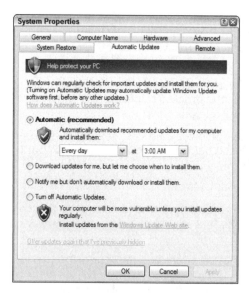

Figure 2-14: Choose an option for Automatic Updates.

✦ **Automatic:** Downloads the updates automatically and installs them without any intervention from you (this is the default setting).

✦ **Download updates for me, but let me choose when to install them.**

✦ **Notify me but don't automatically download or install them.** This option lets you know when an update is available. You can then choose to download and choose to install it.

✦ **Turn off automatic updating.** I want to update my computer manually. If you do not want Windows XP checking for updates automatically, use this option. You can then manually check for updates when convenient by clicking Start ⇨ All Programs ⇨ Windows Update.

Installing and Configuring Hardware

3

Hardware, which presented many problems in previous versions of Windows, is, for the most part, much more user-friendly in Windows XP. With better Plug-and-Play performance and generally better hardware, you are not likely to spend much of your computing time trying to install various hardware devices. However, you need to manage hardware and solve any potential problems that occur. In this chapter, you find the quick and easy help that you need, and you learn how to update device drivers and manage hardware in a way that is helpful to your work and play.

In This Chapter

Installing and Removing Hardware

Working with Devices and Drivers

Managing USB Devices and Display Adapters

Installing Hardware

Windows XP is the most hardware-compatible Windows system, and it has an extensive hardware device-driver database. As a result, in many cases you can simply plug a device, such as a digital camera or a USB flash drive, into your computer. An actual installation process is not usually necessary. You simply plug the device into the correct port on your computer, and Windows XP detects and installs the hardware by locating a generic driver that works with the device.

Naturally, you should always follow the hardware device manufacturer's instructions for installing hardware, and if you are installing an internal hardware device, such as a new video card or modem, ensure that you follow the directions.

 If you need to install an internal hardware device, play it safe. Follow the device manufacturer's instructions carefully and make sure the computer is unplugged from the power outlet. Even if the computer is turned off, there is still electricity running to the computer, and you may be electrocuted! Here's a simple two-word rule that you can follow to avoid problems with hardware installations: "Don't guess." There are no hard-and-fast rules that apply to installing all hardware devices. Rather than guessing how to install a device, follow the instructions that came with the device.

When you plug a new external device into your computer, such as a printer, camera, scanner, or USB drive, you see a balloon pop-up in the Notification area telling you that the device is being installed. After that, you can to use the device.

What if things do not work as they should? When the device does not seem to install, the culprit is typically the driver. A driver is simply a piece of software that Windows XP uses to communicate with the external device. Without the driver, Windows XP can't *drive* the device. If you have problems installing a device, then you probably need to install the device and the appropriate driver. Typically, the hardware device has installation instructions as well as a CD that contains the correct driver. If not, visit the hardware manufacturer's Web site, where you can usually download the correct driver for the device.

If you have problems, you need to locate the correct driver for the device, after which you can use Windows XP's easy Add Hardware wizard to install the device. Follow these steps:

1. **Click Start ➪ Control Panel**.

2. **Double-click the Add Hardware icon**. This opens a wizard.

3. **Click Next on the Welcome screen**. The wizard tells you that Windows XP will now search for any plug-and-play devices on your computer. A report appears, containing all currently installed devices. If the device *is* in the list but is not working, select it and click Next to tell Windows to troubleshoot it for you. If the device *is not* in the list, follow the remaining steps. Select the Add a new hardware device option, shown in Figure 3-1, and click Next. The next window asks whether you want Windows to search for the device again or manually select it from a list.

4. **Make your selection and click Next**. If Windows does not find the device or you want to select from a list, the hardware types window appears.

5. **Select the type of hardware that you want to install and click Next**. Depending on the type of device you select, a new wizard may appear, such as in the case of a modem. You can also click the Have Disk button if you have installation files on a floppy disk or CD-ROM.

6. **Make your selection and click Next.**

7. **Follow any additional screens that may appear, and click Finish.**

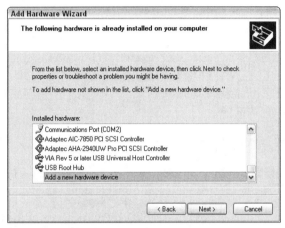

Figure 3-1: Choose to add a new hardware device.

Tip

Remember, if you are struggling with a hardware device installation problem, the issue is usually the driver. Check the device manufacturer's Web site for troubleshooting help and updated drivers. If you are wondering if a particular device will work with Windows XP, be sure to check out www.microsoft.com/ windowsxp for updated information about hardware issues.

FYI: IRQ Conflicts

Interrupt Request Lines (IRQ) is an internal computer process that allows a hardware device to use the processor. Because the processor performs all calculations, hardware devices use the processor like any other component. However, only one device can use a processor at any time, and that is where IRQs come into play. Because processors in Windows XP can handle only one processor task, or thread, at a time, the IRQ enables the device to access the processor in an organized way. The IRQ prevents two different devices from trying to access the processor at the same time (although certain devices can share an IRQ). IRQ conflicts were very common problems in the past because devices would try to use the same IRQ. This forced you to manually set IRQ numbers and related hardware settings, a task that drove most of us crazy. Windows XP now automatically handles these settings for you. With Windows XP using newer hardware, IRQ conflicts are now quite rare. Should they ever occur, you can manage them with the device's properties pages on the Resources tab, which are explored later in this chapter.

Removing a Hardware Device

You can easily remove a hardware device from Windows XP. If you are using an external device, such as a camera or USB flash drive, simply unplug the device from the computer. Windows XP detects that the device has been removed and internally uninstalls it.

If you need to remove an internal device, shut down the computer and unplug it from the power outlet. You can then remove the internal device and restart Windows XP, which detects the change.

Using Device Manager

Device Manager is a simple little tool that has been around in Windows for a long time. Essentially, it functions as a basic Microsoft Management Console (MMC) interface. Its purpose is to give you access to all of the devices on your computer, where you can manage them in several different ways. Follow these steps in use the Device Manager:

1. **Right-click My Computer and click Properties.** The System Properties dialog box appears.

2. **Click the Hardware tab and click the Device Manager button.** This opens the Device Manager window (Figure 3-2). You can also open System Properties in Control Panel, or you can open the Administrative Tools folder in Control Panel and double-click the Computer Management option. In the Computer Management window (Figure 3-3), select Device Manager from the list. No matter which option you choose, the same standard Device Manager list appears.

Once you open Device Manager, notice that the tool contains different categories, such as Computer, Disk drives, and Display adapters. You can expand each category to see where hardware devices are installed, as shown in Figure 3-2. The Device Manager console does not do a lot in terms of the actual console, but you can quickly change the view. By default, devices are listed by their type, although you can use the View menu and change to Devices by connection, Resources by type, and Resources by connection.

Disabling a Device

You can use Device Manager to disable a device. As you use Windows XP, you may want to disable a device for troubleshooting purposes, or to save battery power if you are using a portable computer.

Cross-Reference   **Also, you can use the disable feature when you create hardware profiles, which you learn about in Chapter 4.**

Figure 3-2: Device Manager

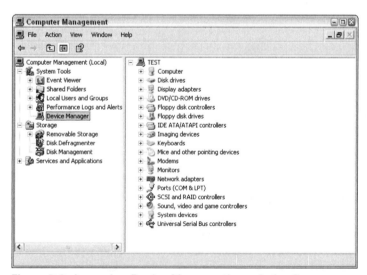

Figure 3-3: Accessing Device Manager through the Computer Management console

When you disable a device, you do not uninstall the device. The device driver is not uninstalled, nor is any configuration changed; the device is simply disabled until you re-enable it again. To disable a device, do this:

1. **Expand the desired category in Device Manager, and locate the desired device.**

2. **Right-click the device and click Disable on the context menu that appears, as shown in Figure 3-4.**

Figure 3-4: Right-click the device and click Disable.

3. **To re-enable the device, repeat the first two steps and choose Enable.**

Accessing Device Properties

If you expand the desired device category and double-click the device, you access the properties pages for that particular device. The tab options that you find may vary, depending on the actual device. Generically, you can use the device's properties to troubleshoot the device, manage the driver, and check resources.

In the General tab, shown in Figure 3-5, you can check the status of the device and click the Troubleshoot button to open the Windows Troubleshooter. Also, notice that you can use the General tab to disable a device as well.

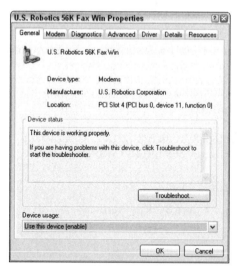

Figure 3-5: The General tab

The Resources tab, shown in Figure 3-6, displays what computer resources the device is using. For some devices, you can use this tab to manually change the resource allocation that Windows XP has established for the device. Generally, however, Windows XP does a good job of managing these settings, and you do not need to do anything on this tab. The best thing about this tab is that it tells you whether there are any conflicts with other devices. As you can see in Figure 3-6, there are no conflicts with this device. However, if there were conflicts, this dialog box would indicate the kind of conflict as well as the other device that was conflicting with it.

Figure 3-6: The Resources tab

Managing Drivers

It is important to remember that a driver is simply software that enables Windows XP to interact with a hardware device. Because the driver is software, you may need to update it from time to time. Driver installation and configuration have been very difficult for Windows users in the past, so Windows XP now includes tools that make driver management much easier than before.

First of all, if you access the Hardware tab of System Properties, as shown in Figure 3-7, you can manage the way that Driver Signing and Windows Update (concerning drivers) work.

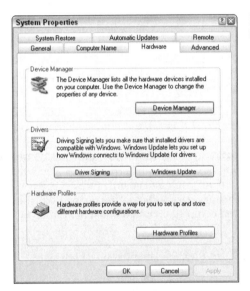

Figure 3-7: The Hardware tab of System Properties dialog box

Managing Driver Signing

Driver Signing, which was first introduced in Windows 2000, is a process that enables you to install only drivers that have been digitally signed by Microsoft. This feature tells you that Microsoft has tested the driver and that the drive will work with hardware on Windows XP. It also tells you that the driver is authentic, and not malicious code that you have downloaded from the Internet, posing as a driver.

Because they have a digital signature stamp that cannot be altered without altering the entire driver package, signed drivers give you some measure of protection and trust. However, many drivers are not signed by Microsoft because it is up to the individual hardware manufacturers whether the driver is sent to Microsoft for testing. You should use your common sense; make sure that you only obtain drivers for your devices from the actual hardware manufacturer, and not some third-party Internet site.

When you install a device driver, the system checks the driver and selects one of the following options in the Driver Signing Options dialog box, shown in Figure 3-8, depending on your configuration:

Figure 3-8: The Driver Signing Options window

✦ **Ignore:** If the driver is not digitally signed, this option tells Windows to ignore the software's unsigned state and install it anyway. You receive no warning messages if this option is used.

✦ **Warn:** If the driver is not digitally signed, a warning dialog box appears telling you so. At that point, you can choose to install the driver or not. This is the default setting.

✦ **Block:** If the driver is not digitally signed, the operating system does not allow it to be installed.

✦ **Administrator option:** This check box option enables you to specify the Ignore, Warn, or Block setting that you choose as the default option for all users on your computer. You must be logged on with a local Administrator account to invoke this feature.

If you click the Driver Signing button on the Hardware tab, a list of options becomes available to you. You can leave the default settings as they are or change them as desired. As a general rule, the Warn option is the best setting because you are alerted to an unsigned driver, but still maintain control over what happens.

Getting Newer Drivers Using Windows Update

Drivers are pieces of software, and so they need to be updated from time to time; otherwise, when you install a new device, Windows XP may need to use Windows Update to look for a driver that works. This is a great feature that requires only an Internet connection. On the Hardware tab, click the Windows Update button to display the three options in the Connect to Windows Update dialog box, shown in Figure 3-9:

Figure 3-9: You can choose a Windows Update option.

✦ If my device needs a driver, go to Windows Update without asking me.

✦ Ask me to search Windows Update every time I connect a new device.

✦ Never search Windows Update for drivers.

By default, the second option is selected, although you can choose another option here and click OK, if desired. As a general rule, you want Windows XP to check Windows Update for new drivers. This way, you always have the most updated software.

Updating a Driver

To update drivers, click the Hardware tab of System Properties, and then click the Device Manager button. Expand the desired category, and double-click the device whose driver you want to update. The Properties dialog box appears for that device, and you can click to display the Driver tab, as shown in Figure 3-10.

If you click the Driver Details button, you see information about the driver, such as the location, provider, file version, copyright, and digital signer information, as shown in Figure 3-11. This data can be helpful when you simply want to gain basic information about the driver.

Figure 3-10: The Driver tab

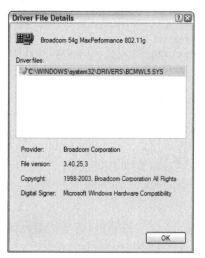

Figure 3-11: The Driver File Details dialog box

If you want to update your driver, you can download and install a new one by clicking the Update Driver button on the Driver tab. When you click Update Driver, the Hardware Update wizard appears and enables you to replace an older driver with a newer one. The installation steps are self-explanatory. Make sure that you have downloaded the updated driver first.

On the Driver tab, you also see buttons labeled Roll Back Driver and Uninstall. If you install a new driver for a device and the new driver does not function well, you can use the Roll Back feature to use the old driver. This feature pulls the old driver out of a backup file and reinstalls it. If you want to completely remove a driver, simply use the Uninstall button. You see a warning message that tells you that you are about to remove the device from your system.

Note

When you uninstall the driver, the device is uninstalled. At this point, Windows XP plug-and-play detects the uninstalled hardware device as new hardware and attempts to reinstall it. In some cases, this can help you uninstall and reinstall a problematic device, especially if you are having driver problems.

Configuring the Display Adapter

Your computer ships with a display adapter card. You plug in your monitor to this card to see what is on the screen. Of course, the display adapter card that you have depends on your needs and your budget. Display adapters vary widely, from basic display adapters to expensive adapters for playing 3D games. In the end, an adapter is just a piece of hardware that must work with Windows XP, and so the standard rules about installation and driver management are the same.

The display adapter has some additional settings that you can configure using Display Properties. When you use Display Properties, you may think that you are configuring the "display," but in reality, you are configuring the display card. The following steps guide you through the process of configuring the display adapter.

1. **Right-click an empty area of the desktop and click Properties.** In the Display Properties dialog box, click the Settings tab. You see the standard settings options, as shown in Figure 3-12.

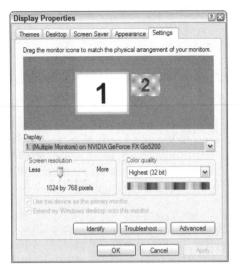

Figure 3-12: The Settings tab of the Display Properties dialog box

2. **Set the Screen resolution.** In the left portion of the tab, you see the option to adjust the screen resolution. In order to change the screen resolution, simply drag the slider bar to a different location. Click Apply. A Monitor Settings window appears, where you can choose whether or not to keep the new settings (you have 15 seconds, after which the setting reverts to the previous setting).

3. **Adjust the Color quality.** You can next adjust the color quality settings by using the drop-down menu. You should use the highest color quality settings that the video card can support (such as 32 bit).

4. **Click the Advanced button on the Settings tab**. Several additional tabs appear. The standard tabs are General, Adapter, Monitor, Troubleshoot, and Color Management (if your adapter supports it). You may see additional tabs, as well. These tabs are specific to the computer's video card and are determined by the video card software that you install.

5. **Change any General tab settings that you want to apply.** On the General tab shown in Figure 3-13, you see two sections, Display and Compatibility. Under Display, you can change the Dots Per Inch (DPI) setting to compensate for small screen items under your current resolution. The default is 96. However, this feature does not adjust font or color sizes. Under Compatibility, you can tell the computer to restart after changes are made to display settings. This feature is available because some programs may not work correctly if there is no reboot after setting changes. The default setting is to apply the new display settings without restarting, although you can choose a different radio button option, depending on your needs.

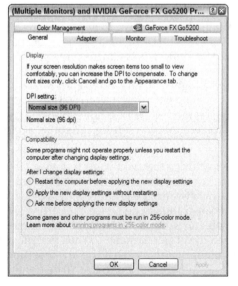

Figure 3-13: The General tab of the Monitor Properties dialog box

6. **Change any Adapter tab settings you want to apply.** On the Adapter tab, you can read basic information about your video adapter. You can also click Properties button to access the Device Manager's properties pages for the video card. If you click the List All Modes button, you see all screen resolution modes that are supported by the video card, as shown in Figure 3-14.

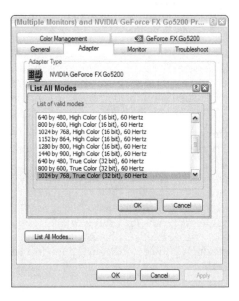

Figure 3-14: The Adapter tab gives you additional information about your adapter.

7. **Change any Monitor tab settings that you want to apply.** On the Monitor tab shown in Figure 3-15, you can access the Device Manager properties for the monitor by clicking the Properties button. You can also adjust the screen refresh rate. Higher refresh rates reduce "flicker" that may appear on the screen, and naturally, you need a higher-quality video card to use a higher refresh rate. Default settings typically fall around 60 to 85 Hertz. Also note the setting that allows you to hide modes that are not supported by the monitor — this ensures that an incompatible setting cannot be accidentally selected on the Settings tab.

8. **Change any Troubleshoot tab settings that you want to apply.** On the Troubleshoot tab, you have two setting options, shown in Figure 3-16. The first enables you to adjust the hardware acceleration of the video card. The typical setting is Full, but you can gradually decrease the setting in order to troubleshoot performance problems with the video card. Of course, lower acceleration settings also mean lower performance. When you move the slider bar down, you see a description of the impact that the lower setting will have on video performance. You also have the option to use Write Combining.

Write Combining provides graphics data to your screen more quickly, which improves performance. However, some video cards cannot keep up with this setting. If you are having distortion problems, try clearing this check box.

Figure 3-15: The Monitor tab gives you information about monitor settings.

Figure 3-16: Check the Troubleshoot tab for additional settings.

FYI: Multiple Monitors and Windows XP

Windows XP continues to support multiple monitor configurations. Multiple monitors are useful to many different people, especially those working with multiple documents and graphics files. Using Windows XP, you can connect up to ten individual monitors to a single PC.

When using multiple monitors, you can place different applications or files on different monitors, and you can stretch items between monitors. One monitor serves as the primary monitor where older applications and the Windows logon screen appear. You can use multiple video cards with different settings, or you can use a single video card that has multiple outputs where you can connect the monitors. Regardless of the configuration that you choose, you can use Display Properties to adjust the appearance of each monitor. Incidentally, Windows XP also supports a dual-view feature. This is the same as multiple monitors, except that it is used on laptop computers where the LCD screen is always the primary monitor, and the attached monitor serves as a second viewing area (you can see this option in Figure 3-12).

When you set up multiple monitors, keep in mind that the monitors need to plug into either a PCI slot or an AGP slot. Make sure that you are only using Windows XP-compatible drivers. Then install the new video card and attach the monitor. Windows XP detects it. At this point, return to the Display Properties and display the Settings tab. Select the monitor that you want to use as the secondary monitor. If the primary monitor is an onboard video adapter that is built into the motherboard, it must be the primary monitor. Click the Extend my Windows desktop onto this monitor option check box, and click OK. *David Dalan*

9. **Change any Color Management tab settings that you want to apply.** The Color Management tab allows you to choose a color profile for your monitor, assuming that your adapter card supports this feature. If you click the Add button, you see a list of profiles that are available by default. You can choose a color profile specific to your monitor's make and model, and this may improve color performance. However, you normally do not need this feature, and unless you are having problems, don't change it.

10. **When you are done examining all of these settings, click OK.**

Managing USB Devices and USB Hubs

Universal Serial Bus, or USB, is an industry-standard bus architecture that has made all of our lives much easier. In the past, you had to connect different devices to specific ports. For example, you had a port for the mouse, one for the keyboard, a different port for your printer, and so on. With USB, most peripherals can now plug in to the USB port, which gives you more flexibility and makes your computing experience less complicated.

Essentially, USB bus technology allows multiple devices to connect to the same port. You probably have several USB ports on your computer, but you can greatly extend them by using USB hubs, which allow you to connect multiple devices to one port. The USB ports that you find on your computer are labeled USB roots, in that there is one USB root with multiple ports that go directly to the computer's motherboard. From these standard ports, you can plug in devices, or a hub, or even a device that has additional USB ports. Using this tiered approach, you can plug up to 127 USB devices in to a single USB port on the computer. However, the types of devices and the types of hubs also have an impact here.

USB hubs are sold as either bus-powered hubs or self-powered hubs. Bus-powered hubs draw their power from the USB bus, or more specifically the power flowing into the computer system from the AC/DC outlet. For most USB peripherals, such as keyboards and mice, the power available from a bus-powered hub is all that you need. However, some USB devices may require more power. For example, if you have a USB bus-powered hub, and you connect a USB external hard drive to it, the drive will not work when you plug it into the USB hub. This is because the external drive needs more power to operate than the USB bus-powered hub can provide. In this case, you need a USB self-powered hub, which has a separate AC/DC connection. The point to remember is that self-powered hubs provide the necessary power to prevent power limitations, and so if you are looking to buy a USB hub, you may want to spend the little bit extra for a self-powered hub.

Troubleshooting: Device Error Codes

Naturally, things can go wrong with hardware. In fact, there are over 30 Windows XP Device Manager error codes that may pop onto your screen if something goes wrong. Fortunately, most of them are self-explanatory. For example, error code 14 states, "The device cannot work properly until you restart your computer."

Although you may see error codes that are not particularly helpful, keep in mind that most hardware problems result from a bad driver or a simple hardware failure. For example, if you are using older devices, there could be some conflict with other system processes or resources. Should you get one of these error messages and need more information, you can easily find an explanation and suggested action(s) at microsoft. com. The direct URL at the time of this writing is http://support.microsoft.com/default. aspx?scid=kb;en-us;310123. If this URL doesn't give you the results you want, just search Microsoft.com for "Device Manager error codes." *Curt Simmons*

If you want to check out the power use on your USB controller, you can do so by using Device Manager. Open Device Manager and expand the Universal Serial Bus controllers category. Double-click a desired host controller and click the Advanced tab. You can see how much bandwidth a particular controller uses, as shown in Figure 3-17. Devices that are attached to the controller must share the USB bandwith (which is often around 10% as set automatically by Windows XP). You can also double-click a root hub in Device Manager and click the Power tab on the Properties dialog box to get more information about the power consumption of the hub, as shown in Figure 3-18.

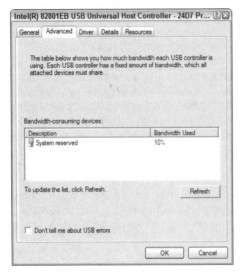

Figure 3-17: The Advanced tab displays USB Host Controller bandwidth.

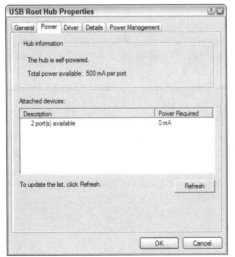

Figure 3-18: The Power tab displays power needs and hub information.

Are you using USB hubs with your laptop running on batteries? If your batteries seem to run down quickly, this is because the USB hub is pulling power from the batteries. Avoid using external USB hubs when your laptop is running on batteries. In fact, you can save more power with a Hardware Profile, which you can learn more about in Chapter 4.

A Word about Printers...

For the most part, installing and using printers has become very easy, thanks to good drivers and a friendly Windows XP environment. If you need to install a new printer, the best thing to do is to follow the manufacturer's instructions. Windows XP contains an Add a Printer wizard in the Printers and Faxes folder, but you seldom need it. Instead, use the manufacturer's setup CD and instructions to make sure the correct drivers and printer tools are installed.

The questions you are most likely to have about printing concern shared network printers, managing the print queue, and getting digital photos to print the way you want. I explore these various topics throughout the book in the appropriate chapters; refer to the index for more information.

Managing Power Options

4

Power options have come a long way in the past several years, and this benefits all of us. With so many of us using portable computers, we all need the flexibility to control power usage in a variety of ways, and we need to control power usage in a way that is helpful to our particular home and work environments. Fortunately, Windows XP gives you the ability to do just that. Using Windows XP, you can determine how a computer should manage power, when certain features of the computer should turn off, and how hibernation should work. In this chapter, you explore the power options that are available to you in Windows XP — how to configure them, how to control them, and how to use them in a way that is helpful to you.

Working with Power Schemes

Windows XP provides you with some default power schemes. You can use one of the defaults if it meets your needs, or you can customize a scheme to create your own. Both options are quick and easy.

Naturally, you need to ask yourself how you want Windows XP to use power, and your decisions will most likely be based on the type of computer that you are using and how you use the computer during the day. For example, if you are using a laptop, then power schemes become much more important because they can help you conserve battery power. As a result, you should first think about your needs, and then take a look at the default schemes to see if one works for you. If not, you can customize a scheme and make it your own.

Choosing a Default Power Scheme

If you click Start ⇨ Control Panel ⇨ Power Options, the Power Options Properties dialog box appears, as shown in Figure 4-1. The first tab, Power Schemes, enables you to either choose a default scheme or create a new one. Note that the appearance of the Power Schemes tab varies, depending on your computer. For example, Figure 4-1 shows a laptop power scheme, and so there is a section for battery power as well.

Figure 4-1: You can choose a default Power Scheme option in the Power Options Properties dialog box.

Tip   **Do not worry if the tab options are different from computer to computer — this is normal. Power options enable you to configure power management for a particular computer's hardware. As a result, the options that you see on this tab vary from computer to computer because the power options only let you configure what you can actually control.**

FYI: How Power Options Work

Power options work through a computer industry design called Advanced Configuration and Power Interface, or ACPI. ACPI is the foundation of the OnNow industry specification that allows for specific control over parts of the system board. Windows XP works with this specification in order to control power to the different hardware devices and system components. Because of this specification and your computer's hardware, the power options that you have on your particular computer may vary, although Windows XP's Plug and Play system is able to detect what you can control with power options.

To choose a default power scheme, simply click the Power Schemes drop-down menu and choose a scheme you want. Notice that the Settings section of the tab changes according to the scheme that you select. Generally, the following settings apply:

✦ **Home/Office Desk — Plugged In:** The monitor turns off after 20 minutes of inactivity, but the hard disk never turns off. The system never goes into standby mode or hibernation. Batteries: The monitor turns off after 5 minutes of inactivity, and the hard disk after 10 minutes. The system goes into standby mode after 5 minutes of inactivity and hibernates after 20 minutes.

✦ **Portable/Laptop — Plugged In:** The system goes into standby mode after 15 minutes of inactivity and hibernates after 30 minutes of inactivity. Batteries: The monitor turns off after 5 minutes of inactivity, and the hard disk after 5 minutes. The system goes into standby mode after 15 minutes of inactivity and hibernation after 30 minutes.

✦ **Presentation — Plugged In:** Nothing turns off, and the system never goes into standby mode or hibernation. Batteries: The monitor never turns off, but the hard disk turns off after 5 minutes of inactivity. The system goes into standby mode after 15 minutes of inactivity and hibernation after 2 hours.

✦ **Always On — Plugged In:** The monitor turns off after 20 minutes of inactivity, but the hard disk never turns off. The system never goes into standby mode or hibernation. Batteries: The monitor turns off after 15 minutes of inactivity, and the hard disk after 30 minutes. The system never goes into standby mode or hibernation.

✦ **Minimal Power Management — Plugged In:** The monitor turns off after 15 minutes, but the hard disk never turns off. The system never goes into standby mode or hibernation. Batteries: The monitor turns off after 5 minutes of inactivity, and the hard disk after 15 minutes. The system goes into standby mode after 5 minutes and hibernates after 3 hours.

✦ **Max Battery—Plugged In:** The monitor turns off after 15 minutes, but the hard disk never turns off. The system goes into standby mode after 20 minutes of inactivity and hibernates after 45 minutes. Batteries: The monitor turns off after 1 minute of inactivity, and the hard disk after 3 minutes. The system goes into standby mode after 2 minutes of inactivity, and hibernates after 1 hour.

If you are not sure about the use of standby mode and hibernation, read on. These features are explored later in the chapter.

As you take a look at the default schemes, it is important to think about whether they meet your particular needs. Some schemes may not conserve battery power as well as you want, while others, such as Max Battery, may be a bit too restrictive for your needs. If you find a default scheme that works for you, simply choose it from the drop-down menu and click OK. If not, the next section shows you how to create a custom scheme.

You can quickly access the Power Options dialog box by clicking Start ⇨ Run and typing powercfg.cpl in the Run dialog box.

Create a Custom Power Scheme

The default schemes give you a number of options, but you may find that no particular scheme gives you exactly what you want. This often occurs, and so you may find that adjusting certain parts of a scheme work best for you. For example, you may want to use the Portable / Laptop scheme, but not have the system go into standby mode until 30 minutes of inactivity has passed, instead of 15 minutes. To do this, you can easily create a custom scheme.

1. **Open Control Panel and then open the Power Options applet.** You can open the Control Panel by clicking start ⇨ Control Panel.

2. **On the Power Schemes tab, click the Power schemes drop-down menu and choose a power scheme that contains the power management settings that are close to your specific needs.**

3. **Click the drop-down menus and adjust the specific settings as desired, as shown in Figure 4-2.**

4. **When you are done, click the Save As button.**

5. **In the Save Scheme dialog box, shown in Figure 4-3, give your scheme a name and click OK.** You can now access your scheme from the Power schemes drop-down menu. You can create multiple schemes for different needs.

Figure 4-2: Click the necessary drop-down menus and adjust the values.

Figure 4-3: Give the new scheme a meaningful name in the Save As dialog box.

Configure Power Alarms

If you are using a laptop computer, you can configure how Windows XP lets you know that battery power is running low and what action Windows XP takes. More than likely, while the computer is running on batteries, it is preconfigured to go into standby mode and, later, hibernation after certain periods of inactivity. You may also see a pop-up notice from the Notification area. This configuration may work fine for you, but you can reconfigure these default options in a way that works better for you. Follow these steps:

1. **Click Start ➪ Control Panel ➪ Power Options.** The Power Options Properties dialog box appears.

2. **Click the Alarms tab, as shown in Figure 4-4.** Notice that you can adjust the settings for low battery power and critical battery power. Also notice that the default settings are provided for you.

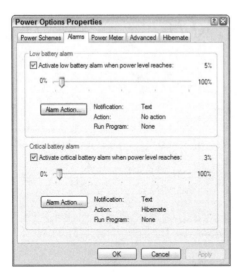

Figure 4-4: The Alarms tab of the Power Options Properties dialog box

3. **If you want to change the default action, click the Alarm Action button for the low battery power or critical battery power option.** In the Low Battery Alarm Actions dialog box, shown in Figure 4-5, you have the option to change the notification action and alarm action, and you can run a program if desired.

4. **Enable the desired check boxes and options to choose the alarm features and actions that you want.**

5. **Click OK and OK again on the Power Options Properties dialog box.**

Figure 4-5: Change default alarm actions in the Low Battery Alarm Actions dialog box.

Work with Standby and Hibernation

Standby and Hibernation are both power-saving features of Windows XP. Their purpose is to put your computer in a power-saving state after a certain amount of inactivity. The actual amount of inactivity depends on the power scheme that you have configured

For more on power schemes, see the section "Working with Power Schemes." earlier in this chapter.

What is the difference between the two features?

✦ **Standby mode** is a power-saving state where the monitor and hard disks are turned off. However, if you want to use the computer, it comes out of standby mode and back to your work. In other words, nothing is shut down. Keep in mind that your work is not saved to the disk, so if the battery fails, you lose any work that you have not previously saved.

✦ **Hibernation** is a power-saving mode that saves everything that you are working on, and then turns off the monitor, hard disks, and finally the computer. When you bring the computer out of hibernation, everything is restored back to the way you left it. For example, applications and files are opened as they were before using hibernation. Hibernation takes longer to come out of than standby mode, but it also saves everything and stops using any battery power. If your computer is configured with user accounts, you need to log on when you bring the computer out of hibernation mode.

Hibernation is a great feature of Windows XP, and I use it all of the time with my laptop computer. In fact, I really never shut down and restart. I simply use hibernation mode every time I am away from my laptop. This way, I do not have to wait for my computer to boot, and I do not have to close down applications and work. The time delay between boot from hibernate to workable desktop is also considerably shorter than is the case when you close down he machine normally and then re-boot. Hibernation is a quick way to get back to your working desktop.

Managing Standby and Hibernation Mode

Standby mode behaves according to the configuration of the power scheme that you have selected at the moment. However, you can also place some additional controls on standby mode and manually put your computer in standby mode if you want. You can do the same thing with hibernation.

Expert's Notebook: Power Options and Air Travel

If you are a frequent flyer, then you know that the Federal air travel regulations require you to power down your computer and cell phones during takeoff and landing. However, it is important to remember that standby mode does not actually turn off your computer. The operating system remains active, as well as any wireless modems. The point to remember is that during air travel, you need to either shut the computer down using Start ➪ Turn Off Computer, or using Hibernation. Either way, all of your computer components actually turn off, and you can avoid any potential trouble. *Curt Simmons*

Note   **Standby mode and hibernation mode are only available on PCs that support the power saving features. If you do not see a Hibernate tab, then the feature is not supported.**

First of all, make sure that hibernation is enabled on your computer. Open Power Options, and then click the Hibernate tab, as shown in Figure 4-6. Make sure that you select the Enable hibernation option check box.

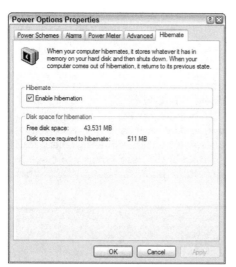

Figure 4-6: Choose the Enable hibernation option check box if it is not already selected.

Note   **Hibernation uses a part of your computer's free hard disk space to save information about programs and files that are in use when hibernation is enacted. You cannot change these settings, nor do you need to.**

Troubleshooting: Standby and USB Storage Devices

If you are using a USB storage device, you might have a problem if you change USB ports when the computer is in standby mode. You may notice that Windows XP does not recognize a USB storage device after you resume from standby mode. This problem occurs when you unplug the USB device and plug it into a different USB port, typically because multiple controllers are in use. Leave the USB device plugged into the same port as it was when the computer went into standby mode.

You can adjust the behavior of Standby mode and Hibernation by using the Advanced tab on the Power Options applet, shown in Figure 4-7. Notice that you can determine the action that you want the computer to take when you close the lid of the laptop or press the power button or sleep button. Also notice that you can choose to have the logon screen re-appear so that a logon password is required. For the best security, keep this option enabled. To come out of Standby mode, press the sleep button on your computer or move the mouse. To come out of Hibernation mode, press the power key on your computer.

Figure 4-7: Adjust the behavior of standby and hibernation

Create a Hardware Profile

Hardware profiles are not new in Windows XP, but with the portable computers of today, they have become more important than ever. Consider this scenario: You use a laptop computer at your small office. When you are at the office, the laptop is plugged in, and you use a portable keyboard, mouse, printer, and several additional

USB devices, including an external USB drive. When you are mobile, you use none of these hardware devices. This is fine, although Windows XP still allocates resources for the installed hardware, even if the hardware is not in use. In addition, you may use a network interface card when you are in the office, but not when you are on the road. However, when you are on the road, you may use a portable printer.

As you can imagine, all of these hardware devices consume system resources. However, when you are mobile, you may want to conserve as many resources as possible. You can easily do that with a hardware profile.

When you install new hardware, it is automatically added to the default hardware profile that Windows XP uses, typically called Profile 1. Under Profile 1, all hardware that is installed is enabled. This is fine when you need all of the hardware. However, when you are mobile, you really need a different hardware profile that does not enable all of the installed devices that are not actually connected to your computer.

Fortunately, you can easily create a second hardware profile and disable the devices that are not used when you are mobile. In fact, you can create as many different hardware profiles as you need for various situations and environments where you use your computer.

Note

Once you create a second hardware profile (or third, fourth, and so on), you see a boot menu option when you start Windows XP. You can choose the hardware profile that you want to use at that time. This feature easily allows you to switch between hardware profiles by simply restarting your computer.

To create an additional hardware profile, follow these steps:

1. **Log on to your computer with an Administrator account.**

2. **Click Start ⇨ Control Panel ⇨ System Properties.** The System Properties dialog box opens, as shown in Figure 4-8.

4. **On the Hardware tab, click the Hardware Profiles button.** In the Hardware Profiles dialog box, shown in Figure 4-9, you see the current default profile.

5. **If you click the Properties button, you can see the basic properties of the default profile, as shown in Figure 4-10.** If you are using a portable computer, you can choose to enable the option and always include the default profile option when Windows XP starts. Click OK.

6. **To create a new profile, click the Copy button in the Hardware Profiles dialog box.** A Copy Profile dialog box appears, as shown in Figure 4-11. Enter a name for the new profile and click OK. Choose a name that is descriptive, such as "travel" or something similar.

   At this point, your new profile appears in the profile list. However, when you copied the default profile, all of the hardware settings were kept, and so you basically have two profiles that are the same. This is okay, because you can edit the second profile later.

Figure 4-8: The Hardware tab of the System Properties dialog box.

Figure 4-9: The Hardware Profiles dialog box.

7. **Select your new profile and click the Properties button**. Select the This is a portable computer option check box, and select the option to include the profile when Windows starts. Click OK.

8. **Click OK to close the Hardware Profiles dialog box, and then restart your computer.** When the computer restarts, you see a boot menu with the two profiles.

9. **Choose the new profile that you created and press Enter.**

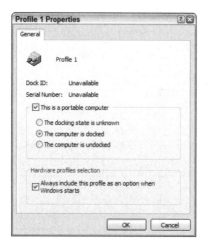

Figure 4-10: The Profile Properties dialog box.

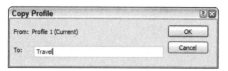

Figure 4-11: Give your new profile a name in the Copy Profile dialog box.

10. **Once Windows XP boots, log on with an Administrator account.** Now you can edit the hardware settings for your new profile.

11. **Click Start ➪ Control Panel ➪ System.** Choose the Hardware tab and click the Device Manager button.

12. **In Device Manager, expand the categories you want to change, and then right-click the device that you do not want to use in this hardware profile.** Choose the Disable option, as shown in Figure 4-12. Repeat this process to disable any other devices that you do not want to use under this profile.

13. **When you are done, close Device Manager and click OK on the Hardware tab.** The next time you boot your computer using this profile, the selected devices are automatically disabled.

Keep in mind that when you disable hardware devices, they are not uninstalled from your system. They are simply turned off under the desired profile. This feature allows you to save system resources, but easily re-enable devices within the profile should the need arise. All devices under the default Profile 1 are automatically enabled if you select Profile 1 when you boot. This easy configuration option enables you to tailor the hardware profiles in any way that is helpful to you, but also to quickly change them if needed.

Expert's Notebook: How I Use Hardware Profiles

I think that hardware profiles are great, and they have helped me to conserve system resources and battery power in several situations. I have a certain laptop that I use in three primary places: in my office, on the road, and in the classroom. When I am at the office, I have several peripherals attached to the computer. I also use wired and wireless network. This configuration serves as my default profile. When I teach, I use an external projector for PowerPoint slides, but no peripherals. For this profile, I disable everything that I do not need, including the network cards. Finally, I also maintain a "travel" profile that essentially turns off everything else, including the CD/DVD drive. Because I use minimal hardware when I am running on batteries, I find that my battery life is extended as unneeded hardware does not consume any power. Hardware profiles are easy to configure and change as needed, and so you should put them to work!
Curt Simmons

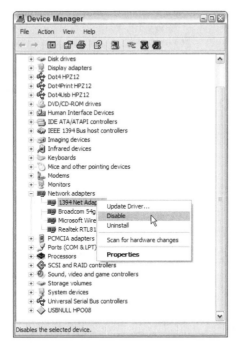

Figure 4-12: Disable unneeded devices in Device Manager.

Customizing Startup and Shutdown

5

I n the olden days of Windows, startup and shutdown of a computer weren't a big deal. You started up the computer and then you shut it down when you were finished. So, why devote a whole chapter to startup and shutdown procedures?

A lot of things have changed in the world of Windows since those early days, and there are now many issues that affect startup and shutdown—issues that stem mainly from programs. For example, maybe startup is slow or shutdown seems to take too long. Maybe you have programs that keep starting when you boot your computer, even though you do not want them to. Regardless of the issue, this chapter helps you to better manage startup and shutdown in Windows XP.

Managing Startup Programs

The Windows XP startup process is complicated. Along with loading the operating system, Windows XP loads your personal user profile data, as well as startup applications that are tied to that user account. Sorting through all of this can be rather complicated and fraught with problems. However, there is a simple tool that can help you to find out what is going on during the startup process and to help you control it in some ways.

That tool is the System Configuration Utility, or MSCONFIG. The following steps show how to access and use the MSCONFIG utility.

Before you jump into MSCONFIG, it is important to note that old drivers will slow down the computer's startup process. When you boot your computer, hardware drivers load, and some older drivers tend to slow down the booting process. The lesson here is to always use the most updated drivers for your hardware devices. See Chapter 3 for additional information about managing hardware drivers.

1. **Click Start ➪ Run.** Type **msconfig** and then click OK. The System Configuration Utility opens. The General tab appears, as shown in Figure 5-1.

2. **Use this tab to make a startup selection.** In most cases, you leave the Normal Startup option selected. With the normal startup, Windows XP loads all device drivers and services during startup. You also have the option to use a Diagnostic Startup, where only basic devices and services are loaded. Finally, you have a Selective Startup option, where you can choose not to process selected startup items, such as system services. Remember to only use Normal startup unless you are trying to troubleshoot startup problems.

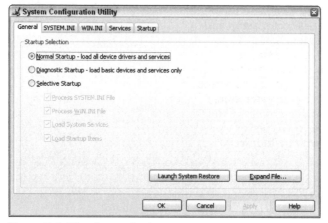

Figure 5-1: The General tab

3. **Click the System.ini and Win.ini tabs.** These tabs are throwbacks to the early days of Windows, where the System.ini and Win.ini configurations were needed for Windows to boot. Unless you are specifically trying to troubleshoot a problem, don't enable or disable anything on these tabs. There are better ways to troubleshoot Windows XP, rather than adding or removing items from these files.

4. **Click the Services tab.** This tab (shown in Figure 5-2) has all of the services that start on your computer when it is booted. Naturally, the more services that have to start, the more time is required to actually boot Windows. You may see services here that you don't need to use. In that case, you can simply clear the check box next to the service in order to stop it from starting when your computer boots. However, a number of these components are needed for all of Windows XP's features to function as they should, so don't disable anything here unless you are sure of what the service does. A helpful feature here is the Hide all Microsoft Services check box. This will hide all services that are developed by Microsoft and leave you with third-party services. This way, you can look through the list of third-party services and disable those that you no longer need. Reducing the number of services that must start will help to reduce the overall boot time.

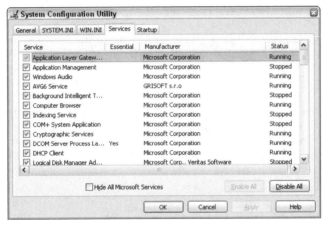

Figure 5-2: The Services tab

5. **Click the Startup tab.** This tab (shown in Figure 5-3) shows you any applications that are configured to start when the computer is booted. Keep in mind that you do not want to disable applications that are configured to start by the system, as you may cause different Windows XP features to stop working. However, you may have other applications that are configured to boot, but that you do not need. For example, in Figure 5-3, you can see that I have a screen capture utility called SnagIt configured to start when the computer boots. If I decide that I no longer want this program to start automatically, I can simply clear the check box here to stop the program from doing so. As with services, the fewer applications that must automatically start, the more quickly your system will boot.

Expert's Notebook: Preventing Programs from Auto-starting

When you buy a computer off the shelf, it may auto-start some programs whether you like it or not. It's not always easy to find a way to prevent a program from auto-starting, because you won't necessarily know what's causing the program to start.

In many cases, the option to auto-start will be in a program's Options dialog box. For example, to prevent a program in the Notification area from auto-starting, you can often double-click that program's Notification area icon to open the program, choose Tools ⇨ Options from the program's menu bar, and then open its Options dialog box. Look through all of the tabs in the Options dialog box for a simple check box to clear to prevent the program from auto-starting in the future.

Some programs auto-start from an icon in the Startup folder for all users, while others may auto-start from an icon in your user account's Startup folder. To prevent the program from auto-starting, you need to remove the icon from the appropriate Startup folder. If you right-click the Start button and choose Explorer, or Explorer All Users, Windows Explorer opens with a Folders list that makes it easy to access either Startup folder. To see Startup icons for all users, expand the Documents and Settings, All Users, Start Menu, and Programs folders, and then click the Startup folder under the Programs folder. To see Startup programs for your user account, expand the folder that has your user account name (under Documents and Settings), and then expand the Start Menu and Programs folders under your user account name. Then click the Startup folder under that Programs folder. *Alan Simpson*

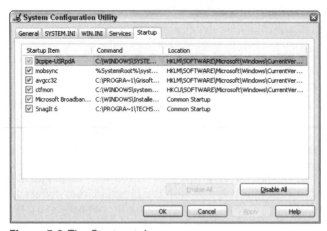

Figure 5-3: The Startup tab

Many malware programs get their auto-start capabilities from the Registry, rather than from a dialog box setting or icon. While the Registry is no place for the technologically faint-of-heart, if you're experienced with it, the key is to look under HKLM\Software\Microsoft\Windows\CurrentVersion\Run for undesirable auto-start programs.

The System Configuration Utility works very well, but it doesn't have as many options as some other programs from third-party vendors. Therefore, I recommend that you check out Startup Cop at www.pcmag.com/utilities. Startup Control Panel is also a great utility. Check it out at www.mlin.net.

Making Windows XP Start Faster

As you noticed in the previous section, there are two major issues that increase the boot time of Windows XP: services and startup applications, and older drivers. You can manage both services and startup applications using the MSCONFIG utility; however, there are a few other tactics that I want to mention in this section that may help reduce Windows XP's boot time.

Using the Services Console

Yes, you can use MSCONFIG to manage services, but the Services Console is a bit easier to use, and it gives you more information about the various services that are configured to start on Windows XP. Open Control Panel ⇨ Administrative Tools ⇨ Services. You can also click Start ⇨ Run, type **services.msc**, and then click OK. You then see the Services command console, as shown in Figure 5-4.

Notice the Startup Type column. The information here tells you whether the service is automatic or manual. Manual services are only started on Windows XP when you start a process that requires the service, or when some other process requires the service that has a "dependency" relationship with the service. These services do not start automatically when you boot Windows XP, and so you do not need to do anything with manual services.

However, all services listed as automatic start when Windows XP boots. These are the services that increase boot time. Many of them are necessary and important, so you should not stop automatic services from booting unless you are sure of the ramifications. The Description column tells you what the service does, but you still may wonder whether you need the service. That all depends on how you use your computer, however. Here are a few services that you may be able to live without:

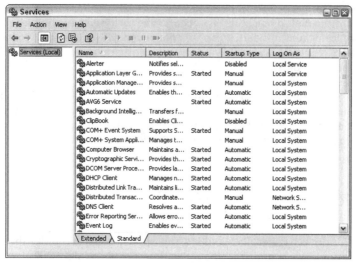

Figure 5-4: The Services command console

✦ **Computer Browser:** If you are not on a network, then you do not need this service.

✦ **DHCP Client**: If you are not on a network, then you do not need this service. If you are, leave it enabled.

✦ **DNS Client:** If you are not on a network, then you do not need this service. If you are, leave it enabled.

✦ **Fax:** If you don't use your computer for fax services, you can disable this one.

✦ **Help and Support:** If you never seem to use the Windows XP Help and Support Center (found on the Start menu), then you can disable this service.

✦ **IMAPI CD Burning COM:** This service enables you to burn CDs on your computer. If you never burn CDs, then you can disable this service.

✦ **Indexing Service:** Your computer keeps an index of files, but if you rarely search for files, the service is sort of a resource hog. You can deselect it to turn the service to manual.

✦ **Internet Connection Firewall / Internet Connection Sharing:** If you do not use these features, then you can disable them.

✦ **Infrared Monitor:** If you do not use infrared devices, then you can disable this service.

✦ **Messenger:** This service is used to send messages on a local area network (it is not the same as Windows Messenger). If you are not on a network, then you can disable this service.

✦ **Print Spooler:** If you do not do any printing from the computer, then you can disable this service. If you print, make sure that you leave it as automatic.

✦ **Remote Registry:** This service allows remote users to modify the registry on your computer. If you are not on a network, then you can disable this service.

✦ **System Restore Service:** This service allows you to use System Restore. If you have turned off System Restore anyway, then there is no need for the service to start (however, I strongly recommend that you use System Restore).

✦ **Windows Image Acquisition:** If you do not use scanners or digital cameras, then you can disable this service.

✦ **Wireless Zero Configuration:** If do not use wireless networking devices, then you can disable this service.

If you double-click any service, you'll see a properties dialog box where you can learn more about the service, as shown in Figure 5-5. Notice that on the General tab, you see a Startup type drop-down menu. If you want to change an automatic service to manual, select Manual on the drop-down menu and click OK. However, before you change a service to manual, it is a good idea to look at the Dependencies tab, as shown in Figure 5-6. This tab will show you what other services are dependent on the service that you are considering reducing to a manual service or even disabling. If you change a service to disabled, other services that need to start may not work either, because you have stopped the first service from starting automatically. This is why you must exercise caution if you want to change services to start manually.

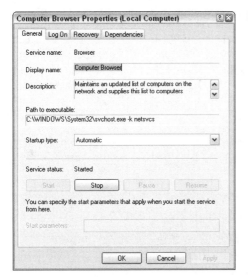

Figure 5-5: The Service General tab

 The indexing service, as well as the System Restore service, takes up a lot of disk space and system resources. I recommend that you use System Restore, but if you are not in the habit of searching your computer on a regular basis, consider changing the indexing service to manual.

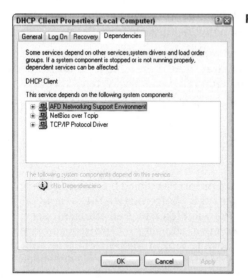

Figure 5-6: The Service Dependencies tab

Disable Recent Documents History

Recent Documents History, which you can access on the Start Menu, is a nice feature that helps you to easily and quickly access recent documents that you have opened. In short, it keeps a history of which documents you have used and places shortcuts to these documents in Recent Documents so that you can open these documents from the Start menu. However, if you don't use Recent Documents, it is one of those features that can slow down boot time, because Windows XP has to determine which documents should be put there each time you boot Windows. As a result, if you never use the Recent Documents History, it's a good idea to disable it. Here's how:

Note   You'll need to edit the Registry to disable Recent Documents History. If you are unfamiliar with editing the Registry, be sure to read the Appendix before performing these steps.

1. **Click Start ⇨ Run.** Type **regedit** and click OK.

2. **Navigate to** HKEY_CURRENT_USER\Software\Microsoft\Windows\ CurrentVersion\Policies\Explorer.

3. **In the right pane, locate the NoRecentDocsHistory value.** Double-click the value to open it.

4. **Set the Data Value to 1 to enable the restriction.**

5. **Click OK and close the Registry Editor.** You'll need to restart the computer for the change to take effect.

Note

An alternative method is to right-click a vacant portion of the task bar and select Properties from the menu. In the Properties window, click the start menu tab and then click the Customize button. In the Customize Start Menu window, click the Advanced tab. In the Recent Documents section, remove the check mark next to the "List my most recently opened documents" option. If you then click the Clear button, all the recently opened document history is removed. To complete the task click OK, followed by Apply in the next window and finally OK to exit the Properties box.

Disable Windows Messenger on Outlook Express 6

If you are using Outlook Express 6, Windows Messenger is configured to start and run in the background when Windows XP starts. That's fine if you use it, but if you don't, you waste boot time and background resources on Windows Messenger, which is always around. However, you can stop this behavior and save yourself a little startup time by following these steps:

1. **Open Outlook Express 6.**

2. **Click Tools ⇨ Windows Messenger ⇨ Options.**

3. **Click the Preferences tab.**

4. **On the Preferences tab, clear the "Allow this program to run in the background" check box, and click OK.**

Configuring Windows XP for Automatic Logon

One thing that you can do to speed up the startup process is to configure Windows XP to log you on automatically. Naturally, this feature works best if you are the only person that uses the computer and you are in an environment where you are not worried about someone else gaining access to your computer. If you configure Windows XP to log you on automatically, then anyone who starts your computer can gain access to it, because no username or password is prompted. Naturally, this can be a huge security risk, depending on how and where you use your computer.

However, if security isn't an issue for you, consider using automatic logon to make startup work more quickly. Do this:

Tip

These steps will not work if your computer is logged onto a Windows domain.

1. **Log on with an administrator account. Click Start ⇨ Run.** Type **control user-passwords2** and click OK.

2. **Clear the "Users must enter a user name and password to use this computer" check box, and then click Apply, as shown in Figure 5-7.**

Figure 5-7: Clear the check box on the Users tab.

3. **In the Automatically Log On window, type the password in the Password box.** Retype the password in the Confirm Password box, as shown in Figure 5-8.

Figure 5-8: The Automatically Log On window

Expert's Notebook: Make Startup Really Fast

OK, the title lies a bit, but if you really want to reduce your startup time, just don't shut down your computer. When used with current hardware, Windows XP's hibernation feature works very well. I primarily use a laptop computer, and I never shut down and restart unless I'm installing software that requires my system to reboot. In all other cases, I simply use hibernation (see Chapter 4). This way, I never have to close documents or programs that I am using, and when I want to use my computer, it is much faster to come out of hibernation than to start up. If you're in the habit of shutting down every time you use your computer, consider giving hibernation a try; you may never shut down your computer again! *Curt Simmons*

4. **Click OK to close the Automatically Log On window.** Click OK to close the User Accounts window.

 If you enable automatic logon, your computer is not secure. If security is important to you, then you may want to go to the other extreme, which is stopping the use of the Welcome screen so that users must type both a user-name and a password. You can find out how to configure this feature in Chapter 10.

Using the Startup Menu

Windows XP contains a startup, or boot, menu that enables you to choose several different startup modes that can be helpful for troubleshooting purposes. Because you won't use those startup modes unless you're having problems, I do not discuss them until Chapter 36.

Making Shutdown Work Faster

You can shut down your computer by clicking Start ➪ Turn Off Computer. You can also shut down the computer by holding down the power key for a few seconds (if you just press it, the computer will hibernate, if hibernation is configured, but if you hold it down, the computer will go through an entire shutdown process). However, this may power off the computer rather than shutting down the operating system, which can cause you to lose data.

However, you may notice that shutting down your computer seems to take longer than it should, and there are probably a few reasons why. The following sections show you a few tactics to make shutdown proceed more quickly.

Reducing Wait Time for Applications

When you start to shut down Windows XP, it has to quit, or kill, any live applications or processes that are currently running. However, Windows XP has some built-in wait time so that those applications have the ability to close on their own. This wait time can slow down the shutdown process, and so you may want to reduce the amount of wait time that Windows XP allows for those applications and processes to close before it kills them. You'll need to edit three different registry settings to change this feature, as follows:

1. **Click Start ➪ Run.** Type **regedit** and click OK.

2. **Navigate to** HKEY_CURRENT_USER\Control Panel\Desktop. Select WaitToKillAppTimeout and set the value to 1000.

3. **Select the** `HungAppTimeout` **value and set it to** 1000 **as well.**

4. **Navigate to** HKEY_USERS\.DEFAULT\Control Panel\Desktop. **Set the** `WaitToKillAppTimeout` **and set the value to** 1000. **Select the** `HungAppTimeout` **value and set it to** 1000 **as well.**

5. **Navigate to** HKEY_LOCAL_MACHINE\System\CurrentControlSet\Control. **Select the** `WaitToKillServiceTimeout` **value and set it to** 1000.

6. **Close the Registry Editor.**

Stopping the NVIDIA Driver

If you use a NVIDIA video card, a service runs that seems to increase boot time and especially shutdown time. The general consensus in the hardware community is that the service doesn't actually do anything, and so you should disable it. Disabling the service should not affect the NVIDIA video card, and it will help your computer to shut down more quickly. Follow these steps:

1. **Click Start, right-click on My Computer, and select Manage.**

2. **In the Computer Management console that appears, expand Services and Applications, and select Services to open the services window.**

3. **Locate and highlight the 'Nvidia Driver Helper' service.** Right-click it and select Properties.

4. **Set the Startup type drop-down box to Disabled.** Click OK and close the Computer Management console.

Automatically End Tasks on Shutdown

You've seen this one before: You shut down your computer, and after waiting a few moments, a dialog box appears, telling that a task cannot end and asking you whether you want to manually end the task. Instead of prompting you, you can make Windows XP take care of the task kill automatically. Here's how:

1. **Open the Registry Editor.**

2. **Navigate to** HKEY_CURRENT_USER\Control Panel\Desktop.

3. **Highlight the value AutoEndTasks and then change the value to 1.**

4. **Close the Registry Editor.**

Customizing and Using Folders

6

The Windows XP system is organized around the concept of folders. Within a folder, you place files or even other folders. If you think of the Windows XP file and folder management system as a filing cabinet, you'll see that the concepts are very similar. As you use Windows XP, you naturally create your own files and folders, and My Documents is the default place to store your data, as well as the subfolders in My Documents, such as My Pictures and My Music.

Although Windows XP makes file storage easy with My Documents, you can create your own folders and completely customize them so that they are useful to you in a variety of ways. In this chapter, we'll explore the use and customization of folders on Windows XP.

Folder 101

If you have been using Windows XP for a while and feel that you know enough about basic folder usage, then you can skip this section. However, many people who use Windows XP still struggle with folder management. There are a few basic skills that you need, as well as an understanding of the basics of folder management.

My Documents

My Documents is simply a folder that is available by default on Windows XP. Within My Documents, you'll find other folders, such as My Music and My Pictures. Other applications may also create folders in My Documents. For example, if you install Jasc's Paint Shop Pro, then you'll see a My PSP Files folder in My Documents.

The point of My Documents is simply this: Microsoft has designed a place where you can put all kinds of documents, photos, and files in one central location without a lot of work on your part. This structure works well for typical home users who do not create a lot of files. However, if you use your computer for work purposes, or you generate a lot of multimedia files, then you may find that the My Documents folder structure just doesn't meet your needs, and that's fine.

The important thing to remember is that My Documents is simply a folder structure, containing subfolders. There is nothing magical about My Documents, and you can decide whether or not to use it.

Folders that Work

You can create a new folder in any folder window by clicking File ➪ New ➪ Folder. You can also right-click the desktop and click New ➪ Folder. Either way, you create a folder that you can name. Using this method, you can create folders for your desktop or other locations, folders within folders, and folders within folders within folders ... you get the picture.

So, how should folders be used? On its own, a folder doesn't do anything; its purpose is to house information. Using that concept, you can create multiple subfolders to organize data in a way that is meaningful to you. There are no hard and fast rules concerning folder creation and usage, but here are some general tips to keep in mind:

✦ **Use a minimal number of folders.** The more folders that you create, the more dispersed your personal data becomes, thus making it difficult to keep track of which folder has which resource. Like a filing cabinet, try to keep folders organized and simple.

✦ **Use minimal subfolders.** Subfolders can be helpful, but once again, too many of them tend to cause more confusion than anything else. Try to keep subfolder structures simple and intuitive.

✦ **Use descriptive names.** As you create folders, be sure to use descriptive names that give you a clue as to what is likely to be stored in the folder. For example, I have a folder for digital photos. Inside, I keep a number of subfolders, all organized by date or event. This way, I can browse through my subfolders to locate photos from a particular date or event. This structure helps me to find what I need quickly and easily.

✦ **If it works for you, then that is enough.** Across the board, if you start to use folders and subfolders in a way that works well for you, then by all means, keep using that system.

Examining Folder Appearance and Functions

Windows folders have come a long way, and the folders that you now create and use provide a lot of functionality. The following sections show you the menu, toolbar, and appearance options that are available in Windows XP folders.

Task and Folder View

By default, Windows XP folders contain a Task pane, as shown on the left side of the window in Figure 6-1. Using the Task pane, you can make new folders, publish a folder to a Web site (this option opens the Web Publishing Wizard), and share a folder on a network. You can also click to access other places on your computer, and view details about the folder.

Figure 6-1: A folder with the Task pane displayed

However, the tasks that you see here also have additional categories, depending on the folder that is open. For example, the My Pictures folder also contains a Picture Tasks area that provides you with tasks related to photos, as shown in Figure 6-2. For example, you can view the photos as a slide show, order prints online, and print photos.

If you do not want to see the Task pane, you can easily change the view to Folder view by clicking Folders on the toolbar. This changes the view to a folder structure so that you can see where the current folder resides, as shown in Figure 6-3. Also, notice that the Address line changes from the Universal Naming Convention (UNC) path to the folder.

Menu Options

The folders in Windows XP all have the same menus and options, which is nice because it allows you to have a streamlined approach to computing. Here's a quick overview of what you'll find under the menu options.

It should be noted that not all of these options are available all of the time. It depends on what type of file or folder you have selected.

Figure 6-2: Some folders have additional task options.

Figure 6-3: The Folder view

FYI: Using the UNC Path

The Universal Naming Convention, or UNC, is a computing standard for accessing folders and files on a Windows computer. Of course, you can browse, which is how most users typically move around Windows. You can also use the UNC path to access files and folders on a network.

You can use the UNC path either in the Run dialog box or on the Address bar of any folder. To access a local resource, begin with the drive, a colon, and a backslash, such as C:\. Next, drill down from folder to subfolder, and eventually to a specific file, if you want. For example, in Figure 6-3, you can see that C:\Documents and Settings\All Users\Documents\My Pictures\Sample Pictures takes me through five folders to finally arrive at my destination. I can simply browse to this folder, or, if I know the path, I can type it in the Run dialog box or in any folder Address line.

In the same manner, you can access a network resource (for which you have permission) using the UNC path. To do this, start at the Run dialog box or the Address line of any folder, and begin with two backslashes (\\), followed by the computer name, the share name, and the filename (if you want). For example, if there is a network computer called Windows2, a share called "Docs," and a file called "procedures," then you can access it directly by typing **\\windows2\docs\procedures**. *Curt Simmons*

File Menu

The File menu enables you to manage files and folders. Aside from using the File menu to create a new folder, you can also select a file and perform any of the following options:

✦ **New**. This pop-out menu enables you to create another folder or a specific type of file. You also see a list of file types available, which vary depending on the applications that are installed on your system. This feature enables you to start a new file of your choice directly from this location.

✦ **Preview**. For picture files, the Preview option opens Image Preview so that you can quickly take a look at the file.

✦ **Open**. This feature opens a window that allows you to select an application with which to open the file. You can use this option if you are having problems opening a file.

✦ **Open With**. You can choose a specific program to open the file from a pop-out menu.

✦ **Send To**. This option allows you to send the file to a drive, folder, or e-mail message. You can also right-click any folder or file and get this same option.

✦ **Edit**. This option opens a program that can edit the file. For example, if you select a picture file and then click Edit, Paint opens by default.

✦ **Print**. You can use the Print option to print the file.

✦ **Others**. In the lower part of the menu, you can perform other basic tasks, such as creating a shortcut for the item, deleting it, renaming it, and even closing the item.

Edit Menu

The Edit menu provides you with several easy features so that you can manage the folders or files within the folder.

✦ **Undo Delete**. Click this option to restore what you have just deleted (if you have performed no other operations since you deleted the item).

✦ **Copy, Cut, and Paste**. You can copy, cut, and paste items from one folder to another using these commands.

✦ **Move or Copy to Folder**. You can move or copy items to another folder by using these options. When you click one of them, a window appears where you can move or copy the file or folder.

✦ **Select All and Invert Selection**. Use Select All to select all items in the folder. This feature is helpful if you want to copy or cut all of the items in a particular folder. You can also use Invert Selection to give you the exact opposite of what is currently selected. For example, let's say you have five files in a folder, and two of the files are selected. If you use Invert Selection, the two previously selected files are not selected, and the three previously unselected files are selected.

View Menu

The View menu enables you to configure the appearance of your folder. You can learn more about this option later in this chapter.

Favorites Menu

The Favorites menu is located in Internet Explorer. You can see your Internet Explorer favorites here and directly jump to them from the current folder. You can learn more about favorites in Chapter 13.

Tools Menu

The Tools menu contains a few important options:

✦ **Map Network Drive**. For computers that are connected to a network, you can use this item to map a network drive. This feature enables you to use a network folder and display an icon on your computer so that the folder looks like it is local to your machine. To map a network drive, just click the option in the Tools menu. A dialog box appears where you can select a drive letter that is not in use, and then enter the network UNC path to the shared folder to which you want to map.

✦ **Disconnect Network Drive**. If you no longer want to use a particular network drive, then use this option to permanently disconnect it from your computer.

✦ **Synchronize**. The Synchronize option enables you to have a folder on a network server that has the same contents as a folder on your computer. As you work with the contents of the folder, you can use this option to synchronize the two folders so that they contain the same data. To use this feature, you must enable and configure Offline Files.

✦ **Folder Options**. You can choose a number of different folder options to customize your folder experience.

Cross-
Reference
For more on Offline Files, see Chapter 19. For more on folder options, see the sections "Customizing Folders" and "Configuring Folder Options" later in this chapter.

Help Menu

The Help menu gives you a quick and easy way to open the Windows Help and Support Center.

Customizing Folders

If you're happy with the default look of folders in Windows XP, you can skip this section. However, if you want to see all that is available to you in terms of customization, you have a number of features at your fingertips. The following sections show you how to customize folders in Windows XP.

Working with Toolbars

If you click the View menu in any folder and point to Toolbars, you see five options:

✦ **Standard Buttons.** This option allows standard buttons, such as Back, Forward, and Search, to display on the toolbar. This toolbar option is enabled by default.

✦ **Address Bar.** Enabled by default, this option allows the Address bar to appear on your folders.

✦ **Links.** The Links bar, which provides all preconfigured links in Internet Explorer, can also be displayed on your folders so that you can easily jump to Internet sites. This option is not enabled by default, but you can enable it by clicking the option.

✦ **Lock the Toolbars.** This option locks the toolbars in one place. Otherwise, you can move the toolbars around within the folder, as in the example shown in Figure 6-4. This option is enabled by default.

Figure 6-4: You can unlock the toolbars and move them around.

✦ **Customize.** This feature enables you to determine what options are on the toolbar.

Creating a Custom Toolbar

The standard toolbar provides you with some basic button options. However, you can change those button options and the overall look that they provide you with. It's easy to do, and you have the option to place buttons on the toolbar that you regularly use. Follow these steps:

When you create a custom toolbar, it applies to all folders. In other words, you can't create a custom toolbar for one specific folder. The changes that you make in the following steps apply to all folders in Windows XP.

1. **In any folder, click View ⇨ Toolbars ⇨ Customize.**

2. **In the Customize Toolbar dialog box, shown in Figure 6-5, you can choose the toolbar buttons that you want to use.** Select an icon, and then click the Add button to move the icon to the current toolbar. You can also select an existing icon and click the Remove button to remove it. Repeat these processes until you have the icons that you want on the toolbar.

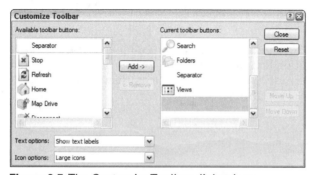

Figure 6-5: The Customize Toolbar dialog box

3. **In the Current toolbar buttons section, select a button icon and use the Move Up and Move Down buttons to reorganize the buttons.** Do this until they are ordered in a way that is useful to you.

4. **In the Text options drop-down menu, choose whether to show text labels with buttons.** In the Icons options drop-down menu, you can choose to use large icons or small icons.

5. **Once you have made your selections, click Close.** Figure 6-6 shows you an example of a custom toolbar.

Figure 6-6: An example of a custom toolbar

You can return to the Customize toolbar dialog box and make changes at any time. You can also click the Reset button on the Customize toolbar dialog box to return the toolbar to the default appearance.

Customizing Icons

The icon appearance in your folders will vary according to your system configuration, but you have several different choices that you can easily apply and change as needed. For example, let's say you have a folder that contains a large number of Word documents. You can choose to view those documents as a list with certain details. You may also have a folder that contains vacation photos. You can choose to view that folder in Filmstrip mode so that you can see a larger representation of each photo that you click. These options are fun and helpful, and you can easily choose how you want to see the icons based on what you want. Here's how.

Open any folder, and then click the Views button. From the drop-down menu, shown in Figure 6-7, choose a view that you want.

You have the following options:

✦ **Filmstrip.** This option allows you to select a photo and see a larger version of it. You have navigation button options, and you can also directly rotate images. Although you can use Filmstrip mode with any kind of files, this feature works best with photos, as shown in Figure 6-7.

Figure 6-7: View options

✦ **Thumbnails.** This option provides a thumbnail look at each file. This feature also works best with photos because you can see a mini picture of each photo.

✦ **Tiles.** This option provides a typical icon view of the files, and additional information about the file, depending on your configuration, as you can see in Figure 6-8.

Figure 6-8: Tiles view

✦ **Icons.** This option also provides an icon view, but the icon is smaller and only provides the name of the file.

✦ **List.** This option provides an even smaller icon and filename, and it organizes the files in a list format.

✦ **Details.** This option provides a list format with additional details about the file, depending on what details you have configured to appear, as shown in Figure 6-9. You can learn more about choosing detail options in the next section.

Name ▲	Size	Type	Date Modified	Date Picture Taken	Dimensions
Blue hills	28 KB	JPEG Image	3/30/2003 8:00 PM		800 x 600
Sunset	70 KB	JPEG Image	3/30/2003 8:00 PM		800 x 600
Water lilies	82 KB	JPEG Image	3/30/2003 8:00 PM		800 x 600
Winter	104...	JPEG Image	3/30/2003 8:00 PM		800 x 600

Figure 6-9: Details view

If you have created a custom toolbar and removed the View icon from your toolbar, you can still easily choose any of these viewing options using the View menu.

If you're using the Tiles, Icon, List, or Details view options, you can control the order in which the icons are displayed. For example, the icons may be orga- nized and displayed by name in alphabetical order. You can also click View ➪ Arrange Icons by, and then choose other options, such as name, size, and type.

Customizing Details

If you choose the Details view option from the View button on the toolbar, then you can see some information about the files in the folder, as shown in Figure 6-9. However, you can also customize the details that display specifically for individual folders, which can be really helpful, depending on the kind of data that you have stored in those folders.

To edit the details that appear, follow these steps:

1. **In a folder, click View ➪ Choose Details.**

2. **In the Choose Details dialog box, select or deselect the check boxes next to the detail items that you want to show (or to hide).** You can also select an item and use the Move Up or Move Down buttons to reorganize the list, as shown in Figure 6-10.

3. **When you're done, click OK.**

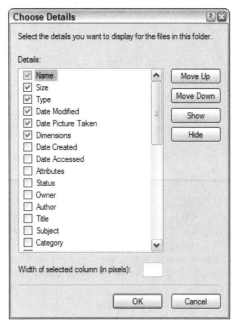

Figure 6-10: The Choose Details dialog box

Other Folder Customization Options

If you click the View menu in any folder, you'll see a Customize This Folder option. This option allows you to quickly access useful features on the Customize tab of the Sample Pictures Properties dialog box:

✦ **In the What kind of folder do you want section:** You see a drop-down menu, shown in Figure 6-11, where you can choose the kind of folder that is in use. For example, if the folder contains photos, you can choose either Pictures or Photo Album from the drop-down menu. If you have a folder of music files, then you can choose music options. What these selections do is adjust the content that displays in the Task pane. For example, if you choose Pictures or Photo Album, you'll see a standard listing of available tasks that have to do with photo management. Also notice that you can apply this setting to all subfolders in the folder by selecting the check box.

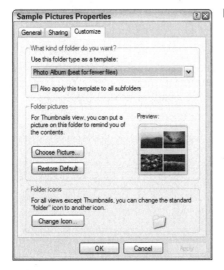

Figure 6-11: The Customize tab

✦ **In the Folder pictures section:** You can put a picture on the folder icon to remind you of what is in the folder. This feature can be helpful for folders that contain multimedia content. Figure 6-12 shows you an example of a folder icon with a picture.

✦ **In the Folder icons section:** For all views except thumbnails, you can change the standard folder icon to a different icon. To do this, click the Change Icon button and choose a different icon.

Figure 6-12: You can put a photo on a folder icon.

Configuring Folder Options

Folder Options govern both the general appearance and the behavior of folders. You can access folder options in the Control Panel, or in any folder by clicking the Tools Menu. For the most part, the configuration options here are intuitive, but you should read the following sections because there are several options available to you that you might want to configure.

General Tab

The General tab, shown in Figure 6-13, displays several options that determine how folders look and how you work with content in those folders. You have three different categories from which you can choose a radio button option:

Figure 6-13: The General tab in the Folder Options dialog box

✦ **Tasks.** This option enables you to display the Task pane options that you have seen throughout this chapter. Although the features of the Task pane are helpful, if you don't want to see the Task pane at all, then choose the Use Windows classic folders radio button.

My Computer and the Control Panel are always displayed with the Task pane view, even if you do not select the option here. The only exception is if you are using Windows Classic folders.

✦ **Browse folders.** This option enables you to choose how your folders display when you are browsing through a folder structure. For example, let's say you open My Computer and then you open the Control Panel. You can have My Computer open in a window, and then have the Control Panel open in a separate window. You can also choose to use the same window so that with My Computer open, when you open the Control Panel, it replaces what you see in My Computer. There is no right or wrong option, but if you work with a number of windows at one time, you may find that the Open each folder in the same window option creates less clutter on your Desktop.

✦ **Click items as follows.** You can have your mouse clicks act as though your Windows XP interface is the Internet. This means that you can open files and folders by single-clicking them rather than double-clicking, as you would do with links on the Internet. You can enable this option and try it out — however, it does take some getting used to. Just click the Single-click to open an item (point to select) radio button to enable it.

View Tab

The View tab, shown in Figure 6-14, contains a number of check boxes that enable you to make different decisions about files and folders. The options found here concern the display of certain file types, folder views, and other lower-level settings. Windows XP does a good job of configuring the standard settings, and so changing them may cause problems; think carefully before you change them. Here are a few of the options that you may want to consider:

✦ **Display all Control Panel options and all folder contents.** This option turns off the Category view of Control Panel so that you always see all items.

✦ **Do not show hidden files and folders** and **Hide protected operating system files.** These two separate options, both of which are enabled by default, keep the hidden files and folders in Windows XP from displaying. Windows XP hides folders that hold operating system files, as well as many of the individual files that make Windows XP run. Obviously, you don't need to do anything with these files, and Windows XP hides them to help prevent tampering or accidental deletion. You should leave these settings as they are so that Windows XP continues to hide system files and folders.

✦ **Hide extensions for known file types.** This option hides file extensions. For example, let's say you create a Microsoft Word document called Resume. The document's official name is Resume.doc. The Hide extensions option hides the .doc extension and all other extensions for files that Windows recognizes. This makes your folder files cleaner and easier to read. This option is enabled by default.

✦ **Remember each folder's view settings.** You can use the View menu in a particular folder to determine how the folder appears and what you can view, as we explored earlier in this chapter. This option tells Windows to remember each folder's view settings. It is enabled by default, and you should keep it enabled.

Figure 6-14: The View tab in the Folder Options dialog box

File Types Tab

The File Types tab, shown in Figure 6-15, provides you with a window that lists every type of file that is supported in Windows XP. Your operating system and applications do a great job of managing this list, and so you do not need to perform any configuration here unless explicitly instructed to do so by some application.

Cross-Reference **You can learn more about file management in Chapter 7.**

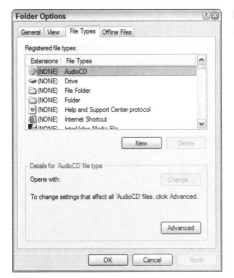

Figure 6-15: The File Types tab in the Folder Options dialog box

Offline Files

Offline files allow Windows XP to store network files locally on your computer, and then synchronize your local copy with the network copy.

Cross-
Reference

We'll explore the use of offline files in Chapter 19.

Managing Files and File Type Associations

7

F ile configuration and usage in Windows XP is rather straightforward and easy. You can determine which application should open which file, manage file properties, manage files in the Recycle Bin, and use the Search function to locate files on your computer. In this chapter, you explore these features and options so that you can make the best use of files on your Windows XP computer.

Managing File Properties

You can right-click any kind of file to access properties pages that contain important configuration options that you need to be aware of. In fact, when necessary, you can configure several important options by using the properties pages; the following sections explore these options.

File Association Options

Each file is a "type" of file, which means that certain applications open the file. For example, Test.doc is a Word file that opens with Microsoft Word, along with some other applications that can open Word documents. Cat.jpeg is a graphics file that you can open with a bunch of different applications.

However, because you can open some files with different applications, you may want to manage which program opens a particular file by default:

1. **Right-click the file that you want to modify, and then click Properties.** The Properties dialog box opens.

2. **On the General tab, click the Change button.** See Figure 7-1. This opens the Open With dialog box.

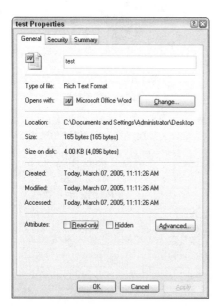

Figure 7-1: The General tab of the test Properties dialog box

3. **In the Open With dialog box, shown in Figure 7-2, choose the program that you want to use to open the file.** Use the Browse button if the program that you want is *not* listed.

Tip

You may have noticed the Advanced button on the General tab. You can click the Advanced button and encrypt the file or compress it. You can learn more about these features in Chapter 8.

Probably the easiest way to associate a document type with a program is to right-click any icon that represents the document type, and then choose Open With ⇨ Choose Program. In the Open With dialog box, choose the program that you want to associate with the document type, choose the "Always use the selected program to open this kind of file" option, and then click OK.

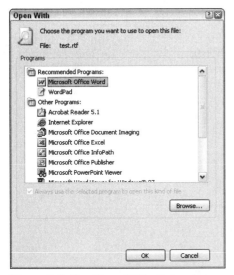

Figure 7-2: The Open With dialog box

Configuring Security

Depending on the security configuration of your Windows XP computer, you may see a Security tab, as shown in Figure 7-3. If you have Simple File Sharing enabled, you will not see this tab. See Chapter 19 to learn more about sharing files and configuring permissions.

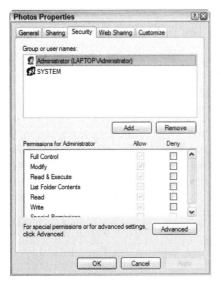

Figure 7-3: The Security tab of the Properties dialog box

Configuring Summary Information

You can configure summary information for a particular file, some of which may already be available. On the Summary tab, shown in Figure 7-4, choose summary data for the particular file type.

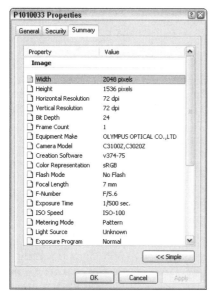

Figure 7-4: The Summary tab on the Properties dialog box

However, if you click the Advanced button, then you see an expanded view of the information. You can click on the configurable areas and change the information that is listed. Depending on the kind of file, you see different information listed. For example, in Figure 7-5, a photo file lists extensive information taken directly from the photo (which was recorded by the camera).

You may be wondering, "How is summary information all that helpful?" It all has to do with information about the file. Using summary information, you can index your file so that you locate the file by searching for specific information. You can also use the Details folder view to see more information about files within folders. You can find out more about folder configuration in Chapter 6.

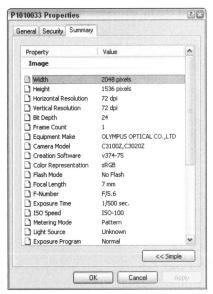

Figure 7-5: The Advanced Summary
Information for a photo file

Configuring a File Association
for a Certain File Type

In the previous section, you noticed that you can configure which application
opens a specific file. However, what if you need a certain application to open all
files of a certain type? For example, let's say that by default, the Windows Picture
and Fax Viewer opens any JPEG file. However, you want JPEG files to automatically
open with Photoshop Elements. Although you can right-click the file and use the
Open With feature, this can take a lot of time.

To save time, you can follow the steps below to configure Photoshop Elements to
open all JPEG files by default. You can apply these steps to any file or application.

1. **Click Start ➪ Control Panel ➪ Folder Options. The Folder Options properties dialog box appears.**

2. **Click the File Types tab, shown in Figure 7-6.** Notice that you can scroll
   through the list of file types, select one, and see what program will open the file.

3. **Click the Change button.** You'll see the Open With dialog box that appears in
   Figure 7-2, where you can select the program that you want to open the particular file type by default. Click OK.

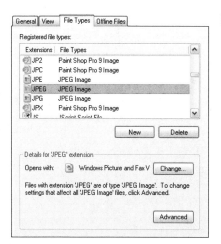

Figure 7-6: File Types tab

4. **Click the Advanced button on the File Types tab.** The Edit File Type dialog box, shown in Figure 7-7, opens. Here, you can change the default file type icon, and even change the action that occurs when you double-click it. For example, you can have the application print the file as soon as it is opened. However, keep in mind that changes that you make are global; they affect all files of the specific file type on your computer. Click OK.

Figure 7-7: The Edit File Type dialog box

5. **Click Apply and Close on the File Types tab.**

To associate CDs and DVDs with programs, based on the types of files on the disk, open your My Computer folder, right-click the icon for your CD or DVD drive, and then choose Properties. Click the AutoPlay tab, and then choose a content type from the drop-down list. Under Actions, choose how you want Windows to react whenever you insert a disk that contains the types of files that you specified.

Expert's Notebook: Open a File with a Keyboard Shortcut

Let's say there is particular file that you use every day. Although you can create a shortcut to the file and put it on your Start menu or the desktop, if you want to save some point-and-click time, you can also create a keyboard shortcut to open the file. Naturally, the keyboard shortcut that you choose should be something unique (in other words, not a keyboard shortcut that is already in use). Here's how:

1. **Locate the shortcut for the file (or create one if necessary).** You must store the shortcut on the desktop. This is because if you store the shortcut in any other folder, and then you create a keyboard shortcut for it, the shortcut will not work.

2. **Right-click the shortcut and click Properties.**

3. **On the Shortcut tab, click inside of the Shortcut Key entry field, and then press the letter for the key that you would like to use.** Windows automatically changes the shortcut to read Ctrl+Alt+*letter,* where *letter* is the letter that you chose, as shown in the following figure.

Use the Shortcut dialog box to create a shortcut key

4. **Click OK, and then test your new shortcut.** If nothing happens, then you have used a letter that is already in use for another shortcut. Reopen the Shortcut properties tab and use another key.

Curt Simmons

Managing Files in the Recycle Bin

By default, Windows XP only provides you with one desktop icon, which is the Recycle Bin. This design is an attempt to keep your desktop cleaner, but if you are like me, you probably have many more icons on your desktop. As you are aware, the Recycle Bin is a place that contains files that are no longer needed. When you delete a file from your system, such as a document, picture, or shortcut, it isn't really deleted; it's actually sent to the Recycle Bin, where it waits to be deleted. The Recycle Bin is an excellent Windows feature that prevents you from losing data that you may actually want to keep. When you delete an item from your computer, it is removed from its current location and placed in the Recycle Bin. It stays in the Recycle Bin until you choose to empty the Recycle Bin, or the Recycle Bin becomes too full. Only then is the item deleted permanently.

Using the Recycle Bin

You can open the Recycle Bin and see what is inside by double-clicking the Recycle Bin icon on your Desktop (you can also right-click the icon and click Explore). You can see the items in the Recycle Bin that are waiting to be deleted, as shown in Figure 7-8.

Figure 7-8: Items in the Recycle Bin

In the View menu, you can select the following views: thumbnails, tiles, icons, list, or details. These options allow you to view your files as large icons, small icons, a list of files, or even a detailed list telling you each item's original location, and the date that it was moved to the Recycle Bin.

You can't open files that are in the Recycle Bin. If you try, you'll open the properties pages for the file. Instead, you must drag the file back to the desktop or to another folder in order to open it.

You have two buttons available in the Recycle Bin Tasks pane, which is found on the left side of the Recycle Bin window. When you click the Empty the Recycle Bin button, it permanently deletes the items in the Recycle Bin. Once you choose to empty the Recycle Bin, all of the items in the Recycle Bin are permanently deleted from your computer. You cannot recover these items once they have been emptied from the Recycle Bin.

Tip

You can also empty the contents of your Recycle Bin by simply right-clicking the Recycle Bin icon on your Desktop and clicking Empty Recycle Bin on the contextual menu.

Nowadays, most people seem paranoid about sensitive material that they delete. Simply pressing the delete button doesn't get rid of the file; it simply marks the space on the hard drive where the file was so that the operating system knows that it can overwrite the area that the deleted files once occupied. Installing third party software such as Eraser (www.heidi.ie/eraser) can ensure that all sensitive data is overwritten at least 35 times. Once you erase it with eraser it's gone for good.

There is also a Restore all items button in the Recycle Bin Tasks pane. This is useful when you accidentally delete a file, and it is moved to the Recycle Bin. You can use the Restore all items button to move the file back to its original location on your computer. However, what if you have 30 files that you have deleted, and you want to restore only one of them? Simply select the file in the list by clicking it. The Restore all items button changes to a Restore this item button. When you click the button, the file is put back in its original location.

Caution

There are a couple of instances where files are not sent to the Recycle Bin, but automatically deleted. One is large files that won't fit. Another is when deleting files on network drives. Windows gives you a warning in the first case. The second is easy to miss. It just says "Do you want to delete?" You have to be paying close attention to see that it does NOT say "Do you want to move this to the Recycle Bin."

Changing the Recycle Bin's Properties

You can also change the Recycle Bin's properties, which basically changes the way it manages files placed there. Right-click the Recycle Bin on your Desktop and click Properties on the contextual menu that appears. You see a Recycle Bin Properties dialog box that has a Global and Local Disk tab, as shown in Figure 7-9.

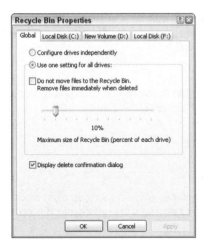

Figure 7-9: The Recycle Bin Properties dialog box

The Global tab has the following options:

✦ **Configure drives independently:** If you have multiple disk drives, you can configure how the Recycle Bin manages files on each drive.

✦ **Use one setting for all drives:** This option applies to you only if you have more than one hard disk in your computer. In most cases, the default setting that configures all of your drives in the same way is all that you need.

✦ **Do not move files to the Recycle Bin:** This option tells your computer to delete items immediately, instead of moving them to the Recycle Bin. As you can guess, this feature automatically deletes items when you click Delete. This provides you absolutely no protection in the event that you accidentally delete a file that you want. Let's say you are writing your life's story and you accidentally delete the document. Selecting this check box means that the document will immediately be gone from your computer without hope of retrieval.

I strongly recommend that you do not click this check box to enable this option. No matter how good your computing skills, you will make a mistake from time to time and accidentally delete an important file. The Recycle Bin is your safety net so that you can retrieve that document. By clicking this check box, you have no protection.

✦ **Slide bar:** This represents the maximum size to which the Recycle Bin can grow. Like everything else on your computer, the Recycle Bin stores items in a folder on your hard drive. The slide bar enables you to set a limit for how big the Recycle Bin can grow before it forces you to empty the contents and permanently delete items from your system. By default, this setting is configured at ten percent. This means that ten percent of your hard drive's space can be used before the Recycle Bin tells you to empty it. That is, if you have a 10GB hard drive, you can store up to 1GB of deleted data in the Recycle Bin before it must be permanently removed from your computer. Under most circumstances, this ten percent setting is all that you need, but you can change it to a higher or lower percentage if you want. Just be sure to ask yourself why you are changing the setting, and make sure that you have a good reason for doing so.

✦ **Display delete confirmation dialog:** This option tells Windows to display that aggravating "Are You Sure?" message every time you delete something. This option is selected by default, but you can disable it if you do not want to see that message.

Aside from the Global tab, you have a Local Disk tab, shown in Figure 7-10 — in fact, you may have several of these tabs if your computer has more than one hard drive. You can't do anything on these tabs if you have selected the "Use one setting for all drives" radio button on the Global tab. If you want each drive to have different settings and you deselected this option on the Global tab, then you can configure each drive independently. The tabs have the same options, such as the slide bar for the percentage of the hard drive that you want to use for the Recycle Bin. Because different drives may have different amounts of space available, you may want to configure different drives individually.

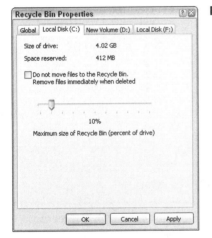

Figure 7-10: The Local Disk tab

Using the Search Feature

Windows XP includes a Search Companion feature that enables you to locate files on your computer. For the most part, the search feature is easy to use and straightforward. Its animation features may even be annoying to you, but if you use the search feature to locate information on your computer, it is important that you use the feature effectively. The following sections examine some important features and functions.

Configuring the Search Features

You can start a search at any time by clicking Start ➪ Search. The basic search window appears. You can turn off the animated character, search the Internet, or change preferences directly from this dialog box, as shown in Figure 7-11.

Figure 7-11: Search window

You can place a Search button on your folder toolbar so that the search feature is always available from within any folder. To do this, you may need to create a custom toolbar. See Chapter 6 to find out more.

If you click the Change preferences link, you'll see several options that you can select or change. For example, you can click the option to use a different character with the Search Companion, in which case the dialog box changes so that you can select an alternate character, as shown in Figure 7-12.

Figure 7-12: You can change the character that appears with your Search Companion.

 You may notice an option here to turn on the indexing service, which gives you faster search results. When the indexing service is in use, your computer's files are indexed when your computer is idle. However, this service is also a resource hog and may slow your computer down. If you use the search feature a lot, then you should use indexing. However, if you rarely use the search feature, do not enable the indexing service because the performance decrease is not worth a feature that you don't regularly use.

Performing a Search

We don't need to spend much time talking about the search feature because the search options that you find are self-explanatory. For the most part, you use the search feature to determine for what and how you want to search, and then you perform the search. For example, in Figure 7-13, I am searching for pictures or photos that have the letters "ps" in the filename.

If you want to perform more advanced searches, simply expand the different categories that are available, such as the last time the file was modified, the file size, and even more advanced options, such as selecting system folders, as shown in Figure 7-14. Naturally, the more restrictive your search, the less returns you see, so you should try to find a balance between restrictions and leniency to avoid being overly restrictive.

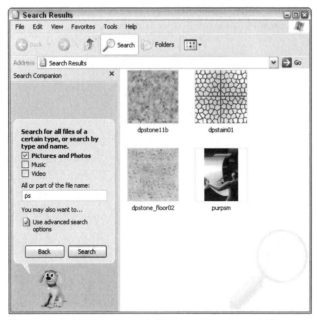

Figure 7-13: You can search for specific types of files.

Figure 7-14: Advanced search options

Compressing and Encrypting Folders and Files

8

Compression and encryption are certainly nothing new in the computing world, but Windows XP was the first Microsoft operating system to have both of these features built-in. *Compression* is computing technology that reduces the overall size of both files and folders, while *encryption* is technology that secures data by making it inaccessible to persons who do not have an encryption key. In short, these technologies save space on your PC's hard disk and help to protect sensitive data from prying eyes.

This chapter examines both compression and encryption and shows you how to get the most from these Windows XP features.

Compressing Files and Folders

There are two kinds of compression that are available under Windows XP: NTFS compression and folder compression. The first type works with the NTFS file system, while the second type uses the standard WinZip technology that has been around for years. For more information, visit www.winzip.com. Both compression types are built into Windows XP and readily available for your use, but each type has specific advantages.

Using NTFS Compression

NTFS compression is a compression feature that only works on NTFS-formatted drives. If you have a drive that is formatted with FAT, then NTFS compression will not work.

More than likely, you are using NTFS on all of your drives (and with the exception of rare circumstances, you should be), but if you are not, or if you need to learn more about NTFS, see Chapter 31.

There are some basic rules that govern how NTFS compression works, and you need to keep these rules in mind as you move forward:

✦ Once again, you can only use NTFS compression on NTFS-formatted drives.

✦ If you move or copy a file into a compressed folder, the file is automatically compressed.

✦ If you move a file from a different NTFS drive into a compressed folder, it is compressed as well.

✦ Files and folders that are compressed with NTFS compression cannot be encrypted, and vice versa.

✦ When you open a compressed file, Windows XP automatically decompresses it for you, and then recompresses it when you close the file. Although this is done automatically, you may find that performance is a bit slower.

✦ If you move or copy an NTFS-compressed file or folder to a non-NTFS drive, the compression attribute is lost.

✦ Although the amount of storage space that you save depends on the kind of file that you compress, you can assume a saving of about thirty percent.

NTFS compression is not available on Windows XP 64-bit Edition. Windows XP encryption is not available on Windows XP Home Edition.

Compressing a Drive

You can compress an entire drive on your Windows XP computer in order to globally save disk space. Generally, you may see about a fifty percent disk space saving. That is certainly a high yield, but is compressing a drive the best thing to do?

The problem with drive compression is performance. Although drive compression saves space, it generally slows down the operation of Windows XP. If you've had Windows XP for any length of time, then you know that it can be difficult to keep things running fast to begin with. Consequently, you have to decide whether the tradeoff between speed and space is necessary. Before

compressing an entire drive, consider uninstalling unused applications and deleting old files or moving them to removable media, such as CDs or DVDs. Also, try running the Disk Cleanup tool to remove old data that you no longer use.

Cross-Reference

For more on Disk Cleanup, see Chapter 33.

If you determine that compressing an entire drive is in your best interest, then follow these steps:

1. **Click Start ➪ My Computer.**

2. **Right-click the desired drive and click Properties.**

3. **On the General tab, click the "Compress drive to save disk space" check box, shown in Figure 8-1, and click OK.** The drive will be compressed, which may take some time to complete.

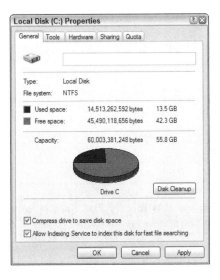

Figure 8-1: You can change the disk compression setting in the General tab of the Disk Properties dialog box.

Note

If you don't see the check box option, this means that the drive is formatted with FAT. You must convert the drive to NTFS to use NTFS compression. See Chapter 31 for more details.

Note

If at any time you want to remove the NTFS compression, simply return to the General tab, clear the check box, and then click OK. This action decompresses the drive.

Compressing a File

You can individually compress any file or folder using NTFS compression, as long as the file or folder resides on an NTFS drive. To compress a file, follow these steps:

1. **Locate the desired file on your computer.**

2. **Right-click the file and then click Properties.**

3. **On the General tab, click the Advanced button toward the bottom of the dialog box, as shown in Figure 8-2.**

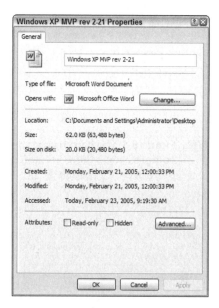

Figure 8-2: Click the Advanced button.

Tip   If you don't see an Advanced button, this means that the file is not on an NTFS drive. You cannot use NTFS compression on a non-NTFS drive. However, you can easily convert a drive to NTFS. See Chapter 31 for details.

4. **In the Advanced Attributes dialog box, shown in Figure 8-3, click the "Compress contents to save disk space" check box option.** Note that you can't select both the compress check box and the encrypt check box. This is because you cannot use these features together, and so the dialog box doesn't allow you to choose both.

5. **Click OK and then click OK again.**

Note   You can decompress the file at any time by returning to this dialog box and clearing the compress check box option.

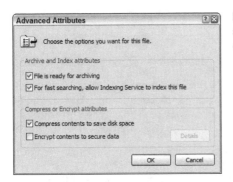

Figure 8-3: You can choose the compression settings for a file in the Advanced Attributes dialog box.

Compressing a Folder

You can compress an entire folder in the same manner. However, when you compress a folder, you have the option to compress only the folder, or all of the files and subfolders within the folder. Typically, you want to compress everything in the folder, because compressing the folder alone doesn't actually conserve much disk space. Follow these steps:

1. **Locate the desired folder on your computer.**

2. **Right-click the folder and then click Properties.**

3. **On the General tab, click the Advanced button toward the bottom of the dialog box.**

Tip

If you don't see an Advanced button, this means that the file is not on an NTFS drive. You can convert the drive to NTFS. See Chapter 31 for details.

4. **In the Advanced Attributes dialog box, click the "Compress contents to save disk space" check box option.** Note that you can't select both the compress check box and the encrypt check box. This is because the features cannot be used together, and so the dialog box doesn't allow you to choose both.

5. **Click OK and then click OK again.** A dialog box appears, asking you to confirm the change. You can also choose to apply the compression attribute to only the folder, or to the folder and all subfolders and files within that folder, as shown in Figure 8-4. Make a selection, and then click OK.

Note

You can decompress the folder at any time by returning to this dialog box and clearing the compress check box option.

Expert's Notebook: Making Compressed Files and Folders Appear in a Different Color

After you compress a file or folder and click OK, you may wonder whether something went wrong. After all, the file or folder doesn't appear to be different. Also, if you start compressing files and folders, how can you keep track of which files and folders are compressed?

A simple way to keep track of which files and folders are compressed is by changing the color of compressed files and folders. You can configure Windows XP so that when you compress a file or folder, the file or folder color also changes. Here's how:

1. **Click Start ➪ Control Panel.**

2. **Double-click Folder Options.**

3. **Click the View tab.**

4. **Scroll and locate the "Show encrypted or compressed NTFS files in color" check box option.** Select the check box, highlighted in the following figure, and then click OK.

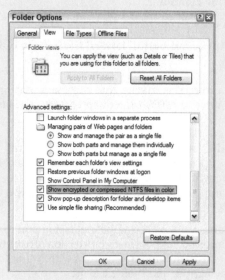

Choose the color check box option.

 So, how much disk space did you save by compressing the file or folder? The only way to find out is to first right-click the file or folder, click Properties, and then read the file size on the General tab. Then, compress the file or folder and check the size again. You'll then be able to see how much space you are actually saving.

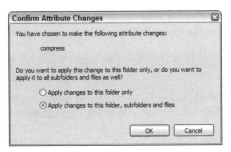

Figure 8-4: Choose what you want to compress.

Managing Compressed Drives, Folders, and Files from the Command Line

If you prefer to use the command line, you can access Compact.exe to manage compressed files and volumes in Windows XP. Using Compact.exe, you can compress, decompress, and view the compression attributes of a folder, file, or drive. You can review the command line switches in Table 8-1. The syntax for Compact.exe is:

```
Compact.exe [/c] [/u] [/s[:dir]] [/a] [/i] [/f] [/q] [filename
[...]]
```

Table 8-1
Command Line Switches

Switch	Explanation
C	Compresses the specified file
U	Decompresses the specified file
S	Performs the specified operation on the files in the given folder and all subfolders
A	Displays file with hidden or system attributes
I	Continues performing the specified operation, even after errors have occurred
F	Forces the compression operation on all specified files, including currently compressed files
Q	Reports only the most essential information
Filename	Specifies a pattern, file, or folder

Using Folder Compression

Aside from NTFS compression, you can also use a basic compressed folders feature in Windows XP that works similarly to WinZip technology, which you have probably used in previous versions of Windows. So, why have two different compression methods in Windows XP? There are several important differences between the two:

✦ Files and folders that are compressed using the compressed folder feature work on both NTFS and FAT drives.

✦ You can directly open compressed folders and files without decompressing them. This is the same as NTFS compression, but you are not as likely to see a performance loss.

✦ When you move compressed folders to any drive, removable storage media, or the Internet, they remain compressed. Anyone can open the compressed folder using either Windows XP or WinZip (and possibly using other third-party compression utilities as well).

✦ You can password-protect compressed folders.

✦ Compressed folders are indicated by a zipper icon.

✦ You can't individually compress files using folder compression technology. You can drag files to a compressed folder to automatically compress them.

As you can see, the primary difference between NTFS compression and folder compression is compatibility. Folder compression uses the *zipped* folder technology and is compatible with both NTFS and FAT drives. You can also move data over the Internet using compressed folders. As a result, if you're sending a folder of vacation photos to friends and family, then a compressed folder is the way to go. Although you manage compressed folders a bit differently, and they aren't as easy to decompress as an NTFS folder, the feature works well overall and can certainly save you some disk space or bandwidth. The following sections show you how to use compressed folders.

Compressing an Existing Folder

When you compress an existing folder, everything in the folder is compressed, and a new zipped icon appears. Basically, a compressed folder duplicates everything in the original folder to create a new folder that is compressed. As you can see, this feature is designed for mobile compression because you can easily put the new compressed folder on a removable media disk, or use it on the Internet. To compress an existing folder, follow these steps:

1. **Right-click the desired folder.**

2. **Click Send To ➪ Compressed (zipped) folder.** The folder is compressed, and a new folder icon (with a zipper) appears. Notice that your original folder and files/subfolders remain unchanged.

Creating a New Compressed Folder

You can easily create a new compressed folder at any time:

1. **Open a desired drive or folder location and click File ➪ New ➪ Compressed (zipped) folder.** The new folder icon appears.

2. **Type a name and press Enter.**

3. **Alternatively, right-click the desktop and click New ➪ Compressed (zipped) folder.** The new folder icon appears.

4. **Type a name and press Enter.**

Creating a Password for a Compressed Folder

You can easily password-protect a compressed folder so that a password is required before opening it. This feature works well if the folder is in a place where different people can access it, or if you are sending it over the Internet. Follow these steps:

1. **Open the compressed folder.**

2. **Click File ➪ Add a Password.**

3. **In the Add Password dialog box, type the password and retype to confirm it, and then click OK.**

Password protection protects the files in the folder. You can still open and browse the folder and subfolders without entering the password. Also, password protection does not stop someone from deleting the folder or from changing properties of the folder. All that it does is prevent people from opening files in the folder without a password.

Decompressing a Compressed Folder

Keep in mind that you can double-click a compressed folder and use the contents as you normally would. However, should you need to decompress the entire folder permanently, you can easily do so. Follow these steps:

1. **Right-click the compressed folder and click Extract All.** The Extraction Wizard appears.

2. **Click Next on the Welcome screen.** The Select a Destination dialog box appears, as shown in Figure 8-5.

3. **Choose the folder where you want to extract the contents.** You can use the Browse button if necessary.

4. **Click Next.** The files are extracted to the new folder.

5. **Click Finish.**

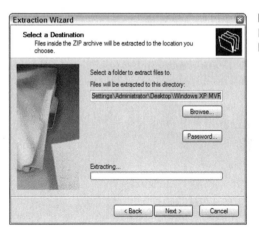

Figure 8-5: The Select a Destination screen of the Extraction Wizard

Encrypting Files and Folders

Windows XP Professional provides built-in encryption, called Encrypting File System (EFS), so that you can encrypt files and folders. The encryption feature enables you to protect files and folders so that other people cannot view them. For example, if several different people use a Windows XP Professional computer, each user can encrypt their own private data so that other users cannot access it. Encryption is seamless and easy to use, and it is a feature of the NTFS file system. You do not have to be aware of any keys or of the underlying encryption technology. You can simply select to encrypt data, and then open the data and use it seamlessly without any kind of manual decryption. If another user attempts to access the encrypted data, that user's key does not decrypt the data, and so it will not be readable.

Before using EFS, there are a few issues to keep in mind:

✦ EFS is a feature of NTFS and only works on NTFS drives.

✦ Encryption and compression are not compatible. You can either encrypt a file or folder or compress it, but you cannot do both.

✦ Encryption tends to affect performance. Encrypted files are slower than regular files because Windows XP Professional must encrypt and decrypt files as they are opened or closed.

✦ You can give several users access to the same encrypted file or folder.

✦ System files or any file in the systemroot directory structure (most files in C;\) cannot be encrypted.

✦ If you encrypt a folder, then files added to the folder are encrypted as well.

Encrypt a File or Folder

You can easily encrypt a file or folder. Follow these steps:

1. **Right-click the desired file or folder and click Properties.**

2. **On the General tab, click the Advanced button.**

3. **In the Advanced Attributes dialog box, shown in Figure 8-6, click the "Encrypt contents to secure data" check box.** Click OK and then click OK again.

   If you are encrypting a folder, you'll see the same dialog box as with compression.

Figure 8-6: You can activate encryption in the Advanced Attributes dialog box.

4. **Choose whether you want to apply the encryption to the folder only, or to all files and subfolders in the folder.** If you encrypt the file without encrypting the folder it is in, it may become a decrypted file automatically when it is next modified. You'll see a warning to this effect when you encrypt a single file.

5. **Click OK.**

At any time, you can remove the encryption attribute from a file or folder by returning to the Advanced Attributes dialog box and clearing the encryption check box.

To be safe, be sure to encrypt all folders that contain any personal documents. If you use My Documents, be sure to encrypt it. Also, consider encrypting the Temp and Tmp folders in C:\Windows.

Giving Other Users Access to an Encrypted File or Folder

When you encrypt a file or folder, you may also want to give certain other local users access to the file or folder. You can easily do that using EFS. Follow these steps:

1. Right-click the file or folder and click Properties.

2. On the General tab, click Advanced.

3. In the Advanced Attributes dialog box, click the Details button.

4. In the Encryption details dialog box, shown in Figure 8-7, click the Add button to add other users to the list of users who can transparently access the file.

Figure 8-7: Click the Add button to enable other users to access the encrypted file.

5. When you're done, click OK, then click OK, and then click OK again.

Accessing Encrypted Data on a LAN

Although encryption can be helpful, there are several situations that can arise that will cause problems. For example, what if you need to access your encrypted data over the network through several different workstations? You can do so in a couple of different ways. First, if you set up a roaming user profile, then the key will be available no matter where you log on. Secondly, if you do not set up a roaming user profile, you can copy your key and carry it with you on a floppy disk. Then, you can use the key to open your encrypted data. This export process is rather easy, and the following steps show you how to do it.

1. **Click Start ⇨ Run.** Type **MMC** and click OK.

2. **In the MMC (Microsoft Management Console), click File ⇨ Add/Remove Snap-in.**

3. **In the Add/Remove Snap-in window, click Add.** In the snap-in list that appears, click Certificates and then click Add.

4. **In the Certificates snap-in window, select My User Account, and then click Finish.** Click Close on the Snap-in window, and then click OK on the Add/Remove Snap-in window.

5. **In the MMC, expand Certificates – Current User.**

6. **Expand the Personal folder, and then select the Certificates folder.** In the right pane, select the desired certificate, as shown in Figure 8-8.

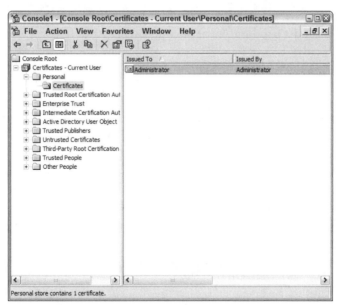

Figure 8-8: The Certificates folder

7. **Click Action ⇨ All Tasks ⇨ Export to start the Export Certificate Wizard.**

8. **Follow the wizard's simple steps.** Make sure that you choose to send your private key with your digital certificate. If you are moving to another Windows XP or 2000 system, choose the Enable Strong Encryption option.

9. **Choose a password, which you will need to import the certificate into the new location.**

10. **The wizard saves your certificate and private key to a Personal Information Exchange file, which is indicated by a *.pfx file extension.** You can now copy this file to a floppy disk and move it to a new computer.

11. **Once you have copied your certificate and private key, you can import the certificate and private key to another computer.** Open the Certificates MMC.

12. **Open Certificates – Current User.** Expand the Personal folder and select the Certificates folder.

13. **Click Action ➪ All Tasks ➪ Import.** This opens the Import Wizard.

14. **Use the Browse option to select the file that you want to import, and complete the wizard steps.** You need to provide the password that you assigned to the file when you were exporting it.

Although the encryption feature in Windows XP provides excellent protection, there is no way to decrypt data if your personal key becomes lost or you accidentally delete it. Use caution when you use the Certificates console, and consider making a backup copy of your personal key.

Recovering Encrypted Data

Another issue that can occur regarding encryption is the recovery of encrypted data. Let's say a user who shares your computer encrypts their data, but the recovery key is lost. Or, in the case of a company computer, the user may leave the company without decrypting the data. Aside from using the private key to encrypt or decrypt data, Windows XP Professional also provides Recovery Agents for this purpose. You can assign the Recovery Agent so that you can recover the data if the user's private key is lost, corrupted, or if the user abandons the data. To prevent data from being hopelessly lost in encryption, a Recovery Agent can decrypt the data. It is important to note that the agent can only decrypt data — not re-encrypt it.

FYI: Encrypting with the Command Line

Like compression, you can also manage encryption from the command line, rather than the GUI console of Windows. If you love the command line, this section is for you. Encryption is managed with the cipher command. You can encrypt or decrypt files and folders using the path to the file or folder and several switches that are available. You can also encrypt multiple files or folders at the same time. To view a listing of the syntax and switches for the cipher command, type **cipher /?** at the command prompt.

The original Administrator account on Windows XP is a recovery agent by default. You can simply log on with this default account and decrypt the file as you normally would. However, if you want to assign other user accounts to be Recovery Agents, you can do so. To configure a Recovery Agent, you must be logged onto Windows XP Professional as an Administrator, and you need to know the location of the certificate of the person who will become the Recovery Agent. Follow these steps to configure a Recovery Agent.

1. **Click Start ➪ Run.** Type **MMC** and click OK.

2. **In the console window, click File ➪ Add/ Remove Snap-in.**

3. **In the snap-in window, click Add.**

4. **In the Add Standalone snap-in window, click Group Policy and then click Add.**

5. **In the Group Policy Object window, leave the Local Computer option selected, and then click Finish.**

6. **Click Close on the Add Standalone snap-in window, and then click OK on the Snap-in window.** You now see the Local Computer Policy in the MMC.

7. **Expand Local Computer Policy ➪ Computer Configuration ➪ Windows Settings ➪ Security Settings ➪ Public Key Policies ➪ Encrypting File System.** This is shown in Figure 8-9.

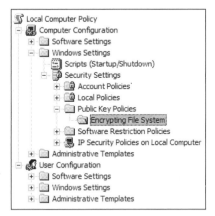

Figure 8-9: Expand Local Computer Policy to open Encrypting File System.

8. **Right-click the Encrypting File System folder, and then click Add Data Recovery Agent.** This starts the Add Recovery Agent Wizard. Click Next on the Welcome screen.

9. **Using the wizard, locate the desired user certificate.** You need to choose a local *.cer file. The certificate must be saved as a *.cer file.

Expert's Notebook: Disabling EFS

If you want to disable EFS on Windows XP, you can do so by editing the registry. Disabling EFS prevents anyone from encrypting files or folders, but it also prevents access to any existing encrypted files or folders. To disable EFS, follow these steps:

1. **Click Start ➪ Run.** Type **regedit** and then click OK.

2. **Navigate to HKLM\Software\Microsoft\Windows NT\CurrentVersion\EFS key.**

3. **Click Edit ➪ New ➪ DWORD value.**

4. **Choose a name, such as Efsdisable.**

5. **Double-click the new value and change the value data to 1.** If at any time you want to re-enable EFS, change this value to 0.

6. **Close the Registry Editor and restart the computer.**

Organizing, Archiving, and Remotely Storing Files and Folders

Computers tend to fill up with information. If you have had your Windows XP computer for a few months, you're likely to notice many more items than you initially had installed on your computer — and rightfully so. After all, one of the main purposes of owning a computer is to create and store files. As a writer, when I am working on a book, I need to store an enormous number of Word documents, screen shots, and other files on my computer. After a while, things can certainly get out of control.

There are two major difficulties with managing files and folders. The first is simply finding what you are looking for. Although the search feature in Windows XP works well, you may find yourself frequently asking, "Where did I put that?" The other problem is storage space. Hard disks have a finite amount of room, and you may find that over time, free space begins to run low, much like an ever-crowded hall closet.

In this chapter, you learn about a few tactics and remedies to help manage files and folders. If you do not have a good organizational method for managing your items in Windows XP, then this chapter can help you.

In This Chapter

Working with Third-party Software

Burning CDs and Using USB Flash Drives

Using Offline Files

Organization 101

In the previous few chapters, you learned how to create folders, manage files and file types, and even compress and encrypt files and folders (see Chapters 6-8). The organization of files and folders is up to you to manage. Windows XP does not automatically help you to organize files and folders, although it tries to help you with the desktop cleanup wizard and with the My Documents folder. In the end, it's all up to you to take care of the files and folders in Windows XP.

Now, if your bedroom closet looks like mine, then I can probably guess how organized your computer is. Let's face it, in the myriad of tasks that you must complete on a daily basis, organizing your files and folders on your computer may not seem like a high priority. However, as with your bedroom closet, you can save a lot of time and frustration if you spend a few extra seconds while you are working to keep things organized. Ultimately, how should you approach the organization of files and folders on your computer? There is no right or wrong way, just as there is no exact way to organize your bedroom closet. However, there are a few issues that you keep in mind as you work and play with Windows XP.

✦ **Keep in mind that folders are designed to help you manage files.** Although you should keep files in folders, and use subfolders as necessary, be careful of overusing subfolders. A top-level folder with multiple sub-level folders that also have multiple sub-level folders often becomes more complicated than it is helpful. Keep it as simple as possible.

✦ **Standardize your method for organizing files.** Some people organize files and folders by date, by the type of information, by the file type, or by projects. In the end, you have to decide what type of organizational method makes sense to you. It is generally a good idea to figure out one type of organizational method and stay with it as much as possible.

✦ **Keep it clean.** Yes, I know that you're planning to wear those jeans from 1985 that are still in your closet, but come on! Your computer can easily end up the same way. Use the tools described throughout this book to keep your computer clean. Remove old items that you know you will never use, or at least copy old items to a CD-ROM (copying to a CD-ROM is discussed later in this chapter).

✦ **Think about redundancy.** This is perhaps one of the most important issues. Try to keep multiple copies of files and folders that you simply cannot lose in different locations — just in case you need a backup. For example, when I finish writing a book, I have one folder for each chapter. What do I do with these folders once I'm done? I don't want to keep all of the information on my computer, and so I typically compress the entire folder, and then copy it to a CD-ROM. I also copy the folder to another computer that I have, or I may use a storage location on the Internet (also explored later in this chapter). In the end, I have two copies of my book just in case something happens to one copy, and I do not clutter up my computer with files that I no longer use.

Using Third-party Organizing Tools

Windows XP doesn't give you any software that directly helps you to manage files and folders. Of course, depending on your usage level, you may not need software to help you manage digital files anyway. However, if you use your Windows XP computer in an office environment where you are constantly generating files and folders that you must organize and manage, you may find that some file- and folder-organizing software can make your life a bit easier. There are a few organizer tools that I thought were really helpful, and so I'll give you a quick overview of them in the next few sections, and you can visit their Web sites to find out more. Unfortunately, none of them are free, but they are generally inexpensive.

Directory Opus 8

Directory Opus 8, from GP Software, is the probably the best directory management software that you can buy at this time. The file manager has a tabbed interface, shown in Figure 9-1, that can display files in just about any way that you would like. This software is generally considered a valid replacement for Windows Explorer, and it can do a lot of stuff—you can even send files through e-mail from directly within the software. I also found the Flat View feature to be helpful. This feature is a display mode that allows you to expand a folder and view everything, including the contents of all subfolders, and subfolders of those subfolders. The software costs about $65 for a single user license. You can find out more about Directory Opus 8 at www.gpsoft.com.

PowerDesk Pro 6

This file organizer software works well, and gives you a simple and easy way to manage files and folders on your computer. It manages just about everything, including multimedia files, and it can also zip files. The interface is simple and easy to use. The software costs about $50, and you can find out more at www.v-com.com.

ExplorerPlus

This file organizer software offers you and simple and easy way to manage files and folders. It uses a simple, two-pane interface, shown in Figure 9-2, that enables you to locate and view files. You can even FTP files using the software. The software is similar to Directory Opus 8, but it doesn't have as many features. However, the ability to view files directly in the interface is a big plus. ExplorerPlus is available from Novatix (www.novatix.com) and it costs about $40. You can find out more at www.pcworld.com.

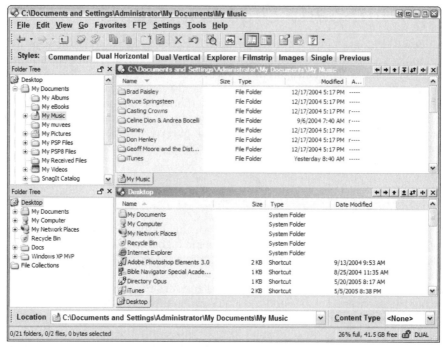

Figure 9-1: The Directory Opus 8 interface

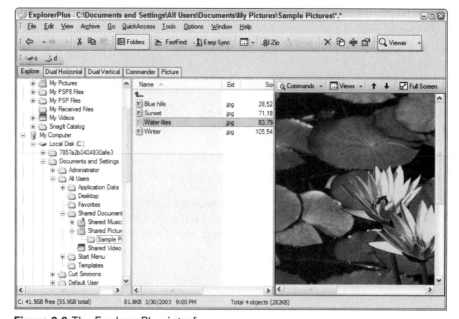

Figure 9-2: The ExplorerPlus interface

You might also be interested in Novatix's RedWall software (the cost is $50 at www.novatix.com). RedWall is actually a security software that is designed to prevent you from opening any virus-infected files. However, it also works great as a simple file viewer utility, and you can even directly convert files into HTML format.

Advanced File Organizer

This tool is technically an "add-in" for Windows XP (see Figure 9-3). It is a simple utility that allows you to organize files into categories, which you can then browse. Basically, you create keywords, and then assign files to those keywords. Depending on how you use files and folders, you may find this feature helpful. Advanced File Organizer costs about $30, and you can purchase it from www.softprime.com.

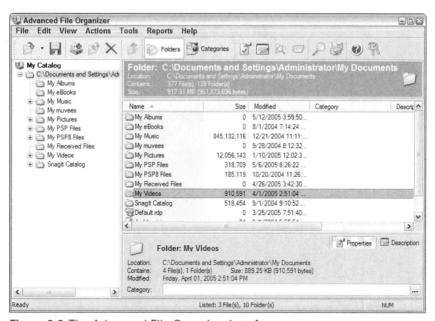

Figure 9-3: The Advanced File Organizer interface

If you work with important data and you're constantly worrying about it being accidentally deleted, you may consider adding a utility to your arsenal that can undelete a deleted file. Check out Undelete 5 (costs about $40) at www.executive.com.

FYI: Don't Forget about Windows Explorer

At one time, Windows XP Explorer was the interface that you used to access and manage files and folders. It has fallen out of favor due to the more friendly, graphical interface of Windows XP. However, Windows Explorer is still available in Windows XP by clicking Start ➪ All Programs ➪ Accessories. The good thing about Windows Explorer is that you can browse through all of your folders, and view subfolders and files in one window configuration. If you're trying to quickly work through your folder structure, Windows Explorer is still one of your best tools, as shown in the following figure. Keep it in mind!

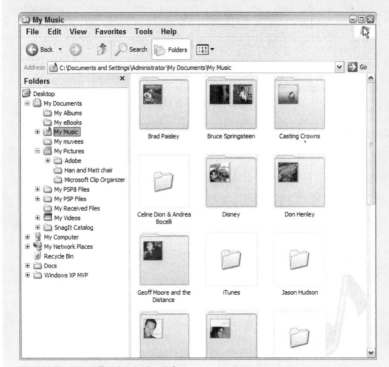

The Windows Explorer interface

Burning Files to a CD

One way that you can manage files and folders is to archive older files and folders onto a CD. This is because you can access the CD when you need the file or folder, and the file or folder doesn't take up space on your hard disk.

Tip

Keep in mind that CDs have a tendency to get scratched, broken, or to simply disappear into never-never land. I use CDs for archiving files, but I also have an older computer that I use as a file server. Everything that is important is kept on both a CD and the file server. In this way, if something happens to a CD (or even the file server for that matter), there is always a redundant copy.

Expert's Notebook: Changing the Default Action When You Insert a CD-R Disc

When you insert a CD-R disc, you see a dialog box where you can choose what you want to do, as shown in the following figure. What you see here depends on the programs that are installed on your computer. As you can see in the first figure, I have several burning and recording software items that are available. I can simply choose what I want, and click the "Always do the selected action" check box, and then click OK. This prevents me from seeing this dialog box again. Of course, if you use multiple applications for different kinds of CD burning sessions, then this dialog box is really helpful because it enables you to choose what you want to do each time you insert a disc.

The CD Drive dialog box

You can also perform this same configuration on the CD drive's Properties dialog box, as shown in the second figure. Access the AutoPlay tab and configure the option that you want. If you want to stop the computer from ejecting the CD when you burn it, then access the Recording tab and clear the "Automatically eject the CD after writing" check box option, as shown in the following figure.

Continued

Continued

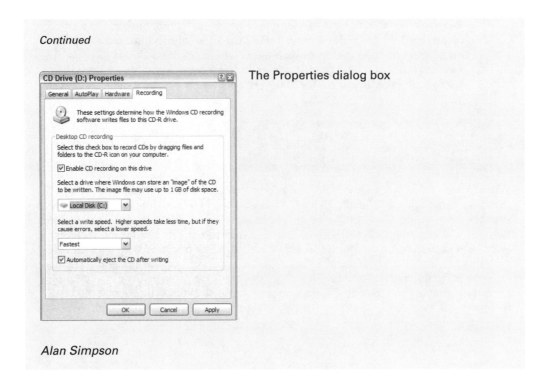

The Properties dialog box

Alan Simpson

Burning files and folders directly to a CD-R or CD-RW disc is easy. Just follow these steps:

Tip

If you want to create a music CD, you can use Windows Media Player. See Chapter 22 for more information.

1. **Insert a blank CD-R disc or CD-RW disc into the drive.** The CD-RW disc doesn't have to be blank.

2. **Locate the file or folder that you want to copy to the CD.** If you want to copy multiple files or folders, use the Ctrl key to select them.

3. **Send your items to the CD Drive.** Right-click the selected items and click Send To ⇨ CD Drive, as shown in Figure 9-4.

4. **Verify the files have been copied.** Once the files have been burned to the disc, you can open the disc by using My Computer, and then verify that the files have been successfully copied.

Figure 9-4: Burn files to a CD

Note

You can either drag and drop the files to the CD drive in My Computer, or use the copy-and-paste method.

Using a USB Flash Drive

USB Flash drives have become very popular over the past two years. With a flash drive, you can store a certain amount of information and easily carry it with you. In fact, some of these devices are combination flash drives and music players. You can easily use a USB flash drive to temporarily store files and folders, and transfer them to other computers. You use a flash drive just like any other drive on your computer. Follow these steps:

1. **Insert the USB flash drive into a USB port on your computer.**

2. **Right-click a file or folder and click Send To ⇨ Removable Disk.** The information copies to the USB flash drive.

3. **You can also manage the contents of the USB flash drive by accessing it in My Computer, as shown in Figure 9-5.**

Figure 9-5: The My Computer window

Storing Files on the Internet

Windows XP allows you to store files on the Internet. You can share files with other people online, or you can use the Internet to store data for redundancy purposes. This feature is a great way to gain extra storage space for free, or at least a minimal cost. I do not recommend that you use the Internet as your only storage solution for files that you can't afford to lose; use this option as a redundancy method.

Note   This section shows you how to use MSN Groups to store data, which is the default method in Windows XP. However, there are other online storage options, which you can find out about in Chapter 21.

1. **Open a folder and select the files and folders that you want to store online.**

2. **In the Files and Folder Tasks pane, click the "Publish this folder to the Web" option, as shown in Figure 9-6.**

3. **The Web Publishing Wizard appears.** In the Welcome screen, click Next.

4. **In the selection window, shown in Figure 9-7, choose the files that you want to publish.** Click Next.

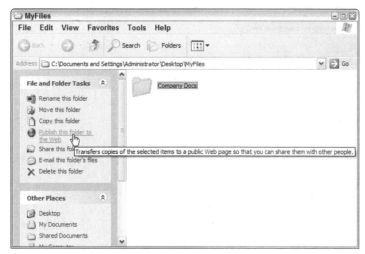

Figure 9-6: The Files and Folders Tasks pane

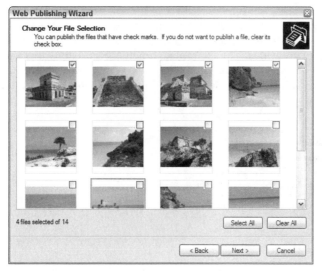

Figure 9-7: Choose the items that you want to publish

5. **Choose a provider.** The example, shown in Figure 9-8, uses MSN Groups. Click Next. A passport sign-in dialog box appears.

6. **Enter your e-mail address and password.** Click OK. Information is downloaded from the Internet, a process that may take a few moments.

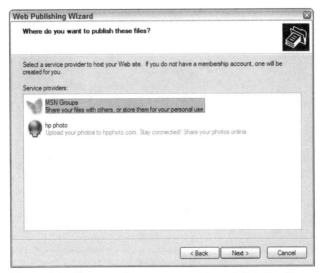

Figure 9-8: Choose where you want to publish the files

7. **Choose where to store your files.** You can choose to store the files in My Web Documents, which is a personal folder, or you can create a new MSN Group to share your files. The example, shown in Figure 9-9, uses the My Web Documents (Personal) option. Then click Next. The wizard tells you that non-image files are uploaded to a Documents folder, while pictures are uploaded to a Documents/Pictures folder.

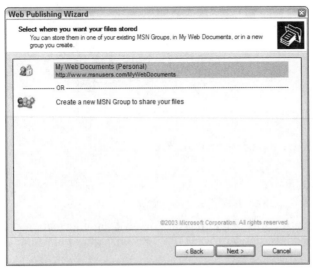

Figure 9-9: You can choose the personal option, or you can create a new MSN Group.

8. **You can change this default by using the Change buttons, seen in Figure 9-10.** Click Next when you're ready. You may see a file size message. Files have a 1MB size limitation, so keep that in mind. Click Next. The file is uploaded, as shown in Figure 9-11.

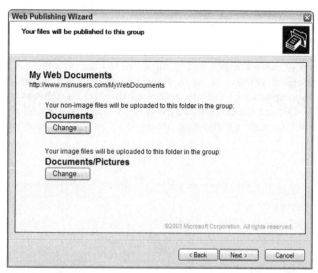

Figure 9-10: You can choose where to publish your files.

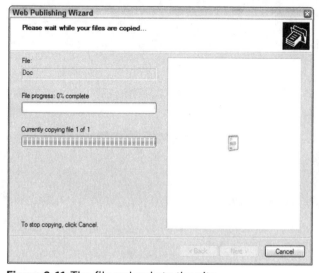

Figure 9-11: The file uploads to the site.

Note

You have a total file size limit of 3MB at the MSN Groups site.

9. **Click Next when the upload process has finished.**

10. **Click Finish.** Notice the URL that you can use to directly access your personal files. From the MSN users' site, you can easily manage your stored items, as shown in Figure 9-12.

Note

If you want to buy more storage space, click the My Storage link on the main MSN Groups page that you access to view your files. You'll see an option to buy more storage space. At the time of this writing, 30 megabytes of storage space on MSN Groups costs you $30 per year, which isn't a bad deal. Also, your files should be safe on the site for as long as you have a valid MSN Passport.

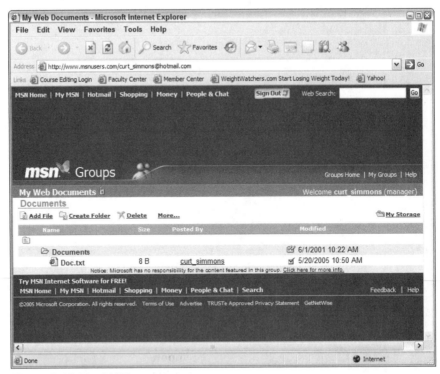

Figure 9-12: The MSN users' site

Using Offline Files

Although the Offline Files feature is not technically a part of file and folder management, you should consider using it if you are on a network. When you use Offline Files, a computer acts as a server to store a collection of network files that other users can access over the network (see Chapters 16 and 17 to learn more about setting up a network). When a file is shared, several different people can access it, collaborate on the file, and use it as needed. With Offline Files, the file is downloaded to the user's computer from the network, where the user can then work with it. Any changes that are made to the file are then synchronized with the server, which can be another Windows XP computer. In an environment where several people use and update the same file, Offline Files ensures that changes from all users are synchronized so that you can always access the most up-to-date copy. To use Offline Files, see the following sections.

Configuring Windows XP to use Offline Files

To configure Windows XP to use Offline Files, follow these steps:

1. **Log on as an Administrator.**

2. **Open Control Panel and then open Folder Options.** Click the Offline Files tab. If you see a message telling you that Fast User Switching is enabled, then you need to change the option in User Accounts so that Fast User Switching is disabled. Offline Files are not compatible with Fast User Switching.

3. **On the Offline Files tab, click the Enable Offline Files check box, shown in Figure 9-13.** You can then set other Offline File options:

   • **Synchronize all offline files when logging on:** This option synchronizes your files whenever you log on.

   • **Synchronize all offline files before logging off:** This option synchronizes your files before you log off.

   • **Display a reminder every *X* minutes:** This option reminds you to synchronize at intervals you specify.

   • **Create an Offline Files shortcut on the desktop:** This gives you easy access to your offline files options.

   • **Encrypt offline files to secure data:** This option encrypts all offline files to make your data secure.

4. **Adjust the amount of disk space temporary files can use.** By default, offline files use ten percent of your hard drive's disk space for storage. You can raise or lower this amount by moving the slider bar.

5. **Delete previously stored offline files.** You can do this using the Delete Files button. This button allows you to view currently stored offline files. This option is simply a way to clean up old offline files.

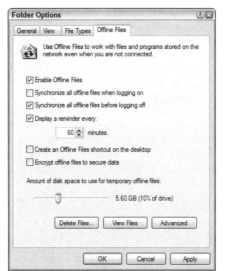

Figure 9-13: The Offline Files tab

6. **Click the Advanced button.** When you click the Advanced button, an Advanced Settings dialog box appears, as shown in Figure 9-14. When you lose your network connection, you have two options. One option enables you to be notified so that you can begin working offline. The other option ensures that you never go offline. You can also generate an exception list. Make any configuration changes that you want, and then click OK.

Figure 9-14: The Advanced Settings dialog box

7. **Choose a network file or folder to make available.** Now that the Offline Files feature is enabled, you can choose which network file or folder you want to

make available offline. Using My Network Places or any other window, simply browse to the network resource, right-click it, and then choose Make Available Offline, as shown in Figure 9-15. The Offline Files Wizard appears.

Figure 9-15: You can make a folder or file available offline.

8. **In the Welcome screen, click Next.** The Synchronization window appears, as shown in Figure 9-16.

9. **Choose whether you want to automatically synchronize files.** If you want to automatically synchronize when you log off and log on, leave the check box selected and then click Next. If not, clear the check box and then click Next.

Figure 9-16: The Synchronization page of the Offline Files Wizard

10. **Enable reminders and create shortcuts.** The final page of the wizard allows you to enable reminders and create a shortcut to the desktop. You can enable these options if you like. Click Finish. The files are copied to your computer.

Synchronizing files

Once you set up Offline Files, you can simply use the file when you want. Depending on your settings, the file may be automatically synchronized with the original file. You can manually enforce synchronization at any time by simply right-clicking the file or folder and then clicking Synchronize. You can also further manage offline files by accessing the Synchronization tool, as follows.

1. **Log on as an Administrator.**

2. **Click Start ➪ All Programs ➪ Accessories ➪ Synchronization.** The Items to Synchronize dialog box appears, as shown in Figure 9-17. Any current offline files or folders appear here.

Figure 9-17: The Items to Synchronize dialog box

3. **Select any items that you want to manually synchronize, and then click the Synchronize button.** You can also click the Setup button to access synchronization settings, which you can change at any time.

4. **Determine when and how synchronization occurs.** The Synchronization Settings dialog box, shown in Figure 9-18, has three tabs, Logon/Logoff, On Idle, and Scheduled. You can use these tabs to specify how and when synchronization occurs. Make any changes that you want, and then click OK.

Expert's Notebook: An Easy Way To Access Internet Resources

If you have a Web site or FTP site to which you can upload files, consider keeping icons to these sites all together in one place: your My Network Places folder. You can use the wizard in the My Network Places folder to create these icons.

To add an icon to your My Network Places folder, open the folder as you normally would. Under Network Tasks in the Explorer bar, click "Add a network place". A wizard appears. Click the "Choose another network location" option on the second Wizard page, and then type the URL of the site in the third Wizard page. For a Web site, use the format http://www.*yoursite*.com. For an FTP site, use the format ftp://ftp.*yoursite*.com. Then just follow the wizard through to completion.

After you have created the icon, you can easily access the remote site by opening your My Network Places folder and then clicking the appropriate icon for the site that you want to access. *Alan Simpson*

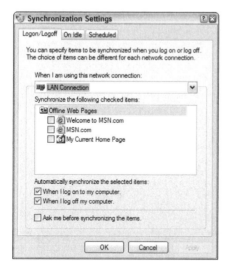

Figure 9-18: You can manage synchronization settings.

Personalizing and Managing User Accounts

10

Windows XP is a multi-user computing environment where several people can easily use the same computer, and yet securely maintain their own files and settings. Although configuration is particularly helpful in office environments where a few people use the same computer, it can also be helpful in home environments where each family member wants to maintain separate user accounts, files, and personalized settings.

User accounts are now easier to configure and manage in Windows XP than in any previous version of Windows. In order to manage user accounts, you'll need to be logged on with an Administrator account, so keep that in mind throughout this chapter.

Working with User Accounts in the Control Panel

The User Accounts applet in the Control Panel is the friendly Windows XP interface for managing user accounts. You can also manage user accounts through the Computer Management console, which is explored later in this chapter. But for now, the User Accounts applet serves as an easy-to-use interface for managing users.

Before you start working with user accounts, you need to make sure that you understand the three types of accounts in Windows XP:

✦ **Administrator:** The Administrator account has full control over the entire computer.

✦ **Limited:** The Limited account is the best account for the standard user. The Limited account can make personal changes to Windows XP, but not system-wide changes. Under most circumstances, the Limited account cannot install or remove programs.

✦ **Guest:** The Guest account is simply that — the guest can log on, but has no rights on the computer. A password is not used with the Guest account. The Guest account is turned off by default, and so you must enable it to use it.

 If you open User Accounts, you may also see an unknown account type. This unknown account appears if you have upgraded to Windows XP from a previous version of Windows.

Creating a New Account

You can create new user accounts at any time, in order to give others access to your computer. To create a new user account, follow these steps:

1. **Click the Create a new account link in the User Accounts window, as shown in Figure 10-1.** A New Account Name window appears.

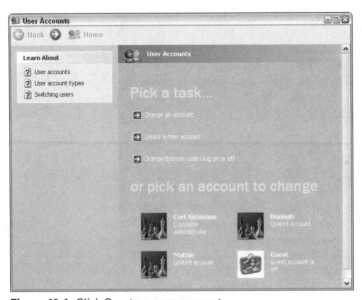

Figure 10-1: Click Create a new account

2. **Enter a name for the new account, and then click Next, as shown in Figure 10-2.** The following window asks you to pick an account type, as shown in Figure 10-3.

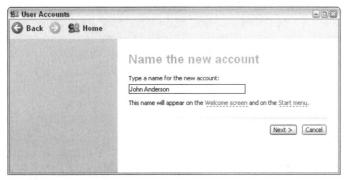

Figure 10-2: Enter an account name.

Tip

Usernames must be unique and must contain up to 20 characters, including numbers. However, user accounts cannot contain any of the following characters: ? \ [ ] : ; | = + * / < >

3. **Choose either Computer administrator or Limited by clicking the appropriate radio button.** If you're not sure which one you want, select each one and read the bulleted list of actions that can be performed by that account type.

4. **When you've finished, click the Create Account button.** The new account now appears in the User Accounts window.

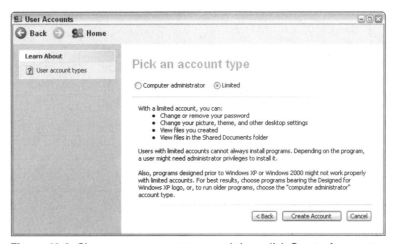

Figure 10-3: Choose an account type and then click Create Account.

FYI: Setting Up a .NET Passport

Windows XP gives you the option to link your user account to your .NET passport, or to create a passport if you do not have one. The .NET passport offers you a single sign-on feature for a number of online accounts and services. If you want to associate your user account with a .NET passport account, open User Accounts in the Control Panel and click your user account. On the What do you want to change about your account? page, click the "Set up my account to use a .NET Passport" link, and then follow the instructions that appear.

Changing an Account

You can easily edit or change any existing account from the User Accounts window. For example, you can edit the password, or you can create a password for an account so that a password must be entered before logging on to the computer. To make changes to an existing user account, follow these steps:

1. **In the User Accounts window, click the Change an account link.** A window appears, asking you to pick an account that you want to change.

2. **Click the account that you want, as shown in Figure 10-4.** A window appears, allowing you to change the name of the account, change the picture, change the account type, create a password, or delete the account, as shown in Figure 10-5.

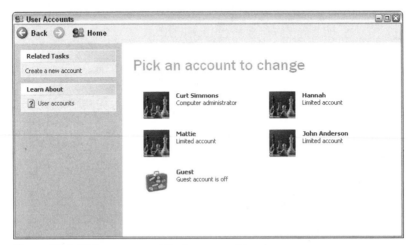

Figure 10-4: Pick an account that you want to change.

Figure 10-5: Choose an account feature that you want to change.

3. **Select the feature that you want to change, and follow the instructions.** An icon represents each user account. For example, if you click the Change the picture link (see Figure 10-5), then a window appears as shown in Figure 10-6, where you can select a new picture or browse for a different one.

Tip   Also notice that you can access a photo directly from your digital camera, assuming your digital camera is attached to your computer.

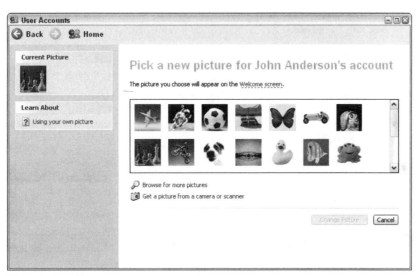

Figure 10-6: Change an account picture.

FYI: Creating Secure Passwords

If you want to make sure that your password is secure, there are a few security tactics that you can use to virtually ensure that no one will be able to break your password:

✦ Make the password at least eight characters long.

✦ Use a combination of letters and numbers.

✦ Use a combination of upper- and lower-case letters.

✦ Consider throwing in a keyboard symbol or two.

✦ Avoid commonly known words, names, or numbers, such as your kids' names, pet names, and phone numbers. Try to use words and numbers that are more random in nature.

✦ Do not write your password down. Keep it only in your head or another secure location.

✦ Never give your password to anyone else under any circumstances.

Curt Simmons

 4. **To change the password for the account, click the Change Password option, and enter the password as you are instructed in the password window**. You can choose to enter a password hint if you like, as shown in Figure 10-7.

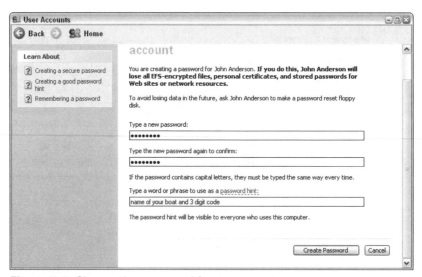

Figure 10-7: Change the password for an account.

Expert's Notebook: Creating a Password Reset Disk

As an Administrator, you can change a user's password. However, if the user has already created a password, your changes will cause the user to lose all EFS-encrypted files, certificates, and stored passwords that they use for Web sites and network connections. Because users have a tendency to forget passwords, thus requiring you to create a new one, you should encourage all users to create a password reset disk. With this disk, you can change your account password without having to know the old password. As a result, you should keep the password reset disk in a secure location. To create a password reset disk, follow these steps:

1. **Log on with your desired account.**

2. **Open User Accounts in the Control Panel.**

3. **Click the Change an account link.**

4. **Click your account.**

5. **In the Related Tasks box in the left pane, click the Prevent a Forgotten Password option.**

6. **The Forgotten Password Wizard appears. Click Next on the Welcome screen.**

7. **Choose to create a password reset disk, and store it on a floppy disk or other removable disk, such as a CD-ROM.**

8. **Enter the current user account password, and then click Next.**

9. **The necessary data is copied to the disk. Click Next, and then click Finish.**

Curt Simmons

5. **Click the Back button to return to the change list, and then make any additional changes that you want.** If you want to delete an account, Windows XP asks you whether you want to automatically save the contents of the user's My Documents folder to a new folder on your desktop. This is a feature to help you avoid losing the user's data; however, e-mail messages, Internet favorites, and other settings cannot be saved.

Changing the Way Users Log On or Log Off

If you click the "Change the way users log on or off" link under Pick a Task (Figure 10-1), you see two options, as shown in Figure 10-8.

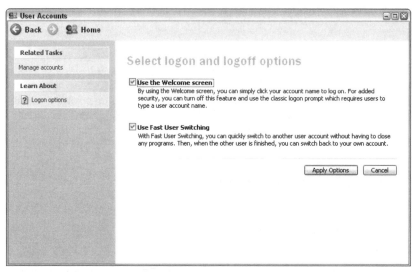

Figure 10-8: Change the password option.

✦ **Use the Welcome screen:** This option uses the Windows XP Welcome screen when you start the computer. Each user account appears on the Welcome screen. Users simply click their account icons and enter passwords, if passwords are used. For security purposes, make sure that each user accesses User Accounts and creates a password, or create a default password for them. If you really want to maintain security, disable the Welcome screen. When you do this, the standard Windows dialog box appears, where the user has to enter both a username and password.

✦ **Use Fast User Switching:** This feature allows you to quickly switch between user accounts without having to close any programs. For example, if several people use the same computer in an office, one person may need to quickly use the computer while another user is logged in. Using Fast User Switching, you can simply click Start ➪ Log Off ➪ Switch User, or you can just press the Windows logo key and then press L to bring up the Welcome screen.

Fast User Switching doesn't work if you are logged onto a Windows domain. It also does not work well with offline files.

If you choose not to use the Welcome screen, then when you press Ctrl+Alt+ Delete, the Windows Security dialog box appears instead of the Task Manager. You can access the Task Manager from this dialog box, or choose to lock the computer, log off, and so forth. This dialog box doesn't appear if the Welcome screen is enabled.

FYI: About Fast User Switching

As I noted previously, Fast User Switching is a great feature when multiple users need to quickly access the computer. Rather than having to completely log off, you can just switch users. However, there are a few quick issues with Fast User Switching that you should keep in mind:

✦ You must enable the Welcome screen.

✦ You must disable Offline files.

✦ You cannot connect the computer to a Windows domain.

✦ For security purposes, it is a good idea to make sure that all user accounts are configured with passwords.

✦ If your computer only has 64MB of memory (which I'm sure it doesn't), Fast User Switching does not work.

Using Computer Management with User Accounts

Aside from the standard User Accounts applet in the Control Panel, you can also use Computer Management to manage user accounts on your computer. The Computer Management console offers you more management features and is faster to use. You can access the Computer Management console by selecting Control Panel ⇨ Administrative Tools or by typing **compmgmt.msc** in the Run dialog box. You can also simply right-click My Computer and click Manage. The following sections show you what you can do with user accounts through the Computer Management console.

Creating a User Account

To create a user account with the Computer Management console, follow these steps:

1. **Using System Tools, expand Local Users and Groups, and then click the Users container.** You see a listing of the current user accounts, as shown in Figure 10-9.

2. **To create a new user account, right-click the Users container and then click New User.** You can also click Action ⇨ New User. The New User window appears, as shown in Figure 10-10.

3. **Enter the user account information and password.** Note that you can use the "User must change password at next logon" option. This feature works well if you want to use a default password, and have the user change it to something private at the next logon.

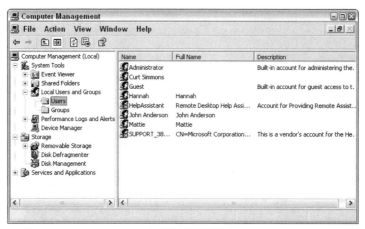

Figure 10-9: The Users container in the Computer Management console

4. **When you're done, click the Create button.**

Figure 10-10: The New User dialog box

Managing a User Account

You can manage existing user accounts within the Computer Management console. Just right-click a user account and click properties, or just double-click the account. Notice that when you right-click a user account, you can choose Set Password, which is the same as resetting the password in User Accounts.

Cross-Reference

See the previous Expert's Notebook sidebar to see how you can create a password reset disk.

Expert's Notebook: Hidden Accounts

The Administrator account is considered a *hidden* account because it doesn't appear on the Welcome screen. However, you can log on using the default Administrator by pressing Ctrl+Alt+Delete twice when you see the Welcome screen. This gives you a default Windows login dialog box, where you can enter the Administrator account information and log on.

On the General tab of the user account's Properties dialog box, shown in Figure 10-11, you can manage some issues with the password and even disable the account.

Figure 10-11: The General tab of the user accounts Properties dialog box

You can also manage the user group of which the account is a member on the Member Of tab, and you can manage profiles on the Profile tab.

Concerning profiles, Windows XP creates and manages local profiles for each user; these profiles include such items as settings, documents, and files. The Profile tab is useful in a domain environment where you need to log on to different network computers, but always receive the same settings. The network Administrator can create a home folder for you on the server that can be downloaded to your computer. You use the Profile tab to configure a connection to that home folder, if your computer was located on a Windows domain.

Fun Tools for Customizing Windows XP

11

Most users like to customize their computer. As you work with Windows XP, you are likely to want features and functions that improve your experience, and for this reason, customizing Windows XP remains a popular task.

You can acquire software to quickly and easily customize Windows XP for a variety of purposes. In fact, Microsoft gives you some helpful software through PowerToys and the Plus! SuperPack. Of course, you can also use third-party solutions to add even more features to Windows XP.

In this chapter, I review PowerToys and the Plus! SuperPack, and I also suggest some tools that you may find useful.

In This Chapter

Using Microsoft PowerToys

Using Plus! SuperPack and Third-Party Options

Using PowerToys

PowerToys are additional programs that the developers at Microsoft create after Windows XP has shipped for manufacturing. Basically, they are little utilities designed to give Windows XP additional functions. You can download the PowerToys for free by going to www.microsoft.com/windowsxp and following the PowerToys link. You can also download and install them one at a time so that you can choose which PowerToys you want.

Before you begin downloading PowerToys, you should note the following:

✦ **Microsoft creates but does not support PowerToys.** This means you cannot access technical support from Microsoft for PowerToy use. Basically, you are on your own, but they are generally easy to use and problem-free.

✦ **You must eliminate older versions of PowerToys.** If you have an old version of PowerToys installed on your computer, you need to uninstall them before downloading and installing the new version.

✦ **PowerToys only work with U.S.-English regional settings.**

✦ **Most PowerToys are user-specific.** This means that you can use PowerToys to customize your Windows XP system, but the customization only applies to you and not to others who have an account on the local computer.

Once you download PowerToys, you can access them by selecting Start ➪ All Programs. The following sections describe some of the PowerToys.

Tweak UI

Tweak UI (User Interface) is a little tool that gives you access to some standard system settings that you cannot configure through the default Windows XP tools and interface. Although a few options may not apply to you, you should find some of these settings really useful. Fortunately, the tool is easy to use, and you can mix and match any of the settings. The Tweak UI interface allows you to change settings just as you would with a standard properties dialog box.

Tweak UI has different setting categories in the left pane, as shown in Figure 11-1. When you expand a category and then choose a setting, the configurable options display in the right pane. The following sections discuss what is available in each category. Note that you must be using at least Service Pack (SP) 1 in order to use Tweak UI.

About

The About category gives you a series of tips for using Tweak UI. The Policy option allows you direct access to the Group Policy Editor, where you can make a number of changes and enforce policies across all users on the Windows XP local computer (assuming you are the computer Administrator).

Figure 11-1: The Tweak UI interface

General

The General category has two options, Focus and Alt+Tab. The Focus option, shown in Figure 11-2, prevents applications from stealing focus from the current window in which you are working. Rather than stealing focus, the taskbar icon for the application flashes, letting you know that the application needs your attention. Simply enable the setting and choose the taskbar flashing option that you want (either flash until user responds, or flash a certain number of times).

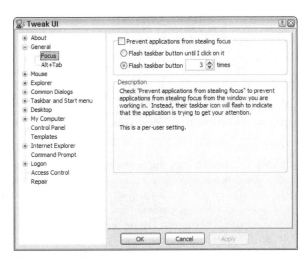

Figure 11-2: The Focus option

By default, the size of the window that appears when you press Alt+Tab is 3 rows by 7 columns. The Alt+Tab option enables you to change the size of the window.

Mouse

The Mouse category gives you several options to control mouse movements and behavior. As you can see in Figure 11-3, you can manage the mouse speed and mouse sensitivity to double-clicking and dragging. The Mouse category contains the following options:

✦ **Hover:** Allows you to adjust your hover sensitivity and hover time.

✦ **Wheel:** Allows you to manage scrolling using the mouse wheel.

✦ **X-Mouse:** Allows you to configure activation for windows as a result of mouse movements. This keeps you from having to click the mouse to bring a window into focus.

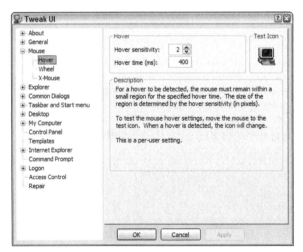

Figure 11-3: The Mouse category

Explorer

The Explorer category allows you a number of options that control the Windows interface. When you select Explorer, options display to manage shortcuts, colors, thumbnails, command keys, customizations, and slide shows. If you simply select the Explorer category, several check box settings appear that you may find helpful, as shown in Figure 11-4. The Colors option, shown in Figure 11-5, enables you to change the color of compressed files, hot-tracking, and encrypted files.

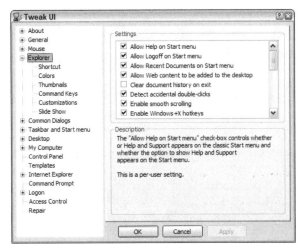

Figure 11-4: The Explorer category

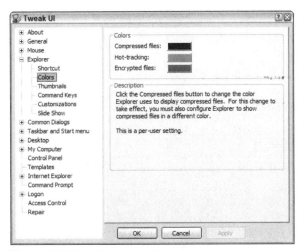

Figure 11-5: The Colors option

Common Dialogs

The Common Dialogs category allows you access to options that make common dialog boxes and entry fields easier to use. For example, you can enable or disable Autocomplete for dialog input boxes. You can also choose to enable a Places Bar when you create different places. For example, you can enable a Places Bar and configure buttons for the desktop, or certain folders.

Taskbar and Start Menu

This category, shown in Figure 11-6, allows you several setting options to manage your Taskbar and Start menu. When you select the category, you can choose to enable balloon tips and receive a warning when disk space runs low. Grouping allows you to configure how applications are grouped on the Taskbar. For example, you can group least-used applications first, and you can also group applications with the most windows first.

When you select Start Menu, you can choose whether to list certain programs on the frequently used programs section of the Start Menu. Simply select or deselect the check boxes next to each application.

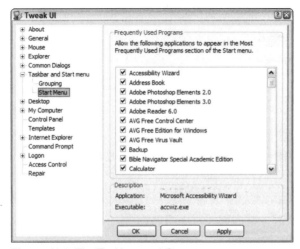

Figure 11-6: The Taskbar and Start menu category

Desktop

The Desktop category allows you to choose which icons you want to display on the desktop. By default, Windows XP only displays the Recycle Bin on the desktop, but you can easily add the following icons by selecting the available check boxes:

  ✦ Internet Explorer

  ✦ My Computer

  ✦ My Documents

  ✦ My Network Places

If you click First Icon, shown in Figure 11-7, you can choose to have My Documents or My Computer displayed first on the desktop. Keep in mind that this is a per-user setting that only works if the user has permission to alter My Computer settings. Also, you may need to log off and back on for the setting to take effect.

As a personal preference, I recommend that you keep as much off the desktop as possible. If you're an old Windows user like me, it is tempting to put every pre-Windows XP folder on the desktop. However, the start menu is a better storage location for folders, so try to get in the habit of using the start menu, and keep your desktop clean for other items.

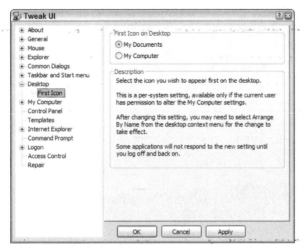

Figure 11-7: The First Icon option

My Computer

The My Computer category allows you to manage which drives and folders you see in My Computer. Simply expand this category and choose Drives, Special Folders, or AutoPlay. You can determine what you see in My Computer from these options and also determine what is done with AutoPlay for each icon or folder.

Under the Control Panel option of My Computer, you can choose to enable or hide certain Control Panel icons, as shown in Figure 11-8. For example, you can hide accessibility options and add Hardware. Some people use this option to make Control Panel neater by removing icons that are not typically used.

Removing the options here only removes the icon from Control Panel — it does not uninstall the control panel option. You can add the icons back at any time by simply returning to this window option and enabling the desired check boxes.

The Templates option allows you to control which kind of document Windows offers to make when you right-click and select New from the menu. You can enable or clear the check boxes that you want.

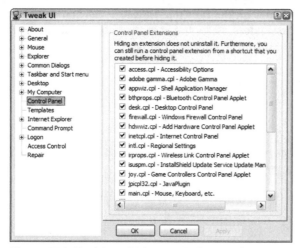

Figure 11-8: Enable or hide certain Control Panel icons.

Internet Explorer

The Internet Explorer category allows you several options for customizing Internet Explorer. You can choose to use a custom toolbar background for Internet Explorer by selecting the Toolbar Background option and clicking the Change button to select a new bitmap image that you have on your computer. This feature allows you to customize Internet Explorer with your own bitmap image.

You can edit the search function so that searches within Internet Explorer are directed to certain search engines. Under View Source, you can specify which program is used to view Web page source code. You can also manage items for animation, as shown in Figure 11-9, as well as the image toolbar.

Under Command Prompt, you can choose a couple of options that determine the character that is used for command-prompt filename completion. You can also specify word separators.

Logon

The Logon category allows you to determine which users appear on the Welcome screen and whether the Autoexec.bat file is parsed at logon (this option is selected by default). You can select the Autologon option to have the system automatically log you on at system startup, and you can also configure whether or not to show unread e-mail on the Welcome screen.

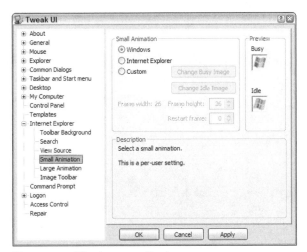

Figure 11-9: The Internet Explorer category

Finally, the Repair option tells Tweak UI to rebuild icons and remove unused icons from Explorer. From the drop-down menu, you can choose different folders that you want to repair, such as the Fonts folder, My Music, and My Pictures.

Open Command Window Here

This tool adds a contextual menu option that enables you to open a command window from any file system window, thus making the command prompt more accessible. As you can see in Figure 11-10, in My Computer, when you right-click any icon, an Open Command Window Here contextual menu option appears. Clicking this option immediately opens a command window. This feature is really helpful if you often use the command prompt. If you rarely use the command prompt, then skip this feature — it just crowds up your contextual menus.

ClearType Tuner

The ClearType Tuner is a little tool that installs in Control Panel, and it is designed to make ClearType easier to read if you're having problems with ClearType in Windows XP. ClearType is a Microsoft technology that is designed to make text more readable on LCD screens. If you open the Control Panel applet, you can run a wizard that can help you adjust the ClearType settings. You can configure them yourself on the Advanced tab, as shown in Figure 11-11.

Figure 11-10: The Open Command Window Here menu option

Alt+Tab Replacement

If you love keyboard shortcuts, then you know that you can press Alt+Tab to toggle between multiple windows on your screen. The Alt+Tab Replacement PowerToys further enhances the Alt+Tab function. After you install the Alt+Tab Replacement PowerToys, a small window appears, showing the actual content of the windows to which you want to switch. This option can make using multiple windows in the same application easier because you can see exactly what you are switching to before doing so. Just press Alt+Tab, then continue holding the Alt key and use your mouse or keyboard arrow keys to select the window to which you want to toggle.

Power Calculator

The Power Calculator PowerToys performs graphing functions and other conversions that are not available on the standard Windows XP calculator. Use the View menu to access numeric, history, and advanced views, and check out File ⇨ Help to learn more about using different functions and features.

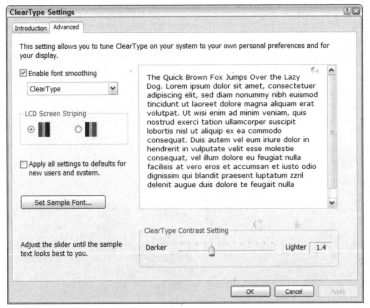

Figure 11-11: The Advanced tab in the ClearType Settings dialog box

Virtual Desktop Manager

The Virtual Desktop Manager allows you to use up to four different desktops on your Windows XP computer at the same time, just by toggling between them using the taskbar. For example, one desktop can have one background and applications open while another can use a different background and applications. You'll see a taskbar icon where you can simply click between the different desktops. It's like having up to four computers in one!

To use the Virtual Desktop Manager, first install it, and then follow these steps:

1. **Right-click an empty area of the taskbar, and then select Toolbars.** In the contextual menu that appears, click Desktop Manager, as shown in Figure 11-12. The Desktop Manager now appears on the toolbar.

Figure 11-12: The Desktop Manager option

2. **To switch between desktops, simply click each one, and then change each desktop.** You can adjust the background and applications that are open on each desktop. After you have configured the desktops that you want, you can simply click between them using the Desktop Manager icons on the taskbar.

3. **To see a preview of your desktops, click the green Preview button next to the desktop buttons on the Desktop Manager.** You see each desktop on the screen, as shown in Figure 11-13, and you can click between them.

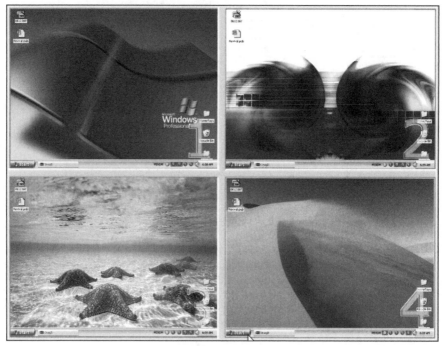

Figure 11-13: You can preview your desktops.

Taskbar Magnifier

If you have problems seeing some things that appear on your screen, you can use the Taskbar Magnifier to magnify portions of your screen. This feature is a lot like the magnifier that you can use through Accessibility Options in Control Panel, but this one stays on your taskbar as an icon until you turn it off.

Simply install the Taskbar Magnifier, right-click an empty area of your taskbar, select Toolbars, and then select Taskbar Magnifier. The Magnifier appears on your taskbar. When you move your mouse over your desktop, that area appears in the magnifier.

WebCam Timershot

The WebCam Timershot PowerToys uses a Webcam attached to your computer to take photos at specified intervals. This is a way to create a collection of photos of a room or office, and is primarily used for security purposes. After you install the WebCam Timershot, click Start ➪ All Programs ➪ PowerToys for Windows XP ➪ Timershot. The window that appears allows you to see the photos that are taken, and you can also adjust the properties for the timershot. For example, you can determine how often to take a photo, where to save the photo, and whether to save all photos or just the last photo taken. You can even save your photos to a network location so that you can take photos of a remote location and see them from a network share.

Cross-Reference

I also describe a few PowerToys in Chapter 25, where I discuss digital photography. For more information about the Image Resizer, HTML Slide Show Generator, and the CD Slide Show Generator, go to that chapter.

Windows XP Plus! SuperPack

If you visit www.microsoft.com/windowsxp, you'll see a link to the Plus! SuperPack. The Plus! SuperPack combines the original contents of the Windows XP Plus! Pack, and the Plus! Digital Media edition. At a price of $30, Plus! SuperPack gives you a number of items that are worth the investment.

One of the most compelling parts of the Plus! SuperPack is the photo slide show option. Although not as complicated as many other existing programs, this fun and easy-to-use tool allows you to create photo slide shows that have narration, music, and even some basic effects. I show you how to use the photo slideshow option in Chapter 25, where I also discuss digital photography projects.

Aside from the slide show, the Plus! SuperPack contains other features that you'll enjoy. Here's a quick review:

✦ **Screen Savers and Themes:** If you miss the additional screen savers and fun themes that you used back in the days of Windows 98 and Me, you can find many of them in the Plus! SuperPack. You'll enjoy the 3D aquarium, and you can even create 3D animated photo albums that can function as your screen saver.

✦ **Games:** You get three additional games with the Plus! SuperPack: 3D bowling, 3D labyrinth, and Tetris.

✦ **Music Options:** You can find some additional features for Windows Media Player, such as more skins, party mode, and desktop dancers. These options are fun, and if you are using Windows XP to play music for a party, the party mode provides an additional security layer. You can also create CD/DVD labels and inserts.

Experts Notebook: Cool Plug-ins for Windows Media Player 10

The Microsoft Plus! SuperPack for Windows XP (available from www.microsoft.com/plus) offers lots of extra toys and goodies for Windows Media Player 10 and Movie Maker 2. At about $29, the Plus! SuperPack is well worth the cost. However, there are lots of other goodies that you can find — many for free — from the little-known WMPlugins page at www.wmplugins.com.

The WMPlugins page is loaded with cool Media Player toys. The site even offers some forums, where you can converse with plug-in fans to find out what's hot and what's not.

✦ **Movie Maker 2:** You can get some additional items for Movie Maker 2, including 50 additional transitions and effects that you can use to liven up your home movies.

Cross-Reference

For more on creating CD/DVD labels and inserts, see Chapter 25. For more on Movie Maker 2, see Chapter 23.

Third-Party Desktop Customization Tools

If you love third-party applications, there are some that can help you customize Windows XP so that it has the appearance and functionality that you want. While there are many customization tools out there, this section focuses on two desktop configuration tools that I have found very helpful and that are well developed. These tools are both safe and I've had good experiences with them, so check them out. You can find more information about other third-party tools in Chapter 27.

Stardock's Object Desktop 2004

Stardock's Object Desktop is a very cool program that is actually a suite of desktop customization and management products all rolled into one. It will cost you around $50, and is found at www.stardock.com. If you love to customize your desktop, then you'll find this suite of products to be very valuable. Keep in mind that you can also purchase and download some of the suite options individually. Here's what you get in the suite package:

✦ **WindowBlinds:** This is a great product that allows you to change the appearance of Windows in a variety of ways. Using this product, shown in Figure 11-14, you can apply skins so that the desktop looks completely different, and you can even add restrictions for other users who use WindowBlinds on the computer.

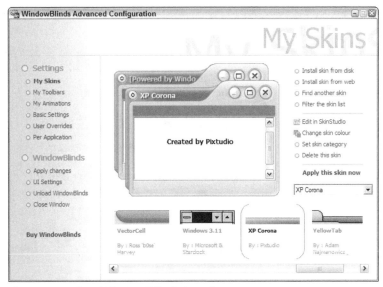

Figure 11-14: The WindowBlinds interface

✦ **IconPackager:** This allows you to change the icons in Windows XP, and to create packages of icons that you can use.

✦ **WindowFX:** This is an older tool for adding visual effects to Windows 98 and 2000 systems.

✦ **SkinStudio:** This is very cool software for creating WindowBlinds skins, and is very easy to use. (See Figure 11-15.)

✦ **IconDeveloper:** You can create icons that you can then use to replace standard Windows icons.

✦ **ObjectBar:** Use this tool to create a new "Start menu" that can combine the features of the Start Menu, Notification Area, and Task Manager.

✦ **Theme Manager:** This tool allows you to manage customization programs from one interface.

✦ **DesktopX:** This great tool enables you to completely design and create your own custom desktop.

✦ **Stardock Central:** This program manages all of the other Stardock programs that you are using so that you can keep them up-to-date.

✦ **IconX:** This program enhances your desktop icons by adding shadows and other effects.

✦ **RightClick:** If you don't like the standard contextual menu that appears when you right-click something, then you can create your own with RightClick!, shown in Figure 11-16.

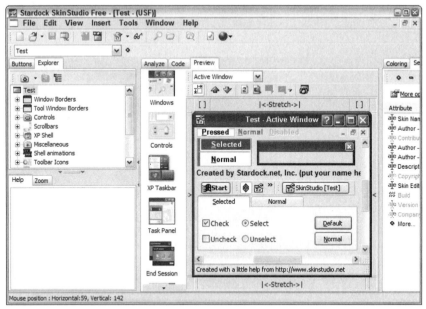

Figure 11-15: The SkinStudio interface

Figure 11-16: The RightClick interface

✦ **Virtual Desktops:** You can add virtual desktops to your Start menu.

✦ **Object Edit:** You can edit objects in Windows XP. This program is for more advanced users.

✦ **Tab LaunchPad:** You can separate programs into a tabbed interface that is easier to use than the standard Windows taskbar.

✦ **DriveScan:** This is a great utility that gives you a graphical display of the hard disk so that you can see what is taking up disk space on your computer.

✦ **Object Sweeper:** This program helps to reduce wasted disk space on your computer.

✦ **Keyboard Launchpad:** This program allows you to create hotkeys to launch any program.

✦ **Component Tray:** This feature gives you a single access location for all of the Stardock Object Desktop components that you install.

3DNA Desktop 1.1

The 3DNA Desktop is a very cool program that replaces your basic desktop with a 3D interface that uses a particular theme. For example, the default theme looks like a studio apartment. The items that you see in the theme are all clickable to give you access to the standard Windows components that you would normally access from the desktop. Each of the 3D environments are customizable, and although they look totally foreign at first, they allow you to easily keep control of Windows XP. This tool is a lot of fun and worth checking out. It will cost you around $30, and you can find it at www.3dna.net.

Tip

If you just can't get enough desktop customization tools and info, check out www.winmatrix.com where you can find a community of people who love to customize Windows XP. You'll learn about many tips, tricks, and different software options there.

Internet and Networking with Windows XP

II

Windows XP has everything you need to access the Internet and create a home or small office network. In fact, the importance of networking and Internet access in today's modern world cannot be overstated, and this part helps you make the most of these features.

In this part, you see how to create Internet connections, configure Internet Explorer and Outlook Express, work with Windows Messenger, create wired and wireless home or small office networks, and manage network security. You also find out about sharing resources, Remote Desktop, and Remote Assistance.

In This Section

Creating Internet Connections

12

As you know, an Internet connection enables your computer to connect with an Internet Service Provider (ISP). The ISP handles the requests that you make to the Internet, and the results are returned to you. In today's Internet connection market, you can find all kinds of super ISP deals, including broadband connectivity, which has finally become affordable. Windows XP makes connections to the Internet easier to create and easier to manage than ever before. In this chapter, you'll find out how to configure and manage Internet connections.

Choosing an Internet Connection Type

Internet connections require the correct hardware, software, and account information. For example, if you want to use a dial-up connection to the Internet, then your computer must have a modem and the appropriate software, and you must have account information so that your computer can connect. Fortunately, Windows XP already has the built-in software that enables you to create an Internet connection. All you need is the correct connection hardware, such as a modem, cable modem, DSL

In This Chapter

Creating Internet Connections

Managing Internet Connections

Working with Modems and Dialing Rules

modem, or satellite modem, and your account information. Once you have the necessary hardware and an account with an ISP, you must use Windows XP to create a connection that can use the hardware and the account to connect to the ISP.

What kind of connection should you choose? That all depends on your budget, your needs, and the available ISP services in your area. Typically, you'll choose one of the following:

✦ **Dial-up:** Dial-up service requires a modem and a phone line. Your computer dials a phone number to connect to an ISP server, and a connection is negotiated. Most dial-up connections cost around $20 per month for unlimited use, but the greatest problem is that all modem connections are slow by today's standards. Phone line limits restrict modems to a 53 Kbps transfer rate, with around a 45 Kbps transfer rate being the reality. Considering the multimedia nature of today's Internet, this speed is rather slow, and you spend a lot of time waiting for pages to download. Additionally, the use of streaming media is next to impossible. If you need Internet access for a small office, then all of the computers in the office probably share the dial-up connection, which further reduces the amount of available bandwidth.

✦ **DSL:** Digital Subscriber Line (DSL) is a broadband technology that has become very popular during the past few years. DSL provides broadband throughput, with speeds generally between 400 Kbps and 8 Mbps, depending on your area. Also, DSL is an "always on" technology. The computer is always connected to the Internet and there is no need to dial a connection. DSL also works with public telephone lines, but different channels are used to transmit high-speed data. DSL requires a special DSL modem that connects to your computer, which is often included free when you sign up for the service. DSL service typically starts at around $40 per month and may be quite higher, but it is not available in all areas. DSL hardware typically requires a USB or Ethernet connection to your computer.

✦ **Cable:** Cable Internet connections are another form of broadband connection, and a direct competitor with DSL. Cable Internet uses a typical coaxial cable that attaches to your computer through a cable modem, just as you would use a coaxial cable with your television. Your computer accesses the Internet over the cable connection, and your cable company or service provider provides an always-on service, just as you would receive cable television. In the past, cable connections worked well, but often did not have the bandwidth of DSL. However, with new cable implementations, the cable access speed is just as fast as DSL and sometimes faster. Like DSL, you can expect to pay around $40 a month for cable Internet. Cable modems typically require an Ethernet or USB connection to your computer.

✦ **Satellite:** Satellite connections are a smaller part of the Internet market and are the least popular type of Internet connection available. However, for people who cannot access other types of broadband connections, satellite connectivity is a good broadband solution, providing an average transfer rate of 300 Kbps. However, it is not as fast as DSL and cable connections, and costs considerably more. The satellite disk equipment generally costs around $500, and unlimited monthly access is around $60. Satellite connections work with a satellite modem that connects to your computer through a USB or Ethernet port. You can find out more about satellite connections at www.starband.net or www.direcway.com.

Tip

Be sure to shop around for an ISP. Depending on where you live, ISPs are very competitive, and you may be able to obtain a great deal. Also, be sure to ask friends and family about the quality of service that they are receiving from their ISPs.

Configuring an Internet Connection

In order to configure an Internet connection, you must first make sure that you have the necessary hardware and account information from your ISP. Keep in mind that some ISPs give you an installation disk and specific setup instructions for your computer, which are often necessary for broadband connections. You should follow the ISP's instructions for creating the Internet connection. However, if you need to create a connection without ISP software, Windows XP can help you create that connection with the New Connection Wizard. The following steps show you how to create an Internet connection using the New Connection Wizard.

1. **Click start ⇨ Control Panel and open the Network Connections folder.** The Network Tasks dialog box appears.

2. **Click the Create a New Connection link.** The New Connection Wizard appears.

3. **Click Next.** The Network Connection Type page opens, as shown in Figure 12-1.

4. **You can choose the kind of connection that you want to create.** Select the Connect to the Internet radio button and click Next.

5. **In the Getting Ready page, if you do not have an account, then you can choose from a list of ISPs.** This process opens a connection to a referral service so that you can sign up with available service providers on the Internet. If you have an installation CD, you can also choose the option to run setup from the CD. Finally, you can choose the manual setup option, which is shown in the following steps.

6. **In the Internet Connection page, choose the type of connection that you want.** You can choose a dial-up, a broadband that is always on, or a broadband that requires a username and password. Make your selection and click Next, as shown in Figure 12-2. Because you are most likely to use the New Connection Wizard to set up modem connections, the rest of the steps focus on that option.

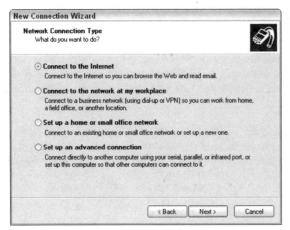

Figure 12-1: The Network Connection Type page

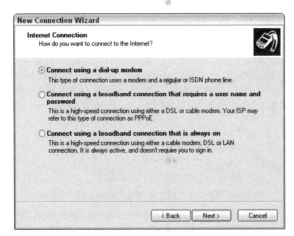

Figure 12-2: The Internet Connection page

7. **In the Connection Name page, enter a name for the connection and click Next.** The name should be something easily recognizable and understandable that distinguishes the connection from other connections.

8. **In the Phone Number page, enter the phone number required to dial the ISP and then click Next.**

9. **In the Internet Account Information page, shown in Figure 12-3, enter your username and password, and then click the check box options that you want to use.** Keep in mind that the account can be accessed by anyone using your computer, or just you.

FYI: Understanding PPPoE Connections

You may have noticed the reference to Point-to-Point Protocol over Ethernet (or PPPoE) when you selected the type of connection that you wanted to create. PPPoE is used with broadband Internet connections that require a username and password (not always connected), and it is a protocol that is used by some broadband connections for access to the Internet. PPPoE is designed for users on a local area network (using standard Ethernet) who access the Internet over that Ethernet network through some broadband connection. In other words, Point to Point Protocol, which is used on the Internet, functions over Ethernet to provide Internet access to these users. With PPPoE, each user can have a different access configuration, even though they all reside on the same LAN. PPPoE is also used by ISPs to control the use of static IP addresses. You can learn more about PPPoE by searching for RFC 2516 on any Internet search engine. *Curt Simmons*

Figure 12-3: The Internet Account Information page

10. **Click Finish.** The new connection now appears in the Network Connections folder.

Starting a Connection

Broadband connections are always connected to the Internet, while dial-up connections require that you start the connection when you want to use the Internet. Naturally, that concept is easy, and you can typically launch a connection by starting an application, such as Internet Explorer or Outlook Express, or by starting the connection using the Network Connections folder. To launch the connection, you can use the connection icon that appears in the Network Connections folder, once you have created the connection. You can also access the connection by clicking start ⇨ Connect To and then clicking the connection. As you can see in Figure 12-4, all connections are found in the Network Connections folder.

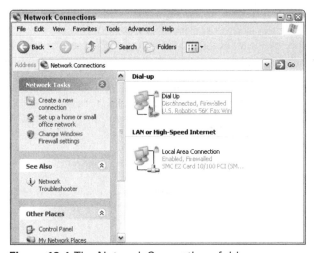

Figure 12-4: The Network Connections folder

When you double-click a connection icon, a connection window appears, as shown in Figure 12-5.

Figure 12-5: The Connect Dial Up window

FYI: Holding the Key with USB Wireless

Suppose you need to provide Wi-Fi access to visitors at your place of business. You'd like to provide easy-to-use access, but you want to retain some control over who can connect and when. One simple way to do this is to use a dedicated access point and USB Wi-Fi network adapters. Because most Wi-Fi access points allow you to configure MAC-based access control lists, you can add only your designated USB network adapters to the "allowed" list. When a visiting user arrives, you turn your access point on and then insert the USB Wi-Fi adapter into the visitor's device. If you adapters are on the Windows XP HCL (which is highly recommended), then the device sees your network and can be joined with minimal effort. If you need additional security, you can disable the SSID broadcast and/or encryption on the AP. The important point here is that you retain physical control of who can access the network. Another application is using this setup at home with a young child's computer. By using a removable network adapter, you can ensure that the child can only access the Internet when an adult allows it. When you no longer want to allow the connection, simply remove the adapter and secure it. Windows XP retains all of its network settings for USB adapters when they are removed. When it is time to surf the Web again, reinsert the adapter in the USB slot where they were originally set up. This allows you to reconnect to the Internet with no additional configuration required. *David Dalan*

Enter your username and password for the ISP. Notice that you can choose to save the username and password so that you do not have to retype it each time. You can save the password for "Me only," which only allows you to use the connection with your user account, or you can choose to allow anyone who uses the computer to use the Internet connection. The phone number that you entered appears by default. Click Dial to make the connection.

There is one security issue that you should be aware of: If you use the "Me only" option, then you are the only who can launch the connection. However, if you leave the computer unattended, anyone who sits at the computer while you are logged on can launch the connection. If you want to make certain that no one else can ever use the connection, simply leave the "Save this user name and password for the following users" check box disabled, which also disables both sub-options. As a result, you must supply the username and password each time that you connect.

Managing Dial-up Connections

Broadband connections tend to be rather simple in terms of configuration, and an installation disk typically handles the setup routine and management. However, with dial-up connections, you'll find some important properties pages that determine how the connection functions when you want to use it. Naturally, if you use a dial-up connection, you should become familiar with the options on the properties pages so that you can both configure the connection and troubleshoot problems. The following sections show you what is available on the properties pages tabs.

General Tab

Right-click the connection in the Network Connections folder and click Properties. On the General tab of the Properties dialog box, you have a few different options, as shown in Figure 12-6:

✦ **Modem Configuration:** If you click the Configure button, you can access the modem's properties pages and make any configuration changes that you want. See the next section to learn more about configuring a modem.

✦ **Phone Numbers:** You can configure alternate phone numbers that can be used with the connection, and you can also configure dialing rules. Dialing rules are explored later in this chapter.

✦ **Notification:** Use the check box at the bottom of the dialog box to display an icon in the Notification Area when you are connected.

Figure 12-6: The General tab

Options Tab

The Options tab, shown in Figure 12-7, gives you a few dialing and redialing options, as follows:

✦ **Display progress while connecting:** If you want to see the progress as the connection is being made, click this check box. If it is cleared, you cannot see any progress information during the connection process.

✦ **Prompt for name and password, certificate, etc.:** If you want to be prompted for information such as the username, password, and certificate during the connection, then check this option. If this information is entered in the connection and you don't want to have to re-enter it each time, do not use this option.

✦ **Include Windows logon domain:** This option, which can only be used in conjunction with "Prompt for name and password, certificate, etc.," requests the Windows domain for logon purposes. Generally, when dialing to an ISP, you do not need this option. If you dial to a corporate server using a Windows domain, then this option is helpful.

✦ **Prompt for phone number:** This option allows you to see, modify, and select the phone number that you use when dialing the connection. If you only use one phone number, then you can simply clear this check box option.

✦ **Redial attempts:** If the first dial connection is not successful, then Windows can automatically redial the number. Use the selection box to determine how many times Windows tries to redial the connection before stopping. The default is 3.

✦ **Time between redial attempts:** By default, Windows XP waits one minute between each redial attempt, but you can change this value.

Figure 12-7: The Options tab

✦ **Idle time before hanging up:** If you want the connection to automatically disconnect after a certain period of idle time, enter the value here. Use the Never option if you do not want the connection to automatically disconnect.

✦ **Redial if line is dropped:** If you lose the connection, this option will have Windows XP automatically try to redial the connection.

✦ **X.25:** If you are logging onto an X.25 network, click the X.25 button and enter the X.25 network provider, as well as the remote server information as required.

Security Tab

The Security tab, shown in Figure 12-8, provides security settings for the dial-up connection. The Typical settings are used by default, and they validate your username and password with the ISP. You also have advanced connection options, but these options are generally used for dial-up connections to corporate networks, and not to ISP servers. Do not change any of the settings on this tab unless explicitly instructed to do so by your ISP. Incorrectly changing these settings stops your computer from successfully logging on to the ISP.

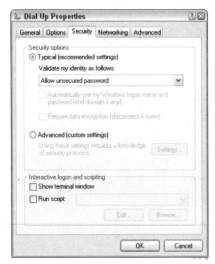

Figure 12-8: The Security tab

Networking Tab

The Networking tab, shown in Figure 12-9, shows you the current networking services and protocols that are used for the connection. If you need additional services or protocols for the connection, use the Install button to add them. In most cases for ISP connections, there is nothing that you need to configure here.

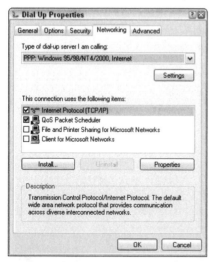

Figure 12-9: The Networking tab

Advanced Tab

The Advanced tab enables you to turn on Internet Connection Sharing and Windows Firewall, which you can learn more about in Chapters 19 and 30, respectively.

Configuring Dialing Rules

As I mentioned earlier in this chapter, dialing rules enable you to configure how the modem dials various phone numbers. For example, some locations require an area code, others do not, and some require you to dial 9 to access an outside line. The dialing rules options enable you to tell Windows XP how to dial your connection, regardless of your specific needs. Just follow these steps:

1. **On the connection type's General tab (Figure 12-6), click the Use dialing rules check box.** Then click the Dialing Rules button.

2. **The Phone and Modem Options window appears, as shown in Figure 12-10.** On the Dialing Rules tab, you see the current location that is configured. You can choose to edit the existing location or to create a new one by clicking the appropriate button. Regardless of whether you choose to edit a current location or create a new one, the same configuration dialog box appears.

   The New or Edit Location window appears, with a General tab, shown in Figure 12-11, containing several setting options.

Figure 12-10: The Dialing Rules tab

Figure 12-11: The General tab of the
New Location dialog box

3. **On this tab, enter the area code and country/region in which the area code is found.** Then use the boxes in the Dialing rules section to determine the rules concerning the use of the area code. You can also choose to disable call waiting, and choose tone or pulse dialing.

4. **Click the Area Code Rules tab.** Area code rules determine how phone numbers are dialed within your current location, as well as other locations. To create an area code rule, click the New button, as shown in Figure 12-12.

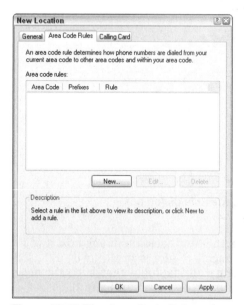

Figure 12-12: The Area Code Rules tab

5. **In the New Area Code Rule dialog box, shown in Figure 12-13, enter the area code to which this rule applies.** You can then enter a list of prefixes that can be used with the area code, or accept the default setting that all prefixes that you use can work with the area code. For example, let's say that the area code is 214, and you only want to use 564 and 569 prefixes with the area code. In this case, click the "Include only the prefixes in the list below" radio button, and click Add to enter those prefixes. If you do not place any prefix restrictions, then Windows XP assumes that any prefix that you dial can be used with the area code. At the bottom of the dialog box, use the check boxes to specify whether a 1 should be dialed when using the area code, and whether the area code should be dialed when using the prefixes. For example, if a dial-out number is 214-564-1234, and the area code is required each time you dial the number, then click the "Include the area code" check box.

6. **Click OK.** The new area code rule now appears in the Area Code Rules tab. You can create new area codes and edit existing ones at any time on this tab.

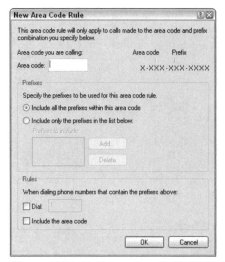

Figure 12-13: The New Area Code Rule dialog box

7. **Click the Calling Card tab in the New Location dialog box.** If you need to use a Calling Card to make the connection—for example, if you dial a long distance number when you are traveling with a laptop—then enter the necessary card information on the Calling Card tab, as shown in Figure 12-14.

8. **Click OK to save your changes.**

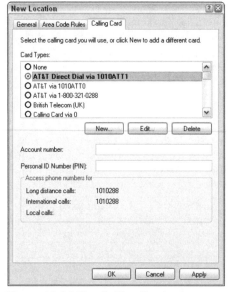

Figure 12-14: The Calling Card tab

Configuring Modem Properties

In order to make modem configuration easier, a Phone and Modem Options icon is included in the Control Panel. If you double-click the icon, you see a dialog box that contains Dialing Rules, Modems, and Advanced tabs. See the previous section for more information about configuring dialing rules. The Advanced tab lists the provider options that are available in Windows XP (which do not require any configuration). However, there are a few options on the Modems tab.

Today's modems do a good job of setting themselves up. You don't have to worry about inputting a lot of information to make the modem work, but you may want to adjust some of the settings to meet your needs. The Modems tab in the Phone and Modems Options dialog box, shown in Figure 12-15, provides a simple interface that lists the modems that are installed on your computer, and it provides you with a few options.

Figure 12-15: Modems tab

At the bottom of the dialog box are the Add and Remove buttons. If you click the Add button, the New Modem Wizard appears and searches for additional modems that are attached to your computer. If the wizard finds one, it automatically installs it. If it doesn't, then you can select it from a list. If you select a modem in the list and click Remove, the modem's software is uninstalled from your computer.

To see the specific properties for a modem, click the modem in the list (if there is more than one), and then click the Properties button. There are several properties tabs. First, the General tab, shown in Figure 12-16, simply tells you the status of the device (whether or not it is working properly). You can click the Troubleshoot button to start the Windows XP troubleshooter if you're having problems with the modem, and you can also use the drop-down menu at the bottom of the screen to disable the device, if necessary.

Figure 12-16: General Modem Properties

The Modem tab in the Properties dialog box, shown in Figure 12-17, displays three basic options. First, you can adjust the slider bar for the modem's speaker volume. Next, you can use the Maximum Port Speed drop-down menu to set a maximum speed at which you want the modem to connect. You should leave this setting at the default so that you have the highest connection speed possible. Finally, the Dial Control section contains the "Wait for dial tone before dialing" check box. This check box is probably enabled, and should generally remain enabled so that your modem checks for a dial tone before actually dialing the number.

On the Diagnostics tab, shown in Figure 12-18, you can run a query, which is simply a test that your computer runs with the modem to make sure that it is working properly. You can also view a log file. The information that you see here consists of a lot of commands, many of which will not mean anything to you, but this information can be helpful if you have to call technical support concerning problems with your modem.

The Advanced tab displays a single dialog box where you can enter additional modem string commands. You don't need to do anything here unless your modem documentation or the technical support explicitly instructs you to make a change. The extra initialization commands that are entered here are most often used to solve problems with modem connectivity.

Finally, the Driver tab is like all driver tabs for hardware in Windows XP. Use this tab to update or change drivers for the device.

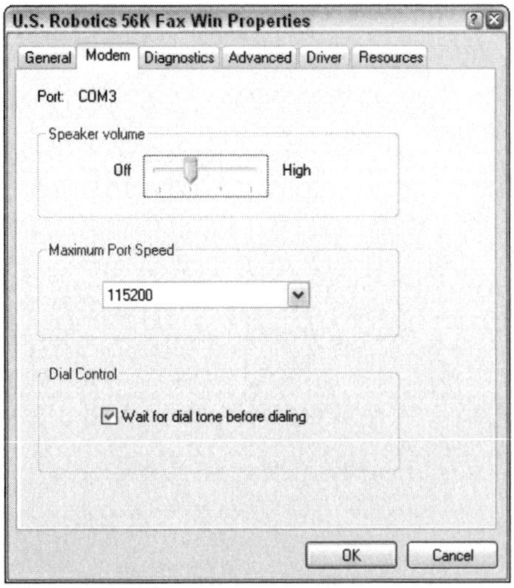

Figure 12-17: Modem tab of General Properties

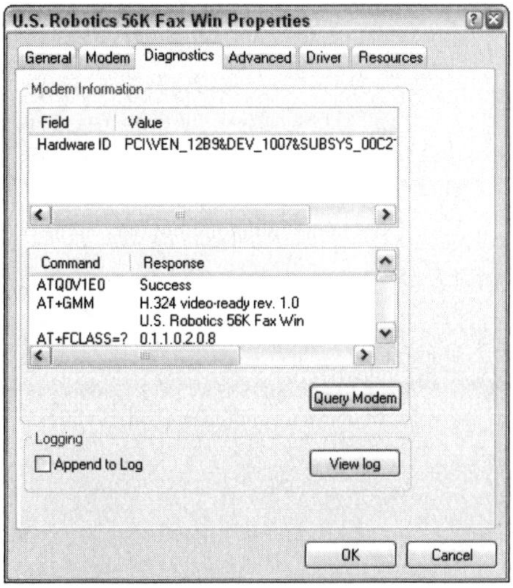

Figure 12-18: The Diagnostics tab

Configuring and Customizing Internet Explorer

13

I nternet Explorer, or IE, is probably the most popular Web browser today, and rightly so; after all, it is included with the Windows XP operating system, and it is integrated with Windows XP. You can easily access Internet Explorer, and you can even jump directly to Web pages directly from the To line in any folder in Windows XP.

For the most part, Internet Explorer is straightforward and easy to use. Because the browser is customizable, you can easily change the appearance of IE and how it displays information.

In this chapter, we'll take a close look at Internet Explorer, focusing on configuration and customization. Although I won't review basic features, I will show you how to do just about everything else with IE.

Managing Connections to the Internet

Naturally, a Web browser doesn't do much if it is not connected to the Internet, and so the connection options are important. If you're using IE from your home or office, it is probably already connected to the Internet and you may feel that you can safely skip this section. However, you may still find this section useful because Internet Explorer has a number of important connection options, depending on how you need to connect to the Internet. This flexibility gives you a number of networking options so that Internet Explorer can meet all of your connectivity requirements.

Choosing a Connection Option

A single tab in Internet Explorer enables you to configure the browser to work with the existing connections on your computer. If you click Start ➪ Control Panel ➪ Internet Options, then you can click the Connections tab, as shown in Figure 13-1. In this tab, you can manage dial-up and Virtual Private Network (VPN) settings, as well as Local Area Network (LAN) settings. You can also choose between dial-up and VPN connections, or LAN connections.

Tip   IE only works with Internet and intranet connections that you have already configured on your computer. You can click the Setup button on the Connections tab to create an Internet connection, as shown in Figure 13-1. This option does the same thing as the Internet Connection Wizard, which you can learn more about in Chapter 12.

Figure 13-1: The Connections tab in the Internet Options dialog box

Choosing a Dial-up or Virtual Private Network Setting

The top section of the Connections tab provides you options to configure dial-up and Virtual Private Network (VPN) settings for Internet Explorer. Keep in mind that Internet Explorer simply uses the dial-up and VPN connections that you have previously created in the Network Connections folder. If you do not have any connections configured, as shown in Figure 13-1, then this window is blank and the options are grayed out. Once you have configured a dial-up or VPN connection, the setting options on the Connections tab are available to you. These are shown in Figure 13-2 and are as follows:

Figure 13-2: The Connections tab with dial-up options

Cross-Reference

You can click the Add button to create a new connection. See Chapter 12 for details.

✦ **Never dial a connection:** This option prevents Internet Explorer from automatically dialing your connection. When you select this radio button option, you must manually connect to the Internet before using Internet Explorer because Internet Explorer is not able to launch a dial-up session. If a connection is never dialed when you open IE, then this option is probably not activated.

✦ **Dial whenever a network connection is not present:** This option automatically dials an Internet connection when you open Internet Explorer if no existing connection is available. If you are already connected to the Internet when you open Internet Explorer, then that connection is used. Keep in mind that when Internet Explorer dials the connection, your default Internet connection is used. This option works well for most users.

✦ **Always dial my default connection:** Let's say you have two different connections to the Internet, but you always want Internet Explorer to use a particular default connection. If you select this option, then Internet Explorer automatically dials the default connection when it is launched. If you need to set the current default connection, just select the connection that you want to use in the Dial-up and Virtual Private Network settings field, and then click the Set Default button.

You may need to contact a proxy server in order to access a dial-up connection. A proxy server is a computer that stands between client computers and the Internet. The proxy server works on behalf of client computers in order to retrieve information from the Internet and acts as a security boundary for the network. If you click the Settings button, you can configure access to a proxy server for the dial-up or VPN account that you have selected in the Dial-up and Virtual Private Network settings field. Keep in mind that the Settings option here is for proxy server settings for dial-up or VPN access only, and not for LAN access.

The Dial-up Connection Settings dialog box, shown in Figure 13-3, offers you three configuration options for a connection to a proxy server:

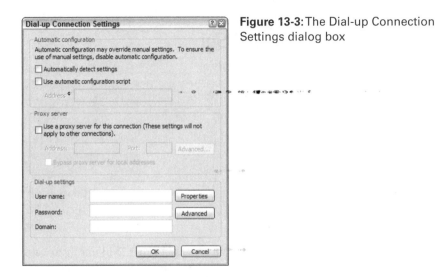

Figure 13-3: The Dial-up Connection Settings dialog box

✦ **Automatic configuration:** If the proxy server is set up for automatic configuration, you can use the "Automatically detect settings" option or point the way to the automatic configuration script. Automatic configuration options and scripts are set up on the proxy server, and so do not use these settings unless you are sure that they are supported. See your proxy server Administrator for details.

✦ **Proxy server:** With this option, you can provide the address to a particular proxy server. If you know that your computer should access a certain server, click the check box and enter the proxy server's IP address. If additional port information is required, you can add the port and click the Advanced button to specify other TCP ports that can be used. See your proxy server Administrator for details.

✦ **Dial-up settings:** You can specify the necessary username and password to access the proxy server. If you click the Advanced button, the Advanced Dial-Up dialog box appears, as shown in Figure 13-4. You can configure the number of times that a connection is attempted, as well as disconnect options.

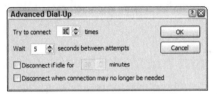

Figure 13-4: The Advanced Dial-Up dialog box

Local Area Network (LAN) Settings

Local Area Network (LAN) settings are used for broadband Internet access, such as DSL modems, cable access, and Internet satellite. You can also use the LAN Settings option if you are using a network adapter to access a proxy server that has a network connection to the Internet or to an ISP.

In order to configure the LAN settings so that Internet Explorer can use the broadband or network connection, you need to enter the correct settings in the LAN Settings dialog box. You can access this dialog box, shown in Figure 13-5, by clicking the LAN Settings button on the Connections tab of the Internet Options dialog box. You can then choose automatic configuration or you can enter the address of the proxy server. Check your broadband documentation for details, or contact your Network Administrator if you are accessing the Internet through a proxy server.

If your computer resides in a domain environment, the settings are often configured automatically through Group Policy. Don't make any changes here if your computer resides in a Windows domain.

Figure 13-5: The Local Area Network (LAN) Settings dialog box

Customizing Internet Explorer

We all like things to look a certain way, which is why we buy different houses, drive different cars, and choose different dogs (or cats, for you cat lovers). You may also want to change some of the configuration options for Internet Explorer. There are a lot of different options that you can choose from, as you will see in the following sections.

The Appearance of Internet Explorer

Internet Explorer uses a collection of default colors, fonts, and languages to display Web pages. However, those default preferences may not meet your needs. You can easily change the defaults by clicking the Colors, Fonts, and Languages buttons on the General tab of the Internet Options dialog box, as shown in Figure 13-6. These configuration buttons open simple dialog boxes, such as the Colors dialog box, shown in Figure 13-7, so that you can make Internet Explorer display Web pages as you want them to appear.

Figure 13-6: The General tab

Figure 13-7: The Colors dialog box

Home Page

Internet Explorer loads a default home page when you first open the browser. This home page may be Microsoft.com, or it may the home page of the computer manufacturer, such as Dell, Compaq, or Gateway. If you want, you can select another home page, or you can choose not to display a home page at all. In the Internet Options dialog box, just click the General tab and enter a new URL in the Address field of the Home page section, or click the Use Blank button if you do not want a page to appear.

Configuring AutoComplete

AutoComplete is a feature that enables Internet Explorer to remember information that you have entered on Web pages. The idea is that you will type less, and Internet Explorer will remember what you want to say. When you attempt to re-enter that information, Internet Explorer tries to complete it for you. Some people find that this feature works well, while others find it annoying — you can decide what works best for you.

You can also adjust AutoComplete's behavior by accessing the Content tab in the Internet Options dialog box and clicking the AutoComplete button. The AutoComplete Settings dialog box appears, as shown in Figure 13-8.

Figure 13-8: The AutoComplete Settings dialog box

You can disable or enable the check boxes to specify whether AutoComplete performs different functions. For example, a notable feature of AutoComplete is its ability to remember passwords. If you log in to a number of Web sites using different passwords, AutoComplete can remember your passwords and make the login process easier. However, keep in mind that someone else using your computer can easily access those passwords as well. Depending on the sensitive nature of your Internet usage, you may want to consider disabling the "User names and passwords on forms" option and click the Clear Passwords button to delete any passwords that Internet Explorer has in memory.

Manage Related Programs

Internet Explorer uses a default listing of programs for certain Internet features. For example, Outlook Express is the default e-mail and newsgroup client, while NetMeeting is the default Internet call program. When you click one of the options on the Internet Explorer toolbar, such as the e-mail icon, Internet Explorer checks the settings on the Programs tab of the Internet Options dialog box and determines which program to open, as shown in Figure 13-9. However, if you have other programs installed on your computer that you want Internet Explorer to use, such as a different e-mail client, you can access the Programs tab and use the provided drop-down menus to change the default options.

Figure 13-9: The Programs tab

Specific Customization Options

The Advanced tab of the Internet Options dialog box provides you with a number of additional check-box settings that control different categories. These categories include Accessibility, Browsing, Multimedia, Printing, Security, HTTP 1.1 Settings, and Search from the Address Bar as shown in Figure 13-10.

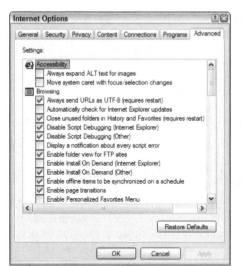

Figure 13-10: The Advanced tab

Under most circumstances, the default settings are adequate for most of your browsing needs. However, there a number of different options that might be important to you, and the following list points out some of the configuration issues that you might consider changing:

✦ **Under the Browsing settings, consider clearing the "Enable page transitions" option if you are using a slow Internet connection.** Some Web sites have page transitions configured so that one page fades into another. While visually appealing, these transitions waste your bandwidth and time, and so you should disable this feature if your connection is slow.

✦ **Under the Browsing settings, consider enabling the "Enable Personalized Favorites Menu" option.** If you use the Favorites menu a lot, the list can become long and disorganized. The Personalized Favorites menu hides the favorites that you haven't used in awhile so that the list is easier to see and use.

✦ **Under the Browsing settings, consider disabling the "Notify when downloads complete" option.** This deactivates that extra OK box notification that you see when a download finishes.

✦ **Under the Browsing settings, click the "Use inline AutoComplete" option.** If you want Internet Explorer to help you automatically complete Web addresses that you have used before, click this option.

✦ **Under the Printing settings, background colors and images on Web pages are not printed by default.** However, if you want the entire Web page to print, you can enable this option.

✦ **Under the Security settings, consider disabling the "Warn if changing between secure and not secure mode" option.** Do this if you do not want to see the Security warning dialog box that appears when you move in and out of secure and non-secure pages.

Tip

To enhance security and prevent other users' tracing the Web sites you have visited during your online activity, you should enable the "Empty temporary Internet files folder when browser is closed" option in the Security section of the Internet options.

Configuring the Internet Explorer Toolbar

You can customize the toolbars that you see in IE, just like toolbars in any folder in Windows XP. If you click the View menu and choose the desired options on the Toolbars and Explorer Bar submenu, you see that the options are almost the same as a typical folder.

You can even move the toolbars around so that they are placed in different locations within the Internet Explorer interface. You can separate toolbars on the top and bottom of the screen, or you can combine them into one long toolbar in order to save more screen space. The choice is yours, so experiment with the options to find what works best for you.

Tip

If you can't move a toolbar, click View ⇨ Toolbars and deselect the check box next to the "Lock the Toolbars" option.

You can also customize the Internet Explorer toolbar by selecting the button items that appear. To customize the toolbar, just click View ⇨ Toolbars ⇨ Customize. In the Customize Toolbar dialog box, shown in Figure 13-11, you can see the toolbar buttons that are available to you, as well as the current toolbar buttons.

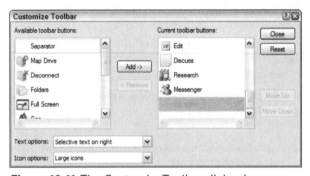

Figure 13-11: The Customize Toolbar dialog box

To configure a custom toolbar, just follow these steps:

1. **In the Available toolbar buttons list, select the toolbar button that you want to add, and then click the Add button.** The new toolbar button now appears in the Current toolbar buttons list.

2. **To remove any existing toolbar buttons, select the button in the Current toolbar buttons list, and then click the Remove button.** You can then configure the toolbar buttons to appear in any order that you want by clicking the Move Up or Move Down buttons.

3. **Finally, click the Text options and Icon options drop-down menus.** You can choose to show selective text on the right, show text labels, or show no labels at all. You can also choose to use large or small icons.

4. **Click OK when you are done.** Keep in mind that you can reconfigure the toolbar at any time to meet your current needs.

Managing History

Internet Explorer keeps track of the Web sites that you or anyone using your computer has accessed. The sites are listed by URL in the History folder, and by default, they are kept for 20 days. However, you can change the default setting on the General tab of the Internet Options dialog box. You can view the History list by clicking the History button on the toolbar. The History Explorer palette appears, as shown in Figure 13-12. By expanding the day and week categories, you can see the sites that have been accessed on those days.

Figure 13-12: The History palette

Expert's Notebook: Using History

Overall, History is a simple feature, but there are few important points that you should keep in mind:

✦ **You can delete History items individually by right-clicking them and clicking Delete.** You can also delete History items from an entire day or week by right-clicking the category and then clicking Delete. You can delete all History items by clicking the Clear History button on the General tab of the Internet Options dialog box.

✦ **Even though you can delete the Today category, it will pop back into place when you use the Internet or when you access History.** In other words, you cannot permanently delete it or the items that it holds. However, you can individually delete the items from the Today list.

✦ **If you change the "Days to keep pages in history" value to 0 on the General tab of the Internet Options dialog box, the current day's history is still recorded anyway.**

✦ **History items can be deleted, and so if you want to keep tabs on what other people are accessing on your computer, you will need third-party software.** Check out www.computersnooper.com and www.spy-patrol.com to get started!

You can use third party software to clear temporary Internet files, cookies and History. The freeware application Crap Cleaner (www.ccleaner.com) completes this task effortlessly. This application also deletes the index.dat files, which are capable of storing all your online activity, even though you may have manually deleted temporary Internet files, cookies and History.

Alan Simpson

Managing Favorites

As you use the Internet, you'll run across sites that you want to remember. The Favorites menu allows you to record URLs so that you can easily access them later. When you choose a favorite, you can also make the favorite available offline. This feature is helpful if you want to read information on a Web site without connecting to the Internet. If you want to make the favorite available offline, enable the "Make available offline" option on the Add Favorite dialog box, shown in Figure 13-13. If you want to customize the offline feature, then click the Customize button. A wizard appears to guide you through customizing how you want to handle the Web site offline. See the following steps for details.

Figure 13-13: The Add Favorite dialog box.

1. **In the Add Favorite dialog box, click the "Make available offline" check box.** Next, click the Customize button.

2. **Click Next on the Offline Favorite Wizard Welcome screen.**

3. **In the next window, shown in Figure 13-14, you can choose to make additional links from the page offline.** When you make a page available offline, that single page is available to you without you having to connect to the Internet. However, if you click a link on the page while you are offline, you are prompted to connect. You can specify that Internet Explorer stores linked pages offline as well. Choose the link depth option to determine how many pages down you want store, but keep in mind that the more pages that you choose to store, the more disk space and synchronization time you will require. Make your selections and then click Next.

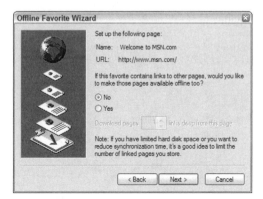

Figure 13-14: The Offline Favorite Wizard

4. **In the next wizard page, choose a synchronization option.** You can either choose to only synchronize when you choose the option from the Tools menu, or you can create a schedule. Click Next. If you chose the schedule option, the schedule window appears. Choose when you want synchronization to occur, and then click Next

5. **In the password window, enter a username and password if the site requires it.** If not, leave the No button selected and click Next.

6. **Click Finish.**

Expert's Notebook: Receive a Notice When an Offline Page Changes

If synchronization occurs, then changes are made to your offline page. To determine whether any changes have been made, you need to keep checking the page. However, there's a nice workaround that enables IE to send you an e-mail notice so that you'll know when the page has changed. Follow these steps:

1. **Click the Favorites menu, right-click the offline favorite, and then click Properties.** You can see a Download tab.

2. **On the Download tab, click the "When this page changes, send e-mail to:" option and enter an e-mail address that you want to use, as shown in the following illustration.** You can also make additional changes to the offline favorite here, such as the link depth and hard-disk space limit.

The Download tab

3. **Click OK.**

Customizing Search Options

You can use any search engine on the Internet to search for any topic that you want. However, you can also do that directly within Internet Explorer. To use the search feature, just click the Search button on the toolbar. If you don't see the Search option, click View, click Explorer Bar, and then click Search. When you enter search information in the Search field, the browser displays Web links, as well a preview of the Web pages. This is a nice feature, as shown in Figure 13-15.

When you first open the Explorer Search page, click the Customize option and make some changes to the default search functions, as shown in Figure 13-16. You can choose the Search Assistant (an animated character), a search engine, and use a Search Companion to help you refine your search. Choose any options that you want, and then click OK.

Figure 13-15: You can use the search feature within Internet Explorer.

Figure 13-16: You can customize your search in this dialog box.

Configuring Internet Explorer Security Settings

Without question, security is the most important issue concerning the Internet, and Internet Explorer is no exception to that rule. Internet Explorer includes a number of security features that you can configure by zone (such as Internet zone, intranet zone, etc.). The different security settings and features enable to you configure a security level that is appropriate for you, as well as for other Internet users who access your computer.

Security Zones

Internet Explorer offers four different security zones, which you can access by clicking the Tools menu in Internet Explorer and then clicking Internet Options. On the Security tab, Internet Explorer displays four zones — Internet, Local intranet, Trusted sites, and Restricted sites — as shown in Figure 13-17. If you select a zone, you can see the current security level of the zone in the lower section of the window.

There are four pre-configured levels of security that you can select for each zone by simply moving the slider bar. They are:

Figure 13-17: The Security tab

✦ **High:** When you use the High setting, all features that are less secure are disabled. Although this is the safest way to use the Internet, it provides you with the least amount of functionality. All ActiveX content is disabled, along with all downloads. Additionally, there are a number of restrictions on accessing and requesting data. ActiveX is a programming language that gives you functionality on the Internet, but it can be used to harbor viruses and other malicious code.

✦ **Medium:** The medium setting does not allow the downloading of unsigned ActiveX controls; as a result, you see the familiar prompt before downloading potentially unsafe content. Browsing is safe but functional under this setting, and in most cases, this is the best setting to use.

✦ **Medium-Low:** The medium-low setting runs most content without prompts, but still does not allow unsigned ActiveX controls. This setting is safe for intranet use.

✦ **Low:** The low setting provides a basic warning and few safeguards. All active content can run. This setting is not recommended unless the site is one that you completely trust.

You can configure different settings for each zone by simply selecting the zone and moving the slider bar. However, you can also customize the settings by clicking the Custom Level button. This opens the Security Settings dialog box, as shown in Figure 13-18. You can scroll through the list of settings and choose the Disable, Enable, or Prompt options for each security setting. This enables you to create a custom security setting that uses the features that you want, instead of the default options.

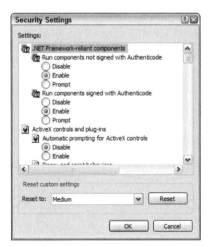

Figure 13-18: The Security Settings dialog box

Although you can use the default settings, you can also customize each zone to meet your needs. The following sections give you some pointers for customizing each security zone.

Expert's Notebook: Additional Local Intranet Sites

If you click the Local Intranet icon on the Security tab, and then click the Sites button, the Local intranet dialog box appears. In this dialog box you can select or deselect a few other options, as you can see in the following figure. You can choose to include all local sites not listed in other zones, all sites that bypass the proxy server, and all network paths. The default setting enables all three of these options, and you should typically leave them enabled. You can also click the Advanced button to add Web sites to this zone. The purpose of these settings is to give you the most flexibility as you work with your local intranet.

Alan Simpson

The Local intranet dialog box

Internet and Intranet Zones

The Internet zone is the place to strike a balance between functionality and security. In the same manner, the intranet zone is typically the place where you go for more functionality and worry less about security.

As a general rule, the default settings that you see are best; however, you can customize these settings using the Custom Level button. If you decide to customize, keep the following points in mind:

✦ **For the Internet zone, use the highest security settings possible, but maintain good usage features.** Low security settings may make browsing easier, but you could be asking for trouble. As you customize, keep the concept of "balance" in mind, and you'll make the best decisions.

✦ **The default setting for the Local intranet zone is Medium-Low.** This means that you can use the intranet in any way, but unsigned ActiveX controls are not allowed. In some cases, you may even want to use the Low setting if you are certain that all of the content on your intranet is safe. If it is, then the Low setting will not prevent any active content from running.

Trusted Sites Zone

If you configure security settings, some content from some Web sites may be blocked. However, you may use a site regularly that has content that would normally not be allowed by IE. To solve this problem, you can configure the site as a "trusted site" in the IE Trusted sites dialog box.

When a site is added to the trusted sites list, IE uses the Low security setting to access that site. This allows you to freely use the site without any security restrictions.

 Do not add a site to the trusted sites zone if the site is not fully trusted. The Trusted sites zone creates a security breach for that particular site, and so you should make sure that the site is trusted because you are letting your guard down for that site.

To add trusted sites to your Trusted sites zone, follow these steps:

1. **On the Security tab, click the Trusted sites zone, and then click the Sites button.**

2. **In the Trusted sites dialog box, enter the URL of the trusted site and click the Add button, as shown in Figure 13-19.** Repeat this process to add other sites. Keep in mind that you can remove sites at any time by using the Remove button, and you can also require server verification (if it is supported by the site) for sites in the zone. Click OK when you are done.

Figure 13-19: The Trusted sites dialog box

 Trusted sites require the use of "https" in order to make sure that a secure connection is made if the "require server verification" checkbox is set. You will see an error message if you don't use https.

Restricted sites zone

In the same way that you can configure a trusted site, you can also configure a restricted site. Sites listed in the Restricted sites zone, shown in Figure 13-20, are given a High security level in order to protect the computer from harmful content. Select the Restricted sites zone, click Settings, and enter the URL that you want to restrict. Notice that by default, IE has already restricted some known dangerous sites.

Figure 13-20: The Restricted sites dialog box

Customizing Privacy Settings

Privacy settings enable you to determine how cookies are handled in Internet Explorer. Cookies are small text files of data that are used with Web sites. Keep in mind that cookies are not bad—in fact, many things that you love about the Internet would not work without cookies. However, because cookies may contain personal information, there is also a privacy issue. In fact, cookies account for many different kinds of privacy invasions, including a lot of the spam that you probably receive in your e-mail inbox. Fortunately, you can use IE to configure how cookies should be handled, thus giving you the Internet functionality that you want and need, along with a certain amount of privacy.

FYI: Understanding IE's Privacy Technology

To protect your privacy, Internet Explorer uses a technology standard called the Platform for Privacy Preferences (P3P). P3P enables Internet Explorer to inspect cookies, determine how they will be used, and then make a decision about how to handle them. The feature is not perfect, but it is a big step forward in handling online privacy. Here are the important concepts that you should understand:

✦ **Compact Privacy Statement:** A Compact Privacy Statement tells how cookies are used on the site, as well as the amount of time that a particular cookie will be used. When you access a Web site, the Compact Privacy Statement is contained in the HTTP header of the Web site, and Internet Explorer can read the Compact Privacy Statement when you first access the site.

✦ **First-Party Cookie:** A first-party cookie is a cookie that is generated and used by the site that you are currently viewing. First-party cookies contain information about you and your browser, and are commonly used to tailor site content to your needs. Online store sites commonly use first-party cookies.

✦ **Third-Party Cookie:** A site other than the one that you are currently accessing, such as a banner ad or an advertisement, uses a third-party cookie. Third-party cookies can be a problem because you do not really know who is using them or what they will do with the personal information that is contained in the cookie.

✦ **Session Cookie:** A session cookie is generated during a single session with a Web site, and then deleted once the session has ended. In many cases, you cannot use a Web site unless a session cookie can be generated.

✦ **Implicit and Explicit Consent:** Implicit consent means that you have not blocked a site from using a cookie — in other words, you have not granted permission, but you have not denied it, either. On the other hand, Explicit consent means that you have acted to allow a Web site to use or gain personal information about you.

Alan Simpson

Default Privacy Settings

Internet Explorer uses some default privacy settings. If you move the slider bar on the Privacy tab, you see the various levels and kinds of protection that are used. Keep in mind that as you move the slider bar towards a higher security setting, the use of cookies becomes more restrictive. Once again, you are faced with choosing a balance between convenience and privacy. The standard privacy setting options are described in Table 13-1.

Table 13-1
Standard Privacy Setting Options

Privacy Setting	Explanation
Block All Cookies	All cookies are blocked. Web sites cannot generate any new cookies, and no existing cookies can be read.
High	No cookies that use personally identifiable information can be generated without your explicit consent. Web sites that do not have a Compact Privacy Statement cannot generate cookies.
Medium High	First-party cookies that use personally identifiable information are blocked without your implicit consent. Cookies are blocked from third-party Web sites that do not have a Compact Privacy Statement. Also, third-party cookies that use personally identifiable information are blocked without your explicit consent.
Medium	First-party cookies that use personally identifiable information without your implicit consent are allowed, but they are deleted when you close Internet Explorer. Third-party cookies that use personally identifiable information without your implicit consent are blocked, along with third-party cookies that do not have a Compact Privacy Statement. The Medium setting is the default Internet Explorer setting.
Low	The Low setting accepts all first-party cookies. Third-party cookies are blocked from sites that do not have a Compact Privacy Statement. However, third-party cookies that use personally identifiable information are allowed without your implicit consent, although the cookies are deleted when you close Internet Explorer
Accept All Cookies	All new cookies are allowed, and all Web sites can read existing cookies.

Customizing Privacy Options

The Advanced button on the Privacy tab displays the Advanced Privacy Settings dialog box, as shown in Figure 13-21. The Advanced Privacy Settings allow you to override how cookies are handled for this particular zone. As you can see, you can choose accept, block, or prompt for first- and third-party cookies, and you can also always allow session cookies.

For some users, the automatic cookie-handling settings do not provide the right support. In this case, you can override these settings and choose how you want to handle all first- and third-party cookies at all sites, regardless of the Compact Privacy policy.

You should typically allow session cookies to be generated so that the Web site can keep track of your surfing selection while you are there. Session cookies are typically harmless, and you may find that Web surfing is hindered without them.

Figure 13-21: The Advanced Privacy Settings dialog box

If you choose to use automatic cookie handling, you can override the privacy settings for certain Web sites. For example, you may regularly use a site that contains first- and third-party cookies. However, the site may not have a Compact Privacy policy, and your current cookie settings may prohibit the use of first-party cookies on sites with no Compact Privacy policy. Rather than changing your entire policy, you can simply create an exception for the Web site.

On the Privacy tab, click the Sites button. You see a Per Site Privacy Actions dialog box, as shown in Figure 13-22. Simply enter the URL of the Web site, and click the Block or Allow button. Web sites that you have added appear in the Managed Web sites list, which you can edit and change at any time.

Figure 13-22: The Per Site Privacy Actions dialog box

Viewing a Privacy Report

You can check out cookies that are blocked, and also view a site's Compact Privacy policy, if you are so inclined. When a cookie is blocked for the first time, you will see a notification dialog box. The status bar is typically at the bottom of the window in Internet Explorer, but if you do not see it, just click View, and then click Status Bar. You'll see a little icon telling you that a cookie has been blocked. Click the icon to see a privacy report, as shown in Figure 13-23. If you want to find out more about the blocked cookies, just select one and click the Summary button. You'll get a privacy statement from the Web site, as shown in Figure 13-24.

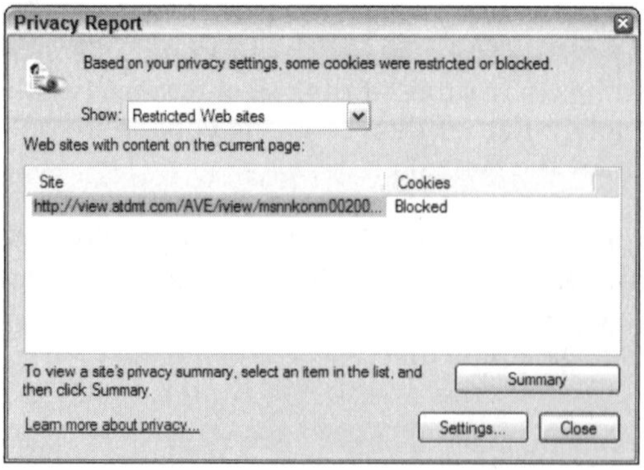

Figure 13-23: The Privacy Report dialog box

Figure 13-24: Privacy Policy

Here's a quick series of steps that you can take to help minimize bad cookies. Choose Tools ➪ Options from Internet Explorer's menu bar. On the Privacy tab, click the Advanced button and choose the Override automatic cookie handling option. Choose the Accept option for First-party Cookies, and the Block option for Third-party Cookies, and then choose the Always allow session cookies option.

Using the Pop-up Blocker

Service Pack 2 includes a simple and helpful Pop-up Blocker that is available on the Privacy tab. If you have been annoyed with pop-ups as much as I have, the pop-up blocker offers welcome relief. To enable it, simply click the Block pop-ups option check box on the Privacy tab. You can also click the Settings button to configure allowed sites for pop-ups, as shown in Figure 13-25. Also keep in mind that when a pop-up is blocked from a Web site, you see a notification in Internet Explorer, on the Information bar. You can right-click the notification and then allow pop-ups from the site from that Web site, as well.

Customizing Content Settings

Internet Explorer provides content settings that enable you to control the sites that it can access. The content settings feature is a great way to control the kind of content that is allowed on your computer, in order to stop pornographic, violent, or other offensive content from being downloaded. Keep in mind that content settings depend on the fair and honest ratings of Web sites, and so the feature is not foolproof. If you want to configure settings that help prevent your children from seeing offensive content, then you can use the Content Settings option that is explored in the following section. However, I would recommend that you also use a third-party software product, such as Cybersitter or Net Nanny. With these tools and your supervision, the Internet can be a safe place for your family members.

Figure 13-25: The Pop-up Blocker Settings dialog box

FYI: How Content Rating Works

The Content Advisor works by getting rating information from Web sites. A Web site can provide a rating so that Internet Explorer knows whether to allow or block the site. If a Web site wants to provide a rating, the Web site Administrator completes a form at the Internet Content Rating Association (ICRA) Web site. The ICRA then evaluates the Administrator's responses and provides a label that applies to that Web site. The ICRA ratings are based on language, nudity, sexual content, and violence. When you reach the site through Internet Explorer, the site's label is read, and the appropriate action is followed, depending on how you have configured the content settings. The ICRA is an independent organization and is not a censor, and so the rating of the site depends on how the Administrator responds to questions in the application. You can find out more about content ratings at http://www.icra.org

Enabling and Configuring Content Advisor

To enable and configure Content Advisor, open Internet Options and click the Content tab. Click the Enable button. The Content Advisor dialog box appears with four configuration tabs. On the Ratings tab, you see a listing of rating categories. Select a category, and then move the slider bar to the level of content that you want users to be able to see. Keep in mind that each category defaults at Level 0, which is the least offensive setting. Adjust the categories as desired, shown in Figure 13-26, and click the Approved Sites tab.

Figure 13-26: The Ratings tab

On the Approved Sites tab, shown in Figure 13-27, you can override the settings that you configured on the Ratings tab by entering a Web site address and then clicking the Always or Never button. The Never option will always prompt for an Administrator password in order to see the site, and the Always option will allow anyone to see the site without an Administrator password.

On the General tab, shown in Figure 13-28, you have a few different configuration options. First, you see two important check boxes, one that will allow users to see unrated sites, and another that provides a supervisor override option. The first option should not be used if you are trying to secure the computer from harmful content. Just because a site contains inappropriate content does not mean that it has a rating, and so if a site does not have a rating, a prompt will appear for the Administrator override. This may cause some surfing difficulty, but it is the safest setting. You should always keep the supervisor setting selected so that you can override any site restrictions, if needed.

Figure 13-27: The Approved Sites tab

Figure 13-28: The General tab

If you need to change your supervisor password or find rating systems used by other companies, you can use the additional options found on the General tab. Keep in mind that the Administrator password that you assign is used to control and even turn off content management, and so you should keep track of it. However, if you should forget your password, then you can override it with a registry edit.

Navigate to HKLM\Software\Microsoft\Windows\CurrentVersion\Policies\Ratings and delete the Key Value that you see.

On the Advanced tab, shown in Figure 13-29, you see the options to locate and use a ratings bureau, and to use PICSRules. A ratings bureau is an Internet site that can check a rating of a site if the site is not rated by the ICRA. However, this can seriously slow down browsing speed. You can also import PICSRules. PICSRules are labels that can help you to determine whether or not sites can be viewed. There are no default rules that are configured, although you can import them if desired.

Figure 13-29: The Advanced tab

Note

Should you decide that you no longer want to use the content feature after you have configured it, you can always return to the Content tab and click the Disable button. You'll need to provide your Administrator password to turn off this feature.

Quick Navigation Shortcuts

As with most Windows programs and features, there a number of keyboard shortcuts that can enable you to use Internet Explorer more quickly and easily. Table 13-2 lists some of the more common shortcuts, but you can also find a complete list in the Internet Explorer help files.

Table 13-2
Common Shortcuts

Shortcut	Explanation
F11	Toggle between full screen view and the browser window
Alt+Home	Go to the Home Page
F5	Refresh the current Web page
Esc	Stop downloading a Web page
Ctrl+N	Open a new browser window
Ctrl+E	Open the Search window
Ctrl+I	Open Favorites
Ctrl+H	Open History
F4	Display a list of addresses that you have typed
Ctrl+Enter	Adds www. to the beginning of a word entered in the Address Bar, and .com to the end
Ctrl+D	Adds the current page to your Favorites List

Configuring and Customizing Outlook Express

14

Outlook Express is an e-mail client that has been included with the Windows operating system for years. Although Outlook Express was rather basic in the past, it has developed into a more comprehensive e-mail client that is capable of handing all of your personal and small-office e-mail requirements. In this chapter, we'll show you all of the helpful options and configuration features that Outlook Express has to offer.

Managing Accounts

With Outlook Express, or OE, you can configure several different e-mail accounts so that OE can check your e-mail from several different sources. For example, although you may receive mail from one or more POP3 or IMAP mail accounts, you can also receive your mail from HTTP mail accounts, such as Yahoo or Hotmail. This flexibility makes it easy for you to check and manage your e-mail, and account creation is not difficult. In order to use Outlook Express, you must configure at least one account. This account can be an e-mail account, but it can also be a newsgroup or a directory service. If you open Outlook Express and click Tools ⇨ Accounts, the Internet Accounts dialog box appears, as shown in Figure 14-1.

IN THIS CHAPTER

Setting Up Accounts

Customizing Outlook Express

Working with Messages

Understanding Message Rules, Blocked Senders, and Address Book

Figure 14-1: The Internet Accounts dialog box

Creating an E-mail Account

To create an e-mail account, follow these steps:

1. **In Outlook Express, click Tools ➪ Accounts.**

2. **In the Internet Accounts dialog box, click the Mail tab, and click Add ➪ Mail.** The Your Name page of the Internet Connection Wizard appears (see Figure 14-2).

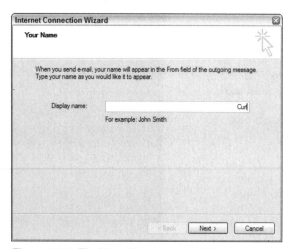

Figure 14-2: The Your Name page of the Internet Connection Wizard

3. **In the Your Name page, enter your name.** This is the name that all users will be able to see when you send e-mail (it will appear in the From field on their e-mail clients). Click Next.

4. **In the Internet E-mail Address page, enter your e-mail address, and then click Next.**

5. **In the E-mail Server Names page, shown in Figure 14-3, click the drop-down menu to select the type of mail server to which you are connecting.** If the server is a POP3 or IMAP server, you need to enter the incoming and outgoing mail server names. If you are using an HTTP server (such as Hotmail), click the drop-down menu and choose your mail service provider. Consult your ISP documentation for details. Click Next.

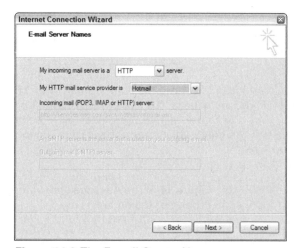

Figure 14-3: The E-mail Server Names page

6. **In the Internet Mail Logon page, shown in Figure 14-4, enter your username and password as provided by your ISP.** If your ISP uses Secure Password Authentication, or SPA, click the "Log on using Secure Password Authentication (SPA)" check box. SPA is a security feature that may require you to manually log on to the mail server. You cannot use SPA unless your mail server requires it. Consult your ISP documentation for details. Click Next.

7. **Click Finish.** The new account now appears in the Mail tab of the Internet Accounts window.

Once you have configured the e-mail account, you can access the account's properties by selecting the account in the Mail tab of the Internet Accounts window, and then clicking the Properties button. Should any of your account information change, you can access the Properties dialog box and adjust the settings as needed.

Figure 14-4: The Internet Mail Logon page

The General, Servers, Connection, and Security tabs in the same Properties dialog box are all self-explanatory. If you are using a POP3 or IMAP account, then you'll also see an Advanced tab, shown in Figure 14-5, that provides some helpful configuration options. With them, you can configure server ports, server timeouts, as well as sending and delivery options:

Figure 14-5: The Advanced tab of the Properties dialog box

✦ **Server Port Numbers:** If your mail servers require Secure Sockets Layer, or SSL, connections, click the appropriate check boxes in the Server Port Numbers section. See your ISP documentation for details.

✦ **Server Timeouts:** By default, the server timeout value is configured for 1 minute. This means that the mail delivery fails after 1 minute of timeout from the server. As a general rule, the 1-minute setting is all you need, but if you know that there are some slow connectivity issues with your mail server, you can increase this value.

✦ **Sending:** In the Sending section, you can have Outlook Express break apart messages that are larger than a certain value. This can be useful when you need to communicate with older servers that cannot handle messages larger than 60 KB. However, don't use this option unless you are sure that you will need it.

✦ **Delivery:** You can choose to leave a copy of the message on your mail server for redundancy purposes, if your mail server supports this feature. See your ISP for more details.

Creating a News Account or Directory Service Account

You can configure a News account by clicking the News tab in the Internet Accounts dialog box, and then clicking Add ➪ News. The same wizard that you used to create an e-mail account (see the previous section) guides you through the steps to create a News account. Once you have entered the news server name, the news server appears on the News tab. If you click the Properties button, you see a Properties dialog box similar to that used to configure e-mail settings.

A directory service enables you to find information about people or services. By default, Outlook Express provides *Lightweight Directory Access Protocol* (LDAP) access to the Active Directory, as well as a few default Internet directory services. If you are not located on a Windows domain, then the Active Directory option is not used. In this case, Outlook Express uses Bigfoot, VeriSign, and WhoWhere Internet directories.

When you run a search, the top 100 matches for the search are provided to you. However, if you want more or fewer results, you can adjust the "matches to return" option on the Advanced tab of the directory service's Properties pages, which you can access on the Directory Service tab by clicking the desired service and clicking Properties.

You can choose additional directory services by clicking Add ➪ Directory Services. Enter the desired directory service name, along with any necessary logon information.

Troubleshooting: Problems with Connections in Outlook Express

Normally, Outlook Express checks your mail using your default Internet connection, which can be a broadband, LAN, or dial-up connection. If you have established an Internet connection, then you should not have problems connecting with Outlook Express, although problems may still occur at this stage. Below are some common problems and how you can solve them:

✦ **You can connect to the Internet, but you see an error message when you try to send and receive:** This problem occurs for two reasons. First, you may have configured the e-mail account incorrectly, such as with an incorrect password or some incorrect security settings. Check to ensure that your settings are correct, and try again. Second, the mail account may work, but the problem is with your ISP or server. In this case, you may want to try again later.

✦ **A timeout occurs when you try to download longer messages:** You can increase the timeout value on the Advanced tab of the e-mail account's Properties dialog box. This will tell Outlook Express to wait for a longer period of time before the connection times out.

✦ **You can't access a newsgroup:** The newsgroup may require you to log on, or some other setting may not be configured properly. Check your connectivity documentation, and then access the Properties dialog box of your newsgroup account. Make sure that all settings are configured as they should be.

✦ **Using a dial-up connection, Outlook Express will not automatically dial the connection.** Try to manually launch the connection from the Network Connections folder. If all seems to be in order, make sure that the default account is available on the Connections tab of Internet Options.

General Outlook Express Settings

Outlook Express has many general settings that enable you to configure how Outlook Express looks and behaves. For the most part, the settings that you'll find on the Options dialog box are easy to understand, and include such items as folder behavior, interface appearance, and so forth. However, there are probably some useful settings lurking about here that you might not know about. You can access all of these features by clicking Tools ⇨ Options. The following sections take a look at the individual tabs of the Options dialog box.

The General Tab

The General tab, shown in Figure 14-6, allows you to configure how e-mail messages are received. There are a couple of important options here:

Figure 14-6: The General tab

✦ **In the General section, notice that the "Automatically log on to Windows Messenger" option is selected.** If you are not using Windows Messenger, deselect this option to save time and aggravation.

✦ **In the Send/Receive Messages section, select the "Check for new messages every" option if you want Outlook Express to automatically check for new messages.** By default, messages are checked every 30 minutes, but you can change the time interval. Also, you can use the drop-down menu to tell Outlook Express what to do when you are not connected. For example, if you are using a dial-up connection, you may want to choose the "Connect only when not working offline" option from the drop-down menu.

The Read Tab

The Read tab, shown in Figure 14-7, offers you a few important options for reading e-mail and news messages. They are as follows:

✦ Normally, e-mail messages that are not read appear in bold type. However, if you are using the Preview pane, the message is marked as read after you preview it for five seconds. This may work fine for you, but if you receive a lot of e-mail, you may not want the messages to appear as read until you have actually opened them. If this is the case, deselect the "Mark message read after displaying for ...second(s)" check box option, in the Reading Messages section.

✦ In the Reading Messages section, you can choose to read all messages in plain text, rather than HTML.

Figure 14-7: The Read tab

✦ By default, 300 headers are used with newsgroups, but you can change this value in the News section.

✦ If you are having problems reading e-mail messages, use the Fonts button at the bottom of the tab to change the font option.

Tip

Although the default 'mark message read after....seconds' is set at 5. I much prefer to reduce this 'waiting' time down to 1 second. This enables me to quickly skip from one email to the next without leaving the odd unread message untouched.

The Receipts Tab

When you send a message, you can request a receipt when the message is read. This feature is helpful when you are sending urgent messages or when you want to make sure that the receiving party has received your message.

On the Receipts tab, shown in Figure 14-8, you can select the option "Request a read receipt for all sent messages." This option applies to all messages that you send. The best option is to request a read receipt on a message-by-message basis, which you can do using the new mail message toolbar. Also notice that you when read receipts are requested of you, you can choose to never send them, to receive a prompt for each one, or to always send one. The default setting is to notify you so that you can make a decision on a message-by-message basis.

Finally, if you are using digitally signed messages, you can also request a secure receipt. If you click the Secure Receipts button, you can access the same options to request receipts for all digitally signed messages, as well as the radio button options that allow you to determine how you want to respond to secure messages.

Figure 14-8: The Receipts tab

The Send Tab

The Send tab, shown in Figure 14-9, offers you a few different options for sending e-mail. By default, all check box options are selected, but you can deselect any that you don't want to use. The options here are self-explanatory.

Figure 14-9: The Send tab

The Compose Tab

The Compose tab, shown in Figure 14-10 gives you three additional features that enhance your e-mail composition — Compose Font, Stationery, and Business Cards:

Figure 14-10: The Send tab

✦ **Compose Font:** You can choose a Mail and News font, style, and color that you want to use. Arial will probably be the default font, and it is a good font to use because it is found on all computers. You can change these settings to whatever you want, but keep in mind that the font and color settings that you choose may not actually appear in your recipient's e-mail — that all depends on your recipient's e-mail client settings.

✦ **Stationery:** You can use a background image when you create your messages. This feature works like wallpaper on your desktop. Use the Select button to choose one that is available. If you want to create your own stationery based on a picture file, then you can click the Create New button, after which a wizard appears to guide you through the process. Although stationery is nice feature, it does increase transmission time. Also, if your recipients are not using HTML mail, the stationery will be downloaded to them as a file, and not as background image.

✦ **Business Card:** You can also create a business card with your new messages. The business card contains any information that you want to include about yourself or your company; recipients can place the business cards in their Address Books.

The Signatures Tab

The Signatures tab, shown in Figure 14-11, allows you to create and format a signature for each of your messages. Signatures can contain your name, e-mail address, Web page, and phone number if you like. Keep in mind that you do not have to include any information that you want to keep private. The signature is then automatically inserted into your e-mail message.

Figure 14-11: The Signatures tab

To create a signature, follow these steps:

1. **Click the New button.** A default "Signature #1" appears. You can click Rename to give the signature another name.

2. **Enter the desired signature text in the Edit signature text box.**

3. **Click the Advanced button.** This specifies the accounts with which you want to use the signature. You can also use the File option in the Edit Signature section, to import a signature from a text or HTML file. Click OK to apply your selections.

Tip

Signatures are an ideal way to reduce the repetitiveness of sending e-mails. You may not feel they are necessary for general use, but for business they are essential. In two simple steps — Insert ➪ signature — you can not only add your signature but you can also include your telephone number, fax, Web site and any other important information you want people to know.

The Spelling Tab

The Spelling tab gives you the option to always check your spelling before you send a message, and you can have Outlook Express suggest replacements for misspelled words. You can also choose a few options that determine how spelling works. These options are self-explanatory.

The Security Tab

The Security tab enables you to configure Outlook Express for limited virus protection and for secure mail, as shown in Figure 14-12. It is important to note that Outlook Express does not actually provide any virus protection, as you would expect from anti-virus software. Rather, this tab contains some settings that can help you to reduce the possibility of receiving a virus. Notice that the virus protection feature warns you when other applications try to send you mail or when you receive mail with attachments. Also, images are automatically blocked with HTML e-mail because they can harbor viruses. These features are helpful, but remember that you should always use anti-virus software on your computer.

If you want to use secure e-mail, you must obtain a digital certificate from a provider, such as Verisign. This feature enables you to send e-mail with the certificate so that other users can verify your identity. You can also encrypt e-mail if you like. Keep in mind that the recipient must be able to read the signature or unencrypt the e-mail in order for the feature to work, using your public key. If you have a digital certificate, you can click the Digital IDs button to select the certificate that you want to use.

Figure 14-12: The Security tab

The Connection Tab

The Connection tab provides the basic setup for dial-up connections, as well as how Outlook Express uses Internet Explorer. A noteworthy item on this tab is the option to hang up after sending and receiving. If you are using a dial-up connection and you have configured your mail account to check for messages automatically, you might consider using this option so that the connection will automatically hang up after mail has been checked. Of course, if you are trying to work online, then this setting can become very annoying because it automatically disconnects you every time you send and receive e-mail.

The Maintenance Tab

The Maintenance tab, shown in Figure 14-13, offers you some important options for managing Outlook Express.

Figure 14-13: The Maintenance tab

✦ **You can review the available Empty and Purge check boxes.** These check boxes determine the way Outlook Express manages items that you delete as well as how it deletes items on an IMAP server. Naturally, if you don't connect with an IMAP server, there is nothing you need to do here.

✦ **You can also configure the default handling method for newsgroup messages.** Although the default settings, shown in Figure 14-13, are usually best, you can read through these options to see if there is any thing you want to change.

✦ **You can select the Clean Up Now and Store Folders buttons.** These options let you clean up messages in order to conserve disk space, and change the location of the store folder so that it is easier to back up.

Tip

Changing the store folder location to another partition or hard drive ensures that your e-mails are safe should your main partition/drive fail. If you must reinstall XP, all you need do is change the stored folder location to the partition/drive you originally moved it to and all your e-mails will be replaced.

Choosing a Layout

Outlook Express uses a "pane" feature for displaying mail, folders, and message content to you. You can customize the default interface by changing the layout that you see to something that is more helpful to you. To do this, click View ➪ Layout. You can use the radio buttons to show or hide different components of the Outlook Express interface, as shown in Figure 14-14. You can experiment with the different settings to find a layout that you prefer.

Figure 14-14: The Window Layout Properties dialog box

Tip

You can also customize the Outlook Express toolbar. Click View ➪ Toolbars ➪ Customize to select different icons, or to reorganize the toolbar.

Quick E-mail Tips

Now that you have a general knowledge of Outlook Express, it's time to put it to good use. The following sections give some good tips and tricks for sending and receiving e-mail with Outlook Express. In addition, the Outlook Express basic e-mail folder structure is explained.

Sending E-mail

When you're sending e-mail, keep the following tips in mind:

✦ **Foreign language e-mails:** If you need to send a message in a different language, click Format ➪ Encoding.

✦ **Priority designations:** You can attach a high, normal, or low priority status to messages using the Priority button on the toolbar, or by clicking Message ➪ Set Priority. This feature is useful when you want to get someone's attention for a quick reply, however, the addressee needs to be using Outlook or Outlook Express for the feature to work.

✦ **Multiple recipients:** If you are sending e-mail to multiple recipients, simply separate the recipients with a comma when typing their e-mail addresses in the To, CC, or BCC fields.

✦ **BCC:** You can use the Blind Carbon Copy (BCC) field to copy recipients on a mail message without the To and CC field recipients knowing about the copy. The BCC field may not automatically appear in your e-mail message. If you do not see the BCC field, click View ➪ All Headers, and it will appear.

✦ **Stationary:** If you have not configured Stationery to apply to all messages, then you can add it to individual messages. Simply click Message ➪ New Using, and then select the stationery that you want to use.

✦ **Read receipts:** If you want to request a read receipt for an individual e-mail message, click Tools ➪ Request Read Receipt. You can also use the Tools menu to encrypt or digitally sign a message.

✦ **HTML toolbar:** When you create a new e-mail message with HTML formatting, a formatting toolbar appears above the textbox. Use the options here to apply fonts and styles to your message. However, if you use plain text, this toolbar appears grayed out.

✦ **Insert elements in your e-mail:** Files, business cards, signatures, and hyperlinks can all be inserted into your e-mail using the Insert menu option. You can also use toolbar buttons for many of these features.

✦ **Save e-mails in different folders:** You can use the File menu to save messages to different folders, or you can use the Save As option to save them to a file. You can save e-mail messages as Outlook Express files with the *.eml filename extension, as text files, or as HTML files.

✦ **Type the sender's name, not address:** For contacts in your Address Book, you only need to type their names in the To, CC, or BCC fields. Outlook Express can resolve the names to the e-mail addresses in your Address Book. If you want to make sure that the addresses are resolved, click the Check button on the tool bar. Resolved names appear underlined.

Receiving e-mail

If you're receiving mail, keep the following tips in mind:

✦ **E-mail delivery:** When you receive e-mail, it all arrives in your inbox, and is usually arranged by arrival date and time. All messages appear in the inbox, whether you have read them or not, until you either move them to a different folder or delete them.

✦ **E-mail viewing options:** You can use the View menu in Outlook Express to hide read messages, to hide read or ignored messages, or to show all messages. You can adjust one of the default views by clicking Customize Current View, or you can define your own view by clicking View ➪ Current View. The Define Views dialog box appears, with the currently applied view selected, as shown in Figure 14-15. To create a new view, click the New button. In the New View window, you can select a condition for the view, and then select an action or a description.

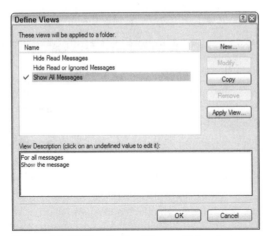

Figure 14-15: The Define Views dialog box

✦ **E-mail sorting:** You can sort messages using the Sort By option on the View menu. By default, messages are sorted in ascending order as you receive them and by priority. You can adjust this behavior so that messages are sorted differently, such as by subject, flags, or attachments.

✦ **Watch, flag, or ignore messages:** If you click View ➪ Columns, you see a dialog box, shown in Figure 14-16, that enables you to choose the column items that you want to see, such as priority, flag, or subject. Make sure that any columns that you want to view are selected. You can also use the Move Up or Move Down buttons to configure the column order.

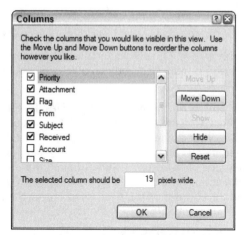

Figure 14-16: The Columns dialog box

Outlook Express Folder Structure

Outlook Express has a basic folder structure that allows you to store e-mail, and you can easily create or delete new folders. For example, when I start writing a new book, I create a folder with that book's name to store all of the e-mail concerning the book. Once I have completed the book, I drag the folder to an "Inactive Items" folder. This way, I can keep the e-mail folder as a reference, and it no longer takes up space as a standard folder in my Inbox. Although folders are easy to use, keep the following tips in mind:

✦ **Inbox:** All e-mail that you receive arrives in the Inbox, unless you have a rule configured to change the item. We'll explore rules later in this chapter.

✦ **Outbox:** All e-mail that you send goes to the Outbox. The mail resides in the Outbox until you are connected, and then it is automatically sent.

✦ **Sent Items:** Outlook Express stores all e-mail that you send in the Sent Items folder so that you can reference it, if necessary. However, you can also open this folder and delete messages. You can also move sent items to another folder or folders for organization purposes, if you like.

✦ **Deleted Items:** Outlook Express stores deleted messages in the Deleted Items folder. If you want to reclaim a message from the Deleted Items folder, just open the folder and drag the message back to a different folder. If you want to delete all messages in the folder, you can click Tools ➪ Options, and choose the "Empty messages from the 'Deleted Items' folder on exit" check box, which is found on the Maintenance tab. You can also open the Deleted Items folder and individually delete items, or click Edit ➪ Empty Deleted Items folder. However, once you delete an item from the Deleted Items folder, it is permanently removed.

Expert's Notebook: Working with Attachments

Attachments are any files that you send with an e-mail, such as pictures, documents, or spreadsheets. You can send any file through e-mail, and you can also send collections of files by first compressing them in Windows XP.

You can attach a file by clicking the Attach button on the toolbar, by clicking Insert ⇨ File Attachment, or you can drag and drop files onto the e-mail. Attached items appear in the Attach field when you are creating a new message. Once you have attached the file, the file is sent with the e-mail. However, if you change your mind before sending, you can right-click the file in the Attach field and click Remove. Keep in mind that files consume bandwidth, and so they may take some time to transfer, depending on the size of the file and the available bandwidth. If you are a DSL user, keep in mind that modem users may have a difficult time downloading large attachments.

When you receive an e-mail with an attachment, you can simply double-click the attachment to open it, or you can drag the attachment to a folder on your local computer for later use. However, e-mail attachments can carry computer viruses, and so you should make sure that you are always using up-to-date anti-virus software. *Curt Simmons*

To keep your e-mail store under control (in terms of size), you can combine a couple of Outlook Express options with a feature of the NTFS file system. First enable file compression on the folder containing your mail store (through Windows Explorer). Next, configure Outlook Express to empty your deleted items on exit, and then use the Compact feature in Outlook Express Local File Cleanup to have Outlook compress and organize its own files. The first two features are "set it and forget it," while the third feature will need to be repeated when your message store grows.

Managing Mail Rules and Senders

You can create a variety of mail rules that determine how Outlook Express handles certain kinds of e-mail, or e-mail from certain people or that contains a particular subject. For example, you can have all messages from a particular person sent directly to a folder that you create for them, or you can have all messages with a particular subject keyword sent to a certain folder. You can use mail rules to automatically place e-mail in your Deleted Items folder, such as junk mail or mail from people to whom you do not want to respond. To create a basic mail rule, follow these steps:

1. **In Outlook Express, click Tools ➪ Message Rules ➪ Mail.** The New Mail Rule dialog box appears, as shown in Figure 14-17.

Figure 14-17: The New Mail Rule dialog box

2. **Follow the steps in the dialog box to select a condition, action and description for your rule.** For example, in Figure 14-17, e-mail that contains specific words in the subject line is moved to a specified folder. In the Rule Description window, you can click the "contains specific words" link to enter the desired words. You can then click the "specified" link to specify the folder to which you want the mail to move, as shown in Figure 14-18. When you download e-mail that meets these conditions, the e-mail is automatically moved to that folder.

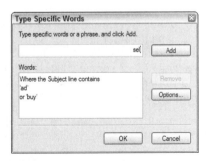

Figure 14-18: The Type Specific Words dialog box

3. **Click OK when you are done, and then repeat the process in the New Mail Rule dialog box to create additional rules.**

In addition to moving specified e-mail to a certain folder, you can use a number of additional rule options. For example, you can mark or flag certain messages. You can also automatically forward messages to users, as well as reply to certain messages automatically with an e-mail that you create and save. If you scroll through the actions list for the rule, you'll see that there are many different actions that you can apply. You should become familiar with the conditions and actions available to you so that you can create customized rules that meet your needs.

Blocking a Sender

Along with creating mail rules that govern certain kinds of e-mail messages, you can easily block a sender from sending you any e-mail. In Outlook Express, when you choose this option, the sender's e-mail is downloaded and automatically sent to the Deleted Items folder, regardless of the message content or attachments. To block a sender, select an e-mail message from the sender in your Inbox and click Message ⇨ Block Sender. A message appears telling you that the sender has been added to your blocked senders list, and Outlook Express blocks all future e-mails from that sender.

Expert's Notebook: Working with Outlook Express Identities

If several different people in an office environment use your Windows XP computer, Outlook Express allows everyone to keep their own identity and e-mail private. Outlook Express 6 provides a feature called "identities." The identities feature allows several different people to use Outlook Express in order to privately access their e-mail accounts, while keeping their e-mail folders and Address Book contacts separate. For example, when you log on with your particular identity, your e-mail folders and contact folders display only to you.

By default, Outlook Express creates a Main Identity for e-mail and for the Address Book. This identity cannot be deleted, but you can add other identities as you like and switch between them. Identities can be password-protected, but this does not guarantee that someone will not be able to see your e-mail or contacts list. If you want to ensure privacy, make sure that you password-protect your entire user account folder, because your e-mail and contact data is stored there.

To access identities, click File ⇨ Identities in Outlook Express. You'll see the option to either create a new identity or manage existing identities. Simply click the New button to create a new identity. A dialog box appears where you can name the identity and provide a password. You can also use the Manage Identity dialog box to determine which identity should be used as the default when starting Outlook Express. When you want to switch identities, just click File ⇨ Switch Identity, and provide the password, if required.

If at a later time, you want to remove the block from the sender, you can click Tools ⇨ Message Rules ⇨ Blocked Senders List and remove the user from the blocked sender's list. You can now receive e-mail from the sender.

You may find that you need to back up and restore your Outlook Express rules and blocked senders list if you have to reinstall or want to duplicate your current configuration onto another computer. To do so, launch regedit and find the HKEY_CURRENT_USER\Identities\{Identity Number}\Software\ Microsoft\Outlook Express\5.0\Block Senders key (for your blocked senders list). Then click the File menu, select the Export option, and save the resulting .reg file where you want it. To back up your rules, perform the same steps on the HKEY_CURRENT_USER\Identities\{Identity Number}\Software\Microsoft\ Outlook Express\5.0\Rules\Mail key. To restore either one, just double-click the relevant *.reg file that you created when backing up your files. You will be asked whether you want to merge the data into the registry, and if you respond in the affirmative, you'll have your items restored.

Importing and Exporting Messages

Outlook Express serves as a primary location to use and store all of your e-mail. However, you can easily import or export messages to and from Outlook Express. When you import mail, you can select the program from which you want to import. When you export mail, you export from Outlook Express to Microsoft Outlook or Microsoft Exchange. To use the import or export feature, click File ⇨ Import or File ⇨ Export, and click Messages. If you are importing, you'll see the option to choose the program from which you want to import, as shown in Figure 14-19. Make your selection, and choose the location of the messages that you want to import.

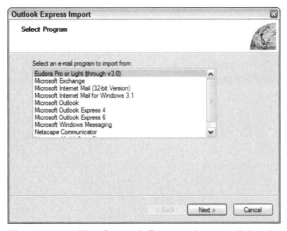

Figure 14-19: The Outlook Express Import dialog box

Using the Address Book

The Windows Address Book is an individual program designed to work with Outlook Express, as well as any other applications that use contact data. You can store all kinds of contact information in the Address Book, and you can even access it directly on the Outlook Express toolbar. You can also access the Address Book by clicking Start ➪ All Programs ➪ Accessories, or by entering **wab** at the run line (Start ➪ Run).

The Windows Address Book gives you a simple interface, as shown in Figure 14-20. You can store contact information in the Shared Contacts database or in the Identity folder for your account. To create new contacts or groups, simply click the New button and select the user or group that you want to create. You can easily add a user to your Address Book directly from an e-mail message that you have received. In the Inbox, just right-click the message and click Add Sender to Address Book.

Address Book is easy to use, but it does not provide security when you use identities. Any user can see all of the contacts by entering wab /a at the run line, and so if you want to ensure that your contacts are private, then you should not use identities.

Figure 14-20: The Address Book

Using Windows Messenger

15

W indows Messenger is a simple
messaging utility that you can
use to exchange instant messages and other
data with users on the Internet. However, it
is also a tool that can do much more. For
example, you can exchange files, data, and
pictures, start a voice conversation, and
even use the features of Remote Assistance
through Windows Messenger.

Windows Messenger is a straightforward
tool that you will find easy to use. If you're
new to Windows Messenger or you need to
strengthen your messaging skills, this chapter is for you.

Connecting with Windows Messenger

You can find Windows Messenger on
your Windows XP computer by clicking
Start ⇨ All Programs, or by looking in the
Notification Area. In order to use Windows
Messenger, you need a connection to the
Internet. You also need a microphone and
Web cam if you want to use the multimedia
features that Windows Messenger has to
offer.

IN THIS CHAPTER

Connect with Windows Messenger

Have Conversations with Others

Use Advanced Features

When you first open Windows Messenger, you're prompted to sign in with your .Net Passport. If you don't have a .Net Passport, then you can get one by clicking the "Get a .Net Passport" link, as shown in Figure 15-1. The instructions guide you through the process.

Figure 15-1: You can sign in to get a .Net Passport through the .NET Messenger Service dialog box.

You use the Windows Messenger window (Figure 15-2) to add contacts and start conversations. You need your online name, as well as online contacts to begin using Windows Messenger.

FYI: Connecting through a Firewall

If you are using Windows Firewall, then it is already configured to allow Windows Messenger traffic, and so you can safely skip this sidebar. However, if your computer is using another firewall product or a firewall on a corporate LAN, there may be additional firewall settings that are needed. If so, Windows Messenger uses the following ports:

✦ **TCP port 1863:** Windows Messenger uses this port when it is available. If port 1863 is not available, then Windows Messenger uses the same port that the Web browser uses, typically port 80. For the best results, a firewall Administrator should open TCP port 1863.

✦ **TCP ports 6891 through 6900:** Windows Messenger uses these ports for file transfers, allowing up to ten simultaneous transfers at a time (one on each port).

✦ **TCP port 1503:** Windows Messenger uses this port for application sharing and Whiteboard communications.

✦ **Dynamically assigned ports:** Windows Messenger uses dynamically assigned ports through UPnP for voice and video.

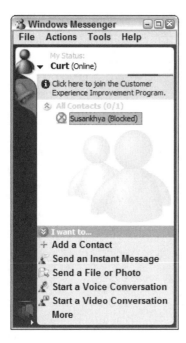

Figure 15-2: The Windows Messenger window

Using Windows Messenger

For the most part, Windows Messenger is an easy utility to use. Once you are signed in, you can access all of its features and configuration options. The following sections show you how to use Windows Messenger.

Choosing a Status

If you click the inverted triangle next to your name under My Status, you can choose a status that shows people on the Internet your availability. You can select from several built-in status settings, as shown in Figure 15-3.

If you click Personal Settings, an Options dialog box appears, as shown in Figure 15-4. The settings you'll find on these tabs are self-explanatory. For example, you can adjust your screen name, message text options, phone numbers, general preferences and so forth. This dialog box allows you to make changes to the personal information that people can see about your phone settings, general usage preferences, and privacy. Keep in mind that you generally do not need to configure anything on the Connection tab.

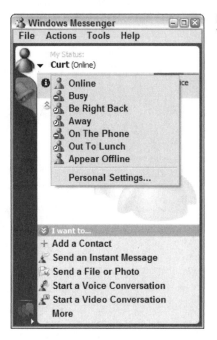

Figure 15-3: The status settings in the Windows Messenger window

Figure 15-4: The Options dialog box

Creating Contacts

The contacts feature in Windows Messenger enables you to control who you communicate with over the Internet or intranet. When you add contacts to Windows

Messenger, they are stored on .NET Passport servers so that you can be contacted directly when you are online.

Contacts appear in the Windows Messenger window. Any contacts that you have added appear under Online if they are connected with Windows Messenger, and any contacts that are not currently online appear under Not Online. You can add a contact by following these steps:

1. **Choose Tools ➪ Add A Contact.** Alternatively, you can click Add a Contact in the "I want to" section of Windows Messenger. In the Add a Contact Wizard that appears, shown in Figure 15-5. you are asked how you want to add a contact.

Figure 15-5: The Add a Contact Wizard

2. **Choose a contact option.** You can choose the "By e-mail address or sign-in name" option, or you can choose "Search for a contact." The search option checks your Address Book or the online Hotmail directory. Typically, if you are adding a contact, you already know the contact's e-mail address, and so you will most often use that option. Click Next.

3. **If you choose to enter the e-mail address, then enter the address on the next wizard page, as shown in Figure 15-6.** The e-mail address that you are using must be an MSN, Hotmail, or .NET Passport e-mail address. If you enter any other e-mail address (or even an MSN or Hotmail account that is not configured for .NET Passport), then you can choose to e-mail that person, telling them about Windows Messenger so that they can download and use it. Of course, until the person downloads the software and configures a .NET Passport, you can't communicate with them using Windows Messenger. Click Next.

4. **This page tells you that the name was added to your list.** Click Next to add another contact, or click Finish.

Figure 15-6: Enter the contact's e-mail address.

Once you choose to add contacts to your list, the contacts are sent a message, alerting them to the fact that you have added them. At this point, the contacts can choose the "Allow this person to see when you are online and contact you" option to allow you to see them when they are online, or they can choose the "Block this person from seeing when you are online and contacting you" option, so that you will not know whether they're online, and therefore will not be able to contact them. Contacts function as a two-way street, and so they have to allow you to see them and communicate with them while you are online.

You can remove a contact at any time by simply right-clicking the contact in Windows Messenger, and then clicking Delete Contact.

The Delete Contact option deletes the desired contact from your contact list; it does not delete your details from the contact list of the person you have deleted. To permanently delete contacts, you need to get in touch with the person you want to delete and ask him/her to also delete your contact details.

Using Instant Messaging

With instant messaging, you can instantly communicate with someone using a chat-like format, only with more privacy. With instant messaging, you simply identify the contact, type the message, and send it. The contact's computer then signals that a message is incoming; the contact opens it, and then responds directly to you. It is much faster than e-mail and allows you to *talk* in real time.

To create an instant message, follow these steps:

1. **In Windows Messenger, right-click the contact's name in the Windows Messenger window, and then click Send an Instant Message, as shown in Figure 15-7.** If the person appears in your Offline list, then you can still right-click the name and click Send E-mail to ask the person to send you an instant message when they are back online.

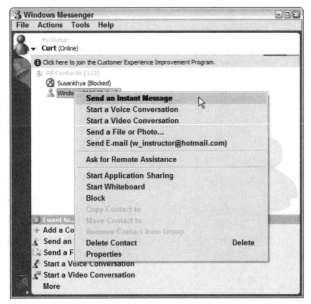

Figure 15-7: You can create an instant message in the Windows Messenger window.

2. **In the Conversation window, shown in Figure 15-8, enter your message in the bottom text box.** You can change the font of the message if you want. Then click Send, or press Enter. Your message now appears in the upper text pane, indicating that your message has been sent.

The message is sent to the contact. If the contact begins to respond to your message, you see a notification in the Conversation window status bar, telling you that the contact is typing a message. When the contact sends it by clicking Send or pressing Enter, the message appears in the upper pane directly beneath your message. This feature allows you to see the conversation thread and scroll it back and forth to review it, as shown in Figure 15-9.

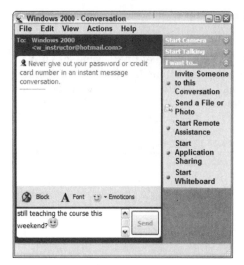

Figure 15-8: The Conversation window

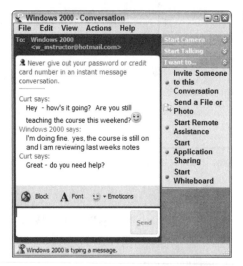

Figure 15-9: You can view the conversation in a chat format.

Can you have a three-person instant messaging session? Yes, in fact, you can even add more people to your session. When you want to add another contact to the conversation, click Actions, and then click "Invite Someone to this Conversation." You can then invite other contacts into the conversation. When a contact accepts the invitation, they see the entire conversation thread, just as though they had been involved in the conversation from the beginning.

FYI: Using Emoticons

Emoticons are icons that you can include in instant messaging sessions to provide some entertainment. They are designed to show emotion to help you further convey the message that you want to send. There are about two-dozen emoticons that you can use, ranging from smiley faces to smooching lips as shown in the following figure. They are all available through the pop-up menu near the bottom of the Conversation window. If you hover your mouse over an emoticon, it will tell you what mood or feeling the emoticon conveys.

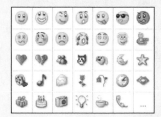

You can use emoticons to enhance your messages.

 You can easily save a conversation for your records when the conversation is finished. In the Conversation window, click File, click Save or File, and then click Save As. You can save the transcript to a text file. You may want to copy and paste the text into Word or Wordpad, and then format it so that you have a cleaner record of the conversation. Keep in mind that emoticons are not saved as a part of the transcript.

Exchanging Files, Voice Conversations, and Video

Aside from simple text messaging, Windows Messenger also gives you the capability to share files with other Windows Messenger users, have live voice conversations, and even share video transmissions. All of these features are generally easy to use and can be fun and helpful with your work and play. The following sections explore these features.

Transferring Files

Windows Messenger provides an easy way to send and receive files to and from your contacts. You can transfer files in basically the same way that you would when using e-mail. The difference is that the file doesn't end up on a mail server somewhere, and so the process is much faster. There are also no file-type limitations or file-size restrictions. The recipient receives a message that tells them how big the file is and about how long it will take to transfer the file over a 28.8 Kbps modem. If you choose to accept a file, a dialog box appears, warning you that Windows Messenger does not inspect files for viruses, and advising you to check the file with an anti-virus program before opening it. As a result, it is up to you to scan files with an anti-virus program before opening them.

Tip

> **There is one restriction to keep in mind. You cannot send a file if your conversation has more than two people.**

When you want to transfer a file, simply choose the "Send a File or Photo" link in the right pane of the Conversation window. A browse window appears, where you can select the file that you want to send. The Conversation window in Figure 15-10 shows you the file transfer progress, and whether the contact has accepted the file.

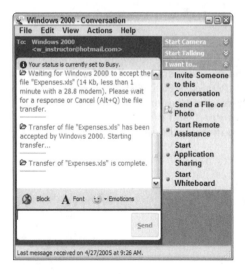

Figure 15-10: You can send a file to another user.

Using the Voice Conversation Feature

Windows Messenger includes a voice conversation feature that allows you to use the Internet to have a spoken conversation with another person. Fortunately, the voice delay has been greatly reduced from previous versions of Windows Messenger, and as a result, the feature works much better. For this feature to work, both your computer and your contact's computer must have a sound card installed, speakers or headphones, and a microphone.

Before using the voice feature, it is a good idea to run the Audio and Video Tuning Wizard. This Wizard helps you to adjust the speakers and microphone, as well as the Web camera, if you are using one. To use the Wizard, follow these steps:

1. **In Windows Messenger, click Tools, and then click Audio Tuning Wizard.**

2. **In the Welcome screen that appears, click Next.**

3. **Select the Camera check box to select the camera that you want to use (if you want to use one).** Click Next. You see a sample screen from the camera.

4. **Adjust the camera and the lighting conditions as necessary.** Click Next.

5. **Adjust your speakers and microphone.** Keep in mind that your microphone should be kept away from the speakers in order to avoid feedback. Click Next.

6. **Select the microphone and speakers that you want to use, as shown in Figure 15-11.** If you are using headphones, make sure that you select the "I am using headphones" option. Click Next.

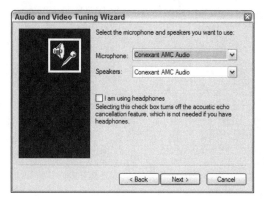

Figure 15-11: You can select the microphone and speaker in the Audio and Video Tuning Wizard.

7. **Adjust the speaker volume using the Test button.** Click Next when you are done.

8. **Speak out loud, reading the provided paragraph if you want to set the sensitivity of your microphone.** Click Next when you are done.

9. **Click Finish.**

In the Windows Messenger window, right-click the person with whom you want to have a conversation, and choose "Start A Voice Conversation" from the shortcut menu that appears. An instant message window appears, and a request for a voice conversation is sent to the contact. If the contact accepts, you can begin the conversation. When you are ready to stop the conversation, click the Stop Talking link in the right pane of the Conversation window, or close the Conversation window.

Using the Video Feature

Windows Messenger also supports a Web cam feature, where you can use a Web camera to communicate over the Internet. Overall, this feature works well and the picture is good, even with slow connections. However, video transfer is limited to Windows XP computers.

To use the video feature, open a Conversation window for the contact with whom you want to communicate, and click the Start Camera option. Your contact must accept your invitation to receive camera transmission. Once the invitation is accepted, the contact can see your video in the Conversation window.

Whiteboard and Application Sharing

Whiteboard and Application Sharing are features that have been added to Windows Messenger to support online meetings. These features enable you to share information and also collaborate on a project. The following two sections explore Whiteboard and Application Sharing.

Using Whiteboard

You can use Whiteboard to create text and graphics that automatically appear on the corresponding Whiteboard of your contact's computer. For example, you can use Whiteboard for online meetings and training, and you can use it in conjunction with voice and video. Keep in mind that Whiteboard is only available in Windows Messenger running on Windows XP; MSN Messenger running on earlier versions of Windows cannot use Whiteboard.

You can start a Whiteboard session in a couple of different ways. First, if you do not already have a session under way, then click Actions, and then click Start Whiteboard. Select the contacts with whom you want to hold a Whiteboard session. Once the contacts accept your invitation, the Whiteboard session begins, and a Sharing Session dialog box appears, which lets you know that you are connected. If you already have a session underway, such as a text session or a video and voice session, click Actions, and then click Start Whiteboard, or click Start Whiteboard in the right pane of the Conversation window. Your contacts must accept the invitation for a Whiteboard session to begin.

Once the session has started, you simply use the Whiteboard to create any text or graphics that you want, as shown in Figure 15-12. Whatever you create appears on the contacts' Whiteboard. Users can save the Whiteboard drawings and text, and even print them from their computers.

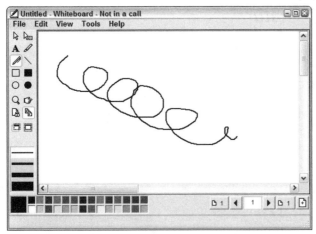

Figure 15-12: Whatever you create appears on the contacts' Whiteboard.

Application Sharing

Application Sharing allows you to work with others on a document or a file. Application Sharing is only available on Windows XP computers, and not on computers running MSN Messenger. To begin an Application Sharing session, click Actions, then click Start Application Sharing, and then select your contacts. You can also right-click a contact and select Start Application Sharing. If you already have an instant messaging session in progress, click Actions, and then click Start Application Sharing, or click the Start Application Sharing link in the right pane of the Conversation window.

The Sharing – Programs dialog box appears and allows you to select the programs that you want to share. You can click the Allow Control button to enable your contacts to control your program. If you don't click this button (or click it a second time when it is labeled Prevent Control), then only you can control the program while others watch.

Wired Networking

16

W indows XP is designed for networking in both the home and small office, and Windows XP Professional is designed for a network domain. The software that you need to create an effective, productive network is already built into Windows XP. You just need to configure it and physically connect the computers together.

Sounds easy, right? Let me emphasize that networking with Windows XP is much easier than it has been in previous versions of Windows. However, networking can still be complicated, and there are many difficulties that you are likely to encounter. In this chapter, you examine wired networks. You take a look at the hardware you need, how to configure the computers, and how to solve common connectivity problems.

Wired Network Hardware Components

In order to create any kind of network connection, you must have two components: hardware that allows your computer to connect to the physical network, and a computer that has the necessary networking software (networking software is already built into Windows XP). To communicate on a wired network, your computer must have a Network Interface Card (NIC), also called a *network adapter card*, a hub, and wiring.

When you attach the network cable to the NIC, the NIC translates data back and forth between your computer and the network. An NIC works like any other internal or external device that you install on Windows XP. NICs are typically sold as internal or external cards. Internal cards plug into PCI-type slots on the computer (inside the case), while external NICs typically connect to a USB port. Because home and small office networking is so commonplace, many NICs are now built into the motherboard on most desktops and laptops. You must install the proper NIC for the kind of network that you want. In most cases, Ethernet networks are used, but there are other kinds, such as HomePNA and Powerline, which are also discussed in this chapter. In most cases, your computer probably already has an installed NIC, and so you should see your computer's documentation for more details.

A hub is a device that provides a central link to the computers on a network. Each computer connects to the hub, and then all communication between computers is routed through the hub. Today, many hubs can perform multiple functions. For example, you can connect your home or small office network through a hub, and also use the hub as a router or residential gateway to manage Internet access. You can find more information about these kinds of products at any computer store.

Note

You may want a hybrid network that contains wired Ethernet computers and that can also include wireless laptops. In fact, that is the kind of home network that I use. You can learn more about wireless and hybrid networks in Chapter 17.

Expert's Notebook: Benefits of Routers and Residential Gateways

Most residential gateways provide security through a feature called Network Address Translation, or NAT. NAT hides the internal IP addresses of a LAN from the Internet (or other destination of the residential gateway). NAT translates the internal IP addresses of the LAN to a different IP address range. These addresses are then used for communications on the Internet. If a hacker decides to break into your network, they must have the real IP address of a computer on your LAN, and with NAT, those IP addresses are not visible. As a result, any hacker attacks that use IP addressing schemes simply fall apart at the residential gateway because the IP address (of the residential gateway) that allows the hacker to access your residential gateway is not the IP address that any of the machines on your LAN is using; therefore, the hacker is stopped at the gateway.

As a second benefit, many routers and residential gateways provide Dynamic Host Configuration Protocol (DHCP) services that make network IP addressing easier. I can recommend both Linksys and NetGear products, and you can learn more about these security features at www.linksys.com and www.netgear.com. Also, if you want to learn more about NAT, you can access RFC 1631 on the Internet. *Curt Simmons*

FYI: Cabling Standards

Installing cable on a large scale is rarely much fun, and so you should plan ahead to avoid problems. New copper wire network cabling standards are not usually quick to emerge, and so you need to determine whether your network cabling is expected to support high-speed LAN technologies. A slower 10/100 Ethernet runs well on any Category 5 (CAT5) cabling. However, if you plan on supporting a 1- or 10-Gbps copper-based Ethernet, you need either CAT5e ("e" stands for "enhanced") or CAT6 cabling. CAT5e is a well-established standard, with much consistency between manufacturers. This is probably the best choice for a scalable, low-risk network cable installation. Today, CAT6 cables have some variation in the specifications that they are built to support, with many specifications exceeding the existing or proposed standards. If you plan to move ahead with a CAT6 cable installation, then double-check your network hardware manufacturer's recommendations against the specifications of the cabling provider. If everything matches up well, then you can move forward with confidence.
David Dalan

The final piece of hardware that you need is wiring. For Ethernet networks, you can use RJ-45 cable (which looks similar to a telephone cable, but is larger). RJ-45, which uses a Category 5 cable, consists of eight wires in four twisted pairs and is the standard for network cabling. You can find RJ-45 cable in all kinds of colors and lengths at your favorite computer store, and usually at an inexpensive price. If you want to use a HomePNA or Powerline network, you can use different cabling.

Types of Wired Networks

From a home and small office point of view, there are only three primary types of wired networks that you are likely to implement: Ethernet, HomePNA, and Powerline. Most users prefer Ethernet, and I also recommend this type. A review of the three network types is as follows:

✦ **Ethernet** is a network standard that is defined by the Institute of Electrical and Electronics Engineers (IEEE) 802.3 specification. You typically see this specification on the box or label for Ethernet products. When you set out to connect a group of computers using NICs, a hub, and RJ-45 cables, you are creating an Ethernet network. Ethernet has been and continues to be an overwhelmingly popular network type, and is the most flexible for small office, home, and corporate networks. Even wireless networks use a form of Ethernet.

Manufacturers adhere to the Ethernet 802.3 specification so that you can mix and match hardware without any problems. This standardization allows you to use NICs, hubs, and wiring that are all made by different companies, so that you do not have to conform to one manufacturer's products.

✦ **HomePNA** is a network standard that was introduced a few years ago when home and small office networking started to become popular. Like Ethernet, a HomePNA network uses internal PCI NICs, or external USB NICs, but these NICs use RJ-11 connectors, which are the type used by telephone connections. Not only are the plugs the same, but when you plug the NIC into a nearby phone jack (one used for a telephone circuit), the NIC uses the home or office's internal phone wiring for network data transfer. Other users who need to access the network can do the same. In homes where most rooms have a phone jack, HomePNA gives you access to a network from virtually any room in the house or office — without a hub. Although Ethernet gives you more flexibility in terms of configuration, HomePNA is helpful in locations where you need non-wireless computers and the flexibility to put them in different locations.

A problem with HomePNA may concern ICS. If you are using a DSL or cable modem, you need an NIC for that connection, as well as the HomePNA NIC. You can set up ICS with the ICS host computer connected to the Internet, and all other computers can then access data from the ICS host. However, if you do not want to use ICS, then you need to configure the ICS host as a bridge so that the two dissimilar networks can communicate. Also, if you want to use a hybrid network made up of wireless computers and wired desktops, you should choose an Ethernet network.

Another problem is that HomePNA is not as fast as an Ethernet. For more info about HomePNA, visit www.homepna.org.

✦ **Powerline** networking is a lot like HomePNA, but instead of using your existing telephone lines, you use your electrical lines. Powerline networking uses an NIC that plugs into a standard electrical outlet. Other computers in your home plug into other outlets, and communication between computers occurs over the electrical lines without disrupting any other electrical services. Powerline networking also provides speeds of 8–14 Mbps transfer, so the system's speed is compatible to that of HomePNA.

So why use Powerline? The main reason is that electrical outlets are more readily available in homes and offices than phone lines, which gives you more networking flexibility. Other than this, there is really no compelling reason to use Powerline networking over HomePNA or Ethernet. However, if you want to learn more about Powerline networking, go to www.homeplug.com.

Setting Up the Workgroup

Once you have determined the kind of home or small office network that you want and you have purchased the hardware, you should follow the manufacturer's instructions to install the NICs, hubs, and other devices. Remember to connect them as required (Category 5 cable is used for wired LANs, phone cables for HomePNA, and power sockets for Powerline). Make sure that you have purchased NICs that are compatible with Windows XP, and be sure to install any drivers that accompany the hardware devices. Keep in mind that some devices require you to install their software drivers before you can connect them. This is often true of USB devices.

FYI: APIPA and TCP/IP

If the mention of TCP/IP and APIPA make you feel intimidated, don't worry. Most people share that sentiment. TCP/IP is a networking protocol that functions by assigning a unique IP address to each client on the network. In large networks, a Dynamic Host Configuration Protocol (DHCP) server, which manages all addresses, usually administers TCP/IP. In the past, if you wanted to use TCP/IP — which is the *de facto* standard for networking these days — in a small office or home network, you had to actually configure those addresses. However, Windows XP can do it for you using APIPA. APIPA is a built-in process where computers on the network configure themselves with a unique TCP/IP address in the range of 169.254.0.1 through 169.254.255.254 with a subnet mask of 255.255.0.0. The purpose of APIPA is to allow home and small office users to use TCP/IP without having to worry about configuring it. This feature saves you a lot of time and many headaches. *Curt Simmons.*

After you install the software drivers and hardware devices and make your connections, you're ready to configure the workgroup. Windows XP provides the Network Setup Wizard to help you set up the workgroup. If you want to use the Network Setup Wizard, and you plan on using ICS, you should first run the wizard on a computer that directly connects to the Internet. You can then run the wizard on the other computers on your network. The wizard automatically configures the computers for TCP/IP networking using Automatic Private IP Addressing (APIPA). If you are using a mixture of Windows XP computers and computers running earlier versions of Windows, such as Microsoft Windows 2000 or Windows 9x, Windows XP provides a way for you to create a network setup disk for those clients when you run the Network Setup Wizard. You'll see how to use the wizard to accomplish these tasks in the next two sections.

Setting Up the Home or Small Office Network

To set up your home or small office network, you should begin with the primary Windows XP PC on the network. To use the Network Setup Wizard, follow these steps:

1. **Make sure that all network computers are turned on and connected to any necessary hubs.** Also, ensure that all NICs are working.

2. **Choose Start ➪ Control Panel and then open Network Connections.**

3. **In the Network Tasks pane of the Network Connections window, click "Set up a home or small office network."** This option is shown in Figure 16-1. If you don't see the Network Tasks pane, click the Folders button on the toolbar to toggle from the Folders bar to the Network Tasks pane. The Network Setup Wizard opens and displays the Welcome page. Click Next.

Figure 16-1: Create a new home or small office network.

4. **On the Before You Continue page, read the instructions and make sure that all of the network components are connected and working.** If you want to use ICS to share your Internet connection but you have not set it up yet, do so now. Make sure that the computer hosting ICS (the one directly connected to the Internet, and the one on which you are running the Network Setup Wizard first) has a working Internet connection. You can find out more about ICS in Chapter 19. Click Next.

5. **On the "Select a connection method" page, select a connect method:**

   • **This computer connects directly to the Internet:** Select the first option, "if the computer will function as the ICS host (see Figure 16-2). Remember, you should be running the Network Setup Wizard on the ICS host first. Click Next and skip to step 7.

   • **This computer connects to the Internet through a residential gateway or through another computer on my network.** If there is already an ICS host computer, choose this option. Click next and skip to step 8.

   • **Other:** If neither of these options applies to you, select Other. Click Next and skip to step 6.

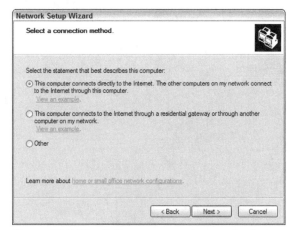

Figure 16-2: The Select a connection method page of the Network Setup Wizard

6. **If you choose the "Other" option in step 5, the following page allows you to select one of three alternate computer configurations (see Figure 16-3).** Select the most appropriate option and then click Next.

- This computer connects to the Internet directly or though a network hub. Other computers on my network also connect to the Internet directly or through a hub.

- This computer connects directly to the Internet. I do not have a network yet.

- This computer belongs to a network that does not have an Internet connection.

7. **In step 5, if you determined that the computer should function as the ICS host, the "Select your Internet connection" page appears, as shown in Figure 16-4.** If you selected another option, your choices will vary, but the ICS host scenario includes most of the same configuration steps as the other choices. Select the Internet connection that you want to share, and then click Next.

8. **If you have multiple network connections installed on your computer, then the "Your computer has multiple connections" page appears.** The wizard asks you for the appropriate network connection. Choose either "Determine the appropriate connections for me to allow Windows XP" (to automatically bridge the connections), or "Let me choose the connections to my network" (if you want to bridge those connections). In this example, choose to make your own connections, and then click Next.

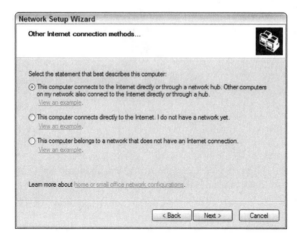

Figure 16-3: The Other Internet connection methods page

Figure 16-4: Choose the connection that you want.

9. **The "Select the connections to bridge" page appears so that you can select the connections that you want to bridge.** Do not choose any Internet connections—you cannot bridge a LAN connection with an Internet connection. See the section concerning bridging later in this chapter for more information. Do not bridge any connections at this time. Click Next. The "Give this computer a description and name" page appears (Figure 16-5).

10. **You can type a short description of the computer in the Computer description text box, and then type an easily recognizable name in the Computer name text box.** The name must be unique (no two computers can have the same name), and should not be more than 15 characters. Do not use special punctuation or spaces. Click Next.

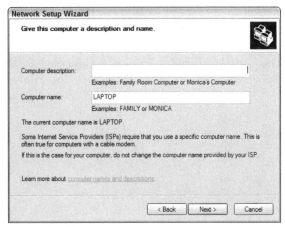

Figure 16-5: You can give the computer a network name.

Remember that the name that you give the computer is the name that other users on the network will see, and the name that they will use to connect to your computer. For this reason, make the name something friendly and descriptive in order to make networking easier for your users.

11. **In the "Name your network" page, shown in Figure 16-6, type a name for your workgroup.** By default, your workgroup is named MSHOME. However, you can change it to anything you like. The name should be short and simple, and all computers on your network must use the same workgroup name to connect with each other. Click Next.

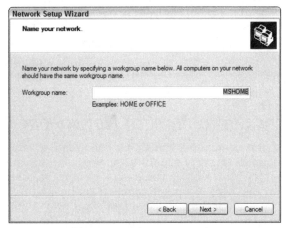

Figure 16-6: You can assign a name for your network.

12. **Review the settings that you are about to apply in the "Ready to apply network settings" page.** Use the Back button to make any necessary changes. When you are sure the settings are correct, click Next.

As Windows XP configures the computer for networking, the Please Wait page appears. You also see a page where you can turn on File and Printer Sharing (Figure 16-7).

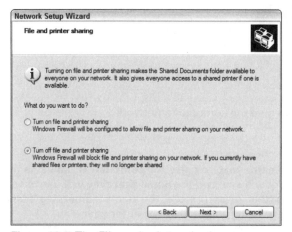

Figure 16-7: The File and printer sharing page

13. **If you want to share files, folders, printers and other resources, then choose this option now.**

14. **When prompted, you can choose to create a network setup disk to apply the network settings to other computers on the network.** You do not need a network setup disk if all of the clients on your network are Windows XP clients. If all of your computers are running Windows XP, choose "Just finish the wizard; I don't need to run the wizard on other computers."

15. **Follow any necessary instructions if you need to create a network setup disk, and then click Finish.**

Configuring Other Computers for Networking

Once the first network client is configured, you should then run the Network Setup Wizard on the other Windows XP network clients. If you are using ICS, then keep in mind that the Network Setup Wizard will ask you to choose how the computer connects to the Internet. Select the "This computer connects to the Internet through another computer on my network or through a residential gateway" option. The Network Setup Wizard will locate the ICS host and proceed with the setup.

Computers running Microsoft Windows 98, Microsoft Windows Me (Millennium Edition), Microsoft Windows NT 4.0, and Windows 2000 clients can also join your Windows XP workgroup. These clients can be configured for networking manually, or you can run the Network Setup Wizard on computers running Windows 98, Windows 98 Second Edition, or Windows Me. To use the Network Setup Wizard on these versions of Windows, you can either use the floppy disk that you created in step 13 when you configured the Windows XP clients, or you can use the Windows XP installation CD to run the Network Setup Wizard.

To run the Network Setup Wizard from the CD, follow these steps:

1. **Insert the Windows XP installation CD into the computer that you want to add to the workgroup.** The Welcome to Microsoft Windows XP screen appears.

2. **Click "Perform additional tasks."** The Perform Additional Tasks screen appears.

3. **Click the "Set up a home or small office network" link in the Network Tasks pane.** Depending on the computer's version of Windows, the Network Setup Wizard may need to copy some additional files to your computer and then restart it.

4. **Click Yes to continue.** At this point, the Network Setup Wizard opens.

5. **Complete the wizard as you did for the Windows XP computer.**

Expert's Notebook: Manual IP Configuration?

If you want to manually assign different IP addresses to the clients in your workgroup, you can easily do so by selecting Internet Protocol (TCP/IP) on the General tab of the connection's Properties dialog box, and then clicking Properties.

However, you should first ask yourself why you want to do this before proceeding. APIPA is designed to service workgroups and was specifically developed for networks where no centralized DHCP server is in use. Manual IP address configuration can be complicated and problematic, and so, before changing your computer's automatic IP addressing to a static addressing scheme, carefully consider your reasons for doing so. Remember that each client on your network must have a unique IP address in the same class range with an appropriate subnet mask. If you use ICS, the default gateway assigned to your network clients must be the address of the ICS host. In short, you can manually configure TCP/IP, but APIPA is designed to be your networking friend, and I advise you to avoid problems by using APIPA rather than a manual configuration. *Curt Simmons*

Troubleshooting: Common Workgroup Problems

Under most circumstances, you will not experience connection problems if you use the Network Setup Wizard to configure your network. However, networking is complicated, and you may experience some difficulties from time to time. Here are some of the most common connection problems and solutions:

✦ **Client computers cannot connect:** Client computers can only connect to each other if they have a proper IP address and subnet mask. Run the Network Setup Wizard again on the clients that are unable to connect. If you continue to have problems, make sure that the computers are physically connected to the network. (In this chapter you can read more about additional tools and features that can help you to troubleshoot connection problems.)

✦ **Problems with Windows 95 clients:** Windows 95 is a very old operating system at this point, and so if you have Windows 95 clients, I would first encourage an upgrade. If that is not possible, remember that the Network Setup Wizard is not supported on Windows 95 clients. However, you can manually configure these computers to access the network. If you are using APIPA, you need to examine each IP address of the other client computers, and then manually assign a different IP address in the same range and the same subnet mask to the computers running the other versions of Windows. Make sure that you also install Client For Microsoft Networks and File And Printer Sharing For Microsoft Networks on each computer. See the Windows 95 help files for more information.

✦ **Problems with manually assigned addresses:** In most cases, your best solution to conflicts caused from incorrectly assigned static IP addresses is to allow Windows XP to automatically assign IP addresses using APIPA by running the Network Setup Wizard. However, if you do assign static addresses manually, you need to make sure that they are all in the same IP address range and subnet. An incorrect network address or wrong subnet mask is usually the problem.

✦ **A client can connect, but no other computers can connect to the client:** When one computer cannot contact others on the network, most likely the Windows Firewall is enabled on the LAN NIC of the computer to which others cannot connect. Windows Firewall does not allow network traffic when it is enabled on the LAN's NIC. To resolve this problem, open the NIC's Properties dialog box, select the Advanced tab, and clear the option to use Windows Firewall.

Working with Connection Settings

You can manage network connections and settings using the Network Connections folder in Control Panel. As shown in Figure 16-8, the connection appears as a Local Area Network (LAN) connection in the Network Connections folder under the LAN or High-Speed Internet heading. If you select the connection and look at the Details section on the task pane in the Network Connections window, you see such information as whether the connection is enabled, and the type of NIC that is used for the connection. You can also see the current IP address, subnet mask, and other details about the connection. In order for the icon to appear as enabled, the NIC must be connected to the network or hub (unless it is a wireless connection, of course). If it is not, then you see an "X" over the icon and a status message, as shown in Figure 16-9.

Checking the Status of the Connection

If you double-click the connection in the Network Connections folder (or right-click the connection and click Status), you see a simple Status dialog box as shown in Figure 16-10. The General tab displays the current connection status, the duration of the network connection, and the current speed of the connection. In the Activity section, you can see the total number of packets sent and received. You can also access the connection's Properties dialog box, and disable the connection using the Disable button.

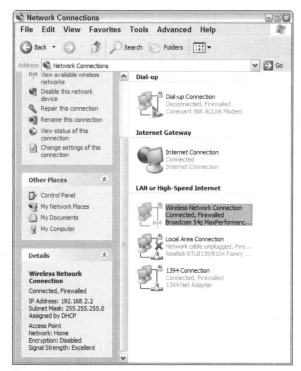

Figure 16-8: The Details section displays information about an enabled connection.

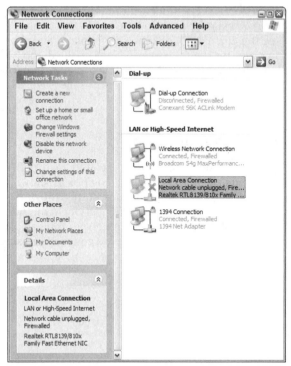

Figure 16-9: The Details section displays information about a disabled connection.

Figure 16-10: The General tab

If you select the Support tab, shown in Figure 16-11, you can see the connection's address type (automatic or manual), IP address, subnet mask, and default gateway (if any). If you click the Details button, you can also see the DNS and WINS server addresses.

Figure 16-11: The Support tab

Notice the Repair button on the Support tab. If your connection is not working, you can click the Repair button to tell Windows XP to try to fix the connection. If you choose the repair option, Windows XP attempts to release and renew its IP address.

Working with Connection Properties

If you open the Network Connections folder, you can right-click the LAN connection icon and click Properties. You can configure several different items on the Connection properties tabs, but I do want to point out that under most circumstances, you don't need to configure anything here. That is the beauty of using the wizard to create a network connection. The wizard can configure these items, and APIPA can configure the IP addressing. However, there are some items that you should take note of on the Properties pages.

The General Tab

On the General tab shown in Figure 16-12, you see a list of the services and protocols that are configured for the connection. By default, a LAN connection includes the following:

✦ **Client for Microsoft Networks.** This service enables the computer to participate on a Microsoft network.

✦ **File and Printer Sharing for Microsoft Networks.** This service allows the client to share files and printers on the network.

✦ **QoS Packet Scheduler.** The Quality of Service Packet Scheduler manages network traffic and related traffic functions.

✦ **Internet Protocol (TCP/IP).** TCP/IP enables the client to participate on a TCP/IP network.

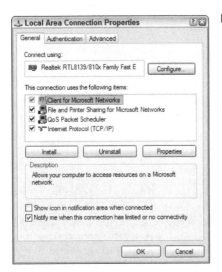

Figure 16-12: The General tab

Notice that you can click the Install, Uninstall, and Properties buttons to work with these different services. You can also click the Configure button to manage the NIC hardware properties. Again, everything that you need to function on a Microsoft network is already installed and configured here.

The Authentication Tab

If network authentication is required on your network, then the Authentication tab, shown in Figure 16-13, enables you to configure authenticated network access for both wired and wireless Ethernet networks.

The authentication option that you see in the figure uses the IEEE 802.1x standard. This standard provides network authentication of devices based on their port or connection to the network. This is why you find the 802.1x option in the connection's Properties dialog box.

Figure 16-13: The Authentication tab

Using 802.1x, you can require authentication using Extensible Authentication Protocol (EAP). Different EAP types are available for authentication, including Message Digest 5 (MD5) – Challenge or a smart card or digital certificate. EAP is a highly secure standard for both wired and wireless Ethernet networks. If you are using a smart card or digital certificate, then click the Properties button to configure the option that you want to use. To implement the 802.1x standard, each network client should use the authentication settings on this tab in order to ensure security.

Note   **The Advanced tab contains settings for Windows Firewall and ICS, which you can learn about in Chapters 30 and 19, respectively.**

Managing Bindings and Provider Order

If you open Network Connections and choose Advanced Settings on the Advanced menu (shown in Figure 16-14), the Advanced Settings dialog box opens and displays advanced settings for adapters and bindings, as well as provider order. These settings give you a summary of which protocols are bound to which connections, and how different services are accessed on your network.

On the Adapters and Bindings tab, shown in Figure 16-15, you see listings of connections and bindings for the LAN connection. Notice that if you select a connection or binding, you can adjust its order on the list by clicking the Up Arrow and Down Arrow buttons to the right of the list. But why would you want to do this? The answer has to do with potential performance when different adapters and bindings are used.

Figure 16-14: Selecting Advanced Settings in Network Connections.

Figure 16-15: The Adapters and Bindings tab

When Windows XP participates on the network, the connections and bindings are used in order. For example, if you have three connections, then Windows XP attempts to use those connections for network communication in the order that they appear in this list. For best network performance, you should move the connections and bindings that you use most often to the top of the list. As you can see in the Bindings For Local Area Connection section, if you have more than one protocol bound to a service, then order the protocols by their relative importance, and disconnect any protocols that are not needed for a given service by clearing their check boxes. Each protocol adds to the overhead of the network, and so turning off those protocols that are unused will improve performance. In a typical home or small office network, there is nothing you can do here, but if you are in a network where several protocols are used, then you should keep this point in mind.

On the Provider Order tab, shown in Figure 16-16, the same rule applies. You see a list of network providers and the services that they provide. Make sure that the services used most often are at the top of each list.

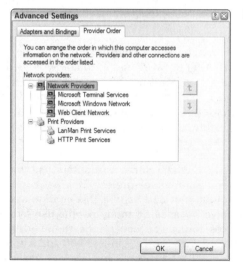

Figure 16-16: The Provider Order tab

Tip

Do not randomly change the settings on this tab unless you have a good reason for adjusting the order of bindings and provider data. In a typical home or small office network, changing the settings here are not beneficial.

Bridging Network Connections

Earlier in this chapter, I mentioned that HomePNA and Powerline networks could have some problems connecting to a shared DSL or cable connection without additional hardware. You can purchase a router that connects with both networks to solve this problem. However, you can avoid purchasing additional hardware by using a software solution, called a network bridge, to connect the two different networks together.

> **When you bridge a connection, the computer that is functioning as the bridge must always be turned on in order for the two segments to have connectivity to each other. This is a negative point of using Windows XP as a bridge, rather than a router.**

A bridge is simply a connection between two dissimilar or incompatible networks. There are a couple of primary reasons why you may need to configure Windows XP to act as a network bridge:

✦ **You can have a small office where there are two different subnets that divide two specific groups.** This configuration often occurs when a second group of users are added to the network, but they are not configured to reside on the primary subnet or segment. Both network segments are Ethernet segments, and in this case you can outfit your computer with two NICs so that it can communicate with each segment. This bridge provides a connection between the two segments.

✦ **You can also bridge different network segments together.** For example, your home network may consist of an Ethernet network and a HomePNA network. In this case, you can install both NICs on a Windows XP computer and let Windows XP bridge the two networks together, creating one IP subnet. Once you bridge the two segments, computers on each segment can then communicate with each other seamlessly. All data flows through the network bridge, but this process is invisible to the user.

> **If you want to create a hybrid network where some computers use wired Ethernet connections while other computers use wireless Ethernet connections, you are better off using a router that can handle this configuration. Routers are common and inexpensive because so many people use hybrid networks in home and small offices today. You can bridge them using a Windows XP computer that is outfitted with both a wireless NIC and a wired Ethernet NIC. However, if you are buying hardware, you are not likely to spend much more money to get the router.**

If you do need to create a network bridge, you need to log on to the computer that serves as the bridge with an Administrator account. You can bridge Ethernet connections (including HomePNA and Powerline), but you cannot bridge an Ethernet connection with a virtual private networking (VPN) connection or with a dial-up connection. Never bridge a connection with your Ethernet NIC and your Internet connection — this creates a security hole that allows Internet intruders to access your private network.

To create a network bridge, follow these steps:

1. **Log on with an Administrative account and open Network Connections.** You log on to the computer that holds both subnets or network types because this is the computer that needs to run the network bridge for the rest of the network.

2. **Turn off Internet Connection Sharing and Windows Firewall if they are enabled for either connection.**

3. **In Network Connections, select the two connections that you want to bridge.** You do this by holding down the Ctrl key and clicking each connection so that they are both selected.

4. **Release the Ctrl key.** Right-click the selected adapters and click Bridge Connections, as shown in Figure 16-17. Windows XP creates the network bridge. When the process is complete, the bridge appears in the Network Connections folder along with the LAN connections that now appear under the Network Bridge, as shown in Figure 16-18.

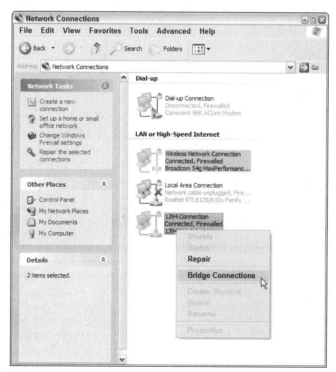

Figure 16-17: Bridging connections in the Network Connections window

Figure 16-18: The Network Bridge

You can add connections to the bridge at any time by right-clicking the bridge icon and clicking Properties. The Network Bridge Properties dialog box appears, as shown in Figure 16-19. Although you can only have one bridge on a Windows XP computer, the bridge can support multiple connections (up to 64).

Creating a Direct Cable Connection

While we are discussing network connections, I want to point out a simple direct cable connection that you can create with another computer. For example, if you are using a laptop at a friend's house, and you want to transfer some files from their computer to your computer without sending them through e-mail, you can create a Direct Cable Connection, or DCC, with their computer and simply transfer the files over. This kind of simple network connection connects two computers using a serial cable, a DirectParallel cable, or a modem. For computers without network adapter cards, or in the case of transfers from handheld devices, such as Windows CE, a DCC connection is a great temporary connection that you can use to transfer files. You can also use a DCC connection to connect a non-networked computer to a network on a temporary basis. When you are connected to a computer that is connected to another network, you may be able to access additional network resources, depending on the permissions that are assigned to those resources.

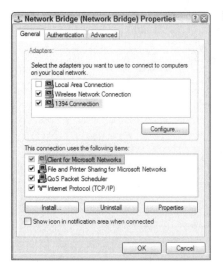

Figure 16-19: The General tab

Although you can use DCC in several different situations, it is not a true networking option, and the transfer speed is slow. If you need to transfer files from one computer to another, then burning a CD is faster. You'll find that connection speeds are often in the modem range of approximately 24 Kbps to 50 Kbps. DirectParallel cables that connect the parallel ports on two computers work faster, and Windows XP supports standard or basic 4-bit cables, Enhanced Capabilities Port (ECP) cables, and Universal Cable Module cables. You can purchase null modem cables at any computer store, and you can also find DirectParallel cables at most computer stores.

You can establish a DCC connection between a Windows XP computer and any other Windows computer that supports DCC (Windows 95, Windows 98, Windows Me, Windows 2000, or another Windows XP computer) using a null modem cable or a DirectParallel cable. When you create a DCC network, you must first attach the two computers together using the necessary cable type.

When you create a DCC network, one computer acts as the host computer and the other computer acts as the guest. The guest computer accesses information on the host computer, but the host computer cannot access information on the guest. Once you have the cable connected between the computers, you can set up the host computer. To set up the host computer, follow these steps:

1. **Log on to Windows XP with an Administrator account.**

2. **Open the Network Connections folder.**

3. **In the tasks pane at the left under Network Tasks (Figure 16-20), click "Create a new connection."** Click Next on the New Connection Wizard's opening page.

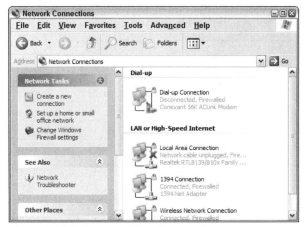

Figure 16-20: Create a New Connection

4. On the Network Connection Type page of the wizard, shown in Figure 16-21, select the "Set up an advanced connection" option, and click Next.

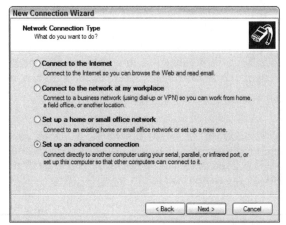

Figure 16-21: Select the advanced connection option

5. On the Advanced Connection Options page (Figure 16-22), choose the "Connect directly to another computer" option, and click Next.

6. On the Host or Guest page, shown in Figure 16-23, choose the Host option and click Next.

Figure 16-22: Connect directly to another computer

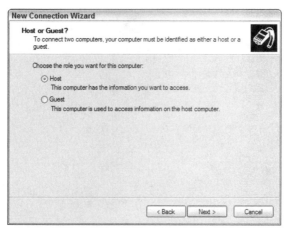

Figure 16-23: Choose the Host option

7. **As shown in Figure 16-24, on the Connection Device page of the wizard, choose the port that you want to use for the connection, such as Infrared Port, DirectParallel, or Communications Port, from the list.** The port that you select is configured for DCC. You cannot use a port that currently has another device attached to it. Click Next.

8. **On the User Permissions page, select which users are allowed to access this host through the DCC connection.** Notice that you can also create additional user accounts directly from this window, as shown in Figure 16-25. Make your selections and click Next.

Figure 16-24: Choose a device for the connection

Figure 16-25: Configure User Permissions

9. **Click Finish.** The new connection appears in the Network Connections window as Incoming Connections.

Once you have set up the host, your next task is to set up the guest computer. For Windows XP computers, simply use the Network Connections Wizard again and choose the Guest option instead of Host on the wizard's Host or Guest page. If you are using another version of Windows as the guest, refer to that operating system's help files for setup instructions. In Windows XP, the connection on the client computer appears under the Direct heading in Network Connections. Simply double-click the icon to make the connection, and then enter a valid username and password.

Helpful Troubleshooting Tools for Your Network

Windows XP includes several built-in command-line tools that can help you both troubleshoot network connections and gain more information about those connections. For the most part, the tools are straightforward and easy to use. This section introduces these tools, and I encourage you to experiment with them to become more familiar with them.

Using Ping

One of the most popular and common connectivity tests is the ping test. Ping uses the Internet Control Message Protocol (ICMP) to send data packets, known as *echo requests,* to a remote computer on a network. You can even use it on the Internet. The echo requests are packets that ask for a reply (an echo), which the remote computer sends back to your computer. This lets you determine whether you have basic connectivity with that computer.

One of the first actions that you should take is to perform a ping loopback test, which tests whether your computer can talk to your own NIC. This test simply lets you determine whether or not your NIC is working. If the loopback test fails, you know something is wrong with the NIC, and that you must fix it before you can gain network connectivity.

The loopback test works by pinging a reserved loopback IP address, which is 127.0.0.1. When you ping 127.0.0.1, echo request packets are sent to your own NIC. To perform a ping loopback test, open a command window, type **ping 127.0.0.1** and press Enter. The loopback test is performed, and if it is successful, you see a reply, as shown in Figure 16-26. If not, you see a "request timeout" message instead.

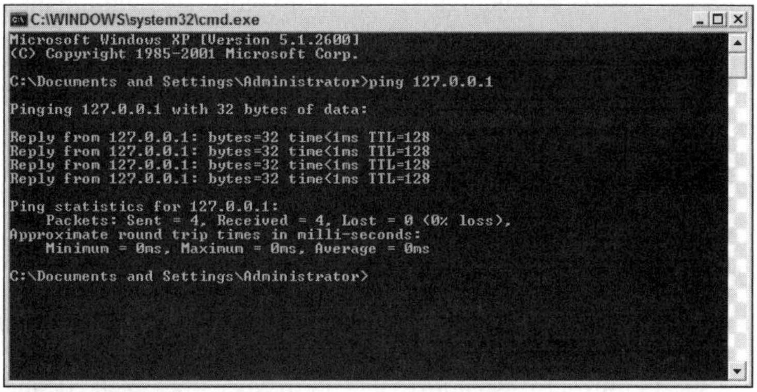

Figure 16-26: Performing a ping loopback test

Tip   **You can also type ping localhost rather than ping 127.0.0.1 for the same result.**

If the loopback test works, your next troubleshooting step is to ping a computer on your network to test for basic network connectivity. This allows you to determine whether you actually have connectivity with other hosts on your network. If it appears that you have connectivity, then you should also ping your computer from another network computer to prove that other computers can successfully ping your computer.

To ping a computer, you first need the computer's IP address. You can then return to the Command Prompt window and type **ping *ipaddress*** where *ipaddress* is the IP address of the remote computer. If the ping test is successful, you see the reply message. In most cases, if you cannot ping any hosts on your network but the loopback test is successful, then your computer has an incorrect IP address or subnet mask.

    You can also ping Internet hosts, such as www.wiley.com. However, the ping test does not work unless Windows Firewall is configured to allow ICMP traffic. You can find out how to configure Windows Firewall in Chapter 30. Also, the ping command, like most command-line tools, has several switch options. You can view them by simply typing ping at the command prompt and pressing Enter.

    A helpful pint switch is the -t option. The "T" is short for "tail" and it simply tells the ping command to continue pinging the host until you stop it. This is useful if you are investigating a connectivity problem and want to see when the connection comes up or goes down.

Using PathPing

PathPing is a ping tool that also traces the route to a host. In a small office or home network, this tool is not very helpful, but if you want to ping a host on the Internet and see the path to the host, then you may find this tool to be helpful. To use this tool, type **pathping *host*** at the command prompt, where *host* is the URL or IP address of an Internet site or network host. You can also specify additional options on the command line to control the information that you receive, and the maximum number of hops allowed. To see all of the available switches, type **pathping** at the command prompt. Figure 16-27 shows you a successful pathping.

Using Ipconfig

Ipconfig is a helpful command-line tool that gives you complete TCP/IP information for the adapters that are configured on your computer. Use Ipconfig to identify an NIC's Media Access Control (MAC) address, IP address, subnet mask, default gateway, DNS server, and DHCP server. Ipconfig is a great tool for troubleshooting because you can quickly gain all of the TCP/IP information about a computer.

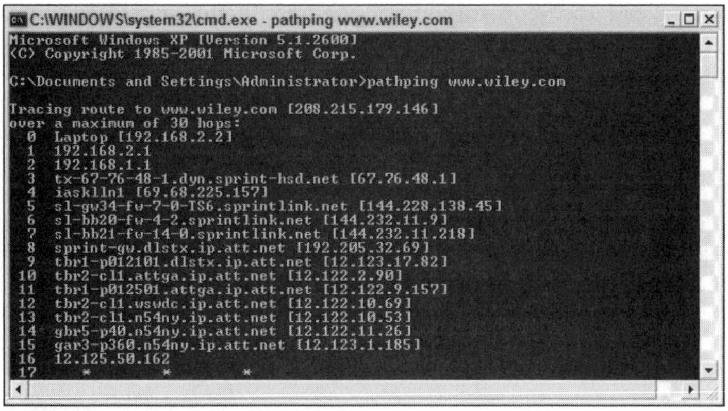

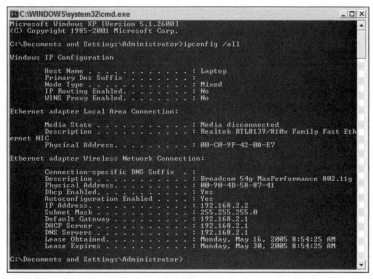

Figure 16-27: A successful pathping

The most commonly used option in Ipconfig is the /all option. At the command prompt, type **ipconfig /all**. You see a listing of the computer's current IP address configuration, as shown in Figure 16-28. To see a complete list of options, type **ipconfig /?** at the command prompt.

Figure 16-28: A listing of the computer's current IP address configuration

FYI: Viewing Network Port Connections

If your network connection or computer is behaving oddly, you can use the Netstat tool to help you to determine whether unscrupulous network connections are the cause. The output shows you which computers are connected to your computer, and which inbound and outbound ports the connection is using. Key things to look for include port traffic on ports 20 and 21 (FTP), 23 (Telnet), 25 (SMTP), and 8080 (Web) attached to the "local address" entry. This means that there is an inbound connection to that service. If you are not running one of those services, this is a cause for concern. Also, if you have outbound connections to common IRC ports (for example, 6667 and 8888), then you should be concerned, unless you are running an Internet Relay Chat program such as mIRC. Unexpected activity on IRC ports may be a sign that you are infected with backdoor applications, bots, or other types of malicious software. *David Dalan*

Using Netstat

Netstat displays all of the active connections to your computer. You can also use Netstat to view the bytes sent and received to and from your computer, as well as any dropped network packets. Typing the basic form of the command, **netstat**, displays each connection's protocol, local (MAC) address, foreign (IP) address, and the current state of the connection. There are a number of helpful command line switches available for Netstat. You can view all of them by typing **netstat /?** at the command prompt.

Wireless Networking and Virtual Private Networking

17

Only a few years ago, wireless networking was a "pie in the sky" idea. Although we knew it could be great, the technology was too primitive, and there were many issues with security in a wireless world.

However, today, as I write this chapter, I'm sitting at my dining room table in my house, and using a laptop. I'm accessing files on a computer in my study upstairs, sending a file to a printer upstairs, and I'm accessing the Internet — all without wires. It's a brave new world and it is about time.

I'll go so far as to say that wireless networking is the best choice for home or small office networks, or at least a hybrid network that uses both wired Ethernet and wireless Ethernet. This configuration gives you the most networking flexibility, and once you try it, you'll never go back to a network that is completely tethered by wires.

In this chapter, you explore wireless networking with Windows XP. You see how to create a wireless network and configure Windows XP computers for wireless access.

In This Chapter

Creating Infrared Wireless Connections

Configuring and Using Wi-Fi

Working with VPN Connections

FYI: Types of Wireless Networking

There are several different standards, or types, of wireless networks (not all of which are supported by Windows XP). These types include:

✦ **Infrared**. Uses an infrared beam to transmit data from one device to the next, just like your remote control transmits data to your television. Infrared networking works well for short-distance networking, and connectivity of devices. For example, wireless keyboards, mice, printers, and game devices can connect with an infrared port on your computer. Laptops and PDAs can also connect with a desktop computer for data transfer. Infrared is a great solution for device-to-computer connectivity, but in terms of an actual LAN, infrared is not a preferred connectivity method. You can learn how to configure an infrared connection later in this chapter.

✦ **Wireless Personal Area Network (WPAN)**. A personal area network that resides in a generalized space, such as a room, a WPAN is useful for wireless network computing in one location, or wireless networking between PDAs, cell phones, and laptop computers. WPANs use infrared connections for close objects, or Bluetooth, which communicates through radio waves with a range of up to 30 feet. The IEEE has established a working group for the development of WPANs, numbered 802.15. For more on this standard, simply search for IEEE 802.15 on any search engine.

✦ **Wireless Local Area Network (WLAN)**. A WLAN is a wireless network that exists within one geographical location, such as in a home, office building, or school. Radio frequencies are used so that all computers within the WLAN can communicate with each other. Although the original IEEE 802.11 standard for WLAN defines transfer rates at 1-2 Mbps, the new IEEE standard for WLAN networking is 802.11b, which defines data transfer rates of up to 11 Mbps using a 2.4 GHz frequency band. 802.11b is the popular standard today, and it provides transfer speeds that are comparable to a typical Ethernet network. 802.11g, a newer standard, also provides a data transfer rate of over 54 Mbps using a 5 GHz frequency band.

✦ **Wireless Metropolitan Area Network (WMAN)**. A WMAN allows communication between different locations within a single metropolitan area. This kind of wireless network is designed for different offices in the same city so that they can communicate with each other wirelessly. The IEEE 802.16 standard is still under development to define the technologies that could be used in WMANs.

✦ **Wireless Wide Area Network (WWAN)**. A WWAN connects to WLANs that are separated over wide geographic areas. WWAN technologies involve the use of satellite communications that are maintained by service providers and use the same technologies as cellular phones and wireless PDAs. Common technologies include Global System for Mobile Communications (GSM), Cellular Digital Packet Data (CDPD), and Code Division Multiple Access (CDMA).

Wireless Networking and Windows XP

Windows XP supports wireless networking, and especially with Service Pack (SP) 2 installed, you'll find that wireless networking is easier than ever before. However, you still need to do some work to create a wireless network, and you need to have a rudimentary understanding of how wireless networks operate. Windows XP supports both the infrared networking, and the 802.11b and 802.11a standards, also known as Wi-Fi. The 802.11b standard provides transfer rates of about 11 Mbps, which makes it comparable with standard Ethernet.

Wi-Fi is the accepted standard among most hardware manufacturers today. Wi-Fi has a range of up to 300 feet from point to point, and it makes use of the best wireless security standards that are currently available. There are already thousands of Wi-Fi public access points, or hot spots, available in the United States today in public locations, such as malls, airports, and even coffee shops. Like I said, it's a new world of wireless connectivity and we are all the better for it.

Note **If you're wondering which hardware will work with Windows XP, just look for the compatibility label on the hardware box, as well as the 802.11 standard. With both of these indicators, you should be in good shape in terms of compatibility.**

Working with Infrared Connections

As I mentioned earlier, infrared connections work well when you need to connect two devices together for data transfer. Typically, you use infrared networking when you want to transfer files between two computers, a PDA and a computer, or for connections to wireless peripherals. Infrared technology uses an infrared beam of light to transfer data from one computer to another. It also uses a *line of sight* transmission method in that you have to align the two infrared ports so that they are pointing to each other. Once the two infrared ports are aligned, they can begin exchanging information with each other over the beam of light, once you configure them to do so.

Most laptop computers ship with an infrared port. If your desktop system does not have an infrared port (many do not), you can purchase an external infrared device that connects to either a serial or USB port on your computer. You should ensure that the device is compatible with Windows XP. Once installed, the infrared port appears in Control Panel as a Wireless Link icon, shown in Figure 17-1, and you are then ready to use the port for communications. You can find infrared USB or serial devices (USB is recommended) at any computer store.

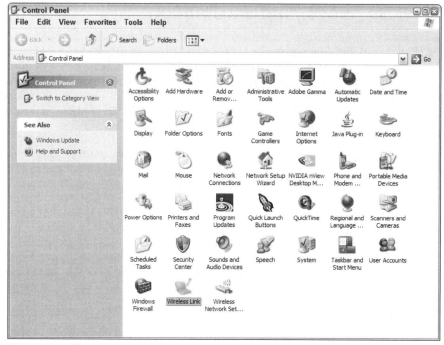

Figure 17-1: The Wireless Link icon in Control Panel

FYI: Infrared Protocols

A *protocol* is a method that computers and devices use to communicate with each other. Windows XP uses several standard wireless protocols that enable infrared devices to communicate with each other. You don't need to remember these, but you might be interested to review what is at work behind the scenes as your computer communicates wirelessly over an Infrared link:

✦ **Wireless Link File Transfer.** Allows you to transfer files over the wireless port.

✦ **Infrared Printing (IrLPT).** Allows you to print to wireless printers using infrared.

✦ **Infrared Image Transfer Protocol (IrTran-P).** Used to transfer digital pictures from a digital camera to your computer.

✦ **Infrared Networking (IrNET and IrCOMM).** IrNET is a point-to-point protocol between two computers, while IrCOMM uses a central infrared hub when several computers need to connect. These protocols are used when several computers need to connect to each other using an infrared connection.

Configuring the Infrared Connection

Infrared wireless connections are generally straightforward to configure and trouble-shoot. You can configure your infrared wireless connection using the Wireless Link icon in Control Panel. If you double-click the icon, The Wireless Link dialog box appears, with three tabs: Infrared, Image Transfer, and Hardware.

The Infrared Tab

On the Infrared tab, shown in Figure 17-2, you have the following options:

✦ **Display an icon on the taskbar indicating infrared activity:** This option allows you to see when you are connected to an infrared link, and when another computer or device is within your infrared range.

✦ **Play sound when Infrared device is near by:** A tone is played when a device first comes into range of your infrared port.

✦ **Allow others to send files to your computer using infrared communications:** If you want to let other devices send files to your computer over the infrared link, make sure that this item is selected. Otherwise, users receive an error message stating that access is denied.

✦ **Notify me when receiving files:** When this item is selected, a Transfer Status dialog box appears when files are being received.

✦ **Default location for received files:** If you choose to receive files, you can configure a default location where those files are stored. Click the Browse button to select the location.

Figure 17-2: The Infrared tab

The Image Transfer Tab

On the Image Transfer tab, shown in Figure 17-3, you can choose to use the wireless link to transfer images from a digital camera to your computer. To do this, enable the option and choose a default storage location for the image files as they arrive. If you choose the "Explore location after receiving pictures" option, the folder in which the pictures are stored automatically opens after you have received the files.

Figure 17-3: The Image Transfer tab

The Hardware Tab

The Hardware tab, shown in Figure 17-4, lists the infrared device that is installed. You can see basic information about the device, such as the manufacturer, COM port location, and the current device status. If you select the device in the window and click the Properties button, either the Device Manager Properties dialog box or the device window opens. You'll see the standard General and Driver tabs.

Using the Infrared Connection

The infrared link is the basic type of infrared connection that you are likely to use. When you create an infrared link, one computer or device can transmit information to another infrared computer or device. You can create a link with Windows XP, Windows 2000, Windows 98, or Windows Me computers. You can also connect to IrDA (infrared enabled) devices, such as printers, digital cameras, keyboards, and PDAs. To establish an infrared link, follow these steps:

1. **Move the infrared computers or devices so that the infrared receivers are facing each other and are within one meter of each other.**

Figure 17-4: The Hardware tab

2. **When the infrared device is detected, an icon appears in your Notification Area, and the Wireless Link icon appears on the desktop.**

3. **Right-click the Wireless Link icon and click Connect.** The connection is made, and data can now be transferred.

Creating an Infrared Network Connection

An infrared network connection provides a direct connection between two infrared computers, over which the two computers can communicate with each other. One computer acts as the host, and one computer acts as the guest, which is similar to a Direct Cable Connection (for more information, see Chapter 16).

This configuration is helpful when one computer needs to access resources on the other computer. The guest computer must have a user account configured on the host computer, just as you would when establishing a direct network connection. The guest computer provides a username and password, after which it can access shared information on the host computer. The guest computer can even map to shared drives and folders, just as you would under a typical network connection. To set up an infrared network connection between two computers, follow these steps:

1. **On the host computer, if you need to, create a user account for the guest computer.**

2. **Align the two computers so that the infrared transceivers are within one meter of each other and are pointing at each other.** The infrared icon appears in the Notification Area, and the Wireless Link icon appears on the desktop.

3. To establish the network connection, open the Network Connections folder in Control Panel, and click Create a New Connection.

4. In the Welcome page, click Next.

5. In the Network Connection Type page, shown in Figure 17-5, choose the "Set up an advanced connection" option. Click Next.

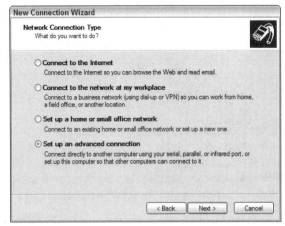

Figure 17-5: Choose the "Set up an advanced connection" option

6. On the Advanced Connection Options page, choose the "Connect directly to another computer" option, as shown in Figure 17-6. Click Next.

Figure 17-6: Choose the "Connect directly to another computer" option

7. **Choose the role of the computer, whether Host or Guest. This example chooses the Host role, as shown in Figure 17-7.** Click Next.

Figure 17-7: Choose the role for the computer

8. **On the Connection Device page, choose the infrared port as the connection device, as shown in Figure 17-8.** Click Next.

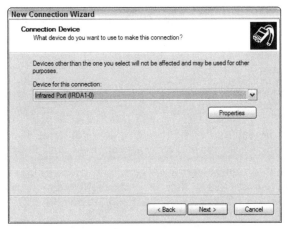

Figure 17-8: Choose the infrared port connection

9. **In the User Permissions page, choose the accounts that can connect over the infrared port, as shown in Figure 17-9.** Click Add if you need to add additional accounts. Click Next.

Figure 17-9: The User Permissions page

10. **Click Finish.** The connection now appears in Network Connections as an "incoming connection."

11. **On the guest computer, repeat this same process, but choose the Guest option.** When the wizard is complete, both computers can open the connection in the Network Connections folder. Click File ➪ Connect to start the infrared network session.

Troubleshooting: Common Infrared Problems

Most of the time, infrared connections are not likely to give you a lot of problems. However, if you're having trouble with the connection, keep these tips in mind:

✦ **Make sure that the infrared transceivers are aligned and close enough to each other for transmission to occur.** Watch the icon in the Notification Area. If it fades in and out, the devices need to be closer or aligned better.

✦ **If you want your digital camera or another computer to send files to your computer, make sure that you have enabled the options on the Wireless Link Properties dialog box.**

✦ **If the transmission seems to work intermittently, access the infrared device's properties in Device Manager. On the IrDA Settings tab, try reducing the maximum connection speed.**

Working with Wi-Fi

Wi-Fi is the *de facto* standard for wireless networking with Windows XP. You'll find that Wi-Fi, also called 802.11b, is a stable and secure network that can provide fast wireless transfer.

Wi-Fi has two different kinds of topologies that you can implement. The first is called Infrastructure mode. In Infrastructure mode, an existing wired LAN is extended to include wireless devices by using a kind of hub called an access point. Although an Infrastructure mode network is also referred to as a *hybrid* because it combines both wireless and wired Ethernet networking components, it is not really a hybrid network because the wired and wireless networks are both Ethernet.

The access point connects to the wired network, and all computers on the wired network communicate with the wireless computers through the access point. In other words, the access point manages all of the traffic between the wireless NICs installed on the computers, as well as any traffic coming to and from the wired LAN. The access point is designed to receive and transmit data over a certain range. If you're creating a new network, you can buy an access point that has both wired Ethernet connections and wireless connectivity—in essence, a hybrid hub and access point. I presently use one of these access points. It was inexpensive, but it provides routing capabilities for my DSL connection.

A second type of wireless connection is called Ad Hoc mode. Ad Hoc mode allows computers to connect directly from one wireless network card to the next without the use of an access point. For example, a collection of wireless networking-enabled computers in a conference room can use Ad Hoc mode to network with each other, and a home without a wired network does not need an access point. However, if you want to access a wired LAN, you need an access point.

You can use both Infrastructure mode and Ad Hoc mode interchangeably because your computer's wireless NIC searches for any and all wireless connections that may be available.

To set up your Wi-Fi network, make sure that you follow the hardware manufacturer's setup instructions and troubleshooting guide, in order to solve problems. Most manufacturers also provide telephone support.

Not all network hardware is created equal. While inexpensive access points can be adequate for most users' needs, and can save cabling costs, choosing the right gear for the task is critical. Inexpensive wireless hardware is typically not designed to provide encryption, routing, and firewall services, nor can it accommodate large numbers of users. For example, a $50 802.11g-access point will fail if you try attaching fifty users that are all trying to move hundreds of megabytes of data across the network using 128-bit encryption and firewall services. Although the radio and network interfaces can probably handle the

traffic, the processor is the "Achilles heel" of inexpensive hardware, and under heavy traffic loads, it is not likely to do well. Just make sure that you do your homework and find out what kind of hardware you need to handle the kind of use that you expect to see. *David Dalan*

By default, 802.11 hardware and Windows XP configure the hardware to automatically look for a wireless network, and the wireless NIC looks for an access point. If no access point is found, the NIC reconfigures itself for Ad Hoc mode and looks for other wireless computers to which it can connect. As the wireless NIC looks for a network to connect to, you'll see a Connect to Wireless Network dialog box, as shown in Figure 17-10. If you don't see the dialog box, then double-click the Wireless Network Connection icon in the Notification Area (lower right portion of your screen next to the clock). If you don't see an icon in the Notification Area, then the wireless NIC is not installed, or there is something wrong with it. If WEP is required, enter the WEP key in the provided dialog box.

Tip

Many laptops actually have an on/off button for the wireless NIC on the keyboard. Make sure that the wireless NIC is turned on before you pull your hair out!

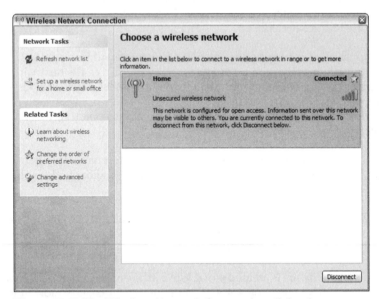

Figure 17-10: The Wireless Network Connection dialog box

Using the Wireless Network Setup Wizard

As a general rule, you should follow your manufacturer's instructions concerning installation and setup. However, you may find that the wireless Network Setup

Wizard helps you to configure the network and to solve potential problems before they begin. SP 2 includes a new Wireless Network Setup Wizard, and the following steps show you how to use it.

1. **Right-click the Wireless Network Connection icon in the Notification Area, and then click View Available Wireless Network.**

2. **In Network Tasks click "Set up a wireless network for a home or small office."** The Wireless Network Setup Wizard appears.

3. **Click Next on the Welcome page.** The Select a Task dialog box appears.

4. **Choose to set up a new wireless network and click Next.**

5. **Type a name for the network and choose how you want to assign network keys, as shown in Figure 17-11.** (The automatic option is recommended). Click Next.

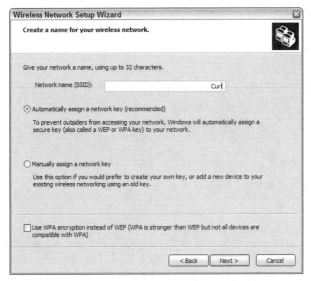

Figure 17-11: Choose the name and configuration options for your wireless network

6. **In the next page, shown in Figure 17-12, choose how you want to set up your network.** You can choose to copy the settings to a flash drive, which you then use to install the settings on other computers, or you can choose to set up each computer manually. Make your decision, and then click Next.

7. **Finish your setup, based on your selection in step 6.**

If you're having problems with your wireless connections, the source of the problem is usually the wrong security information or the wrong wireless channel. You can configure both of these items by accessing the wireless NIC's Properties dialog box. See the next section to learn more about this.

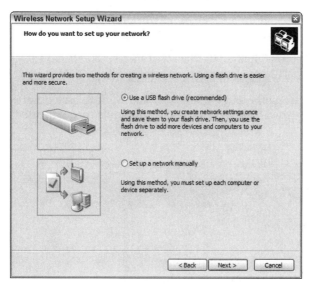

Figure 17-12: Choose how you want to set up the network

FYI: 802.11b Security

Wireless network security is always a concern because the data is "air-borne" and can be easily intercepted by other wireless users. Fortunately, the 802.11b standard provides a high level of security that you can put to work in your wireless network.

The common standard is the Wired Equivalent Privacy, or WEP. WEP is an encryption algorithm that encrypts data as it travels through the air, and that also provides authentication services. You can use a 40-bit encryption key, and some WEP implementations allow up to 104-bit keys. The encryption standard and functions prevent unauthorized access to the network, as well as the theft of data while it is traveling on the wireless network.

In order to communicate with the wireless access point, the client computers must be configured with the correct type of security and channel. If you have problems configuring security on these devices, most 802.11b products have good documentation and Web-site support.

Configuring Wireless Settings

Windows XP does a good job of configuring wireless NICs for access to other NICs or to an access point, and so you typically do not need to configure anything manually unless you are having problems. However, the wireless NIC's Properties dialog box has a Wireless Networks tab where you can manually configure some settings, if necessary. The following steps show you the options and how to configure them.

1. **Open Network Connections and right-click the wireless connection.** Click Properties. You see a General tab, as shown in Figure 17-13.

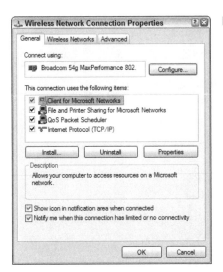

Figure 17-13: The General tab

2. **On the Wireless Networks tab, shown in Figure 17-14, Windows configures the default wireless network settings for you.** This tab contains Available networks and Preferred networks sections. If you need to configure an available network to which you want to connect, select the option in the Preferred Networks list, and then click Properties.

The Properties dialog box appears for the wireless network you selected, as shown in Figure 17-15. By default, the wireless network key and network authentication is enabled. If you need to enter the network key manually, do so in this dialog box, and configure any necessary options. You can check the NIC's documentation for more details. Under most circumstances, the key is provided automatically, and the options here are grayed out. If you are using Ad Hoc mode, then you can disable the settings on this tab by choosing the "This is a computer-to-computer (ad hoc) network; wireless access points are not used" option.

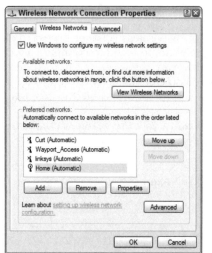

Figure 17-14: The Wireless Networks tab

Figure 17-15: The Properties dialog box for the selected wireless network

3. **On the Wireless Networks tab, in the Preferred networks section, you can reorganize the list if you have more than one network by using the Move up or Move down buttons.** Place the network that you use most often at the top of the list in order to speed up your initial access to that network.

Expert's Notebook: Getting the Most out of Your Gear — High-Gain Antennae

One of the challenges of wireless networking is coverage. Walls, electromagnetic interference, the wireless gear of your neighbor, and distance all complicate your wireless networking experience. One thing that you can do is to invest in additional hardware to create additional access points (APs). This is probably essential if you are supporting large numbers of users. By large numbers, I mean more than 5 to 10 users per access point, assuming that common ($50-$100) APs are being used.

However, if you have few users per AP, then there is a better option: using high-gain antennae. High-gain antennae allow you to increase the reach of your existing hardware. For $20 to $40, you can equip your AP and wireless adapters (if they have external antennae that can be removed) with all of the added strength that you need. Consumer wireless hardware usually comes with a 1- to 2-dBi antenna (dBi is an expression of antenna gain). The replacement gear can easily raise this to 4 to 6dBi. If you really need to extend your reach, there are reasonably priced 12-dBi units. You can really go nuts and purchase costly 24dBi antenna. However, for a large office or location where interference is an issue, 4 to 6dBi should be sufficient, especially if both the network adapters and the APs are using them.

One extremely successful implementation that I am still maintaining uses a series of inexpensive wireless bridges. The central location uses a 9-dBi omni-directional (sprays signal in all directions) antenna, and outlying sites each use a 12-dBi directional (120°-wide signal path) antenna. Before the antennae were used, one location had no signal (I placed the external antenna on a pole to get clear line-of-sight), and the other had an eight to ten percent signal. Both now get a thirty eight to forty two percent signal, and connect at 54 Mbps. The improved net results are due to better antenna performance, more flexible placement options, and higher-quality hardware.

If you are making use of high-gain antennae, and not additional APs, you also save yourself the hassle of trying to connect those additional APs to your network. For about the same price as an additional AP, you can simply increase your output and overcome some typical barriers to wireless networking. High-gain antennae are not ideal for all situations, but they definitely merit consideration in your wireless networking adventures. *David Dalan*

4. **If you only want to connect to access point networks, or you only want to connect to Ad Hoc networks, then click the Advanced button at the bottom of the Wireless Networks tab.** An Advanced dialog box appears, as shown in Figure 17-16. By default, the "Any available network (access point preferred)" option is selected. If you want to restrict the connection to only access points or ad hoc networks, choose the option that you want.

Expert's Notebook: Being a Good Neighbor — Sharing Wi-Fi

If your business is in an area where Wi-Fi usage is high, then you can avoid some headaches by touching base with neighboring businesses. Wi-Fi uses one of eleven channels in the 2.4 GHz or 5 GHz frequency space to transmit, and it is possible that you and your neighbor may end up on the same frequency. This makes both networks operate poorly, if at all. While planning your network (or while troubleshooting), ask neighboring businesses which channels their Wi-Fi gear uses. You can use this information to make sure that you are not using the same channel.

Unfortunately, many people have no idea which channel they are using, especially if they do not have an IT person on staff. In this case, you can use the software, which ships with many aftermarket network adapters, to determine which channel the other user's network is using.

Once you obtain this information, you can eliminate one potential hazard as you are planning your network. You can also eliminate a potential source of interference if you are having trouble with an existing implementation. *David Dalan*

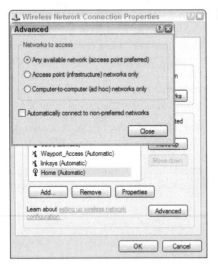

Figure 17-16: Choose a network to access

Virtual Private Networking

By definition, a virtual private network (VPN) is a network that builds secure connections to remote users across an unsecured medium, such as the Internet. In other words, you use a public network to establish a private network connection that is protected from unauthorized users or prying eyes. The end result is that you have a connection that works like a local LAN connection.

For this remote connection to work, data is encapsulated in a manner that allows it to travel the Internet and reach the other VPN host. Encryption ensures that the data on this private network remains private. VPN is extremely useful because a computer with a VPN connection can use virtually any Internet connection to reach the private network.

Creating a Connection to a VPN Server

To create a VPN connection, you need a connection to a VPN server. A VPN server can be an actual computer, or Windows XP can act as a VPN server. This feature allows you to use the Internet to connect one Windows XP computer to another in a remote location. It is helpful to think of a VPN connection as being similar to a dial-up connection. To set up a VPN connection, follow these steps:

Note

Always remember that VPN connections work through the Internet. If your Internet connection is not working, then your VPN connection does not work.

1. **Start the New Connection Wizard found in the Network Connections folder, and then click Next on the Welcome page.**

2. **Click the "Connect to the network at my workplace" option (see Figure 17-17), and then click Next.**

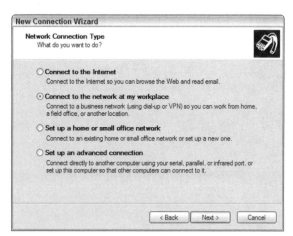

Figure 17-17: Choose a network connection type.

3. **On the next page (Figure 17-18), choose the "Virtual Private Network connection" option, and then click Next.**

4. **Enter a name for the connection, and then click Next.**

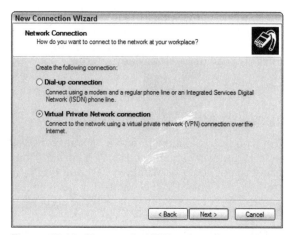

Figure 17-18: Choose the VPN connection option.

5. **On the Public Network page, you can choose to have Windows automatically dial the connection so that the VPN connection can be established, or you can manually dial the connection as needed.** If you are using a broadband connection that is always connected, then choose the "Do not dial the initial connection" option, as shown in Figure 17-19. Make your selection and click Next.

Figure 17-19: The Public Network page

6. **In the "VPN Server Selection" window that appears, enter the fully qualified domain name (FQDN) or IP address of the VPN server to which you will connect.** Click Next.

7. **Click Finish.**

Using Windows XP as a VPN Server

Just as you can allow incoming connections on your Windows XP computer, you can also configure Windows XP to accept VPN connections from remote clients. This process works basically the same as allowing incoming connections. Follow these steps:

1. **Start the Create a New Connection Wizard, found in the Network Connections folder.**

2. **In the New Connection Wizard's Welcome page, click Next.**

3. **In the Network Connection Type page, choose the "Set up an advanced connection" option, as shown in Figure 17-20.** Click Next.

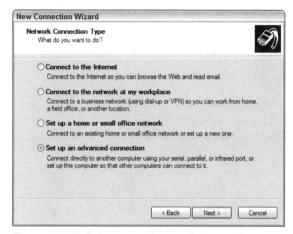

Figure 17-20: Set up an advanced connection.

4. **In the Advanced Connection Options page, choose to accept incoming connections.** Click Next.

5. **In the Devices for Incoming Connections page, choose what hardware will be allowed to accept incoming connections.**

6. **In the Incoming Virtual Private Network (VPN) Connection page (Figure 17-21), choose the "Allow virtual private connections" option, and then click Next.**

7. **In the User permissions page, select the user accounts that are allowed to use a VPN connection.** If the user account does not exist for the client, click New to create one. Click Next.

8. **In the Networking Software page, you can add or remove networking software that can be used over the connection, as shown in Figure 17-22.** This step is helpful if there are some protocols or services that you do not want to use over the VPN connection. Click Next.

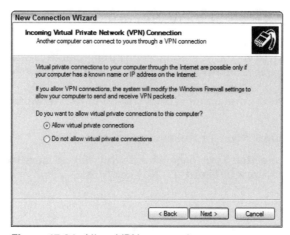

Figure 17-21: Allow VPN connections.

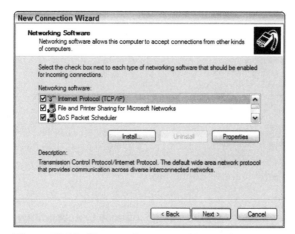

Figure 17-22: Choose the networking software that you want to use.

9. **Click Finish.**

When you set up a VPN, Windows Firewall will automatically enable VPN traffic However, if you are using another firewall solution instead of Windows Firewall, then you need to configure it to allow incoming connections on port 1723. If the firewall uses NAT, then you must configure it to forward VPN traffic to the actual VPN server on the network.

Managing Network Security and Access

18

The big advantage of networking is that you can share resources with other users. The big disadvantage of networking is that you share resources with other users. A paradox? Absolutely. After all, sharing resources is the primary reason for networking in the first place. However, sharing resources opens your computer to possible problems and access issues. For example, you may want some people to access a certain file, while restricting others from accessing the same file. As a result, privacy and protection are very important.

Windows XP gives you everything that you need to effectively share and manage resources on a network. In this chapter, you'll take a look at managing network security on Windows XP, and how to perform related tasks.

Understanding Simple File Sharing

Windows XP includes a file-sharing feature that was not available in previous versions of Windows. This feature, called *Simple File Sharing*, or SFS, is used by default, and it is designed to make file sharing easier for both home and small-office network users. Simple

File Sharing is actually a collection of NTFS settings that govern how Windows XP manages shared files and folders. Because NTFS permissions and settings can be difficult to configure, Simple File Sharing is designed to make sharing among "friendly" computers much easier. Average users can share files and folders and never have to worry about security settings because these settings are configured by default.

When you install Windows XP, or in the case of a default installation or upgrade from Windows 9x, SFS is automatically configured. The SFS configuration creates a collection of shared folders automatically so that you can easily share documents and files with users on other computers, as well as those who have administrative privileges on your local computer. For Administrators on the local computer, all of the files in your user profile are made visible. There is also a shared documents folder that you can use to place shared documents so that any user on your local system can access them. The default location for the shared documents folder is C:\Documents and Settings\All Users\Documents. You can share a folder, or make it private so that no one can access it. If you choose to share the folder, users on your network have read access, but you can change the setting so that users have full control. However, you can't individually manage user access permissions or create other restrictions or privileges with SFS. In other words, SFS is an all-or-nothing approach to sharing, where you can't set different permission levels for different users.

By design, SFS is the only file sharing method available on Windows XP Home edition. This is because with a home or office network, users already trust each other. However, if you use Windows XP Professional edition, and you need access to more security settings and more flexible security, then you can turn off SFS and use NTFS permissions. To turn off SFS, access Folder Options in Control Panel. On the View tab, deselect the SFS check box, as shown in Figure 18-1.

Figure 18-1: You can turn off SFS in the View tab.

Cross-Reference For more information about how to share a resource using SFS, see Chapter 19.

Using Share and NTFS Permissions

NTFS permissions and share-level permissions are advanced sharing features that are available on Windows XP Professional computers. With NTFS, you can share a resource, such as a folder, and specify who on your network can access the folder, as well as what level of permissions they have for that folder. Although assigning permissions allows you a greater level of control, permissions can certainly get out of hand if you don't have a clear vision of what you are trying to accomplish from a security perspective. NTFS permissions can be complicated, and so it is important to assess your security goals first.

Managing File and Folder Permissions with NTFS

You can specify file and folder permissions on the Security tab in the Properties dialog box of the file or folder that you want to share (SFS must be turned off). Simply right-click the file or folder, click Properties, and then click the Security tab, as shown in Figure 18-2. You can select a group or an individual user, and then configure the level of permissions for that file.

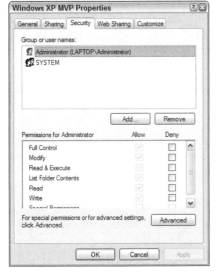

Figure 18-2: The Security tab of the Properties dialog box

The standard permissions are Full Control, Modify, Read & Execute, List Folder Contents, Read, Write, and Special Permissions. You can use the Add button to add a user to the Security tab, and then click the appropriate check boxes to assign the permissions that you want for that user. Each of these permissions is actually made up of a combination of certain special permissions. Before looking at which special permissions make up these standard permissions, let's first consider the special permissions and their definitions, which are described as in Table 18-1.

Table 18-1
Special Permissions and their Definitions

Special Permission	Explanation
Traverse Folder, Execute File	Allows or denies browsing through folders to reach other and affects the ability to run an executable file.
List Folder, Read Data	List Folder allows or denies the viewing of file or subfolder names. Read Data allows or denies reading data in a file.
Read Attributes	Allows or denies the reading of attributes of a file or folder.
Read Extended Attributes	Allows or denies the reading of extended attributes of a file or folder.
Create Files, Write Data	Create Files allows or denies the right to create a file in a particular folder. Write Data allows or denies the creation of new data to a file, or the overwriting of existing information.
Create Folders, Append Data	Create Folders allows or denies the ability to create subfolders in a folder. Append Data allows or denies the appending of data to an existing file (it does not allow the changing of existing data in the file).
Write Attributes	Allows or denies the editing of attributes for a file or folder.
Write Extended Attributes	Allows or denies the writing of extended attributes for a file or folder.
Delete Subfolders and Files	Allows or denies the power to delete subfolders and files within a folder.
Delete	Allows the deletion of a file or folder.
Read	Allows or denies the reading of a file or folder.
Change Permissions	Allows or denies the ability to change permission for a file or folder.
Take Ownership	Allows or denies the power to take ownership of a file or folder.
Synchronize	Allows or denies the power to synchronize data if Offline files are in use.

Standard permissions are combinations of special permissions that allow users or groups of users specific rights. The following list specifies which special permissions are included in which standard permissions.

✦ **Full Control:** Contains all of the special permissions.

✦ **Modify:** Contains the following special permissions:

- Traverse Folder / Execute File
- List Folder / Read Data
- Read Attributes
- Read Extended Attributes
- Create Files / Write Data
- Create Folders / Append Data
- Write Attributes / Write Extended Attributes
- Delete
- Read
- Synchronize

✦ **Read and Execute:** Contains the following special permissions:

- Traverse Folder / Execute File
- List Folder / Read Data
- Read Attributes
- Read Extended Attributes
- Read
- Synchronize

✦ **List Folder Contents:** Contains the following special permissions:

- Traverse Folder / Execute File
- List Folder / Read Data
- Read Attributes
- Read Extended Attributes
- Read
- Synchronize

✦ **Read:** Contains the following special permissions:

- List Folder / Read Data
- Read Attributes

- Read Extended Attributes

- Read

- Synchronize

✦ **Write:** Contains the following special permissions:

- Create Files / Write Data

- Create Folders / Append Data

- Write Attributes

- Write Extended Attributes

- Read

There are two important rules that govern how NTFS permissions work with each other: First, File and Folder permissions are cumulative, and second, Deny permission overrides all other permissions. These rules help you avoid problems, such as when a user is given Read permission to a file, but that same user is also in a group that has been denied that permission.

1. **File and Folder permissions are cumulative.** This means that if a user has Read permission but that same user is a member of a group that has Full Control permission, then the user's effective permission is Full Control. In situations where multiple permissions apply to the same user, then the least restrictive permission takes effect.

2. **Deny permission overrides all other permissions.** This is an exception to the first rule. For example, when a user has Full Control permission but is a member of a group that is denied access, then the user's effective permission is Deny, and therefore the user has no access to the file.

Expert's Notebook: Good Plans = Good Security

With Windows XP you have many tools for managing network security. User accounts, NTFS permissions, firewall settings, diligent system updates, and logging can be combined for a robust solution. Ultimately the effectiveness of your strategy depends on how well you plan before you begin making changes. You need to answer some basic questions: Who needs access? Where will they access the resources from? What services will they need to access those resources? At what times of the day will they access those resources? Once you have answered these general questions, you should build a plan for enabling the network services, as well as for configuring users and file and sharing permissions that you want. Implement according to your plan, and have the user test it. Regularly review configurations and examine system logs for security risks, related errors, or unusual activity. *David Dalan*

Expert's Notebook: "All in the Family" Permissions

Windows XP uses a feature called "inheritance" for shared folders. By default, objects in Windows XP Professional inherit the properties of the parent object. For example, when a particular folder called "Forms" resides in a shared folder called "Public," then by default, the properties and permissions of the Public folder are enforced on the Forms folder, as well. This inheritance behavior keeps you from having to configure folder after folder. Instead, when you configure permissions for the primary folder, all of the sub-folders within the primary folder simply inherit the permissions that you configure. However, there may be times when you need to override this feature, and you can do so in the Advanced Security Settings dialog box. Follow these steps:

1. **Log on as an Administrator.**

2. **Right-click a file or folder, and then click Properties.** Click the Security tab.

3. **Choose a user or a group from the provided list, and then click the Advanced button.** The Advanced Security Settings dialog box appears, as shown in the following figure. The "Inherit from parent the permission entries that apply to child objects..." check box is selected by default.

4. **If you want to override inheritance for this object, deselect the check box option.** Select the user or group in the window for whom you want to change the permissions, and then click the Edit button.

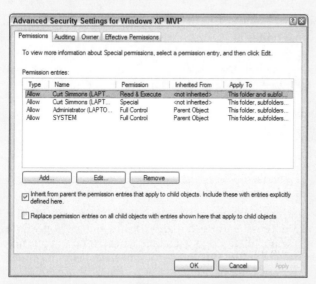

The Advanced Security Settings dialog box

Continued

Continued

5. **In the Permission Entry dialog box that appears (shown in the following figure), click the drop-down menu of the Apply onto box.** Select one of the following: This folder only, This folder, subfolders and files, This folder and subfolders, This folder and files, Subfolders and files only, Subfolders only, Files only.

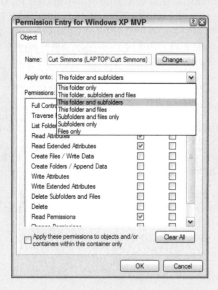

The Object tab in the Permission Entry dialog box

Once you have made your selection, click to select the check box options that you want in order to configure the permissions of the user or group. At the bottom of the page, you can also choose to apply these permissions to objects and/or containers within the existing container. Once you are done, click OK, and then click OK again to leave the Advanced Security Settings dialog box.

Working with Advanced NTFS Permissions

Generally, the standard permissions consisting of Under Full Control, Modify, Read and Execute, List Folder Contents, and Read and Write are all that you will need. Using these permissions, you can effectively manage what users on your network can do with a particular folder or file. However, in some cases, you may need to customize the security settings for a particular user or group. For example, what if you want to give a particular group Full Control to a shared folder without the special permission of Take Ownership? In that case, you must use the advanced NTFS permissions to make the change to the default Full Control settings.

If you select the user on the Security tab, and then click the Advanced button, you'll see an Advanced Security Settings dialog box, as shown in Figure 18-3. From this dialog box, you can see the permissions that are granted, but you can also select a user and click the Edit button to make changes to the general permissions that are already assigned on the Security tab.

Figure 18-3: The Advanced Security Settings dialog box

The Permission Entry dialog box offers you more permissions that you can allow or deny, as shown in Figure 18-4. For example, you can select Full Control here, but then deselect the "Take Ownership" option (found toward the bottom of the list) to restrict the Full Control configuration.

 It is important to remember that advanced permissions offer you an *override* feature that enables you to change the default settings that are normally applied. Although this feature allows you to set specific security settings for a specific purpose, you should not use it too often. If you don't think through permissions carefully, then you can end up causing more problems than you solve, and so you should be careful.

Figure 18-4: The Permission Entry dialog box

Expert's Notebook: Taking Ownership of a File or Folder

NTFS permissions allow you the right of *ownership* when you create a folder and share it on the network. This means that you are the owner of the folder and that you have the right to set permissions on that folder for all other users who might access it. However, you may want to transfer ownership of a folder to another user, or in the case of a local Administrator, you may need to take ownership of a folder from a user who no longer manages it. In either case, Windows XP gives you a way to either transfer the ownership of a file or folder to yourself, or if you are a local Administrator, take ownership. Keep in mind that you can't transfer ownership to someone else once you have forcibly taken it.

If you want to give ownership of a file or folder to another person, you can do so by accessing the special permissions option on the Advanced Security Settings dialog box, as described in the previous sections. Open the Permission Entry dialog box, and grant the Take Ownership permission to the desired user.

If you are an Administrator and you need to forcibly take ownership of a file or folder, follow these steps:

1. **Right-click the folder or file.** Choose Properties.

2. **On the Security tab, click the Advanced button.**

3. **On the Advanced Security Settings dialog box, click the Owner tab.** The Owner dialog box displays the current owner.

4. **Select your account, or another Administrator's account, to change the current owner, and then click OK.** Notice that you can also replace the owner on sub-containers and objects with the folder as well, if the object is a folder.

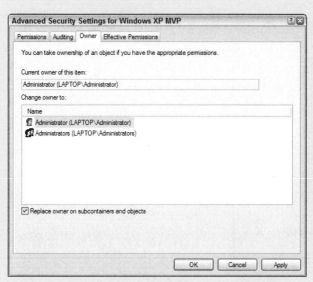

The Owner tab in the Advanced Security Settings dialog box

Share-level Permissions and NTFS Permissions

In addition to NTFS permissions, Windows XP also supports Share-level permissions. Share-level permissions are the only permissions available for shared folders that reside on non-NTFS volumes, such as FAT or FAT32. They are a weaker form of permissions, without all of the advanced options found in NTFS permissions. There are three types of Share-level permissions:

✦ **Read:** The user can view a list of what resides in the shared folder and sub-folders, and can view data and run applications in the shared folder.

✦ **Change:** In addition to being able to do everything provided by Read permissions, the user can also create files and subfolders, and edit existing files. The user can also delete files and subfolders in the share.

✦ **Full Control:** The user can do everything provided by Read and Change, and can also take ownership of the folder and change any existing NTFS permissions.

Share-level permissions can be configured by clicking the Permissions button in the Sharing tab for the folder, as shown in Figure 18-5. This opens a basic dialog box, where you can configure the permission based on a user or a group, as shown in Figure 18-6.

Figure 18-5: The Sharing tab

Figure 18-6: The Share Permissions tab

Like NTFS permissions, a user's cumulative Share-level permissions provide the resulting permission. For example, if a user has Read permission due to one group membership and Full Control from another group membership, then the user has Full Control over that folder. However, when Share-level permissions and NTFS permissions are mixed, the most restrictive permission is applied. For example, a certain folder may have Share-level permissions, but a certain user may have NTFS permissions for that same folder. In this case, the most restrictive permission is applied. As you'll notice, this is the opposite of the cumulative approach of NTFS permissions. Keep these three points in mind:

✦ **NTFS permissions are cumulative:** When a user has several different permissions for the same share, the least restrictive permission applies. The exception is Deny, which overrides all other permissions.

✦ **Share-level permissions are cumulative:** When a user has several different permissions for the same share, the least restrictive permission applies. The exception is Deny, which overrides all other permissions.

✦ **When Share-level permissions and NTFS permissions are combined, the user receives the most restrictive permission.** For example, if a user has Modify NTFS permission for a share, but Read Share-level permission, then the effective permission is Read. As with the other permissions, Deny overrides everything.

Auditing in Windows XP

Auditing is the process of tracking access to a particular folder so that you can see who has accessed resources and what has been done. When you turn on auditing for the desired events, the audit data is recorded to the Security Log, which is available in Event Viewer. Auditing allows you to see how things are accessed, as well as whether there are failed events.

You can audit the following items in Windows XP:

✦ **Account Logon events:** This option audits each instance of a user logging on or off of the system from another computer, where your computer is used to validate the account.

✦ **Account Management:** This option audits account management tasks, such as creating and deleting, or changing users and groups accounts.

✦ **Directory Service Access:** This option audits the access of an Active Directory object that has its own system access control list.

✦ **Logon Events:** This option audits logon events, such as a user logging on or off, or making a network connection to your computer.

✦ **Object Access:** This option audits access to some object in Windows XP, such as a file, folder, registry key, or printer. The object must have its own system access control list.

✦ **Policy Change:** This option audits any local or audit policy change, as well as changes to user rights assignments.

✦ **Privilege Use:** This option can audit each instance of a user exercising a user right.

✦ **Process Tracking:** This option can audit detailed tracking information for different system processes.

✦ **System Events:** This option can audit when a user invokes a system event, such as a restart, shut down, or any other event that affects the system security log or the security log.

Configuring Auditing

In order to configure auditing, you must access the Local Security Settings console. You can access this console by opening Control Panel ⇨ Administrative Tools, and then double-clicking the Local Security Policy console. You can also click Start ⇨ Run, then type **secpol.msc** and then click OK. Either way, the Local Security Settings console opens. Expand Local Polices in the left console pane, and select Audit Policy. The policies appear in the right pane, as shown in Figure 18-7.

Tip

To configure auditing, you must log on as a local computer Administrator. This only applies to Windows XP Professional edition, because Windows XP Home edition doesn't provide a Local Security Settings console, and so you cannot audit events on Windows XP Home edition.

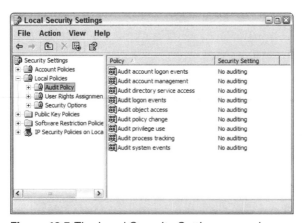

Figure 18-7: The Local Security Settings console

To turn on auditing for a policy, just double-click the policy in the right console pane. For each policy, you can determine whether you want to audit for success, failure, or both, as shown in Figure 18-8. If you audit Logon Events, you probably want to see the failure to logon events in Event Viewer, rather than each successful logon. When you think about auditing, it is best to think about *failure* in this way so that you can see what is not working, rather than every event that does work. To enable the policy, simply click to select the check boxes that you want, and then click OK.

Figure 18-8: The Local Security Setting tab

Setting Up Objects for Auditing

If you want to audit access to objects, you must first enable auditing of objects in the Local Security Settings console (see the previous section). Once you have enabled auditing of object access, you can then configure any file, folder, printer, or other object of auditing. Keep in mind that turning on auditing of object access in the Local Security Settings console simply enables the feature — you must configure each object that you want to audit for auditing. To do so, follow these steps:

1. **Right-click an object, click Properties, and then click the Security tab.** (If you are using SFS, you cannot configure auditing.)

2. **On the Security tab, click the Advanced button.** The Advanced Security Settings dialog box appears.

3. **Click the Auditing tab, as shown in Figure 18-9.**

4. **Click the Add button.** The Select User or Group dialog box appears.

5. **Enter the users and groups that you want to audit for this object, as shown in Figure 18-10.** You can click the Advanced button if you want to choose them from a list. When you are done, click OK. The Auditing Entry dialog box appears, as shown in Figure 18-11.

Figure 18-9: The Auditing tab

Figure 18-10: The Select User or Group
dialog box

6. **Enable the Successful or Failed check boxes for each kind of access that you want to audit on this object.** Click OK when you are done. The entry now appears on the auditing tab.

7. **Click OK, and then click OK again to exit.**

Once you have configured auditing policies, you can view events pertaining to those policies with the Security Log. You can review the Security Log using Event Viewer, which you can access from the Applications folder in Control Panel, or through the Computer Management console. For more information about Event Viewer, see Chapter 33.

Figure 18-11: The Auditing Entry dialog box

Using Disk Quotas

On a home or small-office network, you may decide to use your computer as a storage location, for example, if your small office generates a lot of documents. You can have users store those documents on your Windows XP computer, thus freeing up space on their computers. In other words, Windows XP can act like a file server.

The Disk Quotas feature enables you to control user storage capabilities. This feature is useful when you are using Windows XP as a file server and user storage center, and you want users to store files and folders on the shared hard disk, but you want to limit the available storage space for each user. This feature prevents users from wasting a lot of disk space by storing items that they no longer need. Using Disk Quotas, you can easily configure this restriction. When users begin to run out of storage space, they receive warning messages. Depending on your configuration, users can even be prevented from storing data until they have removed old data, thus keeping them below the limit that you set. As you can imagine, Disk Quotas can be very helpful in a variety of circumstances, and they can help to force users to conserve disk space when users are storing files on local computers.

Note

Disk Quotas management only works on NTFS volumes. Also, users cannot compress data in order to store more than their quota limits.

Disk Quotas are available on the Quota tab on the disk's Properties dialog box. You can enable the Disk Quota management on the Quota tab by clicking the "Enable quota management" check box, as shown in Figure 18-12.

Figure 18-12: The Quota tab

If you enable quota management on this tab, you can then do the following:

✦ **You can deny disk space.** You can use quota management to deny disk space to users who exceed the quota limit, or to warn users that they are running out of storage space without actually denying them disk space. If you want to strictly enforce quota management, you can choose the deny option by clicking this check box.

✦ **You can set the amount of disk space that a user can have in the quota, and set a warning level.** The warning level is generally an amount that is slightly lower than the quota. Once the warning level is met, the event is logged in the Event Log.

✦ **You can use the final two check boxes to log events to the Event Log when users exceed their storage limits or reach the warning level.** These options are not selected by default.

Once quotas are enabled on a disk, they apply uniformly to all network users who store data on the disk. However, what if you need an exception? What if you need to give certain users unlimited access, while giving other users more restrictive access? In this case, you can create a quota entry for specific users. A quota entry further defines the user or groups quota and overrides any existing general settings that are configured on the Quota tab.

To configure a quota entry, just follow these steps:

1. **On the Quota tab, click the Quota Entries button.** This opens the Quota entries window, as shown in Figure 18-13.

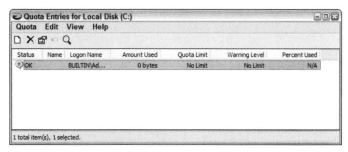

Figure 18-13: The Quota Entries window

2. **Click Quota ⇨ New Quota Entry.** This opens a Select Users window, where you can search for and select the user that you want to add.

3. **When you have selected the user, click OK.** The Add New Quota Entry dialog box appears, as shown in Figure 18-14.

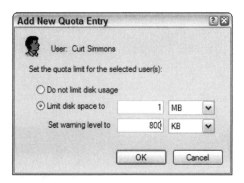

Figure 18-14: The Add New Quota Entry dialog box

4. **You can choose to not limit disk space, or you can set the quota and warning level for that particular user.** This feature offers you flexibility for users who need more storage space. The new entry now appears in the Quota Entries window.

5. **You can edit and change the entry at any time using this console.**

Sharing Resources

19

When you stop and think about it, the only purpose for networking is to share resources. Whether it is your home or small office network, the Internet, e-mail, or any other online resources that you can access, the purpose of all networking is to share information and data in one way or another.

With a home or small office network, you can easily share resources so that other users on the network can access those resources. You can share all kinds of items, from files to an Internet connection. In this chapter, you'll explore the sharing process, and see how to effectively share and manage resources on your network.

Considering NTFS Security and Simple File Sharing

If you're using Windows XP Professional, then you have the option of using either NTFS security or Simple File Sharing on your network. If you're using Windows XP Home Edition, then you are limited to Simple File Sharing, and so you can safely skip this section.

In This Chapter

Sharing Folders and Drives

Sharing Printers

Sharing an Internet Connection

It is important that you decide what kind of security you want to use on your home or small office network before you start sharing resources. NTFS Security is much stronger and gives you more sharing options for controlling users. However, Simple File Sharing is easier to use and you won't have to worry about complicated permissions issues. As you think about NTFS Security and Simple File Sharing, make sure that you have read Chapter 18, and think about the following questions before you start sharing resources:

- ✦ **How much security do you need?** In other words, if you share resources, is it imperative that you carefully control what users can and cannot do with the shared resources? If so, then you should use NTFS Security.

- ✦ **Do you want to make things as easy as possible with basic security controls in place?** If so, then you should use Simple File Sharing.

- ✦ **Are you sharing sensitive information that you want to keep certain people from viewing?** If so, then you should use NTFS Security.

- ✦ **Are you using a home network where security isn't a big issue?** If so, then you should use Simple File Sharing.

In the end, the decision concerning NTFS Security and Simple File Sharing is all about control. If you need a particular level of control over your resources so that you can control what people can and cannot do with those resources, use NTFS Security. However, for simple sharing and access, Simple File Sharing is sufficient.

Sharing a Folder or a Drive

When you share items on a network, you'll likely place those items in a folder and then share that folder. A shared folder can contain any resource that you want to share, including different files, printers, and even shared applications. Just as shared folders enable you to keep things organized on your computer, they also enable you to organize what you want to share. For example, on my office network, most of my shared files are placed in a single folder with different subfolders. This way, when others need to access a file, they only have to access a single folder in order to browse several shared folders. Using Windows XP Professional, you can either share folders through Simple File Sharing (SFS), or you can share folders and set permissions using NTFS permissions. You can also configure how shared network documents are cached on the user's computer, and you can share an actual drive as well. The following sections address these issues.

Sharing a Folder

Sharing a folder is quick and easy if you are using SFS. Just follow these steps:

1. **Access the Properties dialog box.** You can share any folder by simply accessing the folder's Properties dialog box. To share a folder, simply right-click the folder, click Properties, and then click the Sharing tab.

2. **Select a security option.** As shown in Figure 19-1, the Sharing tab has two types of security options when you use SFS: local sharing and network sharing. If you only want to share a folder with users of your local computer, then you need to drag the folder to the Shared Documents folder that is available in Windows XP. When a user logs on to the computer, the Shared Documents folder is available to the user, and anything stored in the folder is also available.

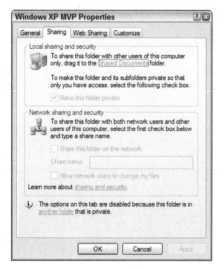

Figure 19-1: The Sharing tab

3. **Decide whether you want the folder to be private:** You can make the folder private by clicking the "Make this folder private" option. If you choose this option, there are a few issues you should consider. First, when you choose the option, no one else that uses your computer will be able to access the private folder. However, the configuration only applies to folders within your user profile. In other words, you can't make an application folder private. Also, when you use the private option, all files and subfolders within the private folder are also private. You can't individually manage subfolders and files for privacy purposes. Finally, if you later decide to move the private folder to another folder, the folder then inherits whatever settings are configured on the target folder.

4. **Share the folder.** To share the folder on the network, click the "Share this folder on the network" option, and then enter a share name. To stop a folder from being shared, simply deselect this check box. If you want network users to be able to change files in the folder, just click the "Allow network users to change my files" option.

Expert's Notebook: Managing Shared Folders with the Computer Management Console

You can also use Computer Management's Shared folder feature to manage shared connections. In this console, you can see how many users are connected to a particular shared folder and view open files. You can also forcefully disconnect sessions from this console. The following steps show you how to use the Computer Management console.

1. **Log on as an Administrator.**

2. **Open Control Panel ⇨ Administrative Tools ⇨ Computer Management.**

3. **In the Computer Management console, shown in the following illustration, expand Shared folders.** You can then view the shares, sessions, and open files. To close sessions and open files, right-click Sessions or Open Files in the left console pane, and choose either Disconnect all Sessions, or Disconnect all Open Files.

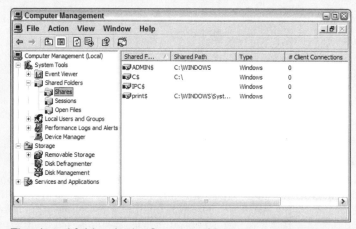

The shared folders in the Computer Management console

4. **Close the console when you're done.**

When you turn SFS off using the folder options, the Sharing tab changes, and a Security tab appears on the folder's Properties dialog box, as shown in Figure 19-2. You can choose to share the folder, give the folder a name and comment, limit the number of users who can connect at any given time, and configure permissions and caching functions. You can learn more about the security settings in Chapter 18. The next section examines caching functions.

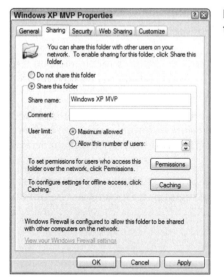

Figure 19-2: The Sharing tab with SFS turned off

Managing Caching Settings on Shared Folders

When a folder is shared on a network, you have the option to configure a caching level for the information in that folder. This feature enables network documents to be stored locally on the user's computer in a *cache*, which is a temporary storage location. The benefit of this feature is better network performance. This is because cached files are stored locally, and so less information needs to traverse the network. However, caching is not a great tool for user information that changes frequently.

To configure caching settings, follow these steps:

1. **Right-click the shared folder and click Properties.** Return to the Sharing tab and click the Caching button. The Caching Settings dialog box appears, as shown in Figure 19-3.

Figure 19-3: The Caching Settings dialog box

2. **Enable caching.** To enable caching, click the "Allow caching of files in this shared folder option," and choose one of the three options from the Setting drop-down menu. The options are:

   - **Automatic caching of documents:** This option is recommended for folders containing user documents. They are automatically downloaded and made available when working offline.

   - **Automatic caching of programs and documents:** This option is recommended for folders with read-only data or applications that are run over a network. Opened files are automatically downloaded and made available offline.

   - **Manual caching of documents:** Users must specify any files that they want to make available when working offline. Documents are not automatically downloaded.

3. **Click OK.**

Sharing a Drive

Just as you can share a folder, you can also share a drive on your computer. This includes hard disks as well as removable drives, such as CD/DVD and USB flash drives. Keep in mind that when you share a drive, you give everyone permission to everything on that drive. As with anything on a network, always think carefully before you act.

To share a drive, simply access the drive's Properties dialog box and click the Sharing tab. You'll see the same sharing tab as if you were sharing a folder, as shown in Figure 19-4.

Figure 19-4: The Sharing tab

When you click the Sharing tab, you may see a message telling you that sharing a drive is not recommended, but that you can click a link if you want to share the drive anyway. This message is just an additional security feature of Windows XP, to ensure that you understand the balance between the security risks and your personal needs for sharing the drive.

Sharing a Printer

On your home or small office network, sharing a printer is likely to be one of the more important networking functions. After all, when you share a printer, you can save hardware resources by letting each computer on the network connect to the shared printer, instead of using separate printers. Shared printers work well in Windows XP networks. The following sections show you how to access, share, and manage shared printers.

Sharing a Printer and Managing Permissions

You can configure a LAN printer when you install the printer using the Add a Printer Wizard, or you can share the printer later, once installation is complete. To configure sharing after installation is already complete, access the printer's Properties dialog box and click the Sharing tab, as shown in Figure 19-5. Click the Share this printer option and enter a share name in the text box.

It is helpful to use a descriptive name for the shared printer. Although your default computer name will appear as the share name, you should give the printer a name that clearly identifies it to users.

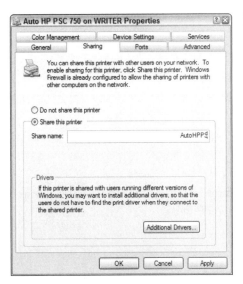

Figure 19-5: The Sharing tab

FYI: Internet Printing

You can also configure a printer for Internet or intranet access. This feature enables users to print to a URL and to open a printer from Internet Explorer. To configure a printer so that you can access it through a URL, you must install Internet Information Services (IIS) on your Windows XP computer. You can install IIS from Windows Components in Add/Remove Programs. When IIS is installed, the printer is automatically made available through Web services when you share the printer. You can think of the Internet printing options as just another way for users to access the shared printer, which is helpful in the case of intranet printing. All permissions and related configurations apply to an Internet printer as they do for a standard printer.

If you have network clients using systems other than Windows XP or 2000, you can also use this tab to install additional drivers. When a down-level computer wants to connect to the printer, Windows XP downloads the drivers to that computer so that the printer can be used. If you click the Additional Drivers button, a list of options appears, as shown in Figure 19-6. Simply click the check box next to the drivers that you want to install, and then click OK. You may be prompted to insert your Windows XP CD-ROM or to provide the driver that you want to make available. You can usually obtain down-level drivers from the manufacturer's Web site.

Figure 19-6: The Additional Drivers dialog box

Connecting to a Shared Printer

You can easily connect to a network printer by using the Add a Printer Wizard in the Printers and Faxes folder. Follow these steps:

1. **Open the Printers and Faxes folder in Control Panel.** Click the Add a Printer Wizard. The Add a Printer Wizard, shown in Figure 19-7, appears.

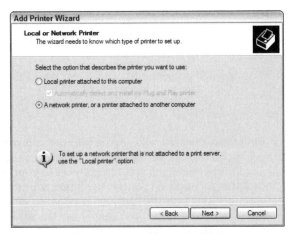

Figure 19-7: The Local or Network Printer page

2. **In the Welcome screen, click Next.**

3. **In the Local or Network Printer page, click the "A network printer, or a printer attached to another computer" option, and then click Next.** In the Specify a Printer page, shown in Figure 19-8, you have a few different options. When you select an option and follow the directions below, the printer is installed on your computer.

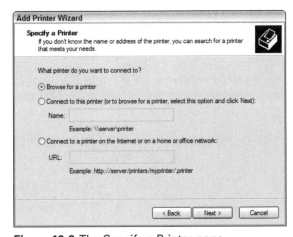

Figure 19-8: The Specify a Printer page

- **Browse for a printer.** If you click this option and then click Next, you see a selection window. You can select a shared network printer and click Next to install it.

- **Connect to this printer.** If you know the Universal Naming Convention (UNC) path (such as *servername**printername*) of the printer to which you want to connect, then click this radio button option, and enter the path. Make your selection, and then click Next.

4. **The Test Page window appears.** If you want to print a test page, choose Yes, and then click Next.

5. **Click Finish.**

Windows XP also supports printing to a print device on the Internet. Internet printing allows you to have remote access to a printer, such as if your business operates out of two different locations. Using Internet printing, you can connect to your remote location and print to a printer at that location. Of course, the Internet printer has to be configured to provide Internet printing (see the previous section for more information). If you want to connect to an Internet printer, you simply use the Add a Printer Wizard, as shown in the following steps.

1. **Open the Printers and Faxes folder in Control Panel.** Click the Add a Printer Wizard.

2. **In the Welcome screen, click Next.**

3. **In the Local or Network Printer page, select the "A network printer, or a printer attached to another computer" option, and then click Next.**

4. **In the Specify a Printer page, choose the option to connect to a printer on the Internet, and then enter the URL of the printer, as shown in Figure 19-9.**

5. **Click Next and then click Finish.**

Figure 19-9: Locate the Internet printer to which you want to connect.

Once the printer is set up, you can then print to it as you would a local printer. If you have more than one printer configured, you'll see a selection screen that allows you to choose the printer to which you want to print, as shown in Figure 19-10.

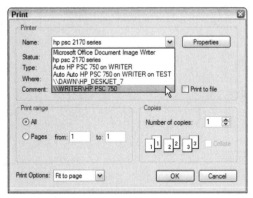

Figure 19-10: The Print dialog box

Although you can follow the same steps if you need to print to an Internet printer, you can also connect to an Internet printer using Internet Explorer 4.0 or later. If you know the URL, simply enter it in the Address bar. If you do not know the URL, then enter the server's name, followed by **/printers**, to see a listing of Internet printers on that server. Once you locate the printer that you want, you can click the Connect button. Windows XP will copy the necessary drivers, and the new printer will appear in your Printers and Faxes folder. This allows you to use a Web browser to access the Internet printer, rather than using the Add a Printer Wizard to set it up.

Managing Permissions

Like any other shared resource, you can manage a shared printer by using permissions. If you are using SFS, then there is nothing else for you to configure in terms of permissions. However, if you are using NTFS permissions, you can place restrictions on users in much the same way as a shared folder. Naturally, the permissions that you can grant or deny are a bit different for shared printers.

In order to modify the permissions for a printer, you need to access the Security tab of the printer's Properties dialog box, as shown in Figure 19-11. There are three primary permissions that you can assign concerning printing:

✦ **Print:** This allows a user to print to a printer.

✦ **Manage Printers:** This allows a user to open the printer's Properties dialog box and to configure options.

✦ **Manage Documents:** This allows a user to open the print queue and to manage documents.

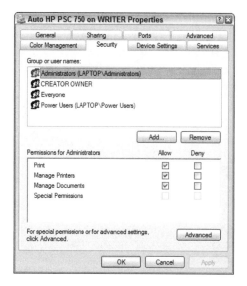

Figure 19-11: The Security tab in the Properties dialog box

In Windows XP, local Administrators are given all three permissions. The Creator or Owner is given the Manage Documents permission, everyone is given the Print permission, and Power Users are given all three permissions. Obviously, most users in your environment will have Print permission for the printer, while only a select few will be given the Manage Printers and Manage Documents permissions.

You can also click the Advanced button to view a listing of permission entries for particular groups, as shown in Figure 19-12. For more information about advanced permissions, see Chapter 18.

Managing Print Queues

The print queue is the holding area that the computer uses for documents that are either currently printing or waiting to be printed. If you have permissions to access the print queue on a Windows XP computer, then you can double-click the printer icon in the Printers and Faxes folder, or you can click the printer icon that appears in the Notification Area when items are being printed. You must have permission to open, view, and modify the print queue. If you do not, then either an access denied message appears if you try to open the printer in the Printers and Faxes folder, or you will not see a printer icon in the Notification Area.

The print queue displays a listing of documents that are printing or are waiting to be printed, as shown in Figure 19-13.

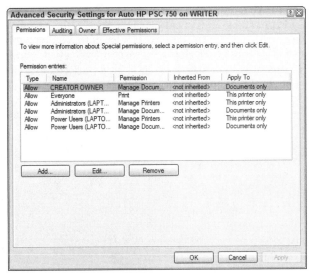

Figure 19-12: The Permissions tab in the Advanced Security Settings dialog box

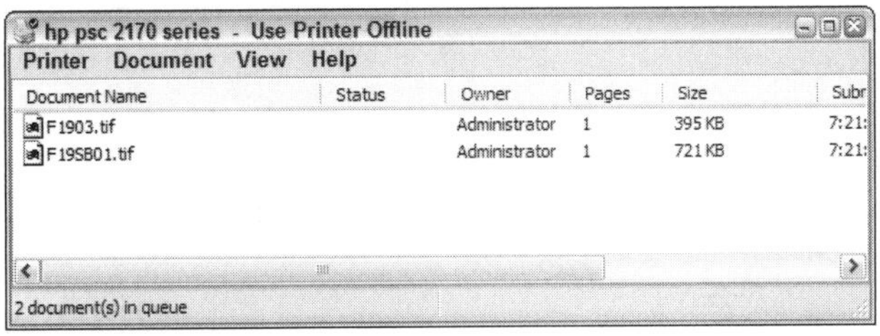

Figure 19-13: The print queue

You can manage the print queue in a few different ways. You can click Printer in the menu bar and then choose Pause Printing or Cancel all Documents. The pause feature is useful when you need to perform maintenance on the printer without deleting everything that is waiting in the queue. You can select Document in the menu bar to manage individual documents. For example, you can select a document and then click Document to display the Document menu, where you can Pause, Resume, Restart, or Cancel printing of the document. These features can be helpful if a document seems to be stuck in the queue—you can cancel it to allow the other documents to resume printing. You can also perform these same actions by simply right-clicking the document icon in the print queue.

You can make a few adjustments to a document's printing by right-clicking the document and then clicking Properties. As you can see in Figure 19-14, a standard Properties dialog box appears, with several tabs. In the General tab, you can change the priority of the document in the queue. Under most circumstances, documents are set to a priority of 1. For example, you may want to print a particular document first, even though there are several documents ahead of it in the print queue. To change the priority, access the document's Properties dialog box and change the priority setting to Highest — this will ensure that the document prints first, assuming no other documents have a Highest setting.

Figure 19-14: The General tab in the Properties dialog box

Sharing an Internet Connection

Internet Connection Sharing (ICS) enables you to have one computer connected to the Internet, with all other computers on the network sharing the Internet connection. This feature is specifically designed for home networks or small office networks with ten or fewer computers. With ICS, you only need one Internet connection and one piece of connection hardware — each computer does not need its own modem or broadband hardware, such as a cable modem or DSL connection. Through sharing, you save money and aggravation because you don't have to configure each computer for Internet use.

However, while ICS is still useful for the home and small office user, its importance has diminished over the past several years. When you use ICS, all computers connect through one host computer, which is then connected to the Internet. However, because of the popularity of networking routers, you can easily connect all of your computers to the Internet through the router, which holds the Internet connection. For example, my home-office network contains five computers that are wired to a hybrid router. I also have a wireless laptop that connects to this router. My DSL connection is connected directly to the router, and so the Internet is always available, regardless of which computer may be turned on at the moment. When ICS first appeared with Windows 98, routers were not that popular for the home and small office user. Because routers provide you with more flexibility, I highly recommend that you use one of them rather than ICS.

Tip

A major drawback with ICS is that one computer is the "sharing" computer. Therefore, that computer must be turned on at all times in order for the Internet to be available to all of the other computers on the network.

When you use ICS, your Windows XP computer should be the ICS *host.* All other computers on your network, called ICS *clients*, access the host to get information from the Internet. As a result, all Internet communications flow from your home network to the host computer and then to the Internet, and vice versa. Using this setup, your host computer has a connection to the Internet and a connection to your home network. All of the client computers need only a network adapter so that they can connect to the host. As far as the Internet is concerned, it only appears as though one computer is accessing the Internet. You don't have to use the Windows XP computer as the host—you can use a different computer, such as a Windows Me system. Keep in mind that you will have fewer operational problems if the Windows XP computer is the ICS host.

Once you have all of your hardware, and your computers are connected to each other, you can run the Home Networking Wizard, which sets up home networking on your computers. The Home Networking Wizard is supported only on computers using Windows 98, Windows Me, or Windows XP. The following steps guide you through the Home Networking Wizard.

1. **Turn on all of the computers on your home network so that they are all booted and operational.**

2. **On your Windows XP computer, click Start ⇨ All Programs ⇨ Accessories ⇨ Communications ⇨ Network Setup Wizard.**

3. **Read the information on the Welcome screen and then click Next.** The next page gives you more information about home networking.

4. **Make sure that you have completed the preparation tasks listed, and then click Next.** The Select a connection method page appears, as shown in Figure 19-15.

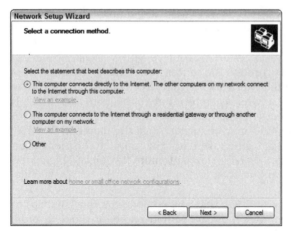

Figure 19-15: The Select a connection method page

5. **Click the radio button for the option that best describes how the Windows XP computer connects to the Internet.** This example assumes that the Windows XP computers connect to the Internet, and the other computers on your network connect to the Windows XP computer.

6. **Click Next**. The Internet Connection page appears.

7. **In the box listing all entries in your Network Connections folder, select your connection to the Internet; then click Next.** If you're using a dial-up connection, then the wizard prompts you to dial a connection to the Internet.

8. **In the provided window, enter a description for your computer and a computer name.** Keep in mind that if you are using a cable broadband connection to the Internet, you should probably not change the name of your computer, because the Internet Service Provider (ISP) may require a certain name.

9. **Review the changes that will be made to your computer, and then click Next.** Windows XP automatically configures all of your computer's software and hardware components for networking, according to the selections you made when running the wizard.

10. **Click Finish.** You will need to restart the computer for the new changes to take effect.

Once you have run the Home Networking Wizard on the Windows XP computer, you need to run the wizard on each computer that you want to include in the home network. You can use your Windows XP CD-ROM to run the Home Networking Wizard on those computers.

Configuring and Using Remote Desktop and Remote Assistance

20

A s networks have grown and developed over the years, the need for remote networking has become more important. Remote networking has actually existed for years, and if you have ever used Windows servers, you may be familiar with Terminal Services, and the functions of "dumb" desktops that work with a server. With Windows XP, remote networking is much more complicated, but the concept of Terminal Services can still be applied to Windows XP through some newer features, called Remote Desktop and Remote Assistance. These features are useful in a variety of ways. You can connect to an office computer from home, or vice versa. You can help a friend, relative, or colleague solve computer problems, and generally access computers without sitting in front of them. In this chapter, you'll see how to configure and use these important features.

Enabling Remote Desktop

Remote Desktop is a feature that enables you to connect with a remote desktop and use the desktop as though you were physically sitting at the computer. The Remote Desktop feature can be helpful to you in a variety of ways. For example, you may have an office desktop computer, and when you are home from work, you may need to print some documents at home. You can do this when your office computer is turned on and configured for Remote Desktop. You can then use your home computer to connect to it and access your documents. Remote Desktop can also be used in office environments so that users can access another computer for which they have an account.

You can easily enable the Remote Desktop feature on your Windows XP computer so that others can connect to it, if you are currently logged on as the computer's Administrator. Access System Properties in the Control Panel and click the Remote tab. As you can see in Figure 20-1, you can enable both Remote Assistance and Remote Desktop on this tab.

Figure 20-1: The Remote tab on the System Properties dialog box

Once you have enabled Remote Desktop, there are two issues that you should address. The first is a user account. The second issue that you should address is Windows Firewall:

◆ **User account:** The remote computer must log onto your computer with a username and password, just as if you were actually sitting at the local computer. When you log on locally, you can use a blank password, but the remote desktop connection requires a password. As a result, you should think about the account that you will log on with and ensure that a password is configured for the account. You may also consider creating a specific Remote Desktop account to use just for the Remote Desktop connection.

◆ **Windows Firewall:** By default, Windows Firewall will not pass Remote Desktop traffic. However, because of updates in Service Pack 2, when you choose to enable Remote Desktop on the Remote tab, Windows Firewall is automatically configured to allow Remote Desktop traffic.

Once you have enabled Remote Desktop, the next thing that you need to do is to determine which users are allowed to connect from a remote location. For example, you may use Windows XP Professional at your office, and three other people may use that computer with Limited accounts. You may also want to ensure that only your account can connect remotely. You can do this by specifying which users can connect to the remote computer. Click the Select Remote Users button on the Remote tab of the System Properties dialog box. Then click the Add button on the Remote Desktop Users dialog box, as shown in Figure 20-2. A Select Users dialog box appears. Enter the user account to which you want to give permission, or click the Advanced button and select the user from a list. When you're done, click OK.

Figure 20-2: The Remote Desktop Users dialog box

Note   Although you can choose which accounts can connect to the remote computer, keep in mind that Administrator accounts can connect, even if you do not select them. In other words, the Administrator automatically has Remote Desktop rights. Also, keep in mind that blank passwords are not allowed. Accounts that will be used to access the remote desktop must use an actual password.

FYI: Making the Connection

To use Remote Desktop, you must first connect to the remote computer. How you make the connection depends on the type of connection that you have available, and other related issues. Here are a few scenarios to consider.

✦ **Connecting over a LAN or WAN:** This is the easiest way to connect. The client computer uses the host computer's IP address DNS name to make a direct connection. No additional configuration is required. For a business LAN or WAN that cannot connect with another LAN or WAN segment, seek help from your Network Administrator.

✦ **Connecting Using a Dial-up Connection:** You generally use this scenario when your work computer resides in a small office and has a modem. To access your work computer from a home computer, you must first use the Create a New Connection Wizard on your work computer to configure it to accept incoming calls. Then, from your home computer, you must configure a dial-up connection to dial the work computer's number. You can then dial the work computer directly and create a Remote Desktop session.

✦ **Connecting Using the Internet:** This process is a little complicated. When a computer connects to the Internet, whether via modem, cable, or DSL, the ISP assigns it a new dynamic IP address each. You must use this address to make the Remote Desktop connection; however, the public IP address changes frequently. There is no direct workaround for this issue; the simple fact is that you must know the IP address of the computer to connect to it. To find the public IP address, connect to the Internet, and then double-click the connection in Network Connections. When you click the Details tab, you'll see the current public IP address. You can then use this IP address to connect to the host from the client computer. For a dial-up connection, you must leave the host computer connected to the Internet to connect to the Remote Desktop.

✦ **Connecting over a Firewall:** Internet Firewalls cause difficulties for Remote Desktop connections because, by default, most firewalls do not allow Remote Desktop traffic. If the host computer resides on a LAN that is protected by a firewall, or if another individual firewall product is used, an Administrator must configure the firewall to allow incoming access on TCP port 3389. This is because Remote Desktop uses TCP port 3389, and the connection will fail if the firewall is not configured to allow incoming access on this port.

✦ **Connecting through a Remote Access Server:** To a Remote Desktop host over the Internet and through a remote access server, you should use a Virtual Private Network (VPN) connection. This connection gives you the most security when using the Remote Desktop host over the Internet. An Administrator must configure the remote access server to allow VPN traffic. Once connected, you start the Remote Desktop session with the host by simply connecting to it using the host's IP address.

Configuring the Remote Desktop Client Computer

Once you have enabled Remote Desktop on the host computer, you can then configure the remote computer to connect to the host. If the remote computer is running the Windows XP Professional or Home edition, then there is nothing that you need to install. The Remote Desktop connection software is already built-in and ready to use. However, if you are using an earlier version of Windows, you'll need to install the Remote Desktop connection software. This software, called Remote Desktop Client, is found on your Windows XP Professional or Home edition installation CD-ROM. You can also download it directly from www.microsoft.com/windowsxp/pro/downloads /rdclientdl.asp. The Remote Desktop Client software will work with any version of Windows 95, Windows 98, Windows Me, Windows NT, or Windows 2000.

To install the software from your Windows XP CD-ROM, just insert the CD-ROM and click the Perform Additional Tasks option on the Welcome screen. Then choose the Remote Desktop Connection option that appears and follow the instructions.

Making a Remote Desktop Connection

Once you have configured the host computer and the remote computer (if necessary), you are ready to make the Remote Desktop connection. On the remote computer, click Start ⇨ All Programs ⇨ Accessories ⇨ Communications ⇨ Remote Desktop Connection. In the Remote Desktop Connection dialog box that appears, shown in Figure 20-3, you can enter the name of the computer that you want to connect to if the computer resides on your local area network. If you are connecting over the Internet, then enter the TCP/IP address of the computer that you want to connect to, and click the Connect button.

Figure 20-3: The Remote Desktop Connection dialog box

When the connection is made, you are presented with a standard Windows dialog box where you can enter a username and password, and then click OK. Once you log in, you can use the host computer just as if you were physically there.

Troubleshooting: Conflicts with Other Users

If you are trying to connect to your work computer from a remote location, but another user is logged on to the work computer and using it when you try to log on, there are two basic rules that apply:

✦ **If Fast User Switching is enabled on the remote computer, the remote user sees a dialog box telling them that you need access.** The remote user can then give you access, which logs the remote user off until you are done. The remote user can also reject your request, which keeps you from logging on. If the remote user allows you to log on, then they will see the Welcome screen and will have to wait until you are done. However, the remote user has more control and can simply log in again at any time, thus disconnecting your remote session.

✦ **If Fast User Switching is not enabled on the remote computer, the remote user sees a dialog box telling them that you are about to log in.** If you log in before the remote user saves or opens any files, they will lose that work.

Managing Remote Desktop Performance

If you are using Remote Desktop over a LAN, DSL, or cable connection, then Remote Desktop performance may not be much of an issue. However, if you are using a dial-up connection from your home computer to your office, then downloading all of your remote computer's graphics and other desktop features can be time consuming. Remote Desktop can give you some options to help you use less bandwidth, thus giving you better performance. On the Remote Desktop Connection dialog box, you can click the Options button, and then access the Experience tab to select a connection speed. Depending on your selection, the performance options will change. For example, if you are using a modem, the desktop background is not displayed because it tends to use a lot of bandwidth.

Click Start ➪ All Programs ➪ Accessories ➪ Communications ➪ Remote Desktop Connection. In the Remote Desktop dialog box, click the Options option. You can choose the speed of your connection, as shown in Figure 20-4. If you choose a modem speed from the drop-down menu, then certain Remote Desktop features are not used. The default settings provided to you are just suggestions; you can change any of them by enabling or disabling the check boxes. You may need to experiment with these settings to find the ones that work for you. However, you should always leave bitmap caching enabled because it helps to speed up your connection. This feature allows images to be saved in your local cache so that they can be reused during the session, instead of your computer having to download them individually each time.

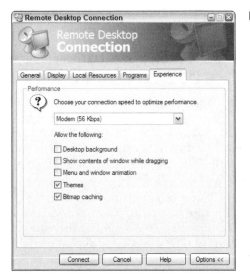

Figure 20-4: The Experience tab

Configuring the Display

The Display tab, shown in Figure 20-5, allows you to modify the options for the window that contains the remote session. The supported resolutions range from 640×480 to full screen. You may also specify the color depth for the connection, as well as whether or not to display the connection bar when in full screen mode. The connection bar simply allows you to see the name or address of the computer that is hosting the session, and to minimize or close the window.

Figure 20-5: The Display tab

Configuring Local Resources

The Local Resources tab, shown in Figure 20-6, allows you to configure some of the newer features that are available with Remote Desktop. Three categories of options are available—Remote computer sound, Keyboard, and Local devices:

✦ **The Remote computer sound section:** You can specify one of three options: Leave at remote computer, Do not play, and Bring to this computer. The last option refers to the Remote Desktop computer. Depending on your choice, Windows event sounds can be heard during your remote session. Keep in mind that sounds also increase bandwidth, and so you may want to choose the "Do not play" option if bandwidth is an issue.

✦ **The Keyboard section:** This section allows you to use keyboard strokes (such as Alt+tab) so that they will operate when the remote session is open. You can configure the special key commands to work only on the remote computer, only on the local computer, or only when in full screen mode.

✦ **The Local devices section:** This section enables you to map the client's disk drives, printers, and serial ports to the Remote Desktop host. For example, you may be connected to your work computer from a home computer, and need to print a document from your work computer to your home computer's printer. The "Printers" option allows you to do that. When you want to access information stored on drives on your local computer while in the Remote Desktop session, the "Disk drives" option makes your disk drives appear in the My Computer window of the remote computer so that you can access them.

Figure 20-6: The Local Resources tab

Configuring Programs

The Programs tab, shown in Figure 20-7, can be used to launch a specific program when the user connects to the Remote Desktop host. In some cases, users will want to launch processes when they connect to the remote host, such as batch files or custom applications. This tab allows the user to specify the location of the programs that should be started.

Figure 20-7: The Programs tab

Using Remote Desktop Web Connection

Aside from a typical Remote Desktop connection using a LAN or VPN, Windows XP also supports connections over the Internet. A Web utility allows you to connect to the remote computer through a Web browser, so that the Remote Desktop client software does not need to be installed on the remote computer. To use the Web connection feature, you must first install it on the host computer. The following steps show you how to install this feature:

1. **Open the Control Panel and double-click Add/Remove Programs.**

2. **Click the Add/Remove Windows Components button.**

3. **In the Setup window that appears, select the "Internet Information Services (IIS)" option and click the Details button, as shown in Figure 20-8.**

Figure 20-8: The Windows Components Wizard

4. **Select the "World Wide Web Service" option and click the Details button again.**

5. **In the Details dialog box, select the "Remote Desktop Web Connection" check box and then click OK, as shown in Figure 20-9.**

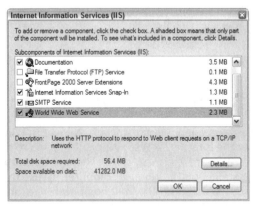

Figure 20-9: The Details dialog box for the World Wide Web Service option

6. **Click OK again, and then click Next.** Windows XP installs and configures the component. You may need your Windows XP CD-ROM to complete this installation.

7. **Once the installation is complete, click the Finish button.**

After you have installed the Web connection, you should be able to start a Remote Desktop session from a remote computer using Internet Explorer. Launch Internet Explorer, and then enter the address, such as http://*ipaddress*/tsweb, where *ipaddress* is the IP address of the Remote Desktop computer.

Using Remote Assistance

Remote Assistance is a new feature in Windows XP Professional and Windows XP Home edition that enables users to help each other over the Internet. With this tool, one user who is termed the "Expert" can view the desktop of another user, known as the "Novice." When properly authorized by the novice, the expert user can remotely use the novice user's system in order to fix problems for the novice user.

In order for a Remote Assistance session to succeed, both users must be connected to the same network (such as the Internet), they must be using Windows XP, and the account requesting assistance must have administrative rights to the computer. Unfortunately, because no other operating systems work with Remote Assistance, both computers must be running Windows XP. Remote Assistance is easy to use and easy to configure, and can be helpful in many situations.

Remote Assistance works by sending Remote Assistance invitations. The novice computer uses either Windows Messenger or e-mail to send a Remote Assistance invitation to another user. The expert user accepts the invitation, which opens a terminal window showing the desktop of the novice. The expert can see the novice's desktop and exchange messages with the novice. If the novice wants the expert to actually fix the computer, the novice can give the expert control of the computer. From this point, the expert can manage the novice's computer remotely.

Enabling Remote Assistance

As with Remote Desktop, you must configure your computer for Remote Assistance. Open Control Panel and double-click System Properties. Click the Remote tab. Select the "Allow Remote Assistance invitations to be sent from this computer" option, as shown earlier in Figure 20-1.

Note   **Remote Assistance only needs to be enabled if you are planning to ask for assistance. You can assist another user through Remote Assistance without configuring anything on your computer.**

Once you have enabled Remote Assistance, click the Advanced button. As you can see in Figure 20-10, you can use this dialog box to allow remote control of your computer. Keep in mind that if you do not enable remote control, the expert user cannot see your computer, but can make any configuration changes. You can also specify a period of time during which the invitation remains active. By default, an invitation is good for 30 days, but you can change this value, if necessary.

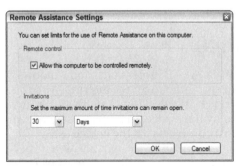

Figure 20-10: The Remote Assistance Settings dialog box

Requesting Remote Assistance

When the end user, or novice, has reached a point where remote assistance is needed, the novice can request help from another user. The novice user needs to end files to the expert user who answers his or her call for help. This help may take one of several forms, from using messaging software, to saving a file to a floppy disk and hand-delivering it to the expert. The logical place for the novice to start is the Windows XP Help and Support Center. This help feature provides easy access to the various methods of requesting a Remote Assistance session, as follows:

1. **Click Start ⇨ Help and Support.**

2. **Click the Support button on the toolbar, and then click the "Ask a friend to help" link.** The Remote Assistance page of the Help and Support Center opens.

3. **Click the "Invite someone to help you" link, as shown in Figure 20-11.** The Remote Assistance page displays up to three possible methods for sending a request from a novice to an expert, as described below and shown in Figure 20-12. Once you make a selection, simply follow the instructions that appear.

   • **Windows Messenger.** Click the Sign In button in the Windows Messenger section. Once you are signed into Windows Messenger, choose a name, and click Invite This Person. The expert receives the request in Windows Messenger and can accept your invitation. Keep in mind that you can bypass the Windows Help and Support Center and use Windows Messenger directly to start a Remote Assistance session. To do this, in Windows Messenger, click Actions ⇨ Ask for Remote Assistance.

- **E-mail.** You can send the invitation through e-mail by entering the e-mail address in the e-mail section, and then clicking the "Invite this person" link. In the next window that appears, enter your name and a message, and click Continue. In the next window, specify duration for the invitation, and enter a password that the user must enter to access your computer. Click Send Invitation. The message is entered in your default e-mail client (such as Outlook Express). The e-mail contains instructions and a file called rcBuddy.MsRcIncident. When the user receives the file, they can double-click it to start the Remote Assistance session.

- **Invitation file.** If you cannot e-mail the invitation or use Windows Messenger, you can save the invitation as a file, which can then be hand-delivered to the desired recipient. Using this option, you can also enter duration for the invitation and a password. The file is saved as RAInvitation. You can then transfer the file by hand, in an e-mail, or through a network share.

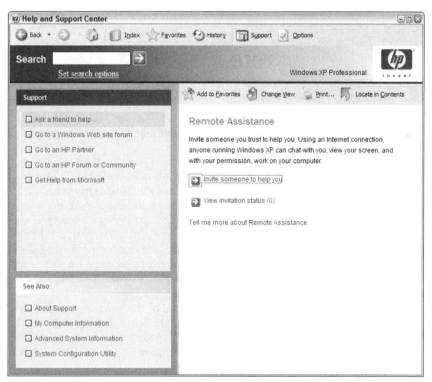

Figure 20-11: The Remote Assistance page

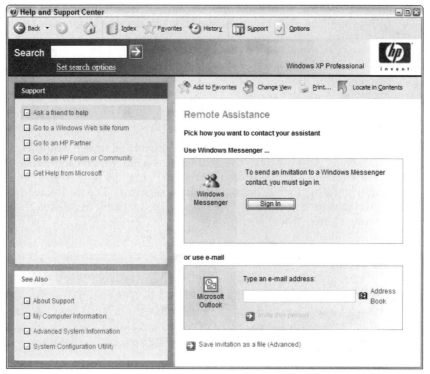

Figure 20-12: The Remote Assistance page displaying invitation options

The expert will receive the invitation, based on how you sent it. The example in Figure 20-13 uses the e-mail option. In this example, the expert can then use the Remote Assistance e-mail attachment to access the remote computer. After the expert accepts the invitation, the novice user's computer validates the password and ensures that the invitation is still valid. The novice user must then complete the process by initializing the Remote Assistance session. Once the session begins, the chat dialog box appears on the novice user's computer; on the expert user's computer, a console window opens displaying the desktop of the novice user.

At this point, the expert user can take control of the novice user's computer. To do this, the expert simply clicks the Take Control button that appears on the console, as shown in Figure 20-14. Once the expert has taken control of the novice user's computer, the novice and the expert are essentially sharing the same computer. Should the novice decide that they want to end the session, they may do so in one of three ways: by pressing the Esc key; by using the Ctrl+C key combination; or by clicking the Stop Control button that appears next to the chat window on the novice user's computer.

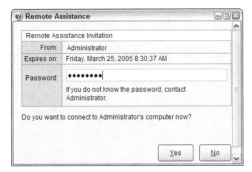

Figure 20-13: The Remote Assistance dialog box

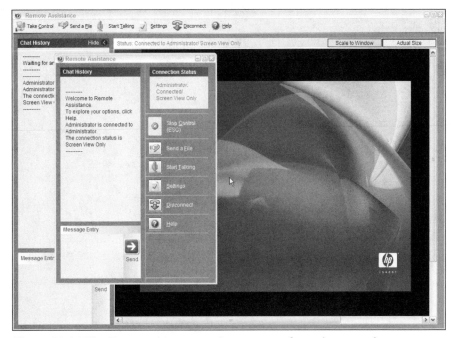

Figure 20-14: The Remote Access session, as seen from the expert's computer

Multimedia Solutions with Windows XP

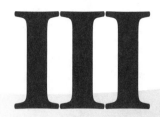

III

O nce a passing fad, multimedia is a vital part of any computing experience. From managing digital photos and video files to viewing movies on your computer, your multimedia needs are likely diverse — but always important.

In this part, you discover how to organize and manage digital photos, using Windows Movie Maker 2 and Windows Media Player 10. You learn about printing digital photos, and even have some fun with custom projects and features you'll enjoy.

Organizing and Managing Digital Photos and Video Files

21

I'm an avid digital photographer and I also teach several online digital photography courses. As a result, I'm constantly taking new photos and putting those photos on my computer. Unfortunately, all of those 2-megapixel files take up a lot of space, and they are becoming difficult to organize. So how do you manage 1000 digital photos in an orderly way so that you can find and use the one that you need?

In this chapter, you'll take a look at some alternative methods for managing digital photos and other digital media files, and you'll be introduced you to some inexpensive software that you may consider using on your Windows XP computer.

Basic Management Reminders

In order to manage digital media, it is important to keep a few basics in mind that have been covered in other chapters. Be sure to put these techniques to work:

♦ **Use folders in an organized way.** All too often, users store their photos in a disorganized collection of folders. If you spend a little time organizing your collection, you are way ahead of the game. There is not a right or wrong method for organizing digital files; just do what works for you. For example, many users choose to organize them by date, type, and event.

✦ **Use compression.** With NTFS disks, Windows uses built-in compression that can be a real lifesaver. You can quickly and easily compress folders with digital content, but still use the content as you normally would. Consistently compressing folders that contain large files can save you a lot of disk space over time. See Chapter 8 to learn more about NTFS compression.

✦ **Use removable media.** You can transfer photos and other digital files to a CD or other removable disk for storage. This simple and inexpensive solution can help you save disk space by allowing you to archive older data that is on your computer's hard disk.

✦ **Remove digital content that is redundant, of low quality, and unnecessary.** Naturally, you took 200 photos of the Grand Canyon, but do you really need that many? Remember to spend some time culling digital photos and video files, and keep only what you really want. This helps save disk space over time.

Using Online Storage

With digital media, storage is always an ongoing problem. However, you can store your digital media, as well as any files or folders, remotely on the Internet. The sites do charge a fee for this service, but it is very reasonable for the amount of storage space that they offer. How does it work? Simple—you access the Web site that offers this service and sign up. Most sites offer services that include:

✦ A lot of storage space—often 5GB just for the basic fee.

✦ Guaranteed redundancy—Most online storage sites backup their servers, which includes your data. This way, should one of their servers experience a technical problem, your data is still available on another server. The end result is uninterrupted service and data redundancy

✦ Sharing functions so that you can share your files online with selected users.

✦ Security.

✦ Integration with other devices, even your wireless PDA and cell phone.

Different sites provide different services, and so you need to check them out before signing up. Most of them offer you a free trial period so that you can try the service before making a serious commitment. Here are a few sites that I can recommend:

✦ **www.imagestation.com.** This is a great place to store and even share your digital photos. You'll find this site very user-friendly and reasonably priced.

✦ **www.globedesk.com.** This is a good storage solution with an easy-to-use interface.

✦ **www.xdrive.com.** Shown in Figure 21-1, this is a storage solution for both individual users and corporations. You can store, share, and even connect with your mobile device.

✦ **www.streamload.com.** This site, shown in Figure 21-2, provides a way for users, such as small businesses, to store and move big files around the Internet. For only $5 a month, you have unlimited storage and 10GB of downloads.

✦ **www.mydocsonline.com.** This is a great place to store and access your files for a reasonable price (shown in Figure 21-3).

✦ **www.all-the-free-space.com.** If you want to find other online storage providers, check out this free space directory.

Figure 21-1: The Xdrive Web site

Figure 21-2: The Streamload Web site

A common question that users often have about Web-site storage concerns their original data. When you upload data to a Web site, you are sending a copy of the data. Your original pictures and files remain on your local hard drive until you delete them. There is no need to worry about your pictures disappearing into Internet outer space. Your original data is always kept safe on your local computer.

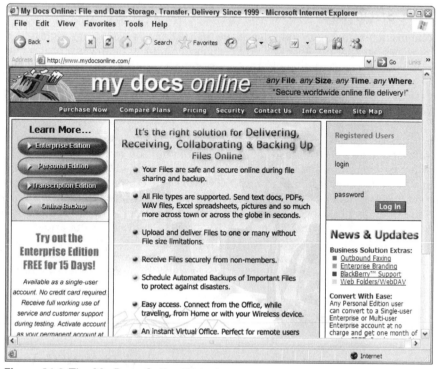

Figure 21-3: The My Docs Online Web site

Using Photo Management Programs

With the popularity of digital photography, there are plenty of programs that can help you to manage and even edit your files. Most of these programs use a catalogue and tagging system that tracks your photos and organizes them in a way that is helpful to you. If you take a lot of digital photos, I strongly recommend one of these programs to help you manage your digital life.

There are five photo management products that I have enjoyed working with and have found very beneficial. If you are a digital photography enthusiast, I encourage you to check them out.

Photoshop Elements 3

Adobe products are highly popular in the digital imaging world, and rightfully so. A few years back, Adobe introduced Photoshop Album, which was a program that helped you to manage digital photos, perform basic editing, and even a few fun tasks with wizard help (such as creating cards, calendars, and such). With the release of Photoshop Elements 3, many of the features of Photoshop Album are incorporated into the Photoshop Elements software.

The Organizer feature, shown in Figure 21-4, allows you to import photos and to organize them into collections that are useful to you. You can tag photos using different category tags in order to make searching easier, view photos by date, use a timeline option to locate photos, and perform basic editing functions. You can automatically transfer photos from your camera directly into Photoshop Elements, and the Organizer catalogs and manages them. Keep in mind that if you are using Photoshop Elements 3 for the Mac, the Organizer software does not appear. The best feature in Photoshop Elements 3 is that you can select a photo and immediately work with the photo in Edit mode. It's a great software program — really a suite — and is a great deal at around $90. Visit www.adobe.com to learn more.

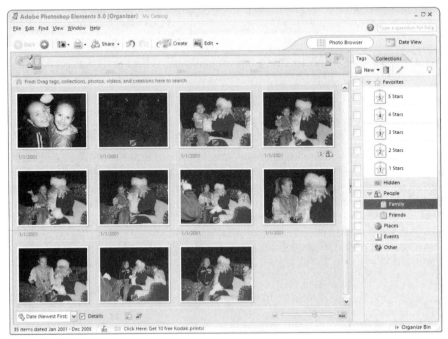

Figure 21-4: The Photoshop Elements 3 Organizer

Paint Shop Photo Album 5

Jasc software has been around for years and has produced the Paint Shop Pro program. Jasc Paint Shop Photo Album is Jasc's answer to photo management. This software does a good job of helping you to manage your digital library. You can work with thumbnail images in a catalog, perform basic editing on your photos, and organize, manage, and tag them in a variety of helpful ways. I really like the interface with this software—it is highly intuitive and easy to use. You can also create album pages, greeting cards, a printed book, e-cards, calendars, and CD labels. The software also makes it easy to share photos with other people in a variety of formats. Figure 21-5 shows you the Enhance feature, where you can easily fix common image problems.

Version 5 costs around $40, and you can download a free trial version at www.jasc.com.

Figure 21-5: The Jasc Paint Shop Photo Album 5 interface.

ACDSee

ACDSee, shown in Figure 21-6, is a popular photo management program from ACDsystems. It allows you to easily download images from your camera and perform basic editing functions, as well as organize them in a variety of ways, using helpful tagging options. The software displays a lot of information about each photo; however, this makes the interface a bit more cluttered than other photo management programs. Overall, I found this software easy to use and helpful, and it is certainly one that you should consider. ACDSee costs around $50, and you can find out more about it and download a free trial version at www.acdsystems.com.

Picajet

Shown in Figure 21-7, Picajet is a less well-known photo management program. It does a good job of organizing your photos, importing directly from your camera, photo tagging, and performing basic editing functions. Picajet doesn't provide the additional bells and whistles of Paint Shop Photo Album, but it costs the same. However, you may prefer the flexibility and ease of use that it provides. The software costs around $40 for a single user license, and you can download a trial version. You can find out more at www.picajet.com.

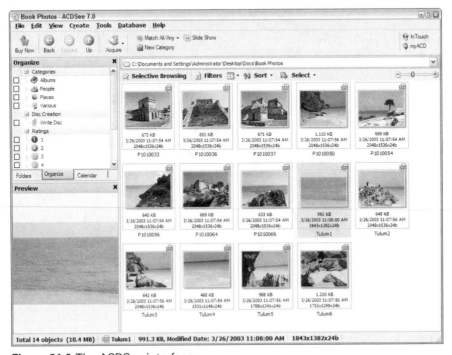

Figure 21-6: The ACDSee interface

Figure 21-7: The Picajet interface

Picasa

If you prefer free software programs (and who doesn't), Picasa (Figure 21-8) is most likely the photo manager for you. Provided by Google, it is a standard photo management package that helps you to find, edit, and share photos on your computer. It creates management folders, enables you to create labels and groups, and provides simple editing functions. For a free software product, it can't be beat. You can read more about Picasa and download the free software from www.picasa.com.

Figure 21-8: The Picasa interface

Using Windows Media Player 10

22

If you enjoy making music CD-ROMs, using portable MP3 players, managing a music collection, or watching videos and DVDs, then Windows Media Player 10 could easily become one of your favorite programs. Not only does Windows Media Player allow you to play music and watch videos, it also allows you to create collections of your favorite songs and videos. With today's dirt-cheap hard disks, you now have room to store hundreds, or even thousands, of songs on your hard drive. From those songs, you can create custom playlists, burn music CDs containing any songs that you like, and even copy music and video to and from portable media players.

When Windows XP first launched in 2001, it came with Windows Media Player 8. Since that time, the program has evolved, and the new-and-improved Windows Media Player 10 is now available as a free download. If you're not already using Windows Media Player 10, you can download a copy from Microsoft's Web sites. Because Web site URLs change often, I'll give you three possible pages to check for the free Windows Media Player downloads (just in case):

- ✦ www.windowsmedia.com/
- ✦ www.microsoft.com/windows/ windowsmedia/mp10/
- ✦ www.microsoft.com/windows/ windowsmedia/download/

In This Chapter

Creating a Media Library

Ripping and Burning CD-ROMs

Using Portable Media Devices

Using Skins, Visualizations, and Plug-ins

Interface Options and Solutions

You can start Windows Media Player from the All Programs menu. When the program first opens, it looks something like Figure 22-1. If you're already familiar with older versions of Windows Media Player, then the new program interface may come as a bit of a shock. To get you quickly up-to-speed, this chapter starts with a general discussion of the new interface and techniques for using the application.

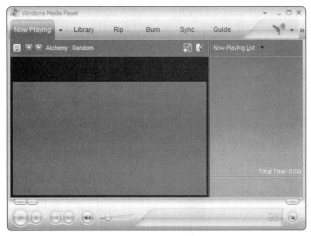

Figure 22-1: The Windows Media Player 10 program window

Where's the Menu Bar?

The traditional title bar and menu bar that are located at the top of most program windows may not be visible when you first open Windows Media Player 10. However, the bar across the top of the window acts as a normal title bar and includes the usual Minimize, Maximize/Restore, and Close buttons. You can access the menu commands for Windows Media Player either by right-clicking the title bar, shown in Figure 22-2, or by clicking the "Access application menus" button just to the left of the Minimize button.

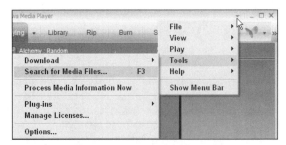

Figure 22-2: The Windows Media Player menu

If the lack of a normal menu bar drives you to distraction, then you can choose Show Menu Bar from the bottom of the menu to see the more familiar title and menu bars at the top of the program window.

After maximizing Windows Media Player by clicking its Maximize button, you can double-click the title bar to make the menu bar visible.

Tip

Umpteen Ways to Look at Things

Windows Media Player 10 offers a plethora of visual options that you can turn on and off, mostly through the View menu, as shown in Figure 22-3. No need to discuss all of those options in depth right now though. Most are self-explanatory when you open them. For example, you can change the interface mode, view options, shop online, and so forth. The more useful optional features are discussed as appropriate in later sections of this chapter.

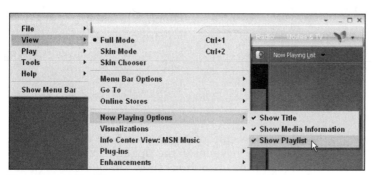

Figure 22-3: The View menu

Files That Windows Media Player Can Play

Windows Media Player can play many types of media files, as listed in Table 22-1. Whether or not Windows Media Player acts as the default player for all of those file types depends on the settings that you choose in the Options dialog box. The term *default player* means that the program opens automatically when you open a file of the supported type. Windows Media Player can also act as the default player that opens whenever you insert an audio CD into your CD drive, or a DVD movie into your DVD drive.

Table 22-1
Windows Media Player 10–Supported File Types

File Format	Extensions
AU (audio)	.au, .snd
Audio Interchange File Format	.aif, .aifc, .aiff
Audio-Video Interleave	.avi
Compact Disc Audio	.cda
Microsoft Recorded TV	.dvr-Thanks! Maureen
MIDI (Musical Instrument Digital Interface)	.mid, .midi, .rmi
MP3	.mp3, .m3u
MPEG (Moving Picture Experts Group)	.mpa, .mpe, .mpeg, .mpg, .m1v, .mp2, .mpv2, .mp2v
Windows Audio File	.wav
Windows Media Audio	.wma, .wax
Windows Media File and Advanced Streaming Format	.asf, .asx, .wm, .wmd, .wmx, .wmz, .wpl
Windows Media Video	.wmv, .wmx

To define file types for which Windows Media Player should act as the default player, choose Tools ➪ Options from its menu. In the Options dialog box that appears, click the File Types tab to see the options shown in Figure 22-4. Choose the file types for which Windows Media Player should act as the default player (or click the Select All button). Then click OK.

Experts Notebook: Stopping Pushy Players

Many computer manufacturers bundle third-party media software, such as MusicMatch Jukebox, with their systems. Such freebies are often *pushy* in the sense that the program acts as your default player, even after you tell Windows Media Player to act as your default player.

In most cases, an easy solution is to choose Tools ➪ Options from the free program's menu bar. Then look through its Options dialog box to find the settings that are making it act as the default player for various media types. Clear those options, then click OK, and then close the program. If that fails, then you can remove that program through Add Or Remove Programs in Control Panel. *Alan Simpson*

Figure 22-4: The File Types tab in the Options dialog box

Accessing Existing Media with Windows Media Player

If you've been using some other program to access song or video files on your hard drive, then Windows Media Player won't know that the files are there by default. To make Windows Media Player aware of the files so that they're available from its Library, press F3 or choose Tools ➪ Search for Media Files from the menu. The Add to Library by Searching Computer dialog box appears, as shown in Figure 22-5.

Figure 22-5: The Add to Library by Searching Computer dialog box

You can use the Search on and Look in fields to specify a drive or folder to search. The default selection, "Local drives, minus program folders," will only search all of your document folders. This prevents little sound effects files from being added to your library. Click Search after making your selections. Wait for the search to complete, and then click Close. Any files that Windows Media Player finds will be available from your Library.

Playing Music, Watching a Video

There are many ways to play music and watch a video through Windows Media Player. For songs and videos that are already in your Library, first click the Library button near the top of the program window, as shown in Figure 22-6. From there, you can use the collapsible list at the left side of the program window to view songs and videos by categories, such as Album Artist, Contributing Artist, Album, and Genre. From there you can:

✦ **Play all titles:** Play all of the titles in that category by right-clicking any category name in the left column and choosing Play.

✦ **Play just one title**: Double-click any single title in the main pane to the right.

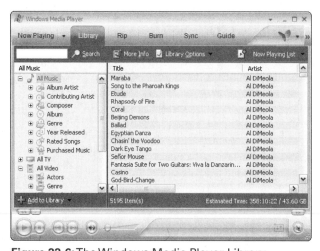

Figure 22-6: The Windows Media Player Library

If you're not already in Windows Media Player, but rather just browsing through files and folders in Windows Explorer, you can double-click the icon for any file type that is associated with Windows Media Player to open it and listen to the song. If you have multiple media players installed, then right-click the file and choose Open With ⇨ Windows Media Player.

To listen to a music CD, insert the disc into your CD drive, close the drive door, and wait for Windows Media Player to open and start playing the CD. If a program other than Windows Media Player opens, close that program and then open Windows Media Player. Then click the small Quick Access Panel button to the right of the Now Playing button (near the mouse pointer in Figure 22-7). Choose your CD drive and the album title from the top of the menu.

Figure 22-7: The Quick Access Panel

If your computer has a DVD drive, watching a DVD movie is similar to playing an audio CD. Just place the DVD in the drive, close the drive door, and wait for Windows Media Player to open and start playing the movie. Use your mouse to make selections from the movie's main menu; this is similar to how you choose options using a remote control with a TV or DVD player.

The first time you try to watch a DVD movie, you may see an error message stating that you need a compatible decoder. If your DVD drive didn't come with a decoder, then you can buy one online through www.wmplugins.com.

Regardless of how you access a song, CD, video, or DVD movie to start playing it, you can use Windows Media Player's Now Playing features, such as control playback, and watch a visualization.

Now Playing Features

The Now Playing area in Windows Media Player is where you watch a video. When you're playing music, you can watch a visualization of whatever song is playing. Figure 22-8 points out the main components of the Now Playing tab. Each is summarized below:

Toolbar   Now Playing List

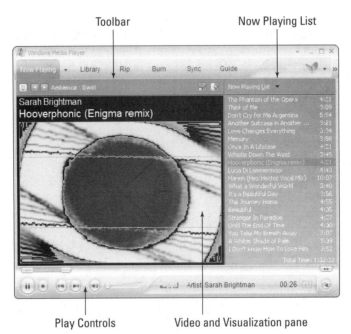

Play Controls   Video and Visualization pane

Figure 22-8: The Now Playing tab

✦ **Video and Visualization Pane:** Displays the video or DVD movie that you're watching, or a visualization (dancing pattern of colors) of a song that you are playing.

✦ **Toolbar:** Contains buttons that provide quick access to commonly used features. Each button also displays a tooltip when you point to it. Going from left to right, the tools are:

- **Choose Now Playing Options:** Provides quick access to optional visual components and enhancements.

- **Previous/Next Visualization:** The buttons allow you to scroll through different visualizations. The name of the current visualization appears to the right of the buttons.

- **View Full Screen:** Expands the video or visualization (which is disabled when nothing is playing). Click anywhere on the full-screen view to return to the normal view.

- **Maximize/Restore the Video and Visualization Pane:** Click to hide the Now Playing List, or to show the Now Playing List if it's hidden.

To prevent your screen saver from starting up while you are watching a video or DVD, choose Tools ➪ Options from the menu. Then clear the "Allow screen saver during playback" option on the Player tab, and click OK.

✦ **Now Playing List:** Shows titles of the songs in the current playlist. When you double-click any song title, the song starts playing immediately.

✦ **Play Controls:** Going from left to right, the buttons are Play/Pause, Stop, Previous, Next, and Mute. The slider controls the volume of the sound. You can use the Seek bar across the top of the play controls to fast forward and rewind.

The Now Playing List at the right side is very flexible and easy to change. If the Now Playing list is hidden, click the Restore the Video and Visualization Pane button at the far right of the toolbar. Clicking the button at the top of the pane shows options for shuffling, sorting, and removing songs and clearing the playlist, as shown on the left in Figure 22-9. Within the list, you can right-click any song for a context menu that is relevant to the individual song, as shown on the right in Figure 22-9.

Figure 22-9: The Now Playing List and context menus

As you will see in later sections of this chapter, you can use the Now Playing List in many ways. For example, you can use it to list songs that you want to burn to CD or copy to a portable music player. However, you first need some songs to work with. Let's take a look at techniques that you can use to copy songs from music CDs into your Windows Media Player Library.

Ripping Music

One way to build up a collection of songs in your media library is to copy any music CDs that you already own. By *music CD,* I mean a CD that you buy in a music store and play in a stereo or CD player. Copying songs from a music CD to your computer is called *ripping* the CD. Before you start ripping songs from CDs, you need to tell Windows Media Player where, and in what format, you want to store the songs. It is important to note that it is perfectly legal to rip music that you already own for your own use. However, you can't distribute that music to anyone else without breaking copyright laws. To rip a song, follow these steps:

1. **From Windows Media Player menu, choose Tools ➪ Options.** The Options dialog box appears.

2. **Click the Rip Music tab to display the rip options, as shown in Figure 22-10.**

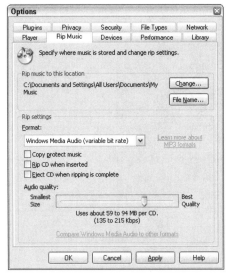

Figure 22-10: The Rip Music tab in the Options dialog box

3. **Make your selections, using the following information as your guide, then click OK.**

Choosing a Folder for Songs

By default, Windows Media Player places all songs that you rip into your My Music folder. In the "Rip music to this location" section in the Options dialog box, you can see that folder expressed as:

```
C:\Documents and Settings\UserName\Documents\My Music
```

where *UserName* is the name of the user account that you're currently logged in to.

If you want to use a different folder, click the Change button, and choose the folder that you want to use. For example, if you want all people who use your computer (or who have access to your computer through a local network) to have access to the songs, then you can place the songs in your Shared Music folder. To do this, just click the Change button and, in the Browse for Folder dialog box that appears, click the Shared Music folder icon, and then click OK. The path to your Shared Music folder will appear as:

```
C:\Documents and Settings\All Users\Documents\My Music
```

where *All Users* is the name of the folder to which all user accounts have access.

Choosing a File Naming Convention

Click the File Name button on the Rip Music tab to open the File Name Options dialog box, as shown in Figure 22-11. Use the check boxes to select or deselect any information that you want to include in the filename.

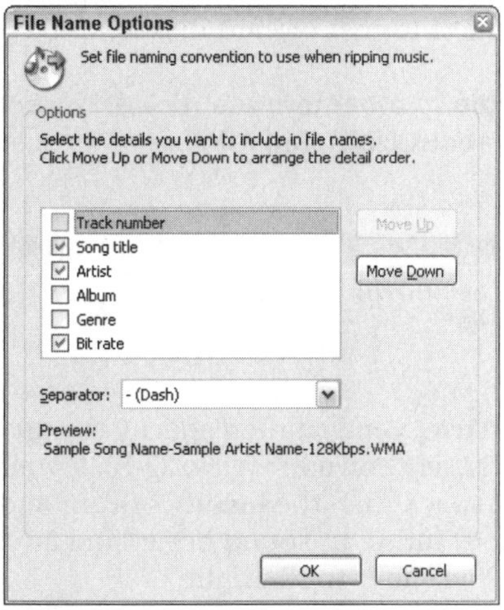

Figure 22-11: The File Name Options dialog box

Once you've chosen which items you want to show in each song's filename, you can use the Move Up and Move Down buttons to choose the order of those items. First click the item that you want to move, and then click the Move Up or Move Down button to move that item. Use the Separator drop-down menu to choose how you want information in the filename to be separated. For example, if you choose Song Title, Artist, and Bit rate as the information that you want in each filename, and then choose the Dash as the separator, shown in Figure 23-11, then each song that you copy shows the song title, followed by a hyphen and the artist name, followed by a hyphen and the bit rate, as in the example below:

```
A Taste of Honey-The Beatles-146kbps
```

Choosing a Format and Level of Quality

You can store songs that you copy from CDs in either Windows Media or MP3 format. The Windows Media format is optimized to work especially well with Windows, but not with other platforms. The MP3 format is a generic format that plays on just about any computer, even a Linux system.

If you use a Windows Media format, you can choose how you want songs to be compressed, as follows:

✦ **Windows Media Audio:** Uses a fixed bit rate of your choosing to store the entire song.

✦ **Windows Media Audio (variable bit rate):** Uses a varying bit rate to reduce the amount of disk space required to store the song, without compromising the quality of the song.

✦ **Windows Media Audio Lossless:** Uses no compression when storing files. The result is professional-quality music at the cost of hard disk space.

> **Tip** Click the "Compare Windows Media Audio to other formats" link at the bottom of the Rip Music tab to learn more about WMA and MP3.

All three of those options, along with the MP3 option, are available from the Format drop-down menu in the Rip settings section, as shown in Figure 22-10.

Choosing Audio Quality

After you choose the format that you want to use, you can then specify the quality of your audio by using the Audio quality slider, as shown in Figure 22-10. If you're more concerned about conserving hard disk space than the quality of your audio, then drag the slider to the left. If you want your music to sound better and are not concerned about hard disk space, then drag the slider to the right.

Expert's Notebook: Settings That I Use for Ripping CDs

I've played around with all of the different file formats and audio quality settings on the Rip Music tab. The settings shown in Figure 22-10 are the ones that I generally use. On average, these settings result in about 1MB of disk storage for each minute of music. As a result, 1GB of hard disk space is enough to store about 300 three-minute songs. My 5,000-song collection uses about 16GB of storage, which seems like a trivial amount of disk space given today's enormous, inexpensive hard drives. *Alan Simpson*

Hard disk space is cheap (about a dollar per billion bytes), so there's no need to put up with low-quality music just to save a few pennies' worth of disk space. However, what's commonly referred to as *CD Quality* is about 128 Kbps, and so that setting, or anything higher, will give you at least the same quality of playback that you're accustomed to from music CDs.

Copy Protection

If you select the "Copy protect music" checkbox on the Rip Music tab, you help to protect the copyrights of the record companies that distribute the music, as shown in Figure 22-10. However, that setting won't protect you from accidentally deleting the song. In fact, you'll find it much more difficult to work with protected content than with normal unprotected files. For example, you won't be able to import the protected music to use as background music in movies that you create.

If you don't select the "Copy protect music" check box, then each song is stored as a "normal" file with no restrictions on how you can use the file. The only thing that you *don't* want to do with the normal, unprotected files is to share them over a P2P network using a program like LimeWire or Morpheus. That is a copyright infringement because you're giving away free copies of songs that the record companies are trying to sell.

Assembly-line CD Copying

When you select both the "Rip CD when inserted" and "Eject CD when ripping is complete" options, you make it easier to copy many CDs in an assembly-line manner, as shown in Figure 22-10. When you place a CD in the drive, Windows Media Player rips the CD, and then ejects it. All you have to do is place in the next CD that you want copy and close the drive door.

If you don't plan on copying every music CD that you place into your CD drive, then you should clear the *Rip CD when inserted* checkbox. This is because you can also use your CD drive to play music CDs without copying them.

Ripping a CD

When record companies switched from vinyl phonograph albums to CDs, they were thinking about stereos, not computers. It didn't occur to the record companies to place textual information, like song titles, on CDs because you can't to see those song titles on a typical stereo or CD player. For this reason, most commercial music CDs do not contain media information such as song titles.

Fortunately, the Compact Disc Database (CDDB) on the Internet does have media information for most CDs. Windows Media Player can retrieve that information automatically, but only if you're online when you rip a CD. When you are ripping CDs, the first thing that you want to do is get online (if you don't have an "always on" account). You can then insert the CD that you want to copy into the CD drive, click the Rip Music button in the toolbar above the Artist column, and wait for the song titles to appear, as shown in Figure 22-12.

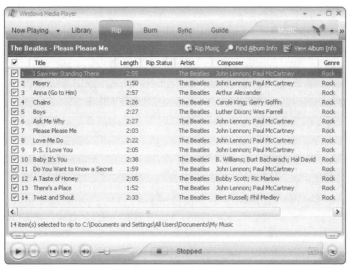

Figure 22-12: Media information for songs that are about to be ripped.

If you chose the "Rip CD when inserted" option in the Options dialog box, you don't have to do anything else. Windows Media Player automatically starts to copy the songs. Otherwise, you can click the Rip Music button in the toolbar above the Artist column to start copying.

As Windows Media Player copies the songs, the Rip Status column keeps you informed of the progress. When all of the songs show *Ripped to Library* in the Rip Status column, you can remove the CD from the drive. The songs are placed in your media library (for more information see the section Using the Library later in this chapter). The songs are also organized into folders by artist and album in whatever folder you told Windows Media Player to place the copied songs.

Purchasing Music Online

Ripping songs from music CDs is just one way to build up your media library. You can also purchase and download music online. Clicking the "Choose an online store" button will list some online vendors, as shown in Figure 22-13.

Figure 22-13: Online media vendors

Each online store has its own way of managing sales. You should shop around and see what online store offers the features that you like the most. To make a purchase, you first need to set up an account with a vendor. Any music, or *content*, that you purchase online is *protected content*, which means that the song won't play on any computer but your own. You can still copy songs to your own portable music player or blank CDs. However, there may be a limit on how many times you can do that. Each online store has its own policies about how you can use protected content.

Using the Library

Clicking the Library button in Windows Media Player takes you to your digital media collection. The Library is divided into two panes. The left pane is called the *Contents pane*. The pane to its right is called the *Details pane*. The Contents pane is a collapsible tree of categories. Click the plus button (+) next to any category to expand it, or click the minus button (–) to collapse it. For example, in Figure 22-14, the All Music and Album Artist categories are expanded.

Contents pane   Details pane

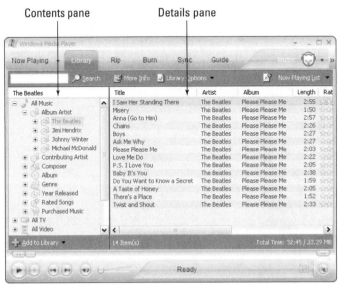

Figure 22-14: Contents and Details panes in the Library

When you click a specific artist's name, all of the songs by that artist appear in the Details pane to the right. Similarly, if you expand the Genre category and click a specific genre, such as Classical or Rock, all of the songs within that category appear in the Details pane to the right. If you want to see all of the songs in your Library, just click All Music at the top of the Contents pane. The Details pane lists every song in your music collection.

Sorting Songs

Like any columnar view in Windows, you can sort songs in your Library just by clicking any column heading. Your first click usually lists items in ascending order and displays a small, up-pointing triangle in the column heading. A second click reverses the sort order, and, in this case, shows a down-pointing triangle to indicate that you're viewing items in descending order.

You can resize any column by dragging the border at the right side of the column heading left or right. You can also move an entire column by dragging the column name left or right.

The columns that initially appear in the Library are the default columns. You can choose which columns you want to view in a variety of ways. The quick method is to right-click any column heading, as shown on the left in Figure 22-15. Then click the name of any column that you want to show or hide. (Column names with check marks are already visible).

If you want to spend a little more time arranging columns, choose "More..." from the bottom of the shortcut menu. Alternatively, you can choose View ➪ Choose Columns from the menu to access the Choose Columns dialog box, as shown on the right in Figure 22-15. Regardless of which method you use to choose columns, you can scroll left or right through columns using the horizontal scroll bar at the bottom of the list.

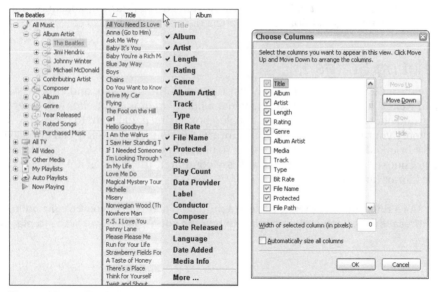

Figure 22-15: Choosing columns to display in the Library

Editing Media Information

You can edit any item of information in the Library by simply right-clicking the text that you want to change, and then choosing Edit. If you want to make the same change to several songs, you can first select the songs that you want to change, and then edit any one of them. Selecting songs in your library is similar to selecting icons in folders. For example:

✦ **Select all songs:** To select all of the songs in the Details pane, click any song title, and then press Ctrl+A.

✦ **Select a range of songs:** To select a range of songs, click the first song title that you want to select. Then hold down the Shift key and click the last song that you want to select.

✦ **Select non-adjacent songs:** To select multiple non-adjacent songs, click one song to select it. Then hold down the Ctrl key as you click the titles of other songs that you want to select.

After you're finished selecting songs, right-click any select item within the column that you want to change, and choose Edit. Make your change and press Enter. Your change is applied to all of the selected songs.

You can also use the Advanced Tag Editor to make changes to any single song, or any group of selected songs. Just right-click any selected song, and then choose Advanced Tag Editor instead of Edit. The Advanced Tag Editor opens, allowing you to add or change media information using a dialog box format.

Deleting Songs

To delete a song from your Library, just right-click the song title and choose Delete. If you want to delete several songs, select all of them first, right-click any selected song, and choose Delete. You'll see a dialog box asking if you want to delete the songs from only your Library, or from your Library and your computer. If you choose to delete from only your Library, the song remains on your hard disk as a file. However, if you choose "Delete from library and my computer," the song is deleted from both your Library and hard disk.

Caution

As a rule, you don't want to delete protected songs that you bought online, because you may end up having to buy the song again if you want to play it.

FYI: How the Library Works

The information that you see in your Library is from properties of the songs that you copied. The songs aren't actually "stored in" Windows Media Player, because Windows Media Player is a program, and you cannot store files in programs. Like all documents, songs are stored in folders, most likely your My Music or Shared Music folder.

To view the properties of a song outside of Windows Media Player, open a folder that contains the songs that you downloaded or copied from a CD. Then right-click any song's icon and choose Properties. In the Properties dialog box, click the Summary tab, and then click the Advanced button. *Alan Simpson*

To minimize the likelihood of accidentally deleting songs, choose Tools ➪ Options from the Windows Media Player menu, and then click the Library tab in the Options dialog box. Clear the check mark next to "Delete files from computer when deleted from library" option, and click OK. The setting won't prevent you from deleting songs. Rather, it will simply ensure that the default option is always "Delete from library only."

Burning Your Own CDs

A big advantage of having a large collection of music is that you can easily create your own custom music CDs with minimal hassle. If you buy CD-R discs by the spindle, they're cheap enough to be disposable. Therefore, you need never play your expensive original CD again and risk scratching it up. Just create your own CDs from your collection. If a CD that you created gets lost or ruined, you can make another.

Most stereos and CD players can't play CD-RW discs, and so you'll probably want to use CD-R discs to create music CDs. There are two types of CD-R discs:

✦ **Data CD-R**: Has a capacity of 650MB, or 74 minutes worth of music.

✦ **Audio CD-R**: Has a capacity of 700MB, or 80 minutes worth of music.

You can use either type of disc to create your own music CDs. The extra capacity of an Audio CD-R disc just allows you to place more songs on the disc than a Data CD-R generally allows.

The only drawback to using CD-R rather than CD-RW discs is that you only get one shot at burning a CD-R. Once you've burned *anything* to a CD-R—even if it's just one song—you can't go back and change the CD later or add any more songs to it. For this reasons, it's a good idea to plan what you want on a CD by creating a Burn List.

Creating a Burn List

As the name implies, a Burn List is a list of songs that you want to copy to a CD. When you're in the Library area in Windows Media Player, you can create a new, empty Burn List by clicking the Now Playing List, and choosing Burn List from the drop-down menu. Initially the list is empty except for some brief instructions, as shown in Figure 22-16.

To add a song to your Burn List, just drag the song's title from the Details pane, and drop it into the Burn List. Optionally, you can select a lot of song titles, using one of the selection techniques described earlier in this chapter, and drag the selected titles over to add them to the Burn List.

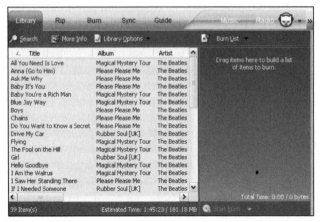

Figure 22-16: An empty Burn list to the right of the Details pane

As you add songs to the Burn List, the Total Time indicator shows you how much time you've used up. The goal is to get within a minute or two of the total capacity of the drive without going over. Don't bother trying to get exactly 80 minutes of music on the list. On an 80-minute Audio CD-R, 77 or 78 minutes worth of music is plenty. For example, I've chosen about 77 minutes (1 hour, 17 minutes, and 27 seconds) to burn, as shown in Figure 22-17. For a Data CD-R, 72 or 73 minutes is enough.

About 77 minutes of music

Figure 22-17: Music in a Burn List

To rearrange songs in the Burn List, just drag any song title up or down within the list. To remove a song from the Burn List, right-click the song's title and choose "Remove from list." To widen or narrow the Burn List, drag its left border to the left or to the right.

You can save any Burn List that you create, which can make it easier to create multiple CDs from the same list. Just click the Burn List title at the top of the list and choose Save Playlist As. Enter a name for the list and then click Save. All playlists that you save in this manner are saved under My Playlists in the Contents pane at the left side of the Library tab.

Burning a CD

Once you decide which songs that you want to copy to a CD, creating the CD is easy. You need to place a blank CD-R in your CD drive first, and give the drive a moment to read the CD. Then click the Burn button near the top of the Windows Media Player program window. The Burn List automatically appears in the left column. If you want to burn songs from a playlist that you have burned previously, just choose that playlist's name from the drop-down list at the top of the left column.

The right column should display the message "There are no items on the CD" when there's a blank CD in the drive, as shown in Figure 22-18. If a different message appears in the right column, just choose your CD drive from the drop-down list at the top of that column (where you see "CD Drive (E:) - Audio CD"), as shown in Figure 22-18.

Figure 22-18: Ready to burn songs to a blank Audio CD-R

When the songs that you want to copy are in the left column, and the blank CD is in the right column, just click the Start Burn toolbar button to start the burning process. Each song is converted to CDA format (as is required on standard music CDs) and then copied to the CD. When the copying is complete, you can remove the CD from the drive and play it in a stereo or a computer.

Syncing Music

If you have a compatible MP3 player or other portable media player that doesn't require CDs, you can copy songs to it using Windows Media Player. Unlike CDs, where you burn music to a disc, you *synchronize* music to a portable device, which is essentially a transfer process. The Sync button near the top of the Media Player's program window is the place to go.

The first time you connect a compatible player to your computer, a Wizard may open, asking if you want to synchronize your music automatically or manually. If you choose the automatic option, Windows Media Player automatically copies new items to the device as soon as you connect it. If there's not enough room on the device for the new items, then Windows Media Player deletes some of the items that are currently on the device to make room.

Most people prefer to use the manual option of synchronizing songs to a compatible player, because it gives you complete control of the player's contents. As with music CDs, you can create a playlist of songs, called a Sync List, to copy to the device. To create a Sync List, click the Library button at the top of Media Player's program window. Then choose Sync List from the Now Playing List button at the right side of the toolbar. The Sync List opens and displays instructions, as shown on the right of Figure 22-19. Using the Sync List, you can perform the following operations:

Figure 22-19: An empty Sync List on the right side of the program window

✦ **Add songs:** To add songs to the Sync List, just drag song titles from the Details pane in the center, over to the Sync List. You can select groups of songs to copy, remove songs from the Sync List, and rearrange songs in the list by dragging song titles up or down in the list. To save a list, click the Sync List button at the top of the list, and choose Save Playlist As.

✦ **Copy songs:** To copy songs to a portable player, first connect the player to the computer (typically through a USB port). Then click the Sync button at the top of the Windows Media Player program window. The screen splits into two panes. The left pane displays the Sync List that you just created. If you prefer to copy songs from a different playlist, choose that playlist's name from the drop-down list at the top of the left column.

✦ **Remove songs:** The pane on the right represents songs that are already in the portable player (if any). If you need to remove a song from the player, just right-click that song's title and choose Delete from Device. If you want to remove all of the songs from the player, drag the mouse pointer through all of the song titles that are currently on the device. You can also click the first song title and then press Shift+End. With all of the song titles highlighted, press the Delete (Del) key, or right-click any song title and choose Delete from Device.

When the left column shows the songs that you want to copy to the device, click the Start Sync button in the toolbar above the left column, as shown in Figure 22-20. Each song is converted to a format that's compatible with your player, and then copied to the device. When the copying is complete, just unplug the device from the computer, and you're ready to go.

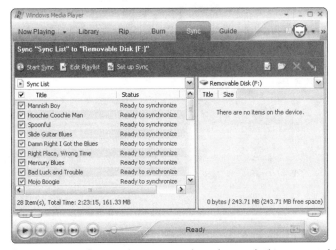

Figure 22-20: Songs that are ready to be copied to a portable player

Using Visualizations, Skins, and Plug-ins

A visualization is a "visual" display that provides entertainment while you listen to music. Quite a few visualizations come with Windows Media Player 10, and you can try them out using techniques described earlier in this chapter (see the section "Now Playing Features").

Windows Media Player 10 is also *skinnable*, meaning that you can change its appearance without changing how it functions. Follow these steps to select a skin:

1. **From the Windows Media Player menu, choose View ➪ Skin Chooser.**

2. **Click the name of any skin in the left column.** This lets you view how the skin will look on the screen, as shown in Figure 22-21.

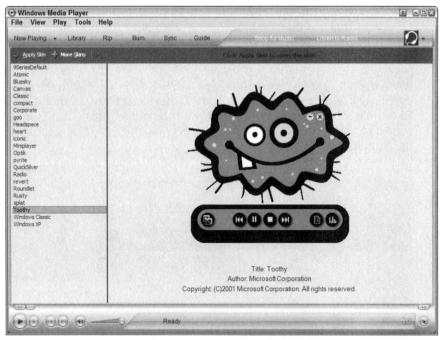

Figure 22-21: Media Player Skin Chooser

3. **When you find a skin that you like, click Apply Skin in the toolbar.**

Windows Media Player applies the skin to its interface. Buttons and controls for working media player vary with different skins. Typically, you just have to point to various buttons and gizmos on the skin to find out which button or symbol controls which function. When you want to remove the skin and go back to the normal Windows Media Player window, you can do either of the following:

✦ Press Ctrl+1.

✦ Click the large anchor button in the lower-right corner of the screen, and choose Switch to Full Mode.

The visualizations and skins that come with Windows Media Player 10 may be enough to keep you busy for a while. However, there are many more to choose from at the Windows Media Player Plug-ins Web site at www.wmplugins.com. In fact, there are lots of goodies — not just visualizations and skins — that you can download to enhance your copy of Windows Media Player 10. To see for yourself, just browse to www.wmplugins.com and have a look around. You're sure to find lots of fun stuff!

Making Movies with Windows Movie Maker 2

23

Windows Movie Maker 2.1 is the current version of Movie Maker at the time of this writing. If you worked with the first version of Movie Maker that appeared back in the days of Windows Me, then you will find that Windows Movie Maker 2 is certainly an improvement. With Movie Maker, you can assemble video clips, pictures, audio, and even effects into a "movie" that you can then save and play in Windows Media Player. Although Movie Maker can only export Windows Media files, it is a great tool for beginners, and is included for free with Windows XP. In this chapter, you can explore Windows Movie Maker 2.1 and learn how to use it. Before you get started, make sure that you have downloaded the latest version of Movie Maker, which you can find at www.microsoft.com/windowsxp.

Note　Windows Movie Maker 2.1 is included in the SP2 download, and so if you have upgraded to SP2, then you already have Windows Movie Maker 2.1.

In This Chapter

Capturing and Importing Data

Editing Clips

Assembling a Movie

Saving a Movie

Movie Maker 2 Requirements

Before you start working with Movie Maker, it's a good idea to review the hardware requirements. If you're using a newer computer, then you have probably met these requirements, but it is a good idea to review them just to be safe:

✦ Pentium 600 MHz or equivalent

✦ At least 128MB of RAM

✦ 2GB of storage space if you intend on saving a lot of movie files

✦ A video card or video capture device

✦ A sound card or sound capture device

Note

Movie Maker will look for and expect to find both a video and sound card or other capture device. If it doesn't find one of these, you'll receive a message telling you that your computer does not meet the Movie Maker requirements.

A Quick Look at the Interface

You can access Movie Maker by clicking Start ➪ All Programs ➪ Accessories ➪ Entertainment ➪ Windows Movie Maker. The Windows Movie Maker interface is primarily made up of four panes — Movie Tasks, Collections, Monitor, and Contents — as shown in Figure 23-1. These panes combine to provide you with an intuitive workspace, as follows:

✦ **Movie Tasks pane:** This pane provides a place where you can select a variety of tasks. The tasks are organized under major headings, such as capturing video and editing movies.

✦ **Collections pane:** This pane shows you the current video clips and photos that you have imported or captured. All of the items that you see here are considered "clips."

✦ **Monitor pane:** This pane allows you to watch a video or view a photo that you have selected in the Collections pane. You can also work with a clip in the monitor in several different ways.

✦ **Contents pane:** This pane runs across the bottom of the interface and it shows you the contents of your movie. You place clips from the Collections pane on the Contents pane, and then apply transitions, effects, and sound. Think of the Contents pane as your assembly area.

Figure 23-1: The Windows Movie Maker interface

Capturing or Importing Movies and Pictures

You can import movies and pictures into Windows Movie Maker in two different ways. The first way is to capture live video from your digital camcorder, and the second way is to import existing movies or pictures. The following two sections describe each of these options.

Capturing Video

To capture video from your camcorder, your computer must first be outfitted with the right kind of connection. For example, your computer may need an IEEE 1394 card, unless your camcorder can connect to a USB port. Your computer needs to detect the camcorder in order for Movie Maker to capture video from the camcorder.

Tip

Under most circumstances, the camcorder must be turned on for Windows XP to detect it.

FYI: Movie Maker...

Begin Soap Box: I've used other video-editing software from other vendors that was much, much better, so I don't mind telling you up front that if you are really interested in getting into movie editing and production, you might want to look for a different software package that will really give you the power and tools that you need. Windows Movie Maker is a free application included with your Windows XP system — this should indicate to you that video-editing software is not Microsoft's main focus, and Movie Maker is, in fact, a basic video-editing package. However, Windows Movie Maker is free and it is very intuitive and easy to use.

There are several caveats regarding Windows Movie Maker: When you create a movie in Movie Maker, you are forced to save the movie as a Windows Media Video file (WMV). You do not have the option to use other standard video formats, such as AVI or MPEG. Windows Movie Maker can read these types of files, but you cannot save your work as one of them. Also, you must use a computer that has Windows Media Player installed to be able to play Movie Maker files. If you want to play a WMV file on a system that does not automatically have Windows Media Player, such as a Macintosh, you'll need to install Windows Media Player for the Mac. I personally think Microsoft should give us more options here, and not force us to stay in the Windows Media Player land with our movies. *Curt Simmons*

You may need to read through your camera documentation to find out how to connect your camcorder to your computer. Once you have connected the camcorder and Movie Maker detects it, you can click the "Capture from video device" link in the Movie Tasks pane under Capture Video. You can also use the File menu to connect your camcorder. Movie Maker captures the streaming movie from your camcorder and automatically breaks it into clips for you.

It is not unusual to have problems capturing video. This is because different devices and hardware tend to create software problems. One easy solution is to use the software that came with your camcorder to capture video, and to save the movie to Windows XP as a simple AVI or MPEG file. Then, you can import the file into Movie Maker. See the next section for information about importing clips.

Importing Clips

Windows Movie Maker can recognize all kinds of graphics files, from AVI and MPEG to basic Web files, such as JPEG and GIF. Once the files are loaded and saved onto your hard disk, you can use Windows Movie Maker to import them and to begin working with them. To import an existing clip, click the Import video, Import pictures, or Import audio or music links in the Movie Tasks pane under Capture Video. These links open a typical browser window so that you can locate files on your Windows XP computer. Once you import the clips, they appear in the Collections pane.

Editing Clips

Whenever you record or import media, by default, Windows Movie Maker creates clips to break apart the video sequences into manageable pieces. Windows Movie Maker examines the video stream and attempts to segment it when the picture sequence changes. This doesn't always work perfectly, but it does work well enough so that Windows Movie Maker can help you more easily manage and edit your video. Using Windows Movie Maker, you can record or import the video or still-shot clips that you want to use, organize them into collections, edit them, and then save the project. Keep in mind that you can combine video and still shots into one collection and blend them together. You can also import background music and narrate a movie by recording your voice. The following sections show you how to perform the basic tasks of editing clips.

Splitting Clips

Windows Movie Maker creates clips for you; however, you may need to split those clips into more manageable pieces. You can perform this function by using the *Split* command, as follows:

1. **In the Collections pane, select the clip that you want to split.**

2. **In the Monitor pane, click the Play button.**

3. **When the clip reaches the point at which you want to split it, click the Split Clip button in the Monitor pane.** You can also click the Clip menu, and click Split, or simply press Ctrl+Shift+S on your keyboard. In the Collections pane, the clip is split in two — the first clip retains its original name, while the second clip contains the original name followed by (1), as shown in Figure 23-2. If you want, you can change the name.

Figure 23-2: A movie split into two clips

Windows Movie Maker 2
Sample File

Windows Movie Maker 2
Sample File (1)

Combining Clips

Just as you can split a clip into two or more clips, you can also combine clips. If you want to combine two or more clips, just follow these steps:

1. **In the Collections pane, select the first clip, hold down the Shift key on your keyboard, and then select the remaining clips that you want to combine.**

2. **Click the Clip menu, and then click Combine.** The clips are combined using the name of the first clip.

Note
You can also trim a clip so that only part of it appears in the movie, without deleting the unused part. You'll see how to do that later in this chapter.

Creating Your Movie

The Contents pane at the bottom of the interface is the area where you edit and assemble movies. If you examine the interface, shown in Figure 23-3, you can see buttons at the top left of the area that correspond to areas in the Workspace. You can access volume and zoom controls, narration options, play and rewind buttons, and use a button to toggle between Timeline view and Storyboard view. Timeline view enables you to more easily work with all of the components in the movie, such as audio and narration, as shown in Figure 23-4.

Figure 23-3: The Storyboard view

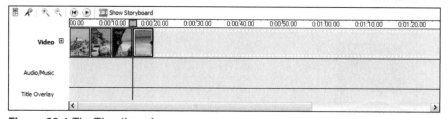

Figure 23-4: The Timeline view

Creating a Storyboard

You can use the Contents pane to create a storyboard or to sequence your clips together. First, drag clips onto the Contents pane to create the storyboard. Begin by dragging the first clip in your movie to the video area of the Contents pane. Once the clip is in position, the first frame of the video displays in the box. If you change to Timeline view, you can see how much time the clip consumes. By using the timeline, you can connect pieces of clips together, while keeping a watch over the time frame of the entire movie. However, you will probably find that the Storyboard view is initially easier to use when you are visually assembling your movie, as you can see in Figure 23-3.

The zoom in and zoom out buttons let you see more detail concerning the timeline (click the Timeline button to switch to Timeline view). While zoomed out, the storyboard appears in increments of ten seconds. You can zoom in and zoom out to see the clips in whatever time measure you want.

Note

By default, imported still shots are given five seconds of time on a storyboard. You can change that value on the timeline by simply grabbing the edge of a photo and dragging to increase or decrease its duration on the timeline.

Trimming Clips

As you work with clips in the storyboard, you may notice areas of your video that you want to cut out, or trim. These are often dead spots in the video where not much is happening. The trim feature is very powerful because it gives you a fine level of control over your clips. You can use the timeline feature in the Contents pane and trim away seconds of a clip that you do not want to use. However, when you trim a clip, you do not actually delete that part of the movie; you simply "hide" it so that it is not used. As a result, you can always go back later and remove the trim points (the place where to started and ended the trimming) to restore the full clip. The following steps show you how to trim a clip:

1. **In the Contents pane, select the clip that you want to trim.** The first frame of the clip appears in the Monitor, as shown in Figure 23-5.

2. **Switch to Timeline view. Click the Show Timeline button in the Contents Pane.**

3. **Grab the edge of the clip and drag to trim the clip, as shown in Figure 23-6.**

4. **To manage trim areas, use the Clip menu.** Notice that you can clear trim points to take the clip back to its original state. You can also use the Clip menu to set starting and ending trim points.

Tip

Throughout the process here, make sure that the clip stays selected. You cannot do anything with the Clip menu if the clip isn't selected on the timeline.

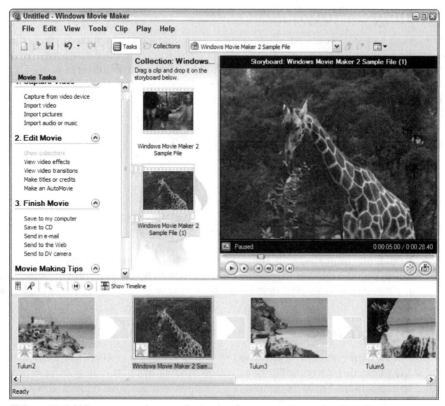

Figure 23-5: When you select a clip in the Contents pane, the first frame appears in the Monitor.

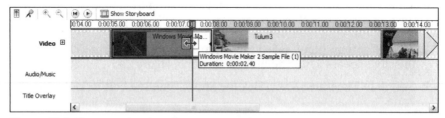

Figure 23-6: Drag to trim the clip.

Creating Transitions

Windows Movie Maker provides several transitions that you can use between clips. You can also access more transitions by installing the current Windows Plus pack, available at www.microsoft.com/windowsxp. Although you don't have to use any transitions, they improve the flow from clip to clip by making it appear more natural and less choppy. To create a transition, follow these steps:

Note   Video transitions also work with transitions between photos, so don't let the title fool you.

1. **In the Contents pane, ensure that you are in Storyboard view. If not, click the Show Storyboard button.**

2. **Click Tools ⇨ Video Transitions, or in the Movie Tasks pane, click the "View video transitions" link in the Edit Movie category.** The available transitions appear in the Collections pane, as shown in Figure 23-7.

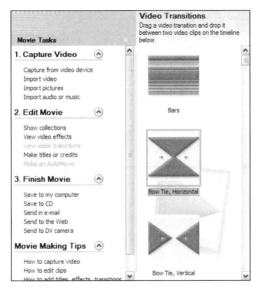

Figure 23-7: The Video Transitions window

3. **Drag a transition to the transition box on the storyboard.** The transition boxes appear between each clip or photo. Once you drag the transitions to the storyboard, you see an icon for each of them between each clip, as shown in Figure 23-8.

4. **Press Play in the monitor to see your movie play with the transitions.**

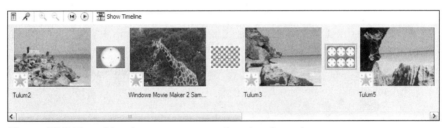

Figure 23-8: Transition icons appear on the storyboard

Expert's Notebook: Speed Up or Slow Down a Transition Effect

A transition duration works a lot like a clip duration. You can change it by trimming the transition, which is actually a clip. To do this, go to Timeline view. Click the little plus sign (+) next to the Video category to expand it. A Transition row appears. Locate the transition, click it, and then drag to adjust the length of the transition. You can experiment with different lengths until you get the transition that you want, as shown in the following figure.

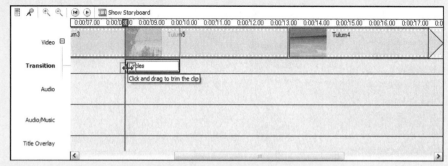

Click and drag to change the transition duration.

Adding Effects

Movie Maker 2 also includes a number of effects that you can add to any clip or photo. Like transitions, you can use the default effects, or you can install more effects by purchasing the Windows Plus! pack. These include all kinds of video or photo effects, such as blurring features, lighting features, and even an aged-film effect. These features are not necessary, of course, but they can add some cool features to your movies. To add an effect, just follow these steps:

1. **Click Tools ➪ Video Effects.** The video effects appear in the Collections pane.

2. **Scroll through the effects and locate one that you want to use.**

3. **Drag the effect to the Star icon on each clip.** Repeat this process for other clips to which you want to add effects. Clips that have an effect added show an enabled Star icon in the left corner, as shown with the Tulum3 clip in Figure 23-9.

4. **Press Play in the Monitor to see your effect in action.**

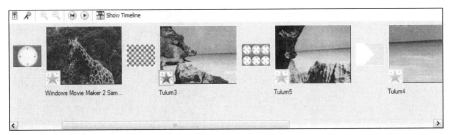

Figure 23-9: The Tulum3 clip has an effect added.

Adding Titles or Credits

In much the same way that you can add an effect to clip, you can also add a title or credit to a clip. Windows Movie Maker has an easy process for you to follow:

1. **Click Tools ⇨ Titles and Credits.** The Titles and Credits window, shown in Figure 23-10, appears.

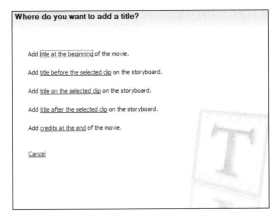

Figure 23-10: Choose a title or credit.

2. **Click a link based on the kind of title or credit that you want to create.** A screen appears that allows you to enter the text for your title, as shown in Figure 23-11.

3. **Enter your text.** You can also use the More Options links to change the title animation, or to change the text font and color.

4. **When you're done, click the "Done, add title to movie" link.**

Figure 23-11: Enter and format your text.

Audio Files and Your Movies

Once you have placed, trimmed, and added transitions to your clips on the storyboard, you can add audio to your movie. For example, you can add narration, background music, or even additional background noise. As long as it's an audio file, you can add it to your movie.

In some cases you may already have audio on your video, such as with a family reunion, where everyone is talking and laughing. You may want to add soft background music to that movie without losing the original audio. In this section you learn how to do this.

Adding Audio to a Movie

In the Contents pane, there is an audio section of the storyboard at the top left side where you can manage audio levels and add narration. To record your voice, or some background music or sounds, you click the Microphone button. You should have your computer microphone connected and tested, or you should make sure that the other sound input device that you want to record is ready. To record an audio file, just follow these steps:

1. **In the Contents pane, click the Microphone button.** A window appears, listing the sound device that you will use to record the audio, as shown in Figure 23-12.

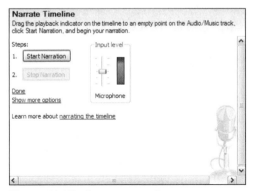

Figure 23-12: Create narration

2. **If you have more than one sound device installed on your computer, use the drop-down menu to select your device.** When you are ready, click the Start Narration button.

3. **Give the file a name, and then save it**. The file now appears in your timeline. You can see an example in Figure 23-13.

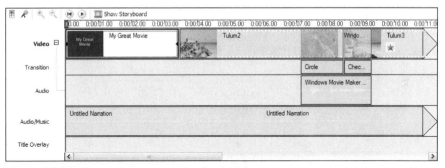

Figure 23-13: An audio segment in the timeline

Adjusting Audio Levels

Once you add audio to your movie, you can adjust the audio level. This is particularly helpful if you have two streams of audio — for example, a primary audio stream, such as voice, and a secondary audio stream, such as background music. By default, Movie Maker sets both streams to the same audio level, and so you may need to adjust them for your movie. To adjust audio levels, click the Timeline button, and then click the Set Audio Levels button in the Contents pane. This action opens a simple dialog box, shown in Figure 23-14, which enables you to adjust the audio source volume.

Figure 23-14: The Audio Levels dialog box

Saving Movies

As you finish your movie, make sure that you proof everything for accuracy. When you're done, you can choose to save your movie to your computer, or to a CD. You can also send it in an e-mail or post it on the Web, as well as send it back to a DV camera. To save the movie, in the Movie Tasks pane, and under the Finish Movie option, click the option that you want, and then follow any steps that appear.

Printing Digital Photos with Windows XP 24

Many people love digital photography today, and for several good reasons. For example, they have complete control over their photos: they can edit them, take experimental photos without having them developed, and, of course, print them. The ability to print digital photos from home has become very popular in recent years, and printer manufacturers have scrambled to meet the needs of the growing photo-printing market. You'll find mini-printers just for printing photos, and printers that actually call themselves "photo printers." Fortunately, printing technology is better than ever, and with Windows XP and a good printer, you can create great prints of your photos. In this chapter, I discuss printing from Windows XP. I'll describe built-in printing tools that are available to you, online printing, and a few third-party products that you may find helpful.

Understanding Resolution

Once you purchase a digital camera and begin to print photos, you move beyond the arena of "basic photographer." Before, you simply took photos and had someone else do all of the processing. Now, you are not only taking photos, but you are processing them as well, which requires that you know a few more things about photo processing, such as resolution. In fact, you'll have difficulty printing great photos without understanding the concept of resolution.

Every digital picture is made up of *pixels*. Pixel stands for picture element. You can think of a pixel as a little block of color that helps to create an entire picture. The more pixels a picture has, the higher the color and quality. Resolution refers to the number of pixels per inch (ppi). The more pixels per inch, the better the quality of your pictures is. Digital cameras provide different resolution capabilities. Less expensive cameras may only support around 75 to 100 ppi, while higher-end cameras support much higher values. The fewer pixels you have, the bigger the pixel must be in order to make up the image. The more pixels, the smaller they are, which provides a very fine level of appearance and quality. As a result, fewer pixels mean loss of color control and quality.

In order to get higher-quality printed photos, you must have a camera that supports higher resolution levels. Depending on what you want to do, a less expensive digital camera may be all that you need. If you want to view pictures on your computer or post them on Web sites, then you really only need a resolution of about 75 to 100 ppi, because computer monitors do not display more than this resolution. However, if you want to print high-quality photos, then you need pictures that have a higher resolution. The greater the number of pixels, the greater the quality, or the higher the resolution. High-resolution digital photos result in high-resolution print photos, and so the importance of resolution cannot be understated.

Your camera is capable of a certain maximum resolution. With today's digital cameras, resolution is expressed in megapixels. A megapixel is equal to one million pixels. For example, if your camera is a 1.3-megapixel camera, then you can take a photo that has 1,300,000 pixels. If your camera is a 5-megapixel camera, then you can take a photo that has 5,000,000 pixels. Obviously, the 5-megapixel camera can give you much greater resolution than a 1.3-megapixel camera.

When you want to take a photo, you can use the camera to choose a resolution value for the photo. Your camera lists resolution values as photo pixel height times width. Rather than giving you the option to shoot a 1.3-megapixel image, you see the option to shoot a 1280 x 1024 image (1280 x 1024 equals 1,300,000, or 1.3 megapixels). If you have a 4-megapixel camera, your highest resolution would be 2240 x 1680 (which equals 4,000,000, or 4 megapixels).

Keep in mind that when you want to print an image, you must have a high enough resolution in order to recreate all of those pixels when you print. For this reason, you cannot take a 640 x 480 image and print it as an 8 x 10 photo with good results. The pixel count is too low, and so the print quality will be poor.

Although it is difficult to give you an exact guideline, the following resolution values generally give you good-quality print sizes:

FYI: Dots per Inch (DPI)

Keep in mind that printers measure an image in dpi (dots per inch), and not in ppi. As a general rule, the printer needs to print an image with a resolution of at least 300 dpi in order for the image to look good, although this 300-dpi value depends on the kind of printer. For example, laser printers often provide a resolution of 1200 x 1200 dpi, while inkjet printers provide much higher resolutions. The point here is really this: your printer probably has the capability to print a sharp-looking photo, and so you typically don't have to worry about your printer's resolution settings. Spend your time thinking about resolution and shooting photos at a high enough resolution to do what you want. The printer will handle the issue of converting ppi to dpi.

✦ If you want to print small images or use the images for computer viewing and the Internet, you can shoot at 640 x 480.

✦ To create 4 x 6 prints, you need to shoot an image that is at least 1024 x 768.

✦ To create 5 x 7 prints, you need to shoot an image that is at least 1280 x 1024 (1 megapixel).

✦ To create 8 x 10 prints, you need to shoot an image that is at least 1600 x 1200 (2 megapixels).

✦ To create 11 x 14 prints, you need to shoot an image that is at least 2048 x 1536 (3.3 megapixels).

More pixels mean larger file sizes. In other words, the more pixels that you have in a photo, the greater the file size in terms of megabytes. For example, a typical 75-ppi JPEG file may only be about 50KB, while a 300-ppi TIFF file may be 2 or 3MB in size — 50 to 100 times bigger!

Your camera may allow you to adjust the resolution as needed. Keep the purpose of your pictures in mind, and adjust the resolution accordingly. Always try to take images at a slightly higher resolution than you may need. You can always reduce pixels, but you can't add pixels later to produce a high-quality photo.

Printing Photos with the Photo Printing Wizard

Windows XP includes a Photo Printing Wizard that is designed to help you select the photos that you want to print, choose the quality and size of the photos, and print the photos. To use the Photo Printing Wizard, follow these steps:

1. **In the folder containing the photos that you want to print, click the Print pictures option in the Picture Tasks pane (see Figure 24-1.).** If the folder contains multiple items other than photos, first select the photo in order to see the Picture Tasks options. You can also right-click any photo and click Print, or select multiple photos by Ctrl-clicking them, then right-clicking them, and then clicking Print.

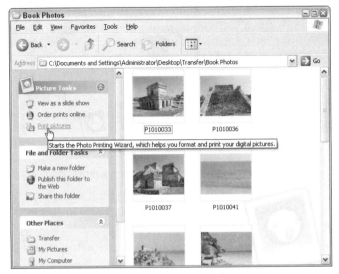

Figure 24-1: Click the Print pictures option

2. **The Photo Printing Wizard appears.** Click Next.

3. **In the Picture Selection page (Figure 24-2), select the photos that you want to print.** Deselect the check boxes next to any photos that you do not want to print.

4. **In the Printing Options page (Figure 24-3), use the drop-down menu to select the printer to which you want to print.** Then click the Printing Preferences button.

5. **In the Properties dialog box that appears (Figure 24-4), make your selections.** Be sure to choose a photo paper option from the Media drop-down menu. When you are done, click OK. This returns you to the Printing Options page. Click Next.

6. **In the Layout Selection page that appears (see Figure 24-5), choose a print layout.** You can choose from full page, contact sheets, and a variety of other sizes. In the example in Figure 24-5, I am printing three 4 x 6-inch photos on a single page. Each photo is printed only once. Make your selections and click Next.

7. **The photos are sent to the printer.** Click Finish.

Figure 24-2: The Picture Selection page

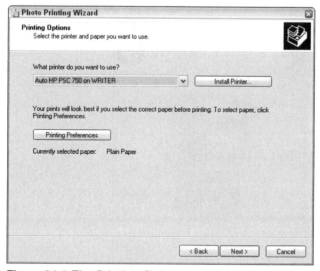

Figure 24-3: The Printing Options page

Before you print, you need to choose a paper that is compatible with your printer. There are many to choose from, and so it may be difficult to find the paper that you really like. Start with the brand that matches your printer. Try some test prints and then try other brands to see which one gives you the best prints. Like most things in life, you get what you pay for, and so you should avoid deals that seem too good to be true.

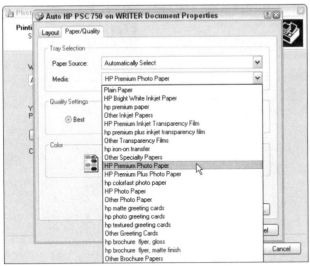

Figure 24-4: The Paper/Quality tab of the printer Document Properties dialog box

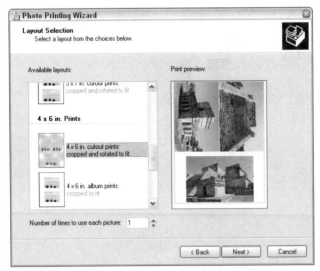

Figure 24-5: The Layout Selection page

Ordering Prints Online

Windows XP includes a feature that helps you connect to an Internet service that prints your photos for a fee and mails them to you. Although you can do this online without using Windows XP, XP makes it much easier to order prints online. The following steps show you how:

1. **If you have a dial-up connection, connect to the Internet.**

2. **Open the folder where your photos reside. In the Picture Tasks pane, click Order prints online (see Figure 24-6).** The Online Print Ordering Wizard appears.

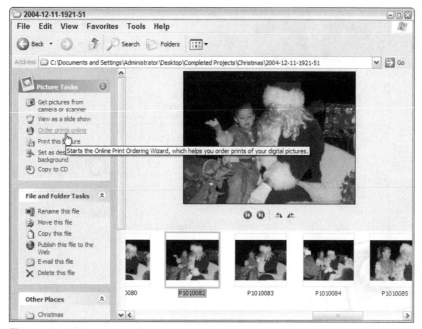

Figure 24-6: You can order prints online

3. **Click Next on the Welcome page.**

4. **In the Change Your Picture Selection page, shown in Figure 24-7, choose the photos that you want to order.** Deselect the check box of any photo that you do not want to order. Click Next when you are done.

   The wizard connects to the Internet and downloads information. This may take a few moments, depending on the speed of your connection.

5. **In the selection page that appears, shown in Figure 24-8, select the photo company from which you want to order.** Click Next. The wizard downloads ordering information from the company that you selected and displays it to you, as shown in Figure 24-9.

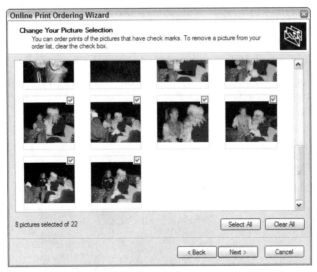

Figure 24-7: Select the photos that you want to order

Figure 24-8: Choose a printing company

Figure 24-9: Order your prints

6. **Use the ordering page to select the number of each print that you want, as well as the size.** Scroll to the bottom of the window to see your sub-total when you are done, and click Next.

   Depending on the company that you selected, you progress through a series of pages where you establish an account and release your credit card and shipping information.

7. **Follow the remainder of the wizard pages to place your order.**

Other Printing Options

The Photo Printing Wizard can help you to easily print photos using Windows XP. However, the Photo Printing Wizard may not be as flexible as you would like in that you can't print different picture packages exactly to your needs. There are a number of free or inexpensive third-party tools that you can download for more printing options. The following sections describe my favorite tools, as well as where to get the software.

Print Six

One of the things that you may want to do is create pages for photo albums where you typically display six photos. One easy way to do this is with the Print Six photo-printing software (shown in Figure 24-10), which is available from www. sixdigitalphotos.com. You can easily print six photos per page, or just about any other combination that you want. If you print a lot of photos for photo albums, you'll find this software easier to use than the Photo Printing Wizard in Windows XP. This software costs about $20.

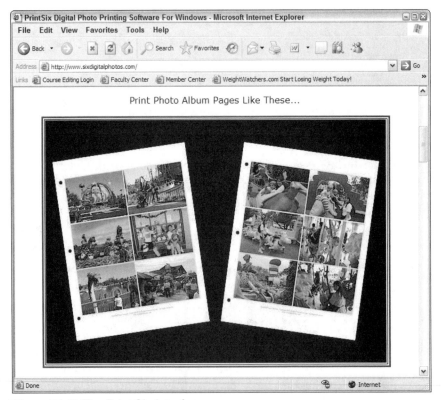

Figure 24-10: The Print Six interface

Pics Print

Pics Print, shown in Figure 24-11, is very flexible printing software that gives you a standard interface. You can select what you want to print and then choose the sizes you want. This is the great advantage over the Windows XP Photo Printing Wizard because you can manually choose the sizes you want for the photos you are printing. You'll find the software easy to use, and it only costs about $40. Find out more at www.picsprint.com.

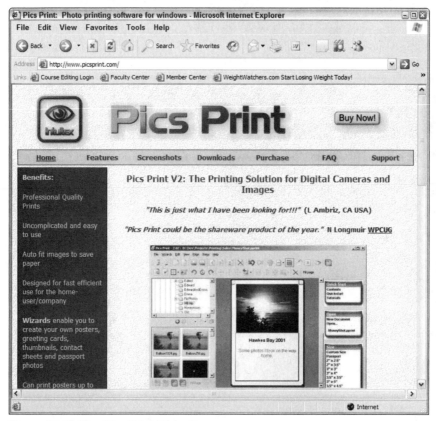

Figure 24-11: The Pics Print Web site

Photo Elf

Photo Elf (Figure 24-12) is another printing software package that enables you to combine photos and print different picture package options, a feature which is lacking in the Photo Printing Wizard in Windows XP This software package is inexpensive and easy to use. You can find out more at www.photoelf.com and buy the software from the site for about $25.

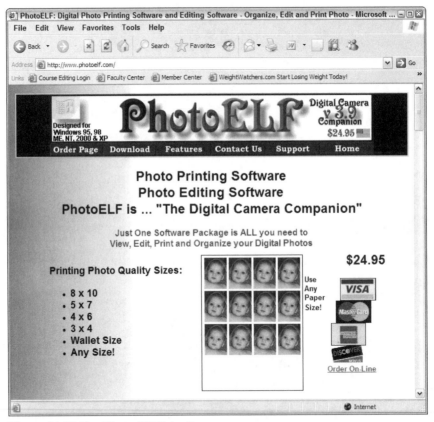

Figure 24-12: The Photo Elf Web site

Photo Cool

Photo Cool, shown in Figure 24-13, is an easy-to-use software package that gives you many options when printing your photos. You can even print passport photos and other creative options, which you can't do with the Windows XP Photo Printing Wizard. You can check it out at www.ussun.com. Photo Cool costs about $30.

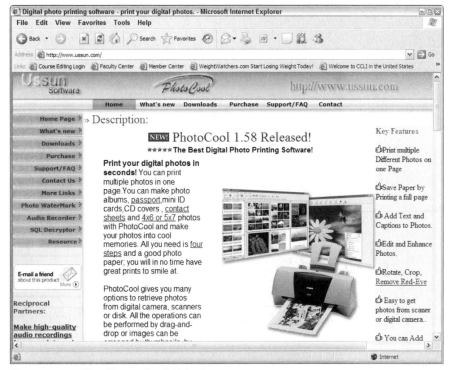

Figure 24-13: The Photo Cool Web site

Custom Projects and Fun Activities with Digital Photos

25

D igital photos are here to stay. Just walk into any department store and check out the number of digital cameras that are available. After all, digital photos are easy to edit and work with, and you can use them for all kinds of projects.

One way to create fun projects with your digital photos is to use image-editing software. Although you can purchase expensive image-editing programs and production software, in this chapter I concentrate on a few free or inexpensive image-editing tools that I enjoy using.

Resizing a Photo for E-mail

You may need to resize a photo for an e-mail attachment. For example, you may have a high-resolution TIFF file that you are using for printing, but that you also want to send to a colleague. If both you and your recipient use a broadband service, then you can take some liberties with file sizes. However, for dial-up users, a large file takes a long time to download, and your recipient's e-mail server may even reject the file for its large size.

As the above example shows, you may need high-resolution photos for printing, as well as low-resolution JPEG versions of these photos for sending by e-mail. In the past, this meant that you had to use an image-editing program to alter your original file size. Now, Windows XP can easily do this task for you if you follow these steps:

1. **In the folder where you store your pictures, select the photo that you want to e-mail.** You can select multiple photos by Ctrl-clicking the files. Then, either click the "E-mail the selected items" option, found in the File and Folder Tasks pane, or right-click the photos and click Send To ➪ Mail Recipient.

2. **In the Send Pictures via E-mail dialog box, choose the "Make all my pictures smaller" option.** If you click the "Show more options" link, you can determine the size that you want to make your photos, as shown in Figure 25-1. Make your selections and then click OK. Your pictures are resized and attached to an e-mail message.

Figure 25-1: Send pictures through e-mail

PowerToys for Digital Photos

In Chapter 11, I introduced several PowerToys, which were created after Microsoft released Windows XP. You can download PowerToys for free from www.microsoft. com/windowsxp. In the following sections, I discuss three utilities that you may want to download and use when working with your digital photos.

Image Resizer

Image Resizer is a great tool if you frequently work with digital images. Because resizing is a common task, this utility enables you to quickly resize an image, or even a group of images, rather than having to open the images in an image-editing program. Once you install it, just follow these steps to resize your images.

1. **Right-click an image or a collection of images.** On the contextual menu, click Resize Pictures. The Resize Pictures dialog box appears, as shown in Figure 25-2.

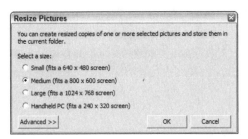

Figure 25-2: Choose a size option

2. **Select an option for the size that you want the photos to be.** Windows XP creates a copy of the original photos and stores them in the current folder. It does not alter your original photos.

3. **Click the Advanced button for more options, as shown in Figure 25-3.** You can create a custom size, make photos smaller but not larger, and resize the original photo. Click OK when you're done.

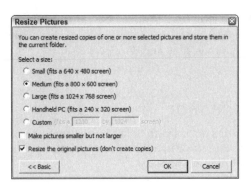

Figure 25-3: The Advanced options

CD Slide Show Generator

The CD Slide Show Generator enables you to put a collection of photos on a CD that you can play as a slide show. When you open the CD, you see an autorun file that you can double-click to start the slide show, as shown in Figure 25-4. When you double-click the file, the photos display, one at a time in a full screen, and the photos automatically advance after a period of a few seconds, although you can also manually advance them by clicking your mouse button. The slide show continues to loop through all of the photos until you press the Esc key.

To create a slide show, you must install the software and then copy the photos to a CD. When you burn the CD, the CD-burning wizard asks you if you want to make the view as a slide show option available on the CD.

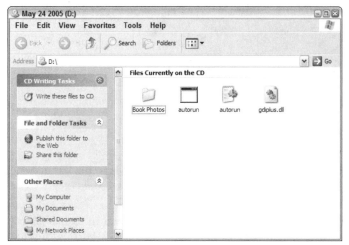

Figure 25-4: You can click the autorun icon to start the slide show.

Note CD Slide Show Generator slideshows can be played on older versions of Windows as well, such as Windows 2000 and Windows 98.

HTML Slide Show Generator

The HTML Slide Show Generator uses a wizard to help you to create a slide show of photos. You can then view the slide show in a Web browser. After you install the HTML Slide Show Generator, just follow these steps:

1. **Click Start ➪ All Programs ➪ PowerToys for Windows XP ➪ Slide Show Wizard.** The Welcome page appears.

2. **Click Next.** The Images page appears.

3. **Use the Add Image or Add Folder buttons to add images and folders to your collection**. You can use all of the photos that you add here in the slide show, as shown in Figure 25-5.

4. **In the Select options for your slide show page, give a name for the slide show, and add your name as the author.** By default, although Windows XP saves the slide show in My Documents\My Slide Shows, you can change the location by clicking the Browse button and selecting a different location. In the Picture size section, choose the picture size that you want. In the Slide show type section, you can choose between simple and advanced (which simply changes the layout option), and you can also choose to display the slide show in full screen, as shown in Figure 25-6.

Figure 25-5: Add your images or folders of images to your slide show

Figure 25-6: Configure the slide show options

5. **Make your selections and then click Next.** The slide show is created, and you arrive at the Finish page.

6. **You can view the slide show from this page by clicking the View the Slide Show Now button.** Figure 25-7 shows a complete slide show.

Figure 25-7: A complete slide show

Note When creating the slide show, the program creates a folder that contains a default.htm file and a couple of other folders that hold the photos and the Web content. You can e-mail the entire folder to someone to view it, or you can place it on a CD. Keep in mind that the default.htm file must have the other two folders in order to work, and so you must not separate them.

Creating a Plus! Photo Story

Part of the Plus! SuperPack product, Plus! Photo Story works like a mini moviemaker. You assemble the photos that you want, and then you can add panning effects that simulate movement. You can also add narration using the computer's microphone. Plus! Photo Story formats the movie as a Windows Media file that only Windows Media Players can play. Plus! Photo Story costs about $30, and is available from www.microsoft.com/windowsxp.

Cross-Reference For more information about Plus! SuperPack, see Chapter 11.

To create a Photo Story, follow these steps:

1. **Click Start ➪ All Programs.** Navigate to Photo Story.

2. **On the Welcome page, shown in Figure 25-8, you can start by clicking the Begin a Story button, or you can play an existing story from the Media Library.** If you plan on adding narration to your story, you should click the Configure Microphone button and walk through the wizard steps to configure your microphone.

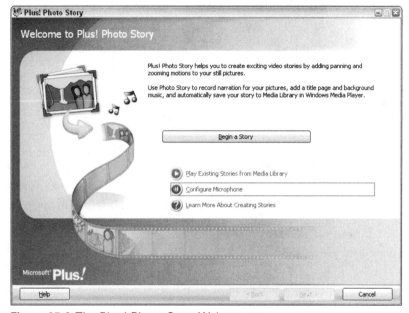

Figure 25-8: The Plus! Photo Story Welcome page

3. **When you're ready to create your photo story, click the Begin a Story button.** In the Import and Arrange your Pictures page, shown in Figure 25-9, use the Import Pictures button to browse for and import photos. The imported photos appear on the timeline, where you can use the Arrow buttons to rearrange them, or you can click and drag them around with your mouse. Do not proceed until the photos are in the order that you want for your Photo Story. Click Next when you're done.

4. **Add narration to your story.** In the next page, you can record your narration, preview the story, or click the Advanced button to configure additional features:

Figure 25-9: Import and arrange your pictures

- **To record your narration:** Click the Record button and begin talking. Use the large arrow button to advance the photos as you record your narration. You can also stop recording or reset the picture — this erases the narration that you have placed on the picture. Think of the narration as "photo by photo" — this helps you to narrate a picture and easily fix mistakes because the narration is photo-specific. Writing a script beforehand is also helpful. Figure 25-10 shows you a recording session in progress.

- **To preview your story:** Simply click the Preview Story button. You can view your story in Windows Media Player.

- **To access more features:** Click the Advanced button. You can then configure additional options, as shown in Figure 25-11. For example, you can control the panning motion of each photo by selecting start and end points for the pan. You can also prevent the narration from being recorded and determine how long to display the picture. When you're done, click OK. You then return to the previous page, where you can select another photo and configure advanced features for it.

Tip

The panning function is automatically added to each photo. You do not have to manually configure panning here unless you are trying to achieve a certain panning effect. If you don't want to use panning, choose the full screen box for the start and end position. (This is the last box on each row of panning selections.)

Figure 25-10: Narration is built on a photo-by-photo basis.

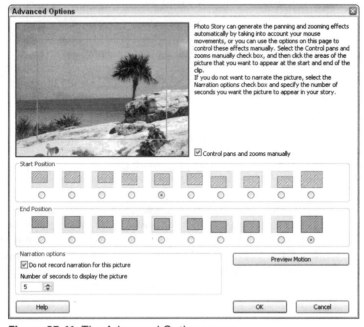

Figure 25-11: The Advanced Options page

5. **On the Add a title page, you can select the "Add a title page to your story" option.** You can input your text, determine the text alignment, and click the Font button to adjust the font style, size, and color. Click the Background Image button to use a photo as a background, as shown in Figure 25-12. Click Next when you're done. In the next page, shown if Figure 25-13, you choose to add background music and specify the duration of photos that have no narration (five seconds is usually enough).

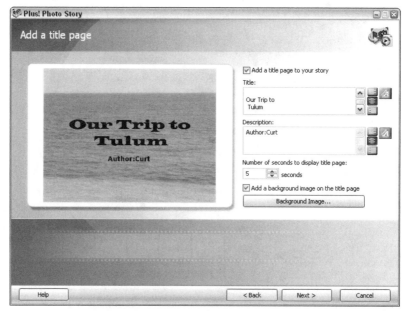

Figure 25-12: Create a title page

6. **Click the Browse button to select a song from your Windows Media Player library**. When you're done, click the Preview Final Story button to check all volume levels and pacing. You can always use the Back button to make adjustments. Click Next.

If you have content protection turned on in Windows Media Player, you're likely to have problems adding a song to the Photo Story because the software sees this as copyright infringement. You cannot use someone else's song, put it on your Photo Story, and then distribute or view the story, except for your own use. If you see this message, you need to turn off content protection, delete the song from your library, and re-copy it to Windows Media Player.

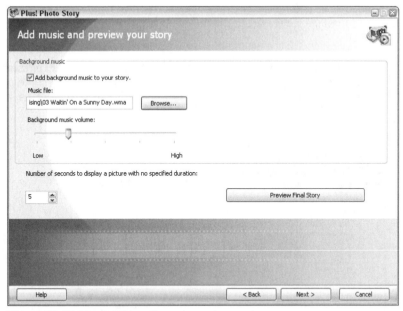

Figure 25-13: The Add music and preview your story page

7. **In the Quality Settings page, you can choose from high and medium quality for both audio and video, and give your story a filename.** You can use the medium quality if you need to keep the file size low; otherwise, go with the high quality settings. Click Next. The story is created and saved in your My Documents\My Videos folder.

8. **You can view the story, burn it to a CD, or even e-mail it to friends and family.**

Creating a Custom CD Label

The Plus! SuperPack includes CD Label Maker software, which allows you to create custom labels for your CDs or DVDs. The software works well, and it is compatible with a great number of CD and CD insert labels that you can find at any department or computer store. If you've never made custom labels, you should give it a try. For example, with every Christmas and family vacation, I make a DVD photo slide show for my family, and I always create a custom label using one of the photos as a background. My family loves receiving these DVDs.

The CD Label Maker software allows you to quickly and easily create labels. I should also mention that many of the label packages that you purchase also ship with a CD that includes label software. My experience is that the Plus! SuperPack software is a bit easier to manage, as shown in the following steps for creating a standard label for a CD or DVD.

1. **Launch the Plus! CD Label Maker by selecting Start ⇨ All Programs, and navigating to the program.** Click the Next button on the Welcome page. The wizard prompts you to choose a CD or playlist for the CD label, as shown in Figure 25-14.

Figure 25-14: Choose a CD or playlist for the label.

The wizard is designed to work with Windows Media Player, and so it checks Windows Media Player for any playlists that you have created. It also checks your CD drive for a music CD. In the left pane, select the CD or playlist for which you are creating a label; the contents of the CD or playlist appear in the right pane. This information is used for a CD case insert. If you are only creating the label, you don't need this information. However, CD Label Maker gathers this information anyway, in case you decide later to make a label for your jewel case insert.

2. **Click Next to continue.**

If the CD or playlist song name isn't exactly what you want, then you can change it later in the wizard.

3. **Locate the label product that you have purchased.** The Plus! CD Label Maker uses templates in order to print your CD labels correctly. As shown in Figure 25-15, you can use the Templates menu and choose the brand and product number that matches the labels that you have purchased. Make your selection and click Next.

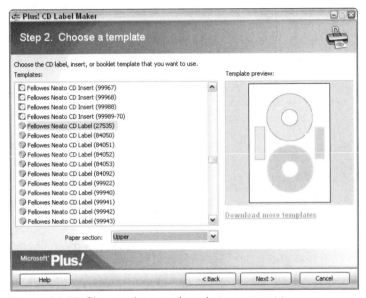

Figure 25-15: Choose the template that you want to use.

> **Note** Depending on your selection, you may notice that the Paper section drop-down menu is enabled, which allows you to choose between the upper and lower label on the page. Unfortunately, you can't make a duplicate label on the same page at the same time. You have to print the first label, run the paper through the printer again, and then choose the other label selection option the second time.

4. **In the next part of the wizard, you design your label.** First of all, orient yourself to the interface, as shown in Figure 25-16. You see a sample label, along with a tab for that label. Depending on the template that you chose, you may have more than one label and more than one design tab for each label. For example, in Figure 25-16, the template can print both a label for the CD and a label for the spine of the jewel case. Choose which label you want to design first by either clicking the sample itself or the appropriate tab.

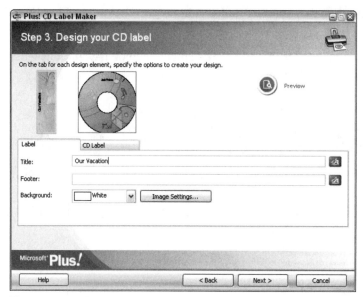

Figure 25-16: The Design page for your CD label

5. **Type the title and footer text into the provided fields on the Label tab.** Try to keep your text short, because it must fit on the label.

6. **Click the formatting button at the end of the text field (it looks like a double A).** A Font dialog box appears, where you can select the font, style, and color for your text, as shown in Figure 25-17. Once you've made your selections, click OK. You return to the wizard.0

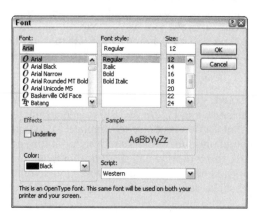

Figure 25-17: The Font dialog box displays formatting options.

Tip

Be careful with fonts, colors and styles. Although your selection may look good, ask yourself if it is easy to read. Keep your text simple, rather than over-stylized. Also, be careful with the contrast between your text and your background. For example, black text is very difficult to read on navy and blue backgrounds.

7. **Preview the label to see how your text will look when it is printed.** Click the Preview button, and then use the drop-down menu to adjust the size of the preview so that you can see it easily, as shown in Figure 25-18. If you do not like what you see, return to the wizard and make adjustments as needed.

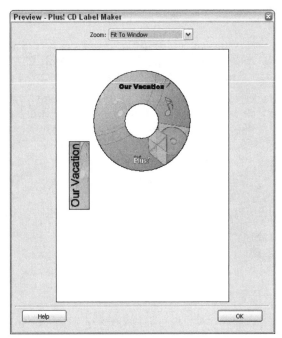

Figure 25-18: Preview the text for your CD label

8. **Create a background.** In this step, you can apply a background, which can either be an image or a simple background color. The following bullets explain your options. You can use any standard photo file as a background. Click the Image Settings button on the Design your CD label page to begin creating the background. The Background Image Settings dialog box appears, as shown in Figure 25-19. If you do not want to use a background image, select the "Do not use image" option, and then click OK. This takes you back to the main wizard page.

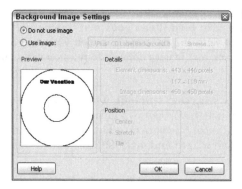

Figure 25-19: The Background Image Settings dialog box

9. **Select a background color**. If you want to use a background color, use the Background drop-down menu to select one, as shown in Figure 25-20. Use this feature when you want a single color label rather than a background image.

If you want to use a background image, then in the Background Image Settings dialog box, select the "Use image" option, and then click the Browse button to locate the image. A standard Open window appears, where you can choose the image that you want to use.

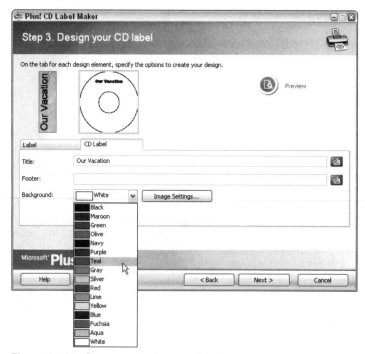

Figure 25-20: Choose a background color.

In the Background Image Settings dialog box, you can see a preview of your image on the label, as shown in Figure 25-21.

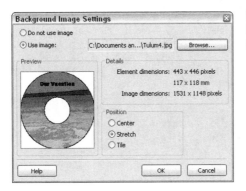

Figure 25-21: You can preview the image in the Background Image Settings dialog box.

10. **In the Position section, you can select the Center, Stretch, or Tile option if your image is not large enough to cover the whole label.** If you are using a digital photo, there is nothing you need to do here.

Note

The Preview image will be grainy and perhaps a bit blurry. This is okay, as the image will not look this way when you print it.

11. **Click OK when you are done to return to the wizard**. To see your background and text, click the Preview button; the background will still look grainy and somewhat distorted. At this time, you may want to return to the Font dialog box and adjust your text so that it looks better with your selected background. Once everything looks the way you want, click Next.

12. **The final wizard page, shown in Figure 25-22 allows you to choose the printer and the number of copies that you want to make.**

You can also use this wizard to create a custom jewel case insert. The process of creating the insert is almost exactly the same as that for the label. You can buy the jewel case insert label paper, select the correct template using the wizard, and then configure the text and background as you like. Generally, the jewel case label allows you to create a front and back insert card that you fold in half and put in the jewel case. You can add your own background image as usual, and manage the titles and fonts.

I mentioned earlier in this section that the song list appears. You can directly edit this text in order to make the CD insert more personal.

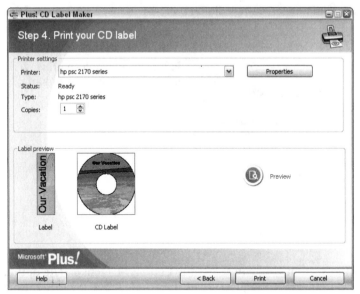

Figure 25-22: Choose your print options for your CD label.

Hacking
Windows XP

IV

I f you feel a need to make unauthorized
changes to Windows XP, you may be a
hack! In this part, you learn about "hacking"
Windows XP for greater customization and
control.

In this part, you discover how to hack your
system using the Registry Editor, put expert
tips and tricks to work. You also learn about
scripting with Windows XP.

In This Section

Hacking Your System

26

I f you've been using Windows XP for a while, you know that there are a lot of settings, in a lot of dialog boxes, where you can choose personal preferences. Many of the dialog boxes are located in Control Panel, while other dialog boxes are located in programs, such as when you choose Tools ⇨ Options from a program's menu bar to choose preferences for just about anything.

The Windows XP Registry stores all of the settings that you choose. In addition to all of your personal preferences, the Registry contains a lot of other configuration data about your computer, including details about every hardware device, program, document, and folder that is on your system.

Once in a blue moon, you may need to *hack,* or edit, the Registry to solve some pesky problem. You can also hack the Registry to make some changes to your system that you cannot make through more traditional means, such as through dialog boxes. In this chapter you learn what hacking the Registry is all about.

Hacking the Windows XP Registry

Before you get started, make sure that you read Appendix A, "A Primer on Registry

Editing." The Registry is no place for experimentation, or for trying to solve problems through guesswork. When you're editing the Registry, even a minor typographical error can have far-reaching and negative consequences, such as chronic crashes, or even the inability to start your computer!

The Registry is not a user-friendly place. Where the dialog boxes show plain-English descriptions of options, the Registry contains only obscure key names. Where dialog boxes allow you to make your selection using familiar numbers and text, the Registry stores much of its data in hexadecimal and binary formats. That's because the Registry is intended to provide information to the system, not to humans. In other words the Registry is more machine-friendly than it is user-friendly.

Starting the Registry Editor

The first step to editing the Registry is to start the Registry Editor. To do so:

1. **Click the Start button, and then choose Run.** The Run dialog box appears.

2. **Type** regedit, **and then press Enter or click OK.**

To make a quick backup of the Registry before you start making changes, follow these steps:

1. **Choose File ➪ Export from the Registry Editor menu bar.**

2. **Enter a filename, such as RegBackup.**

3. **Under Export Range choose All.**

4. **Click the Save button.**

Tip   As an alternative to the registry editors' own backup facility, there are numerous third party applications that can do the job quickly and simply. One such freeware application is ERUNT at www.larshederer.homepage.t.online.de/erunt. I use this application on a regular basis for backing up the registry before making any alterations. It is simply to use and you don't need install it. Just download the file, unpack the zipped file to a new folder, open the folder and click ERUNT.exe.

FYI: Backing Up the Registry

Always back up the Registry before making any changes. That way, if you really make a mess of things, you can restore the previous settings from the backup copy of the Registry. You can back up the Registry by running a normal Windows Backup (see Chapter 32). You can also recover your system using System Restore (see Chapter 34), or booting into Safe Mode and invoking the Last Known Good Configuration option. See Chapter 36 to learn more about Safe Mode.

How the Registry Is Organized

The Windows XP Registry is a hierarchical database containing *configuration data*. In other words, the configuration data determines how Windows operates. A hierarchical database is different from a relational database in that the data is not organized into rows and columns stored in tables. Instead, the Registry stores the data in a hierarchical format — where file paths represent specific data items — similar to a family tree or organization chart. For example, a file path to a file named KEYBOARD.DRV in your Windows System folder might look like this:

```
C:\WINDOWS\SYSTEM\KEYBOARD.DRV
```

The path starts with the most general location, drive C:. The next item in the path, WINDOWS, refers to a folder named WINDOWS on that drive. SYSTEM refers to a subfolder within the WINDOWS folder. Finally, KEYBOARD.DRV refers to a specific file within the SYSTEM folder.

The same idea applies to configuration settings in the Registry. For example, here's the path to data that contains the computer's CPU in the Registry:

```
HKEY_LOCAL_MACHINE\HARDWARE\DESCRIPTION\System\CentralProcessor\0
```

Figure 26-1 shows how the path corresponds to selections made in the left side of the Registry Editor window, called the *Key pane*. Each folder in the Key pane represents a *registry key*. A minus sign (–) to the left of a folder icon indicates that the folder is expanded to display its contents. In Figure 26-1, you click the plus sign next to HKEY_LOCAL_MACHINE, HARDWARE, DESCRIPTION, System, and CentralProcessor folders, and then finally click the 0 folder or, more accurately, the 0 *key*. The status bar at the bottom of the Registry Editor window displays the same path, with the folder names separated by backslashes.

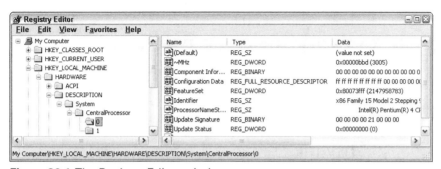

Figure 26-1: The Registry Editor window

To the right of the Key pane in the Registry Editor is the *Value pane*, which displays the values (data) stored in the key. In Figure 26-1 the 0 folder icon is selected and open, and therefore the Value pane to the right displays the values found in the 0 folder.

Common Abbreviations for Root Keys

If you collapse all keys in the left pane of the Registry Editor, leaving only My Computer expanded, you see the five *root keys*, as shown in Figure 26-2. When specifying the path to a specific registry key, use the abbreviations shown in the left column of Table 26-1.

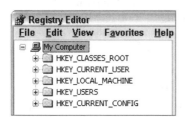

Figure 26-2: The five root keys

Abbreviation	Root key name
Table 26-1	
Abbreviations for Root Keys	
HKCC	HKEY_CURRENT_CONFIG
HKCR	HKEY_CLASSES_ROOT
HKCU	HKEY_CURRENT_USER
HKLM	HKEY_LOCAL_MACHINE
HKU	HKEY_USERS

For example, the path:

```
HKLM\SOFTWARE\Microsoft\Windows\CurrentVersion\Run
```

is short for:

```
HKEY_LOCAL_MACHINE\SOFTWARE\Microsoft\Windows\CurrentVersion\Run
```

Registry Key Values

Earlier in the chapter, it was mentioned that Registry data is stored in machine-friendly, rather than human-friendly, format. The Value pane is divided into three columns: Name, Type, and Data. Here's what each column represents:

✦ **Name:** Every value within a registry key has a unique name, which appears in the left column of the Value pane.

✦ **Type:** Defines the type of data stored in the key, such as REG_SZ (fixed-length text) or REG_DWORD (double-word). For example, the ~MHz key stores its value as a REG_DWORD.

✦ **Data:** This is the value that is stored in the key, if any. For example, in Figure 26-1, the ~MHz key contains the double-word value 0x00000bbd. The number in parenthesis, 3005, is the more familiar decimal representation of the hex number 00000bbd.

Tip

The ~MHz key is the speed of the processor expressed in megahertz. The 3005 reflects the fact that the CPU for this computer runs at 3.05 GHz.

Each entry is a placeholder for data. In many cases the value is null (nothing), in which case the Data column shows *(value not set)*. Hacking the Registry is largely a matter of locating the appropriate key and value name, and then changing the data stored under the value name. You can see many examples in the sections to follow, which provide some sample Registry hacks that you may need, or may want to try out for the fun of it.

Windows XP Interface Hacks

Most of the Registry settings that apply to the Windows XP interface are accessible from the Display Properties, Taskbar, and Start Menu Properties, as well as Folder Options dialog boxes in Control Panel. The optional Tweak UI PowerToy, available from Microsoft's Web site, provides a few additional settings that the dialog boxes omit. There are a few things on the interface that you cannot easily change without using the Registry. Some examples are in the following sections.

Stopping Error Message Beeps

Here is a simple registry hack that you can use to enable or disable the beep that you hear when an error message pops up on the screen. The key is:

```
HKCU\Control Panel\Sound\Beep
```

To change the setting, navigate to HKEY_CURRENT_USER\Control Panel\Sound in the Key pane. Then right-click the Beep value in the Value pane, and choose Modify. To stop the beep, change the Value Data entry from yes to no, as in Figure 26-3, and then click OK.

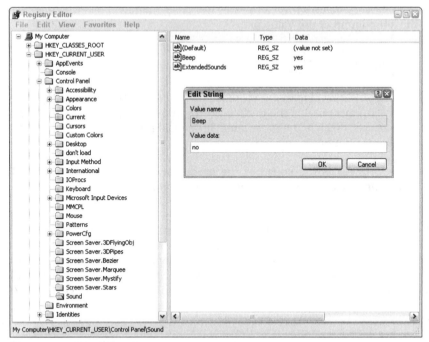

Figure 26-3: Disabling the error message beep

Remove the Username from the Start Menu

By default, whenever you click the Start button, your user account icon and name appear at the top of the Start menu. (Although that's only true if you're using the Windows XP style menu, rather than the Classic Start menu.) You can hide the username by changing (or adding) the following key:

```
HKLM\Software\Microsoft\Windows\CurrentVersion\Policies\Explorer
```

To get started, follow theses steps:

1. **Open the Registry Editor.** Work your way to the HKLM\Software\Microsoft\ Windows\CurrentVersion\Policies\ key, and then click the plus sign to the left of Policies. If you do not see an Explorer key, you can create one by right-clicking the Policies folder and choosing New ⇨ Key. Type **Explorer** as the new key name, and then press Enter.

2. **Once you have an Explorer key under Policies, click its name, as shown in Figure 26-4.** If you do not see the value name NoUserNameInStartMenu in the Value pane, right-click the Explorer folder in the Keys pane, and then choose New ⇨ DWORD Value. Type **NoUserNameInStartMenu** as the value name, and then press Enter. Finally, right-click the NoUserNameInStartMenu value name, and choose Modify. Then:

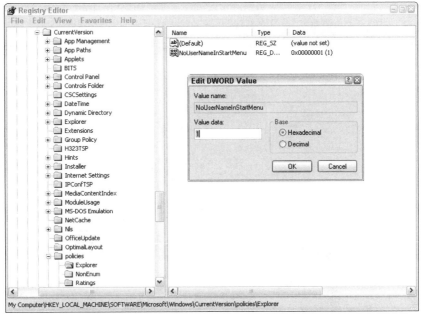

Figure 26-4: Disable username on the Start menu.

- To hide the username from the top of the Start menu, set the value to 1.

- To display the username at the top of the Start menu, set the value to 0.

3. **Click OK.** The username does not disappear from the top of the Start menu automatically. You need to restart the computer for this change to take effect.

Show the Username on the My Computer Icon

This hack is useful if you work in multiple user accounts and you want to see which account you are in by just looking at the My Computer icon. The registry key to make this change is:

```
HKEY_CLASSES_ROOT\CLISD\{20D04FE0-3AEA-1069-A2D8-08002B30309D}
```

1. **Once you've clicked on the key name, right-click the LocalizedString value, and choose Modify.** You can type any text you want as the label for the My Computer icon. You can also use the following environmental variables to display system information:

   - **%USERNAME%:** Displays the user account name.

   - **%COMPUTERNAME%:** Displays the computer name.

Figure 26-5 shows an example where the Value Data for the LocalizedString has been changed to %USERNAME% on %COMPUTERNAME%. Make the change and close the Registry Editor.

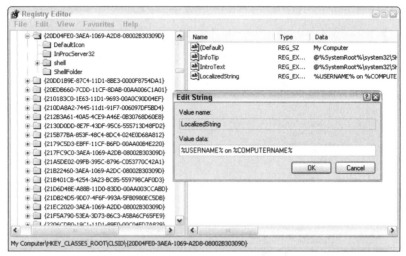

Figure 26-5: Hack the My Computer icon label

2. **You must right-click the Desktop, and choose Refresh (or press F5 at the desktop) to refresh the display and see the new label on your My Computer icon.** The new label also appears on the Start menu's My Computer icon.

To go back to your original label, return to the key and set the LocalizedString value back to its default setting of:

```
@%SystemRoot%\system32\SHELL32.dll,-9216
```

Windows XP System Hacks

Next you'll look at Registry hacks that apply more to the system as a whole than to specific interface features. These hacks include changing your user information, getting rid of programs that are "stuck" in Add or Remove Programs, and enabling and disabling Task Manager. You also learn how to bypass the Welcome screen, auto-start programs, and automatically log into a user account of your choosing.

Changing Your User Information

When you first install Windows XP, it asks for your name and company name. Whatever you enter into the boxes is permanent in the sense that it is not easy to go back and change your information. However, you can change either entry in the Registry using the following key:

```
HKLM\SOFTWARE\Microsoft\Windows NT\CurrentVersion
```

Once you get to the key, shown in Figure 26-6, right-click either the Registered-Organization or RegisteredOwner value in the Value pane, and choose Modify. In the Edit String dialog box that opens, replace the text in the Value Data box with the corrected organization or owner name, and then click OK.

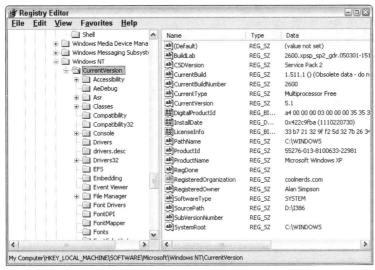

Figure 26-6: Change your registration information

Fixing the List of Installed Programs

When you open Add or Remove Programs in Control Panel, you see a list of currently installed programs. To uninstall a program, you click its name, and then click the Remove or Change/Remove button that appears under the program name.

You may come across a program that has already been removed, but it is still listed in the Add or Remove Programs. When you attempt to uninstall the program, you see an error message stating that the program cannot be removed. When that happens, you can edit the Registry to remove the program from the list of currently installed programs.

When you first expand the Uninstall key, many of the installed programs are listed by a GUID code, such as {282EF7E3-AE54-48AE-A11D-26F512F23AB3}. To see which program the code refers to, click the code and take a look at the DisplayName value in the Value pane. For example in Figure 26-7, the selected GUID refers to a program named Rio Music Manager.

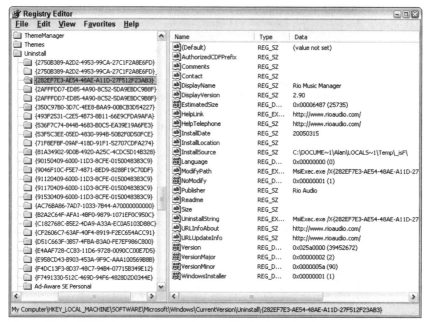

Figure 26-7: GUIDs for programs that can be uninstalled

When you locate the name of the program that should no longer be in the list of installed programs, right-click its name or GUID in the left pane, and choose Delete to delete the entire key. The program no longer appears in the Add Or Remove Programs list.

Enabling or Disabling Task Manager

Normally, you can open Task Manager by pressing Ctrl+Alt+Del, by right-clicking the taskbar, or by clicking and choosing Task Manager. If doing so just results in a message saying that the Administrator has disabled access to the program, then the program may be disabled through Group Policy. You can usually fix the problem by navigating to the following key:

```
HKCU\Software\Microsoft\Windows\CurrentVersion\Policies\System
```

Once you find the key, click it, right-click DisableTaskMgr in the Value pane, and then choose Modify. To make Task Manager work normally, set the Value Data option to 0 (zero). To disable Task Manager, set the DisableTaskMgr value to 1 (one).

Tip

If you don't find DisableTaskManager under the above-mentioned key, it might be under another key, such as Group Policy Objects. To search for the key, choose Edit ⇨ Find from the menu bar in the Registry Editor, and search for DisableTaskMgr. If you find multiple DisableTaskMgr values, change them all to 0 or 1.

Expert's Notebook: Better Spyware Removal

Many malware programs have remarkable stealth and self-preservation capabilities. For example, it may be difficult to remove the Run key for an adware or spyware program that's already loaded. And even if you do manage to delete the key, it magically re-creates itself the next time you restart the computer. As a result, trying to deal with malware through the Registry can be a very frustrating experience.

Your best bet is to access a good anti-spyware program such as Lavasoft Ad-Aware (www.Lavasoft.com) or Microsoft AntiSpyware (www.Microsoft.com/spyware), or both. Either of these can generally find whatever programs have infected your system, and remove them without any trouble at all. You can find out more about spyware in Chapter 30.

Prevent Programs from Starting Automatically

You can auto-start any program when Windows XP starts by adding a shortcut icon for the program to the C:\Documents and Settings\All Users\Start Menu\Programs\Startup folder. If you want a program to auto-start in a specific user account only, you can add a shortcut icon to the Start folder for that user account only. The path to that folder will be C:\Documents and Settings*UserName*\Start Menu\Programs\Startup, where *UserName* is the user account name.

The easy way to stop a program from auto-starting is usually to delete the program's shortcut icon from the Startup folder. Check the Startup folder for All Users first, as that's where most programs get their auto-start capabilities. If you don't find the icon there, check the Startup folder to the specific user account.

Some programs that auto-start do not have a corresponding icon in the Startup folder that you can delete. This is especially true of malware, such as adware that pops ads up on your screen, or hijacks your Web browser. Sneaky programs like that often use only a registry key to start the program. As a result, the only way to prevent the program from starting is by deleting the program's registry key.

There are two keys that you need to check for auto-starting:

```
HKLM\SOFTWARE\Microsoft\Windows\CurrentVersion\Run

HKCU\SOFTWARE\Microsoft\Windows\CurrentVersion\Run
```

 Caution   **Just because a program accesses its start from the CurrentVersion\Run key does not mean that it is a "bad" program. There are likely legitimate programs listed in the key, so you don't want to start deleting keys until you know exactly what you are deleting.**

Figure 26-8 shows an example where HKLM\SOFTWARE\Microsoft\Windows\CurrentVersion\Run is selected in the Key pane. The Values pane lists all programs that are currently configured to auto-start. In this example, they are all legitimate programs related to Microsoft AntiSpyware and McAfee VirusScan, and so you wouldn't delete any of these keys.

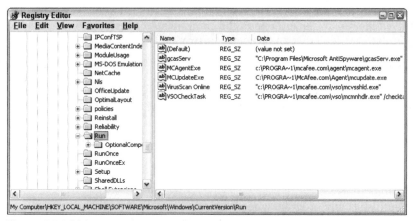

Figure 26-8: Value names represent auto-start programs.

However, if you ever do find a program that you want to prevent from running, you can just right-click the program's name in the Value pane, and choose Delete, to delete the entire key.

Log on Automatically

When you set up multiple user accounts on a Windows XP computer, you generally go to the Welcome screen each time you start the computer. From the Welcome screen, you click your user account name or picture, to log in.

Administrator Account: Setting a Password on Windows XP Home Edition

Unfortunately, the password for the Administrator account is blank by default under Windows XP Home edition. To correct this egregious oversight, boot into Safe mode. Once you reach the Desktop, you can open your Control Panel and then access the User Accounts applet to set a password on the Administrator account. You should consider this a high priority, given the number of exploits, worms, and viruses that have in the past taken advantage of poor password practices and security lapses to abuse operating system software. Every system should have a meaningful Administrator password. Period. *David Dalan*

Forcing Security: Requiring RAS Connections

Users on a WAN often have to cross unsecure networks to reach a server that is on a secure network. It is possible that some WAN sites can use a local network connection for accessing e-mail or the Internet. This may bypass some of the centralized security and monitoring tools that are in place to protect the rest of the network. VPN is a useful tool to ensure that communications are secure. It can also override local network options and tunnel all network communications through the VPN link (and the central network), as well as prevent traffic from flowing out from other network gateways. To ensure that users use a VPN connection, you can create a new String Value called "RasForce" inside the registry key HKLM\SOFTWARE\Microsoft\Windows NT\CurrentVersion\Winlogon. Set the value to 1 to force a RAS connection during logon. Setting the value to 0 disables this item. This is not without risk. You must have a working VPN connection defined. If a VPN session (or other RAS connection) cannot be established, the user will be unable to log on at all. If your WAN links are stable, this is a useful tool for locking things down. If they are not stable, then it is a good way to make your users despise you. *David Dalan*

You can bypass the Welcome screen and go straight to the Desktop using a specific user account as the default user. For example, if you use the computer most of the time and allow other people to log in occasionally, you may want to set up your own account as the default account. The registry key that you need to change is:

```
HKLM\SOFTWARE\Microsoft\Windows NT\CurrentVersion\Winlogon
```

When you get to the key, right-click the AutoAdminLogon value name and choose Modify. Change the Value Data from 0 to 1, as shown in Figure 26-9, and then click OK. Look closely at the DefaultUserName to verify that the user account into which you want to login is selected. Also, if the user account is password-protected, make sure that the DefaultPassword value matches your actual password.

Caution

> There's not much point in password-protecting your user account if you use autologon. After all, anybody who starts, or restarts, the computer is logged into your account automatically!

Once you've activated this Registry hack, the only way to get to the Welcome screen is to click the Start button and choose Log Off ⇨ Log Off. If you ever change your mind and want to go back to starting at the Welcome screen, change the AutoAdminLogon value data from 1 to 0 (zero).

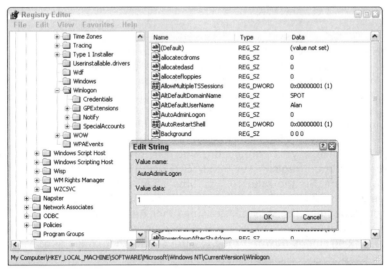

Figure 26-9: Set AutoAdminLogon to 1

Hacks for Fun and Customization

Here are a couple of hacks that are purely for fun, and do not fix any problems or change how your system operates. If nothing else, you can impress your friends by making changes to your system that most people might consider impossible!

Change the Recycle Bin Icon

The Recycle Bin folder on the desktop is one item that seems to be utterly unchangeable in Windows XP. When you right-click its icon, there's no Rename option on the shortcut menu that lets you change the icon's name. But there is a registry key that you can change if you want to rename your Recycle Bin. The registry key is:

```
HKCR\CLSID\{645FF040-5081-101B-9F08-00AA002F954E}
```

To change the name of the Recycle Bin, change the LocalizedString value for that key from the default of @%SystemRoot%\system32\SHELL32.dll,-8964 to whatever text you want to show under the icon. In other words, you need to open regedit and expand the HKEY_CLASSES_ROOT and CLSID folders. Scroll down through the hefty list of class IDs and click the {645FF040-5081-101B-9F08-00AA002F954E} key.

In the Value pane, right-click the LocalizedString value name and choose Modify. Under Value Data, replace the current entry with whatever you want to label your Recycle Bin icon. For example, in Figure 26-10, the icon is renamed Commode. Click OK, and then close the Registry Editor to save your change. Refresh the desktop (press F5, or right-click the desktop and choose Refresh) to see the new name.

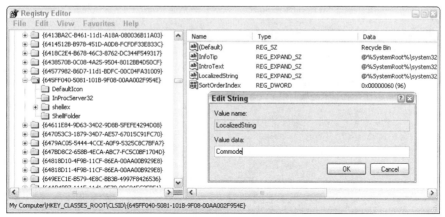

Figure 26-10: Changing LocalString value to "Commode"

The Recycle Bin is unique in that it has two icons, one for an empty Recycle Bin, and the other for a Recycle Bin that contains deleted items. You do not need to use the Registry to change the Recycle Bin's icon. You can do so more easily by following these steps:

1. **Right-click the Desktop and choose Properties.** This opens the Display Properties dialog box.

2. **Click the Desktop tab, and then click the Customize Desktop button.**

3. **Click the icon that you want to change, and then click the Change Icon button.**

4. **Use the Change Icon dialog box to choose a new icon, and then click OK.**

Figure 26-10 shows an example where the Registry Editor was used to change the icon's label from Recycle Bin to Commode. Then the Customize Desktop dialog box was used to change the Recycle Bin icon to one that I just happened to find in my collection of icons, as shown in Figure 26-11.

Figure 26-11: Recycle Bin before (left) and after (right)

To return to the original label for Recycle Bin, change the LocalString value back to the default of:

```
@%SystemRoot%\system32\SHELL32.dll,-8964
```

FYI: Finding Icons

You cannot find the icon shown in the right side of Figure 26-11 in the Change Icon dialog box. It's a freebie icon (.ico file) that you can find on the Internet. You can usually find these icons by searching the Internet or a shareware site, such as www.Tucows.com, for "Free Windows XP Icons," or similar search words. Save any icons that you find as .ico files.

If you want, you can create your own custom icons. For the technical details, see http://msdn.microsoft.com/library/en-us/dnwxp/html/winxpicons.asp. You can also find some easy-to-use icon editors at www.Tucows.com. To use custom icons, click the Browse button in the Change Icon dialog box, and navigate to the folder in which you store the .ico files. Once you have navigated to the folder, use the View Menu button in the Toolbar to choose Icon (or another view) to get a good look at the icons.

To return to the original icon, go back to the Customize Desktop dialog box, click the icon that you want to change, and then click Restore Default.

Changing the Explorer Toolbars

If you ever get tired of seeing the same old gray toolbar in Windows Explorer and Internet Explorer, you can replace it with a picture or pattern of your own choosing. Keep in mind that you need to use a bitmap image. If the image that you choose is larger than the space provided by the toolbars, then only as much of the image as fits in the available space will show. If the image is smaller than the toolbars, then it is tiled to fill the space. You also need to know the path to the image, for example, C:\Documents and Settings*yourUserName*\My Documents\My Pictures*pictureName*.bmp.

The first step is to get to the registry key:

```
HKCU\Software\Microsoft\Internet Explorer\Toolbar
```

Once you click that key, right-click an empty space in the Value pane, and then choose New ⇨ String Value. Name the new value BackBitmap, right-click the new value name, and choose Modify. In the Edit String dialog box that opens, type the complete path and filename of the picture. For example, in Figure 26-12, C:\Documents and Settings\Alan\My Documents\My Pictures\hubble.bmp was entered. This refers to a picture that I downloaded from the Hubble Space Telescope Gallery (http://hubblesite.org/gallery/) and cropped to fit within the area provided by the toolbars.

Figure 26-13 shows the result (although it doesn't look quite as good in grayscale as it does in color). If you ever change your mind and want to get rid of the picture altogether, you can delete the entire BackBitmap key that you added to the Value pane.

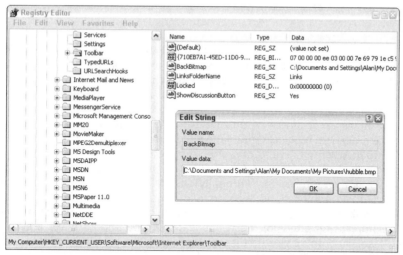

Figure 26-12: Choosing a bitmap for the Explorer toolbars

Figure 26-13: Using a picture for the Internet Explorer background

Hide Folders in My Computer

When you open your My Computer folder, you typically see folders at the top of the folder, followed by icons for hard drives and drives with removable storage. You can hide the folders so that only the drive icons show. To get started, you need to navigate to the following key in Registry Editor:

```
HKCU\SOFTWARE\Microsoft\Windows\CurrentVersion\Policies\Explorer
```

Once you get to the key, you need to right-click an empty spot in the Value pane, and then choose New ➪ DWORD Value. Name this new value NoSharedDocuments. Then right-click the new value name and choose Modify. Enter the number 1 as the Value data, as shown in Figure 26-14, and then click OK. Close the Registry Editor.

The new setting is not applied until you restart the computer. After restarting, when you open your My Computer, it shows the drive icons, but not the folder icons.

Customize the Boot Screen: Personalizing Your System

If you want that "extra something" to personalize your Windows XP installation, you can change your boot screen! Instead of the droll "Windows XP" logon, you can replace it with your favorite picture or company logo. This can be done in a couple of ways. One method is to use a skinning application that essentially hijacks the startup process and replaces the image with an overlay. BootSkin (http://www.stardock.com/products/bootskin/) is an example of an application that can do this. The second method involves creating a replacement image that is used inside the NTOSKRNL.EXE file. BootXP (http://www.bootxp.net/) offers a simple method of modifying this executable. The skinning option is somewhat safer because most of these methods do not require actually modifying the system kernel (NTOSKRNL), although you should confirm this. The kernel modifications tend to use fewer resources during startup. However you do risk corrupting your kernel and making your system unstable or even inaccessible. Before using either of these applications, you should make a system restore point. Also, check to make sure that the tool that you chose is compatible with your version of Windows XP. Review the requirements for the application, and see whether your system meets the service pack and kernel version requirements. *David Dalan*

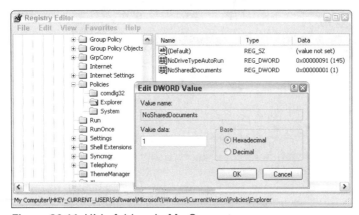

Figure 26-14: Hide folders in My Computer

To return to the default settings, delete the new NoSharedDocuments value, or change its value from 1 to 0.

Expert Tips and Tricks

27

Many users enjoy hacking their system and customizing Windows XP — in fact, there are books available that are only about hacking your computer. However, hacking can be dangerous because it often involves editing the Registry, which can lead to disaster if you're not careful. (For more information, see Chapter 26 and Appendix A.)

With those warnings out of the way, there is nothing quite as fun as hacking Windows XP and customizing your system. In this chapter I share some fun tweaks and changes that I've discovered, as well as some additional third-party software that can help you to make Windows XP your own. Read on... and have fun!

In This Chapter

Fun Hacking Tips

Helpful Tools and Add-ons

Tweaks for Fun and Profit

Okay, not really for profit, but you get the idea. In the following sections, I'll describe some fun tweaks that you can make to Windows XP. Most of these are for customization and fun, and so you can browse through them and try some with your computer.

Note

You should create a system restore point before doing anything in the following sections. This way, if something goes wrong, you can undo it quickly and easily. See Chapter 34 to find out how to create a restore point.

Branding XP

Depending on the computer that you have purchased, you have probably noticed that the brand name shows up in your system interface. For example, if you have a Dell or HP system, then you may notice that their brand name appears on the Start menu and in the Help and Support Center. This is called Original Equipment Manufacturer (OEM) branding, and it is a normal part of the operating system that results from deals that these companies have made with Microsoft.

Of course, you can also brand Windows XP, but without having a deal with Microsoft. This hack allows to you create a registry entry that brands your own icon onto the operating system. Here's how:

1. **Launch Notepad, and then create a new registry file.** Copy and paste the following text into Notepad. Replace the italic text with your custom text or action.

```
Windows Registry Editor Version 5.00

[HKEY_CLASSES_ROOT\CLSID\{2559a1f6-21d7-11d4-bdaf-
00c04f60b9f0}]
@="your title here"

[HKEY_CLASSES_ROOT\CLSID\{2559a1f6-21d7-11d4-bdaf-
00c04f60b9f0}\DefaultIcon]
@="your icon here"

[HKEY_CLASSES_ROOT\CLSID\{2559a1f6-21d7-11d4-bdaf-
00c04f60b9f0}\InProcServer32]
@=hex(2):25,00,53,00,79,00,73,00,74,00,65,00,6d,00,52,00,6f,
00,6f,00,74,00,25,\
00,5c,00,73,00,79,00,73,00,74,00,65,00,6d,00,33,00,32,00,5c,
00,73,00,68,00,\
64,00,6f,00,63,00,76,00,77,00,2e,00,64,00,6c,00,6c,00,00,00
"ThreadingModel"="Apartment"

[HKEY_CLASSES_ROOT\CLSID\{2559a1f6-21d7-11d4-bdaf-
00c04f60b9f0}\Instance]
"CLSID"="{3f454f0e-42ae-4d7c-8ea3-328250d6e272}"

[HKEY_CLASSES_ROOT\CLSID\{2559a1f6-21d7-11d4-bdaf-
00c04f60b9f0}\Instance\InitPropertyBag]
"CLSID"="{13709620-C279-11CE-A49E-444553540000}"
"method"="ShellExecute"
"Command"="your title here"
"Param1"="your function here"

[HKEY_CLASSES_ROOT\CLSID\{2559a1f6-21d7-11d4-bdaf-
00c04f60b9f0}\shellex]

[HKEY_CLASSES_ROOT\CLSID\{2559a1f6-21d7-11d4-bdaf-
00c04f60b9f0}\shellex\ContextMenuHandlers]
```

```
[HKEY_CLASSES_ROOT\CLSID\{2559a1f6-21d7-11d4-bdaf-
00c04f60b9f0}\shellex\ContextMenuHandlers\{2559a1f6-21d7-
11d4-bdaf-00c04f60b9f0}]
@=""

[HKEY_CLASSES_ROOT\CLSID\{2559a1f6-21d7-11d4-bdaf-
00c04f60b9f0}\shellex\MayChangeDefaultMenu]
@=""

[HKEY_CLASSES_ROOT\CLSID\{2559a1f6-21d7-11d4-bdaf-
00c04f60b9f0}\ShellFolder]
"Attributes"=dword:00000000
```

2. **Save this file as brand.reg.** Then reopen it by double-clicking it so that the information is entered into the Registry. When you log on and then log off, you'll see your change in the Start menu. Your system will now be branded with your text.

Change the Browser Toolbar Background

You can easily change the appearance of the Internet Explorer toolbar and make it your own. The process may vary, depending on which version of Windows XP you are using. If you're using Windows XP Professional, then follow these steps:

1. **Log on as an Administrator. Click Start ➪ Run.**

2. **Type gpedit.msc and click OK.**

3. **Navigate to User Configuration\Windows Settings\Internet Explorer Maintenance\Browser User Interface.**

4. **Open Browser Toolbar Customizations and select the "Customize toolbar background bitmap" option.** This dialog box is shown in Figure 27-1.

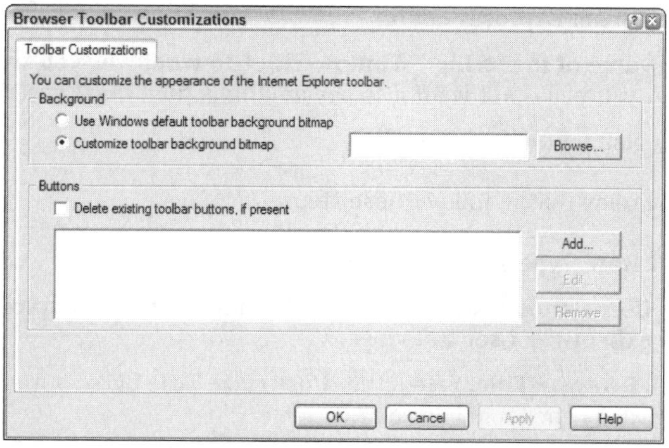

Figure 27-1: The Browser Toolbar Customizations dialog box

5. **Browse for the new background file.** Keep in mind that only bitmap images will work, although you can open any image in Microsoft Paint (or any other image-editing program) and save it as a bitmap.

Windows XP Home edition does not include the Group Policy editor, and so you must edit the Registry to make this change. You should see Appendix A before following these steps if you are not familiar with editing the Registry. Follow these steps:

1. **Open the Registry Editor.**

2. **Navigate to HKEY_CURRENT_USER\Software\Microsoft\Internet Explorer\Toolbar.**

3. **Right-click any empty area and create a new string value.**

4. **Give the value a descriptive name, and then double-click the name and enter the path to the bitmap that you want to use.**

5. **Click OK and close the Registry Editor.**

Changing Internet Explorer's Title

By default, Internet Explorer has a default title of "Microsoft Internet Explorer" on the top of the browser window, as shown in Figure 27-2. However, you can easily customize this title to whatever you want.

You can make this change by either editing the Registry or using the Group Policy console (log on as an Administrator in either case). If you're using Windows XP Home edition, then you don't have Group Policy editor, and so you must use the Registry Editor.

To edit the Registry, follow these steps.

1. **Open the Registry Editor and navigate to HKEY_CURRENT_USER\Software\ Microsoft\Internet Explorer\Main.**

2. **Change the value of the string "Window Title" to whatever you want the title bar to say.** If you don't want it to say anything, then don't enter a value.

3. **Close the Registry Editor.**

To use the Group Policy Editor, follow these steps.

1. **Click Start ⇨ Run.** Type **gpedit.msc** and click OK.

2. **Navigate to User Configuration\Windows Settings\Internet Explorer Maintenance\Browser User Interface.**

3. **Double-click Browser Title.** Select the "Customize Title Bars" option, and enter your text, as shown in Figure 27-3.

4. **Click OK and close the Group Policy Editor.**

Figure 27-2: The default browser title

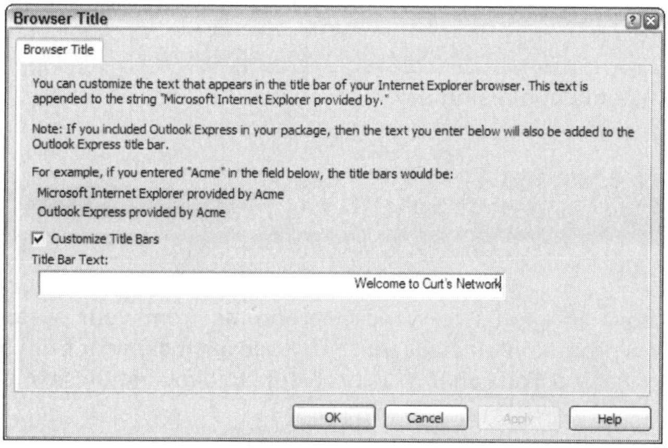

Figure 27-3: The Browser Title dialog box

Creating a Custom Internet Explorer Logo

If you look in the upper-right corner of the Internet Explorer window, you see the little Internet Explorer logo. You can easily change this logo to something else using any image that you want. Note that if you want to use a large logo, it must be resized to 38 x 38 pixels and saved as a bitmap. If you want to use a small logo, then it must be resized to 22 x 22 pixels and saved as a bitmap. Follow these steps:

1. **Click Start ➪ Run.** Type **gpedit.msc** and click OK.

2. **Navigate to User Configuration\Windows Settings\Internet Explorer Maintenance\Browser User Interface.**

3. **Double-click Custom Logo.** In the Custom Logo dialog box, shown in Figure 27-4, click Browse to find the logo that you want. Click OK when you're done.

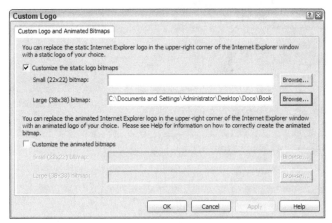

Figure 27-4: The Custom Logo dialog box

Troubleshooting: Removing Troublesome Entries in Add or Remove Programs

You can use Add or Remove Programs to remove programs from your system. However, sometimes when a program uninstalls, the entry doesn't disappear from the Add or Remove Programs interface. You can fix this problem by following these steps:

1. Open Registry Editor.

2. Navigate to HKEY_LOCAL_MACHINE\SOFTWARE\Microsoft\Windows\ CurrentVersion\Uninstall, and remove any unwanted subkeys under "Uninstall."

3. Close the Registry Editor.

Getting Rid of Balloon Tips

If you hate those annoying balloon tips that seem to pop up constantly, then you can disable them. Simply follow these steps:

1. **Open the Registry Editor and navigate to HKCU\Software\Microsoft\ Windows\CurrentVersion\Explorer\Advanced.**

2. **Create an entry called EnableBalloonTips, and set REG_DWORD to 0. If you want to enable balloon tips again, delete the key or set REG_DWORD to 1.**

Customization Software

There are some third-party utilities that allow you to make further changes and customizations in Windows XP. For the most part, these utilities enable you to make changes to different portions of the XP interface that you would otherwise be unable to do. Check these out.

Login King

If you access a lot of online services and forms where you have to constantly log in, you may want some software that helps you to manage your log-ins with a single click. Login King, shown is Figure 27-5, is a good program that is very easy to use. The software will remember your login information and tie that data to your user account in Windows XP so that other users can't access it. Check it out at www.loginking. com. You can download an evaluation copy; the full version costs about $25.

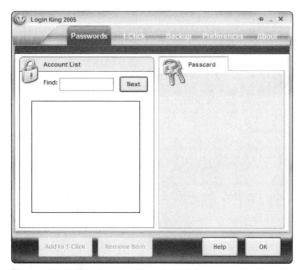

Figure 27-5: The Login King interface

Roboform

While Login King is helpful with passwords and login names, Roboform can remember your address and other personal information so that you can easily complete online forms. If you encounter a lot of online forms, then this software can save you a lot of time and aggravation. Check it out at www.roboform.com. You can download a trial version, and the full version costs about $30. As shown in Figure 27-6, Roboform adds toolbar options to the Internet Explorer interface.

Window Washer

If you need to erase tracks on a Windows XP computer so that no one can see any Internet Explorer, Firefox, Mozilla, Netscape, and Opera traces, then Windows Washer, shown in Figure 27-7, will do this for you. It is great privacy software, and it only costs about $30. You can download a free trial version at www.webroot.com.

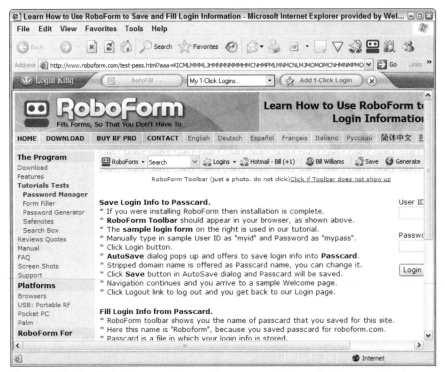

Figure 27-6: The Roboform toolbar options are added to the Internet Explorer interface.

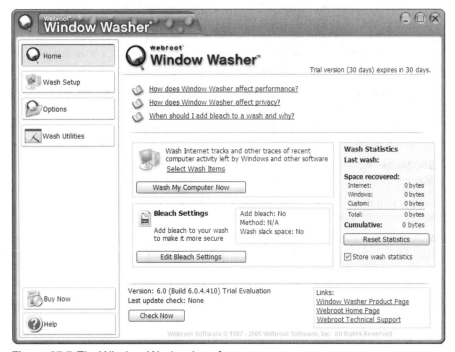

Figure 27-7: The Window Washer interface

Absolute Startup

If you want complete control over what applications start when you boot your computer, then you should like Absolute Startup. This software tracks almost every program that has startup extensions and enables you to manage them. It also helps you to see all of the services that start. You can learn more about this program at www.absolutestartup.com and you can purchase the software for about $30.

Tip

If you are an online game player and you have trouble accidentally hitting the Windows key, killing the game, try I Hate This Key Deluxe Edition, which costs $10 at www.bytegems.com. The software disables these problematic keys during online games.

WinPlosion 2

This is a nice little software package that shrinks and rearranges all of the Windows on your screen to make them all visible at one time. You essentially choose a "hot corner" where you can point and see all of the windows jump to life and rearrange. This is great software if you use a lot of windows and often find yourself fumbling in a sea of confusion. Check it out at www.winplosion.com. It costs about $10.

Expert's Notebook: Browser Add-ons

There are tons of add-ons for Internet Explorer. Some are good, some are junk, so I thought you might like to know which ones I've found useful. Check out these:

✦ **Bookmark Buddy:** A good software add-on that can help you manage bookmarks. Check it out at www.bookmarkbuddy.net.

✦ **Web Picker:** A nice tool that let's you right-click a Web page and save everything on it. See www.superlogix.net.

✦ **Googletoolbar:** This is still one of the best search engine toolbar helps for Internet Explorer. Get it from http://googlebar.mozdev.org.

✦ **Search Panel:** Search Amazon, Google, Yahoo and LookSmart from one single pane. It's helpful and free at www.naturallyopen.com.

✦ **Alexa toolbar:** This product provides instant reviews and extra information about the site you are visiting. It's helpful to get more information quickly and easily. Access www.alexa.com.

Scripting With Windows XP

28

W indows XP supports scripting
with a wide range of programming
languages through the Windows Scripting
Host (WSH) application. You can use scripting to automate a wide range of useful tasks
for both networked and stand-alone computers. For those who are not familiar with
programming languages, scripting can seem
intimidating at first. Fear not! In this chapter,
you learn about the process of running
scripts, and about resources for accessing
more information. This chapter also walks
you through many sample script implementations. By the end of this chapter, you should
have some handy tools at your disposal, and
enough information to continue working
with scripting.

In This Chapter

Scripting 101

Useful Scripting Samples

Scripting 101

Two forms of scripting are available in
Windows XP: Batch file programming, and
Windows Scripting Host (WSH) technology
with higher-level computer programming
languages such as VBScript. Batch file programming involves creating a BAT or CMD
file, and a text file, as well as entering system
commands. For example, a BAT (called
batch) file can contain any code that you
can run from a command prompt. Batch file
scripting is not as powerful or as flexible as
scripting that utilizes higher-level languages.
Most tasks that you can complete with

either the WSH supported languages, or with batch scripting, perform better with WSH-based scripting. WSH supported languages can typically accomplish the task in question faster and with less code than a comparable batch script. The example below uses the Echo command.

1. **Click Start ⇨ Run.**

2. **Type** cmd **and then click OK.** A command prompt opens.

3. **Type** echo this is my first test **and then press Enter.** You should see a message similar to the one in Figure 28-1.

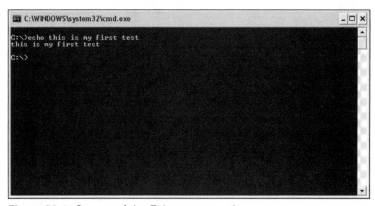

Figure 28-1: Output of the Echo command

4. **Create a new text file called sample.txt.** Then rename the file to sample.bat.

5. **Right-click the file and select Edit from the context menu that appears.** Enter the following code into the file, with each code on a separate line, and then save the file.

```
cd \
cls
echo This is my first test
pause
```

6. **Double-click the .bat file that you have already created.** You should see a screen identical to the one you saw after step 3.

As you can see, batch files allow you to automate a series of commands that you would normally need to manually execute at the command line. This feature is handy for very basic tasks. It can store information in variables, as well as make use of some rudimentary logical statements (if/else logic) to make some decisions based on the outcome of previous commands. However, batch programming becomes cumbersome when you're trying to perform a large number of tasks or very complex processes. It is simply not designed to provide an elegant interface for extensive programming.

The other, more robust, scripting solution involves using higher-level languages with the WSH technology. Specifically, this means running a script with either the command line tool CScript or the GUI-based WScript application. By default, WSH supports the processing of VBScript, JScript, and JavaScript. On a clean installation of Windows XP, you can simply double-click a supported file type such as *.vbs and the script is processed by the WSH engine. You can also run the script in a more interactive manner. Both CScript and WScript support a series of runtime options that you can access by using the /? switch when running either command. The syntax is shown in Figure 28-2.

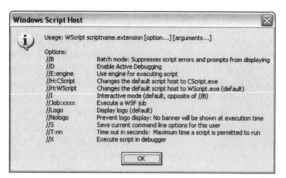

Figure 28-2: A list of WScript /? output

>
> **Note**
>
> **CScript and WScript share all of the same runtime options with one exception: \\U is an option only with CScript. This option is used to enable I/O tasks from the console environment.**

The available runtime options are useful when invoking the script. In some cases there are security concerns, and restrictions with allowing many types of scripts to execute without user interaction. However, one of the benefits of automated scripting is the ability to make things happen without involving the actual user. As a result, you can use a BAT file to access your WSH script files. A particularly useful command option is //B, which runs the script in batch mode, regardless of which launching program (CScript or WScript) you are using. With this option enabled, errors are not displayed, and the user does not see prompting. For example, a batch file that runs a script called user.vbs from the C: drive could use the following commands:

```
Cscript //B C:\user.vbs
```

Learning through Immersion

If you are not familiar with any of the supported scripting languages, how can you start making script files? It is highly recommended that you find out what other people have done, and use their work as a starting point for your own understanding of a particular programming language. In this way, you can see the language in action. You can access little bits of syntax and logic, all in the context of creating something that you can immediately put to work. There are several reputable sources for this kind of additional information. The most useful sites tend to be user-oriented Web sites, so these sites are listed first in the following list. If you do not find the script idea that you need, there are user forums or bulletin boards where you can access additional assistance.

✦ **The DevGuru Homepage:** Located at `http://www.devguru.com`, this site contains a wealth of information on programming in general. Start your search in the VBScript or WSH sections. The information on the Web site is sparse at times, giving you the name of the function, call, and operator, as well as some explanation of what they do. With a bit of experimentation, you'll find this information very useful.

✦ **Win32scripting:** Located at `http://cwashington.netreach.net`, this is an active warehouse of scripting conversations, information, and samples. It is quite possibly the most useful site for systems-management scripting samples. For example, there are samples for collecting remote system information, and there are discussion groups and a forum for posting sample scripts. If you are looking for a particular script, check out the ScriptDepot. The link to the depot is located in the lower-left corner of the Web site, and the icon looks like two connecting cogs. When you click the link, various sub-depots are listed. The VBScripts section has the largest number of samples. Make sure that you check out the command-line script examples. There are only a few, but some of them are quite creative.

✦ **Microsoft's Official WSH reference:** Located at `http://msdn.microsoft.com/library/default.asp?url=/library/en-us/script56/html/wsconWSHWalkthroughs.asp`. This site contains a sub-page on accomplishing common tasks. The information is presented using both JScript and VBScript examples. The site also includes a wealth of in-depth information about WSH. The menu that appears on the left allows you to navigate easily though both the WSH site and the greater Microsoft scripting site in which it resides.

There are more scripting sources on the Internet than one human can ever visit. If you find yourself struggling to implement an idea with script files, use a search engine, such as Yahoo or Google. It is a good idea to keep your query simple, such as "map drive wsh" or "search registry VBScript." WSH is a good element to include as it is commonly used in explanations of Windows scripting, and it is included in object (such as WshNetwork) and method (such as WshArguments) names.

Security

You need to ensure that scripts are securely managed when you anticipate that many people will run them. For example, if you use logon scripts, you may have security issues if unauthorized users can edit those scripts. If you provide access to scripts through a network share (such as the NETLOGON folder), then you need to ensure that non-Administrative users can only read and execute the items inside your scripting folder. One way to do this is to assign the "Read & Execute" right to the "Authenticated Users" group, and then to give additional rights to any Administrative users who may need to connect remotely to modify their scripts.

You can also ensure the integrity of your scripts by using the Microsoft CryptoAPI tools to digitally sign your scripts. By using the CryptoAPI tools, you can prevent a user from executing scripts that are not signed by you; this tool can prevent unauthorized script execution of any kind. Digital signatures are also useful in that they can prevent unauthorized modification of scripts. Illicitly changed scripts no longer have a valid signature if they were signed with a security certificate. For more information about implementing signatures, visit the Microsoft CryptoAPI reference site at http://msdn.microsoft.com/library/default.asp?url=/library/en-us/seccrypto/security/cryptoapi_tools_reference.asp.

Future Security Player: Microsoft AntiSpyware

Although scripts can ease administrative burdens, they can also carry malicious code. Because of this, many companies have developed tools to catch and stop a variety of malicious software, much of it using scripts, in one form or another, to complete their nefarious deeds. Microsoft's AntiSpyware application is proving to be an effective tool for securing end-user systems from new and known script-based and software threats, shown in the following figure. AntiSpyware uses signatures to identify known pieces of malicious code (similar to anti-virus software), as well as to clamp down on certain executable file types, including script files. AntiSpyware does not interfere with scripts that are called with the CScript or WScript applications, but by default, they halt and ask the user if they try to directly launch a script. The user then has the option of allowing or blocking the action, and then deciding whether AntiSpyware should remember this action or prompt the next time the script is executed. Why use Microsoft's solution and not a third party? First, because it's free for now (I am betting it stays that way), and second, because it currently has comparable features to any of the retail spyware or adware blocking software, as well as some elements of home network firewall software. You can find out more about Microsoft AntiSpyware in Chapter 30. *David Dalan*

A Microsoft AntiSpyware popup

Useful Script Samples

Now you can start to make some basic (and not so basic) Windows Scripting Host (WSH) compatible scripts. In the following examples, the WSH objects and methods are used, which means that the examples use the natively supported script language. You also see some examples that make use of VBScript. You can use the .vbs file extension for all of the examples. By using the VBScript file extension, you can have WSH process your script as if all of the code were VBScript. This allows you to freely mix the native objects and methods of WSH with the functions, statements, and operators of VBScript. Other scripting languages (JavaScript, JScript) use different syntax, and have other complexities that are beyond the scope of this chapter.

To get you started on your scripting adventures, take a look at some scripting solutions. In the following examples, you need to look at some common tasks that you can automate with scripting.

Launching Applications

You can use the following process to create a basic sample script as well as other scripts in this chapter.

1. **Click Start ⇨ Programs ⇨ Accessories ⇨ Notepad.**

2. **Save the file as firstsample.vbs, and leave the file type as ANSI text.** See Figure 28-3 for an example.

3. **Type in the code shown in the Figure 28-4.** You can set the run option (in this case, it is www.google.com) to any Web site that you prefer.

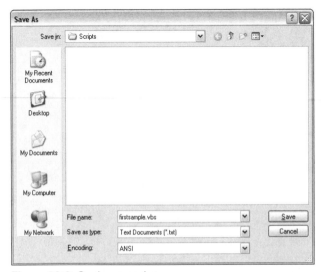

Figure 28-3: Saving a script

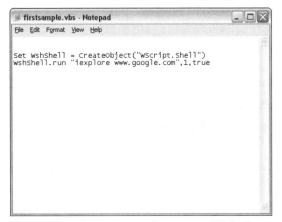

Figure 28-4: The code used to open a Web site with Internet Explorer

4. **Save the file, and then close Notepad.**

5. **Right-click firstsample.vbs and select the Open option.** Alternatively, you can double-click the file. You should now see the Web page that you specified in your script.

In this script, you use the WshShell object. By using the command *Set WshShell = CreateObject("WScript.Shell")* you enable the WshShell object for use in the script. This object provides access to a number of Windows functions, such as the ability to launch applications. In the example here, you use Internet Explorer with the WshShell.run method, which allows you to run an application. Basically, you can run any application that is located in one of the defined system "PATH" entries. You can also see that at the end of the line that reads *WshShell.run "iexplore www. google.com", 1, true,* there is a "1, true." This code illustrates the syntax of the WshShell.run methods.

```
WshShell.Run strCommand [,intWindowStyle] [,bWaitOnReturn]
```

The intWindowsStyle option allows you to specify the kind of window in which the application opens. Your options are 0 (not visible), 1 (normal window), and 2 (minimized). In the example, options 1 and 2 leave you with a usable window, while option 0 really makes it uninspiring. Unfortunately, if you run this script with the 0 option, Internet Explorer just runs in a hidden window until you either end the task or log out. The bWaitOnReturn option tells the script whether it should wait for the launched application to run and exit before moving on with the script. Because you are not doing anything else, you just set the value to True (the other option is False for "don't wait"). The values used in this script are the default values (just spelled out), and if you remove them from this script, and use just *WshShell.run "iexplore www.google.com",* the script works just the same.

Adding a Printer

Your users log on to a networked computer and need access to a networked printer. The script below connects the printer *staffPrinter* on the server *printServer*.

1. Click Start ⇨ **Programs** ⇨ **Accessories** ⇨ **Notepad.**

2. Save the file as addprinter.vbs, and leave the file type as ASCII text.

3. Type in the code as shown in Figure 28-5.

Figure 28-5: Script syntax for mapping a printer

4. Save the file, and then close Notepad.

If you want to test this script, you need a network printer available and you must make the appropriate changes for the server and printer names. If you have a stand-alone computer with a printer connected, you can share the printer and then use your local host name and the shared printer name to execute this script. The syntax of this command is as follows:

```
WshNetwork.AddPrinterConnection strLocalName, strRemoteName
[,bUpdateProfile] [,strUser] [,strPassword]
```

In this example, strLocalName is the name of the local device, and strRemoteName is the path to the network server (\\server\printername). The strLocalName is not required, and in most cases is unnecessary. The bUpdateProfile option specifies whether you want the user's profile updated with the printer mapping information. Your options are to write the change to the profile (TRUE), or to not write the change to the profile (FALSE). In the example, the changes are written to the user's profile. The remaining options allow you to specify the logon name and password to use when connecting to the resource. Because using these strings directly (for example,

storing the logon name and password) in the script files could represent a signifi-
cant security risk, it is not recommend that you do so.

Removing Printers

What if you have "problem children" users who have made a habit of attaching to
every networked printer available? While you could (and probably should) restrict
security rights to your printers so that only authorized users can connect to them,
you can use scripting to help remove undesirable printers. In the following script,
inspired by a www.tek-tips.com forum poster, you can discard all attached network
printers and explore some useful logic.

1. **Click Start ➪ Programs ➪ Accessories ➪ Notepad.**

2. **Save the file as delprinters.vbs, and leave the file type as ASCII text.**

3. **Type in the code shown in Figure 28-6.**

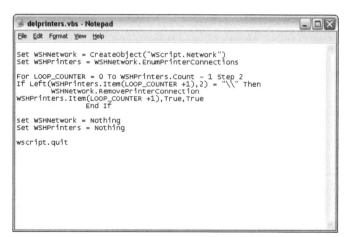

Figure 28-6: Code that removes all network printers

4. **Save the file, and then close Notepad.**

5. **When you execute the script, all network printers are removed.**

There is a bit more going on in this script than in the previous examples. You are
working with two objects and some introductory logic in the form of a loop statement. Essentially, the script enumerates attached printers (using WshNetwork.
EnumPrinterConnections), assigns the value to WshPrinters, and then runs a loop
that deletes printers until all of the 'contents' of the Wshprinter.item have been
removed. Each passing of the loop removes a single printer. Eventually there is nothing left, and the script cleans up our objects out of memory, after which it exits.

Setting the Default Printer

So far, you have removed unwanted devices and added new ones. Next, you want to determine which printer you want as the Windows default printing device. In the following example, you walk through creating a script that sets the default printer to \\printServer\staffServer. If you have more than one printer installed on your computer, you can change the printer name to match one, and practice changing your defaults with this script.

1. **Click Start ➪ Programs ➪ Accessories ➪ Notepad.**

2. **Save the file as setdefault.vbs, and leave the file type as ASCII text.**

3. **Insert the code, as shown in Figure 28-7.**

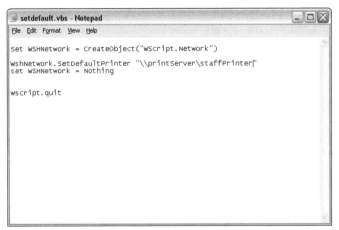

Figure 28-7: Setting your default printer

4. **Save the file, close Notepad, and then launch the script.**

Map and Disconnect Network Drives

Another common task that is performed by logon scripts is the mapping of network drives. The following script samples show you the basics of mapping a drive, as well as how to enumerate group membership information to make some logical determinations about who should access to mapped drives.

1. **Click Start ➪ Programs ➪ Accessories ➪ Notepad.**

2. **Save the file as an ASCII text file named mapdrive.vbs.**

3. Add the code shown in Figure 28-8 to your script.

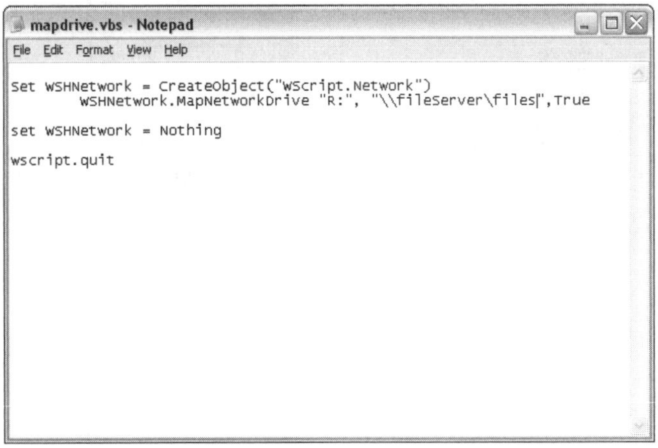

Figure 28-8: Mapping a drive

4. Save the file, and then close Notepad.

The syntax for the method used to map network drives is:

```
WshNetwork.MapNetworkDrive strLocalName, strRemoteName
[,bUpdateProfile] [,strUser] [,strPassword]
```

The WshNetwork.MapNetworkDrive script uses the same variables as the WshNetwork.AddPrinterConnection script does. StrLocalName in this case is the drive letter (for example, E:), and strRemoteName is the UNC path to the folder that you want to map in the form of \\servername\sharename. In the WshNetwork.MapNetworkDrive method, you can also specify whether the user profile should be modified to permanently reflect these changes. You can also specify an alternate username and password to use when connecting to any of the remote shares.

To expand on this functionality, you can add some additional logic to the previous script idea. In Figure 28-9, you can see part of a script that is adapted from a sample script that was posted by Mark MacLachlan (http://www.thespidersparlor.com). This script maps network drives based on their Active Directory group membership.

The script collects the user's group membership and then performs the commands to map network drives if the users are either Authenticated Users or in the Domain Admins group. If a user is in both groups, then they meet both criteria and can access all of the mapped drives.

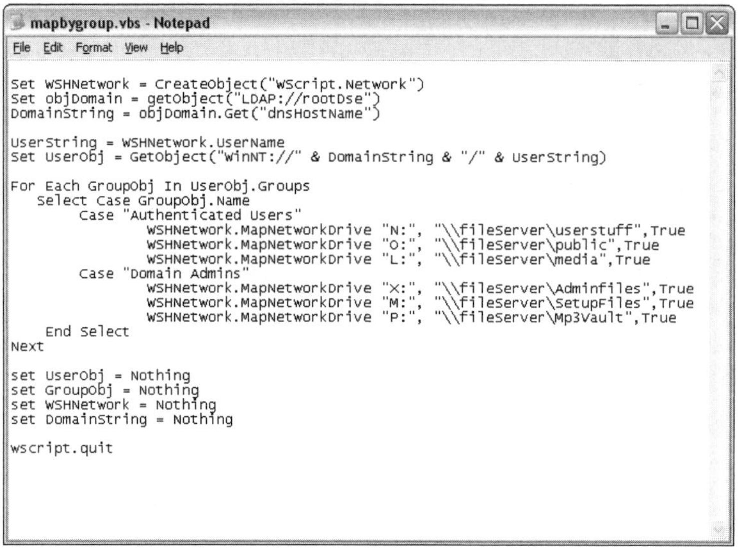
mapbygroup.vbs - Notepad

File Edit Format View Help

```
Set WSHNetwork = CreateObject("WScript.Network")
Set objDomain = getObject("LDAP://rootDse")
DomainString = objDomain.Get("dnsHostName")

UserString = WSHNetwork.UserName
Set UserObj = GetObject("WinNT://" & DomainString & "/" & UserString)

For Each GroupObj In UserObj.Groups
   Select Case GroupObj.Name
        Case "Authenticated Users"
                WSHNetwork.MapNetworkDrive "N:",  "\\fileServer\userstuff",True
                WSHNetwork.MapNetworkDrive "O:",  "\\fileServer\public",True
                WSHNetwork.MapNetworkDrive "L:",  "\\fileServer\media",True
        Case "Domain Admins"
                WSHNetwork.MapNetworkDrive "X:",  "\\fileServer\Adminfiles",True
                WSHNetwork.MapNetworkDrive "M:",  "\\fileServer\SetupFiles",True
                WSHNetwork.MapNetworkDrive "P:",  "\\fileServer\Mp3Vault",True
    End Select
Next

set UserObj = Nothing
set GroupObj = Nothing
set WSHNetwork = Nothing
set DomainString = Nothing

wscript.quit
```

Figure 28-9: Mapping by user group

Securing and Trouble-shooting Windows XP

V

Security and problem solving are ever-important aspects of computing these days. The good news is that Windows XP gives you plenty of tools that help you keep your computer secure and troubleshoot problems.

In this part, you find out how to manage local security, keep your computer safe on the Internet, manage disks and drives, take care of Windows XP, use Event Viewer, and use System Information and System Restore. You also put some tips and tricks to work in order to speed up Windows XP. Finally, you learn how to recover from a crash or other serious problem.

Managing Local Security

29

L ocal security involves keeping your computer secure in a physical location (thus it is also called "physical security"). If your computer is at home, then you probably don't need to worry about local security. However, in an office you may be very concerned about how other users can physically access your computer.

Keep in mind that network security and local security are two different things. When you configure network security, you are configuring how users can access your files, folders, and other resources over the Internet. Local security concerns how other users can physically access your computer using your keyboard and mouse.

If your computer contains sensitive information that you want to protect, then you should read this chapter. Also, if you want to have more control over what local users can do on your computer, this chapter will show you how to configure additional restrictions.

User Accounts

This section continues the discussion from Chapter 10 on configuring and managing user accounts. It is important to understand that user accounts are your main defense against unauthorized access to your computer. However, user accounts are often treated in a careless fashion, a lot like fire alarms in your home — you may not worry too much about them working until it's too late. Although many people are concerned about local security, they still configure many accounts on their computers, and some use blank passwords.

Ultimately, you must have a good user account policy in order to have good local security. To do this you can use the following tactics:

✦ **For the best security, there should be only one Administrator account, and you should be the only user to know the password.** Also, you should use a limited account for day-to-day use. This way, if someone gains access to your computer while you are logged on, that person is limited by the restrictions placed on the user account.

✦ **Only use the necessary number of user accounts.** For example, if only three people access your computer, then there should be only three limited accounts — one for each person. Keep up-to-date with the user accounts, and make sure that you remove accounts that are no longer necessary.

✦ **Disable the guest account.** Unless you actually use the guest account, you should disable it. In User Accounts, click the guest account and use the "Turn off the guest account" option in the "What do you want to change about the guest account" window, as shown in Figure 29-1.

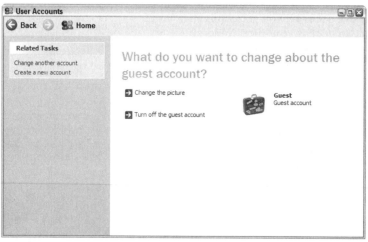

Figure 29-1: Turn off the guest account for added security.

✦ **Use secure passwords.** Although you don't have to use passwords with Windows XP — such as for home users that trust each other — if you are concerned about security, then every user account should have a secure password. A secure password contains at least eight characters, including letters and numbers. Avoid using common words, such as your name, phone number, street address, or your pet's name. It is also helpful to use upper- and lower-case letters because passwords are case sensitive.

For added protection against lost data, create a password reset disk and store it in a safe location. See Chapter 10 to learn how to create a password reset disk.

✦ **Turn off the Welcome page.** The Welcome page is a handy feature that can make it easier to log on and off. With passwords configured, you must enter the password on the Welcome page, but if you want to go an extra step, you can turn off the Welcome page so that users must also enter their user account name. This feature prevents prying eyes from seeing the user accounts that are configured on your computer. To turn off the Welcome page, open User Accounts and click "Change the way users log on or log off." Then, deselect the check box for the Welcome page. Note that the Fast User Switching option does not work if the Welcome page is turned off (it appears grayed out, as shown in Figure 29-2).

Figure 29-2: Fast User Switching is not available when you turn off the Welcome page.

Additional User Account Settings

There are a couple of additional user account settings that I want to mention. The most important setting is to require users to press Ctrl+Alt+Del in order to log on. Ctrl+Alt+Del is a security feature that prevents another application from capturing the key combination. It ensures that the logon dialog box that you see is an actual

Windows logon dialog box and not an application that is designed to capture usernames and passwords. In today's world of troublesome software and security problems, Ctrl+Alt+Del remains an important security feature. To use this feature, follow these steps:

1. **Click Start ⇨ Run.** In the Run dialog box that appears, type **control userpasswords2**, as shown in Figure 29-3, and then click Allow.

Figure 29-3: This command directly opens the User Accounts dialog box.

2. **On the Users tab of the User Accounts dialog box, shown in Figure 29-4, you can specify that users must enter a username and password in order to access the computer.** You can also add or remove user accounts from within this dialog box.

Figure 29-4: The Users tab

3. **On the Advanced tab (seen in Figure 29-5), you can control passwords and .NET Passports that have been stored on the computer.** You can also open the Users and Groups console and enable the secure logon feature (which requires Ctrl+Alt+Del) by selecting the check box. Make your selections and then click OK.

Figure 29-5: The Advanced tab

Using the Local Security Settings Console

If you want to place additional restrictions on users who access the computer, you can do so by using the Local Security Settings console. However, you should think carefully before enabling additional restrictions. As a general rule, the best policy is to only allow as many users as is necessary to access the computer, but no more. You need to think through your security needs and what you are trying to accomplish in terms of local security before you enable any of these settings.

If you log on with an Administrator account and type **secpol.msc** at the run line, you can access the Local Security Settings console, as shown in Figure 29-6.

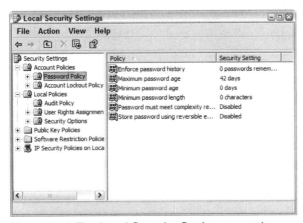

Figure 29-6: The Local Security Settings console

In the left console pane, you see a collection of folders that contain different security policies. You can explore the security policies that are available and enable some of them for your local computer, if necessary.

For example, you may want to set a maximum password age of 24 days. After 24 days, each user would then have to change their password. You can do this by expanding Account Policies and selecting Password Policy. In the right pane, you can double-click the Maximum password age policy icon. In the dialog box that appears, you can adjust the password age and click OK to enforce the new policy, as shown in Figure 29-7. Other policies have similar configurations.

Figure 29-7: You can change the policy settings.

Of all of the policy settings, some are more helpful than others in securing your local computer. There are several policies that I would recommend that you use. Under Account Policies\Password Policy:

✦ **Enforce password history:** It is best to configure this setting to 0 so that the computer remembers no passwords.

✦ **Maximum password age:** Forty-two days is the default setting, although you can lower it. This forces users to regularly change their passwords.

✦ **Minimum password length:** You should configure this setting for eight characters.

✦ **Passwords must meet complexity requirements**: This policy requires that passwords have a combination of letters and numbers. The policy also requires that the password cannot contain all or even part of the user's account name, requires upper and lowercase letters, base 10 digits (0 to 9), and nonalphanumeric characters (such as !, $, #, etc.). You can either enable or disable this option, as shown in Figure 29-8.

Figure 29-8: You can enable or disable password complexity requirements.

Under Account Lockout Policy, you should use both of the following options:

✦ **Account lockout duration:** This option determines how long an account remains locked after failed logon attempts.

✦ **Account lockout threshold:** This option locks an account after a certain number of failed logon attempts. This is a good security feature because it prevents someone who is trying to guess a password from being successful. As a general rule, three attempts is enough to lock the account. If you double-click the policy, then you can specify the number of attempts that you want, as shown in Figure 29-9.

Figure 29-9: You can specify the account lockout threshold.

Once you set the policy, click OK. A Suggested Value Changes dialog box (seen in Figure 29-10) appears, with suggested policy settings of 30 minutes for the "Account lockout duration" and "Reset account lockout counter after" policies.

Figure 29-10: The Suggested Value Changes dialog box

If you expand the Local Policies folder, you see sub-folders for Audit Policy, User Rights Assignment, and Security Options. The Audit Policy concerns policies if you are auditing events on your Windows XP computer. In the User Rights Assignment folder, you can configure policies that control what users can do. Although user rights are already configured by restrictions that are placed on the Limited user accounts, you can configure additional restrictions here. As shown in Figure 29-11, although there are a lot of policy options, you should find most of the default settings to be adequate.

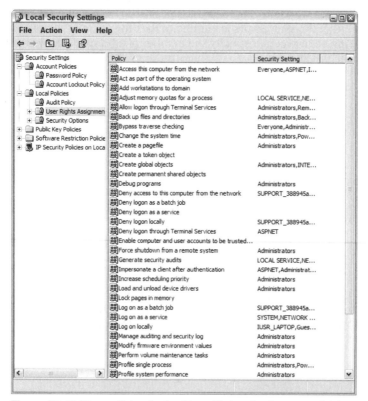

Figure 29-11: The policies in the User Rights Assignment folder

FYI: Locking Your Computer

A simple but often overlooked security tactic in an office environment is to lock your computer. You may need to step away from your desk for a few moments, leaving behind your computer, along with all of your sensitive documents. Because you're logged on, anyone can simply take a quick look at your system. To prevent this, you can simply lock your computer. To lock it, press the Windows logo key and the L key if the Windows Welcome page is disabled. Alternatively, you can press Ctrl+Alt+Del and click Lock Computer. You'll then be required to enter your password to unlock the computer.

The Security Options folder also contains a lot of settings. Although you should find most of the default options to be adequate, there are some that you may want to change:

✦ **Accounts:** This policy limits local account use of blank passwords to console logon only — make sure that this setting is enabled.

✦ **Devices:** This policy allows users to undock without having to log on. Although this option is enabled by default, if you are docking a portable computer, then you may consider disabling this option for added security. Users are then required to log on in order to undock.

✦ **Interactive Logon:** This policy prevents the last username from displaying. Although this option is disabled by default, you should enable it. It prevents a user who is logging on from seeing the username of the previous user who logged on.

✦ **Interactive Logon:** This policy prompts users to change their password before expiration. This is a good policy because it reminds users that their passwords are about to expire.

Keeping Your Computer Safe on the Internet

30

T he Internet, for everything it has to offer, is also full of potential security threats. For example, corporations spend hundreds of thousands of dollars trying to maintain network security when they allow their users to access the Internet, and in order to keep security threats from entering the corporate network.

The Internet also poses a security risk to home computers and small office networks, forcing you to protect your computer from viruses, Trojan horse programs, possible malicious code, and hacker attacks. If you have ever been the victim of an attack, you know how destructive they are.

In this chapter, you take a look at Internet security. You learn how to put tools to work on your computer that greatly reduce the likelihood of your experiencing problems.

Internet Security 101

The concept of Internet security can be a bit overwhelming. You hear many horror stories from coworkers, friends, and television and magazine ads, but what threats are really out there and what do you really need to do to prevent possible problems?

Common-sense Tips

As you read in the previous section, you can stop all Internet threats with programs that are designed to control them. However, you should get into the habit of following some basic common-sense tips that will help you to avoid problems:

✦ **Avoid opening attachments from e-mail senders that you do not know and be careful of those you do.** E-mail attachments can contain viruses and other programs, and so you should use caution and make sure that your anti-virus software is up-to-date.

✦ **Watch out for Web sites that download software to your computer.** While you may need software from the Web site to use the site's features, use only reputable sites. Run a search on the site to see whether there are any issues or complaints that you need to know about.

✦ **Be wary of giving out your personal e-mail address, phone numbers, addresses, and other contact information on the Internet.**

Although Internet threats are real, you don't have to go into panic mode when responding to security problems. You just need to understand what potential problems can come your way and how to avoid them. Some types of code that can cause problems include:

✦ **Viruses:** A *virus* is a piece of software code that accesses your system and does something that you don't want it to do. A virus can cause a simple annoyance, or it can cause major problems such as making your computer unbootable. Although computer viruses include a number of different types and classes, you can generally prevent viruses by using up-to-date anti-virus software.

✦ **Trojan horses:** A *Trojan horse* is a malicious program disguised as legitimate software. The term derives from the story of the wooden horse that the Greek army used to capture the city of Troy. The Trojans believed that the horse was a gift, and brought it within the city walls, but the horse was hollow, and contained Greek soldiers, who opened Tory's city gates at night and allowed the Greek army to capture the city. Trojan horse programs basically do the same thing. The Trojan horse looks like a valid program, but when you install it, it damages your system, sometimes with catastrophic effects. Trojan horse programs are not self-replicating like viruses, and you can generally stop them with an up-to-date anti-virus software.

✦ **Worms:** A computer *worm* is a self-replicating program, similar to a virus. The difference is that a worm is self-contained and doesn't need another program to run like a typical virus. Anti-virus software usually prevents worms.

✦ **Hackers:** A *hacker* is a person who uses networking data to access your computer, often to steal information or cause other problems. You can generally prevent hacker access by using a firewall.

✦ **Spyware or adware:** Spyware and adware refer to a large collection of programs and files that gather information about you, or show advertisements to you. Have you ever had problems with Internet Explorer pop-up windows that kept running advertisements? That happens because spyware or adware has managed to get into your system. You can prevent or solve spyware and adware problems with software designed to recognize and stop them.

Using Anti-virus Software

Windows XP doesn't provide any built-in anti-virus software. You can ignore such "features" found in Outlook Express and other email programs that say they have "virus protection" as these minimal protection options do not identify viruses and do not delete them. You really need to install an anti-virus software program on your computer and update the program regularly. There are many different programs available, but it is best to use well-known software providers to make sure that you have full protection. Although there are many different programs available, the three recommended programs with which I have had personal experience: Symantec, McAfee, and AVG.

Symantec

Symantec is a leader in computer software, including anti-virus software. The basic anti-virus program, called Internet Security, costs about $50, with annual payments to keep the software updated regularly with new virus definitions. You can find out more at www.symantec.com/homecomputing/.

McAfee

McAfee is another industry leader in computer software, including anti-virus software. Their Internet Security suite costs about $50, with annual payments to keep the software virus definitions updated. You can find out more at www.mcafee.com.

AVG

AVG, from Grisoft, is a free anti-virus program to home and small office users. It works great and never costs you a penny. I use AVG on my computers and have been very pleased with the results. You can find out more about AVG and download the product from www.grisoft.com.

 Whatever program you choose, the main point is that you must run anti-virus software and you must enable that software to update regularly. New viruses appear every day, so keep the software enabled and keep it updated for the best protection!

Windows Firewall

A *firewall* is a piece of software or hardware that protects a computer or network from unauthorized network traffic. For a personal computer on a small network, a firewall is a software solution that monitors incoming traffic and determines whether the traffic should be allowed. Windows XP includes a free built-in firewall called Windows Firewall, which is updated in Service Pack 2.

Windows Firewall is an effective tool. However, if you want more features than those in Windows Firewall, you can purchase third-party firewalls from other companies, such as Symantec and McAfee. There is even a good free firewall application called ZoneAlarm that is available at www.zonelabs.com.

Do you actually need a firewall? With today's technology, the answer is yes. Any time that you are using the Internet, your computer is open to potential attacks. With a dial-up connection, the attacks are limited because you are not connected to the Internet all of the time. However, with the explosive growth of broadband connections, the need for a firewall becomes very important because these computers are always connected to the Internet and therefore are always exposed to danger.

Using Windows Firewall

Before you get into more detail about configuring Windows Firewall, you need to know to about a few issues concerning the firewall's default behavior. You should keep these issues in mind as you set up Internet connections on your home or small office network:

✦ **Windows Firewall should be enabled on any shared Internet connection in your home or small office network.** If you are only using one computer at your home, the firewall should be enabled on that computer.

✦ **Windows Firewall works on a per-connection basis, and not per computer.** For example, when your computer has both a DSL connection and a modem connection, you must enable Windows Firewall on both the DSL and modem connections to have full protection.

✦ **In a small network setting that uses Internet Connection Sharing (ICS), you should certainly enable Windows Firewall on the ICS connection.** However, if other computers on the network have other ways to connect to the Internet (such as through modems), you also need to enable Windows Firewall on each of these connections. Again, Windows Firewall works on a per-connection basis.

✦ **Any configuration changes that you make to Windows Firewall are only for that particular connection.** They do not transfer from connection to connection. For example, if you have two connections and Windows Firewall is enabled on each of them, you must individually configure each connection.

✦ **You should only use Windows Firewall for connections to the Internet.** You should not use it for connections between computers on your private network. For example, you should not enable Windows Firewall on any computer's network adapter card if you use the card to local computers. Doing so prevents connectivity.

Windows Firewall and the Security Center

When you upgrade to Service Pack 2, Windows Firewall is turned on by default, although you can turn it off again. You can manage Windows Firewall through the new Security Center, which is available in Service Pack 2. To turn on the firewall (or turn it off), open the Security Center by clicking the Security Center icon in the Notification Area or Control Panel. The Security Center opens, and you can see whether Windows Firewall is turned on, as shown in Figure 30-1. If your firewall is not turned on, scroll to the bottom of the Security Center dialog box and click the Windows Firewall icon under Manage Security Settings. This action opens the General tab of the Windows Firewall dialog box, where you can click the "On" option, as shown in Figure 30-2.

How Windows Firewall Works

Windows Firewall is considered a *stateful* firewall. This simply means that Windows Firewall works with your Internet connection to examine traffic as it is passing through the firewall both to and from your computer or network. Because Windows Firewall is stateful, it examines Internet traffic in terms of its live use. If something attempts to enter the firewall that is not allowed, Windows Firewall simply steps in and blocks the traffic from entering. As a result, no unauthorized traffic ever passes the firewall. To use stateful inspection, Windows Firewall examines the destination of every piece of traffic coming from your computer or the computers on your network. Whenever something is sent to the Internet (such as a URL request), Windows Firewall keeps a routing table to track your requests. When data comes to the firewall, Windows Firewall inspects it to see whether it matches up with requests found in the routing table. If so, it is passed on to your computer or to the requesting computer on your network. If not, it is simply blocked from entering the firewall. The end result is that any traffic that you want from the Internet can enter the firewall, and anything that you have not requested is blocked. When communication is dropped, it is done automatically without any intervention from you. In fact, Windows Firewall doesn't even tell you when communication from the Internet has been dropped, although you can see what has been dropped by viewing a log file.

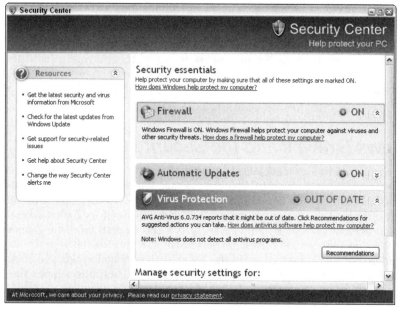

Figure 30-1: The Security Center

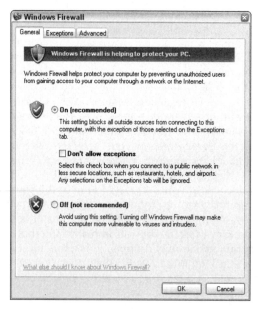

Figure 30-2: The General tab of the Windows Firewall dialog box

Configuring Windows Firewall Settings

If you click the Exceptions and Advanced tabs of the Windows Firewall dialog box, you can view settings that govern how Windows Firewall works, and what kinds of applications and services it allows. Normally, the default settings are all that you need. However, if you are using certain applications or you are providing certain types of content to the Internet, then you may need to configure some of these settings.

The Exceptions tab, shown in Figure 30-3, provides you a list of check boxes concerning programs and services that are running on your computer or network and that you are allowing Internet users to access. For example, you may want to use Remote Assistance on your Windows XP computer. If Windows Firewall is in use, you need to check the Remote Assistance check box so that a Remote Assistance user can contact you. When you click this check box, and then click OK, Windows Firewall reconfigures itself to allow certain kinds of content to pass through the firewall to meet these needs. Another example is when you want to use Remote Desktop with someone on the Internet. By default, Windows Firewall does not allow this kind of communication, and so you have to enable it here.

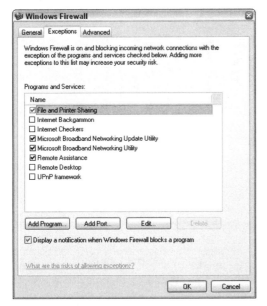

Figure 30-3: The Exceptions tab

If you only want to use Windows Firewall to surf the Web and send and receive e-mail, then you don't need to configure any exceptions; Windows Firewall is already configured, and ready to go.

On the Advanced tab, shown in Figure 30-4, you can see the connections that Windows Firewall has enabled. If you want to allow more or fewer connections, you can use the check boxes in the Network Connection Settings section. However, remember that every Internet connection on your computer should be protected by the firewall. Notice the Settings button option under Network Connection Settings. If you click Settings, you'll also see another list of services that you can configure. These settings are for more advanced users. For example, you may be using your Windows XP computer as an FTP server for Internet clients. To allow FTP traffic, you need to enable the FTP Server check box option, as shown in Figure 30-5. The same is true with any Internet Control Message Protocol, or ICMP, services that you may want to use. Keep in mind that these are advanced options, and so you should not enable any of them unless you are sure that you need them.

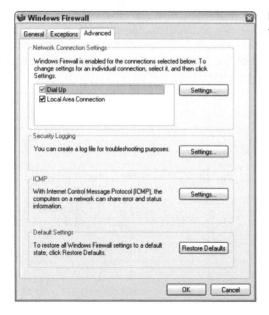

Figure 30-4: The Advanced tab on the Windows Firewall dialog box

Although by default, the security log is stored in C:\Windows\pfirewall.log, you can click the Settings button in the Security Logging section to change the location of the log. The log file has a default maximum size of 4096KB (4MB). You can increase or decrease this space if you like, although this should be enough. To enable logging for successful connections and dropped packets, just click the check boxes in the Logging Options section, as shown in Figure 30-6.

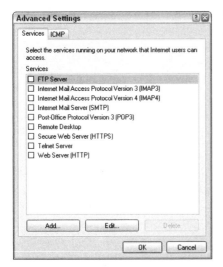

Figure 30-5: The Services tab on the Advanced Settings dialog box

Figure 30-6: The Log Settings dialog box

You can see an ICMP section on the Advanced tab. ICMP is a protocol that handles a number of communication functions that test computer connectivity. A common test is "ping," which tests another computer to see whether it is connected. Although ICMP messages are harmless, some attacks from the Internet act like ICMP messages, and so by default, no ICMP messages are allowed on your network. However, depending on your needs, you may want to enable some, or all, of these ICMP message types. Just click the Settings button and enable the ICMP functions you want, as shown in Figure 30-7. You can select a message type and read more about it in the Description section of the ICMP Settings dialog box.

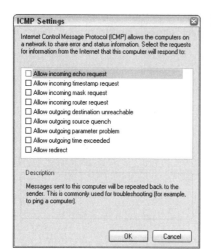

Figure 30-7: The ICMP Settings dialog box

Managing Spyware and Adware

If you use the Internet, you'll most likely end up getting spyware or adware. In fact, the current estimates suggest that as many as ninety-seven percent of home computers are infected with spyware or adware. You often pick up spyware and adware from Web sites and general Web usage, and they can be simply annoying or possibly dangerous in terms of your personal information.

To rid yourself of spyware and adware, you need to use a program that detects threats and removes them. Otherwise, there's nothing you can do to stop spyware and adware.

So, which program should you use? Microsoft has produced a free AntiSpyware utility that you can download from the Windows Web site at www.microsoft.com/athome/security/default.mspx. Overall, this new tool works well and has a friendly, configurable interface, as shown in Figure 30-8. The software scans your system and effectively removes spyware and adware, and it also includes a tracks eraser and browser hijack restore tool. Because the tool is free, you should try it out.

Tip

If you want to use another anti-spyware or anti-adware program, visit http://www.comparespywareremovers.com to get the latest scoop on different programs that are available, and where to get them.

Note

Each anti-spyware application has its own unique way of searching for spyware/malware. For this reason it is not always prudent to stick to one application. Prior to Microsoft's own anti-spyware addition the de-facto anti-spyware applications were Ad-Aware and Spybot search and Destroy. Both Ad-Aware and Spybot take some beating and are a welcome addition to Microsoft's AntiSpyware application.

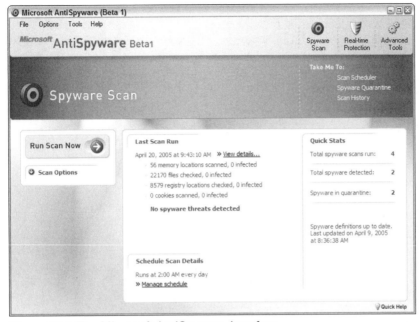

Figure 30-8: The Microsoft AntiSpyware interface

Managing Disks and Drives

31

You may not think about your hard disk and drives until you have a problem with them. However, if you do not have an operational hard disk and a properly configured file system, then you cannot store and manage your data.

Windows XP makes it easier for you to manage your hard disk. You have more flexibility and more ways to manage disk configuration, especially if you have a computer with more than one physical disk. In this chapter, we explore these issues, and you learn how to manage a disk and drives.

File Systems and Windows XP

A file system is a logically organized method that enables a computer to store data on a disk. A file system is similar to a file cabinet, because, like a file cabinet, without organized file folders, a computer's file system cannot manage and locate data. The file system makes the hard disk usable by the operating system so that the operating system can store data on the disk. Windows XP supports both the File Allocation Table, or FAT32 file system, and NTFS.

When a hard disk is installed it is typically unformatted. As a result, the operating system is unable to write and read data from it. In order to use the hard disk, Windows XP must write a signature to the hard disk and format it with a file system. Without file folders, there is no way to organize and store information on the hard disk. When Windows XP formats the hard disk, it creates magnetic rings on the disk and divides the disk into circular areas called sectors. Sectors are then grouped together into clusters. Clusters are the logical areas of the disk to which the operating system writes data. Depending on how the operating system handles cluster size, the disk can hold more or less data because space can be lost when a file is written and space is left over on the cluster.

The cluster-size configuration enables the computer to write data to the hard disk and keep it organized. Over time, hard disks become fragmented, which is a condition where the data is not stored in a contiguous manner. To correct this problem, Windows XP includes a disk defragmenter tool. You can learn more about this tool in Chapter 32.

Getting to Know FAT/ FAT32 and NTFS

If you are new to file systems, then it is a good idea to have some background information about the primary file systems that Windows has used over the years.

The first file system supported by Windows XP was the File Allocation Table (FAT) file system. FAT16 was first developed for 16-bit systems, with a 32-bit version appearing a few years later. FAT16 is a basic file system that was designed for small disks and is supported on Windows 3.1 and higher Microsoft operating systems. Under Windows XP, the FAT16 file system can grow up to 4GB in size and support file sizes up to 2GB. In other words, 4GB is the maximum amount of cluster storage space and management functionality that FAT16 provides. As a result, this size limitation is too small for today's computer hardware. Under most circumstances, FAT16 would never be used on a Windows XP Professional operating system (or even earlier systems, such as Windows 98) unless you needed to dual-boot with an older operating system, such as Windows 3.1 or the original version of Windows 95. Because few people (if any) are using Windows 3.x or Windows 95 any longer, there is no need to use FAT16.

First available for Windows 95b, FAT32 was significantly different from FAT16 in two important ways. First, it supported larger hard drives, and second, it supported smaller file clusters. This allowed you to make use of a large hard drive — up to 32GB — while simultaneously conserving disk space due to the small cluster size. As a result, there was less wasted room on the hard disk compared to FAT16. For these reasons, FAT32 is the operating system of choice for Windows 95b, Windows 98, and Windows Me operating systems.

NTFS is supported under Windows XP and is considered the file system of choice. NTFS has been around since the early days of Windows NT, and the new version, first supported in Windows 2000 (NTFS v5), provides additional features and functions.

NTFS supports a virtually unlimited drive size because it supports up to two ter-abytes of data, which is a theoretical number because hard disks are not yet capable of supporting this much data. NTFS also supports many features that are not avail-able under the FAT (16 or 32) file system, including folder- and file-level security, as well as data encryption and compression.

You should use NTFS on Windows XP, and not FAT32. This is because FAT32 does not support the disk management and security features of NTFS. The only reason that you may want to use FAT32 is if you need to dual-boot Windows XP with Windows 9x, or Windows Me. Because Windows 9x and Windows Me cannot read NTFS, you use FAT32 on the Windows XP partition to access data on it from the Windows 9x or Windows Me partition. Other than this scenario, you should only use NTFS. It is also important to note that this restriction only applies to local files being accessed locally. In a net-working situation, the Server Message Blocks (SMB) protocol handles the translation, so you would be able to access a network file stored on an NTFS drive using a networked Windows 98 computer. This is a common point of confusion, and the best way to remember it is to simply remember that down-level systems cannot access local files stored on NTFS disks, but this restriction does not apply to network files. *Curt Simmons*

Formatting and Converting Drives to NTFS

You can easily format an unformatted drive with NTFS, and you can also convert an existing FAT drive to NTFS. The conversion process preserves any data on the disk. However, this process is one-way; you cannot revert back to FAT32. In the unlikely event that you need to go back to FAT32, you must reformat the drive, and lose all of the data on the disk.

Tip

Keep in mind that this discussion refers to the computer's hard disks. Most removable disks, such as Zip, floppy, and writeable CDs, do not support NTFS. However, you can interact with these removable disks as you normally would, even though the computer's hard disk uses a different file system.

Although the conversion process is safe and effective, volumes that are converted to NTFS lack some of the performance benefits of a drive that was initially format-ted with NTFS. Also, the Master File Table is different on converted volumes, thus affecting performance. Still, conversion is the easiest way to change an FAT drive to NTFS without reformatting and having to restore data that is currently held on the FAT volume. Converting to NTFS is easy, and the following steps show you how:

1. **Click Start ➪ Run.** Type **cmd**, and then click OK.

2. **At the command prompt, use the Convert command to convert the FAT drive to NTFS (see Figure 31-1).** Keep in mind that the conversion process is completely safe, and that all of your data remains as it is. The command and syntax is *convert driveletter:* /FS:NTFS. Press Enter. In Figure 31-1, the C drive is

being converted. Conversion may take several minutes, depending on the size of the drive.

Figure 31-1: Using the Convert command

3. **When the process is complete, simply exit the command interface.** If you converted the boot partition, you are prompted to reboot the computer.

Managing Hard Disks

To manage hard disk configuration, Windows XP uses one centralized location, which is found under Disk Management, shown in Figure 31-2, in the Computer Management console. Click Start ➪ Control Panel ➪ Administrative Tools ➪ Computer Management. Select Disk Management in the left console pane. The disks and their configuration display in the right console pane.

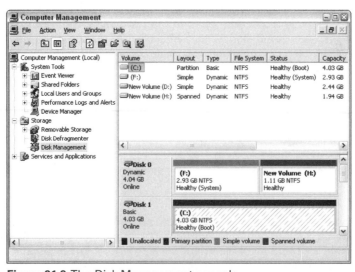

Figure 31-2: The Disk Management console

Understanding Basic and Dynamic Disks

Windows XP Professional supports two kinds of disks, basic and dynamic. A basic disk is a standard hard disk that supports standard configurations. A basic disk can have a primary partition and extended partitions that make up logical disk drives. For example, you can configure the basic disk so that it has a C drive (primary) and a D drive (extended). You can use the D drive for storage or other purposes (or to set up a dual-boot configuration). For example, on a basic disk, you can have up to four primary partitions, or alternative configurations, such as three primary partitions and one extended partition. One of the primary partitions is considered active and is used to start the computer. In other words, this active partition contains your boot files and the master boot record.

A dynamic disk is a drive configured by the Disk Management console so that it can support volume management. A volume is the logical organization of a disk for storage purposes, and it is flexible and easy to use. With volume management, you are not limited to a primary partition and extended partitions. Volumes allow you the flexibility to divide up a disk in any way that you want. In other words, the Disk Management utilities configure the drive so that it can use Windows XP Professional's disk management features. If you want to take advantage of volume management and lose the partition restrictions that are placed on basic disks, you need to convert the disk to a dynamic disk.

Basic disks do not provide the advanced management features supported under Windows XP Professional. Disks are always basic when they are first installed, but you can convert them to dynamic disks in order to take advantage of all that Windows XP Professional has to offer.

If you are dual-booting with a down-level system such as Windows 98, that system will be able to access basic disks because older systems do not support dynamic disks.

Understanding Dynamic Disk States

Dynamic disks are capable of displaying several different states. The state of a disk tells you the current status of the disk and helps you to understand any disk-related problems that may exist. You can see the state of any disk by navigating to Disk Management in the Computer Console. As you can see in Figure 31-3, Disk 1's state is "online," but Disk 3 is labeled as "offline" and "missing."

The following list explains the states that a dynamic disk may display:

✦ **Online:** The disk is online and functioning with no errors.

✦ **Online (Errors):** The disk is online, but there have been some errors. These errors are usually minor and you can fix them by running the Error Checking tool, which is found on the Tools menu of the disk's Properties dialog box.

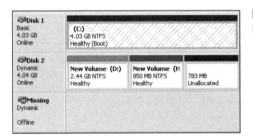

Figure 31-3: Viewing the Disk State in the Computer Console

✦ **Offline:** The disk is not accessible. This problem can occur due to corruption or an I/O problem. Try right clicking the disk and then clicking Reactivate Disk in order to bring the disk back online.

✦ **Missing:** The disk is not accessible or is disconnected, or corruption has caused the disk to not be readable. Try right-clicking the disk and then clicking Reactivate Disk in order to bring the disk back online.

✦ **Initializing:** This message occurs when the disk is temporarily unavailable due to a conversion to dynamic state.

✦ **Not Initialized:** This message occurs when the disk does not have a valid signature. This message also occurs when you install a new disk. When the Disk Management utility appears, the disk appears as Not Initialized. To write a valid signature so that you can format and begin using the disk, simply right-click the disk and then click Initialize.

✦ **Foreign:** This message appears when a physical, dynamic disk is moved from a Windows 2000 or XP Professional computer to another Windows 2000 or XP Professional computer. When this message appears, right-click the disk and then click Import Foreign Disk.

✦ **Unreadable:** This message appears when I/O errors keep the disk from being readable. Click Action ⇨ Rescan Disks to fix the problem.

✦ **No Media:** This message appears on a removable drive when no media is inserted into the drive.

Converting a Basic Disk to a Dynamic Disk

If you want to take advantage of volume management and lose the partition restrictions placed on a basic disk, you need to convert the disk to a dynamic disk. You can easily convert your existing drives to dynamic disks by following these steps:

1. **In Disk Management, right-click the Disk number in the graphical portion of the Disk Management display.** Then click Convert to Dynamic Disk, as shown in Figure 31-4. You can also click Action ⇨ All Tasks ⇨ Convert to Dynamic Disk.

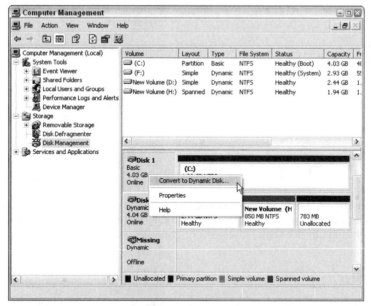

Figure 31-4: Converting to a dynamic disk

2. **In the Convert to Dynamic Disk dialog box, shown in Figure 31-5, select the disk that you want to convert.** Click OK.

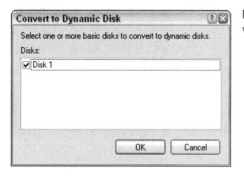

Figure 31-5: Choose the disk you want to convert

3. **In the Disks to Convert dialog box, review the settings, as shown in Figure 31-6.** Click Convert to continue. A message appears telling you that other operating systems will not be able to start from the disk once the conversion has taken place (this means all other operating systems, including NT, 9x, and Me).

4. **Click OK to continue.** You may see a message telling you that any mounted disks need to be dismounted. Click OK to continue.

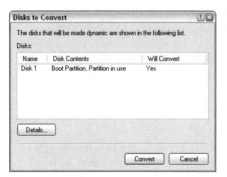

Figure 31-6: The Disks to Convert dialog box

5. **After the conversion process you are prompted to reboot the computer.**
   Once you reboot, you can see that the disk's status has changed from basic to dynamic in the Disk Management console.

Configuring Drive Letters and Paths

Once a basic disk has been converted to a dynamic disk, you can begin taking advantage of the features of dynamic disks. The first thing that you may want to consider is the configuration of drive letters and paths.

You can assign a drive any alphabet letter, and you can also assign a drive to an empty NTFS folder. If you want to change to a dynamic disk volume, right-click the volume in the Disk Management console, and then click Change Drive Letter and Paths. A Change Drive Letter and Paths dialog box appears, as shown in Figure 31-7.

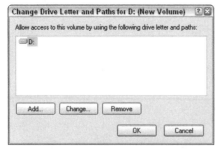

Figure 31-7: The Change Drive Letter and Paths dialog box

You can perform the following actions:

✦ **Add:** If you click the Add button, a second window appears where you can mount the drive to an empty NTFS folder (which is discussed later in this section). Because a drive can only have one drive letter, you cannot assign multiple drive letters for the same drive.

✦ **Change:** If you click the Change button, the Change Drive Letter or Path window appears, as shown in Figure 31-8. You can choose a different drive letter from the drop-down menu.

Figure 31-8: Choose a different drive letter

✦ **Remove:** You can also remove the drive letter. Dynamic disks do not require that a letter or path identify a drive. However, some programs may not function if you remove the drive letter, and you will not be able to access the drive except through any remaining disk paths.

You can also mount a volume to a local, empty NTFS folder. The purpose is to give you freedom and flexibility beyond the 26-letter alphabet limitation. When you mount a volume to an empty NTFS folder, a drive path is used instead of a drive number. For example, if you have a local volume that is only used for storage, then you can create an NTFS folder called "Storage." Then, you can mount the drive to the empty storage volume. You can then access the drive by simply accessing C:\Storage, just as you would a folder. The end result is that you have an unlimited number of drives and can use them like folders rather than standard drive letters that you must remember. You can use both a drive letter and a mounted volume on the same drive, if you like. Keep in mind that the drive must be mounted to an empty folder. Once the mount takes place, you can then move data to that folder in order to store it on the volume.

Note

The Mounting option only works on NTFS folders. You cannot mount a drive to a folder on an FAT drive.

To mount a drive to an empty NTFS folder, just follow these steps:

1. **In the Disk Management console, right-click the volume that you want to mount to an empty NTFS folder.** Next, click Change Drive Letter and Paths.

2. **In the Change Drive Letter and Paths dialog box, click the Add button.**

3. **In the Add Drive Letter or Path dialog box, shown in Figure 31-9, select the "Mount in the following empty NTFS folder" radio button.** Then enter the

path to the folder that you want to mount, or click the Browse button to select the folder.

Figure 31-9: Choose a different drive letter

4. **If you browse for the folder, a Browse window appears, as shown in Figure 31-10.** You can locate the folder or create a new one by clicking the New Folder button. Make your selection and click OK.

Figure 31-10: Browse for a folder location

5. **Click OK again in the Add Drive Letter or Path dialog box.**

If you click the View menu in the Computer Management console, you can see some options that enable you to view the Disk Management console in a variety of ways. You can even assign different colors and wallpaper patterns to different kinds of disks.

Configuring Disk Volumes

When a disk is first converted to a dynamic disk, it appears in the Disk Management console as unallocated space. This means that the disk has no volumes and has not been formatted. In other words, the disk is not usable by the operating system in its current state. Figure 31-11 shows you an unallocated disk in the Disk Management console for Disk 2. This disk has been converted to a dynamic disk, but it has no volumes and no file system. As a result, the operating system cannot use it. In order to use a dynamic disk, you need to create and format disk volumes. The following sections show you the different kinds of volumes that are available to you, and how to create them.

Figure 31-11: This disk has unallocated space.

Creating Simple Volumes

A simple volume is a standard disk volume. It is a unit of disk space that has been configured and formatted so that you can use it to store data. You can format a hard disk as one volume, or you can format a part of it so that you can use multiple disk volumes. The following steps show you how to create a simple disk volume.

1. **In the Disk Management console, right-click the Dynamic disk's unallocated space.** Next, click New Volume, as shown in Figure 31-12. The New Volume Wizard appears.

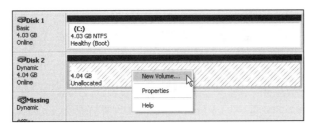

Figure 31-12: Choose the New Volume option.

2. **Click Next to continue.** The Select Volume Type page appears, as shown in Figure 31-13.

3. **Click the Simple radio button and then click Next.** The Select Disks page, shown in Figure 31-14, appears.

4. **Select the disk that you want to configure (it is already selected for you in this wizard).** Next, enter the size of the volume (in megabytes) that you want to create. The maximum amount of space available is listed here for you, as well. Click Next.

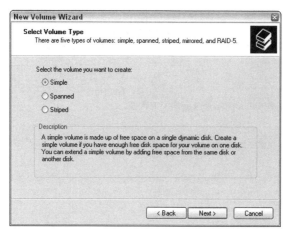

Figure 31-13: Choose the Simple volume option

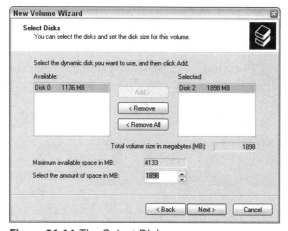

Figure 31-14: The Select Disks page

5. **In the Assign Drive Letter or Path window, choose a drive, assign an empty NTFS folder, or do not assign either, as shown in Figure 31-15.** Click Next.

6. **In the Format Volume page, shown in Figure 31-16, you can choose whether to format the volume.** You can also choose to use the quick format feature and enable file and folder compression for the volume. Make your selections and then click Next.

7. **Click Finish.** The new volume is created and appears in the Disk Management console.

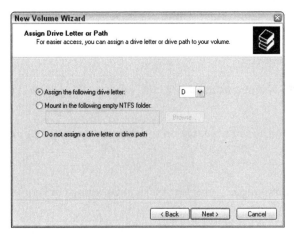

Figure 31-15: Choose a Drive Letter or Path.

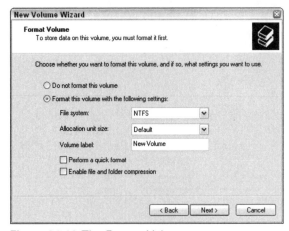

Figure 31-16: The Format Volume page

Extending a Simple Volume

You may create a simple volume and still have extra free space on the same disk. If you decide later that the volume should have been larger, then you do not have to remove your data from the volume in order to create a new one. You can simply extend the existing volume by grabbing some of the additional unallocated space on the disk. This feature allows you to quickly gain additional space without harming any data that is currently stored on the existing volume. For example, you may have a 10GB volume with 2GB of free space available on the same disk. You can extend the 10GB volume to include the 2GB of free space in order to create a 12GB volume. You can do this without damaging the data that is stored on the original 10GB volume.

To extend a volume, follow these steps:

1. **Right-click the desired volume and click Extend Volume.** The Extend Volume wizard appears.

You must have unallocated space available on the disk for the extend option to appear.

2. **Click Next on the Welcome page.** The Select Disks page, shown in Figure 31-17, appears.

Figure 31-17: The Select Disks page

3. **Choose the amount of disk space that you want to extend onto the existing disk.** Click Next.

4. **Click Finish.** The new volume extension is created and appears as an additional volume, although it is an extension of the previous volume.

Creating a Spanned Volume

Aside from the simple volume, Windows XP Professional also supports spanned volumes. A spanned volume combines areas of unallocated space on multiple disks into one logical volume. You can combine between 2 and 32 areas of unallocated space from different drives. For example, your computer may have three hard drives, where each drive has about 500MB of unallocated free space. A 500MB volume is rather small and not very practical for everyday use. However, using the spanned volume option, you can combine all three 500MB areas of unallocated space to create a 1.5GB volume. You can then use the volume, just as if the storage were located on a single disk. Essentially, this configuration gives you more flexibility, and less volumes (and drive letters to remember), and makes good use of left-over space.

Once the spanned volume has been created, it appears as any other volume in My Computer or the Disk Management console. However, it is important to note that spanned volumes are storage solutions only — they do not provide any fault tolerance. If one disk in the spanned volume fails, then all data on the spanned volume is lost. However, you can back up a spanned volume just as you would any other volume.

Like a simple volume, you can easily extend a spanned volume at any time by adding existing free space. However, you cannot remove a volume from a spanned volume without losing the entire volume. Keep this in mind as you plan your disk configuration.

To create a spanned volume, just follow these steps:

1. **In the Disk Management console, right-click one of the areas of unallocated disk space on one of the disks.** Then click New Volume. The New Volume Wizard appears.

2. **Click Next to continue.** The Select Volume Type page, shown in Figure 31-18, appears.

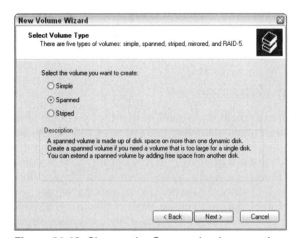

Figure 31-18: Choose the Spanned volume option.

3. **Click the Spanned option, and then click Next.** In the Select Disks page, shown in Figure 31-19, the current disk appears in the Selected field.

Figure 31-19: The Select Disks page

4. **Choose the free space on the desired disks that appear in the Available field, and then click the Add button**. Repeat the process until all unallocated areas that you want to use appear in the Selected field. Click Next.

5. **In the Assign Drive Letter or Path page, choose a drive letter or mount the drive to an empty NTFS folder.** You can also choose not to assign a drive letter or path at this time. Click Next.

6. **In the Format Volume page, choose whether or not to format the volume at that time, and whether or not to perform a quick format and enable file and folder compression.** Click Next.

7. **Click Finish.** The volume is created and now appears in the Disk Management console.

Creating Striped Volumes

Striped volumes are similar to spanned volumes in that they combine areas of free disk space (between 2 and 32 areas of unallocated space on different drives) in order to create one logical volume. However, the big difference is that striped volumes write data across the disks, instead of filling one part of free space first, before writing to the next part. As a result, you are likely to see faster read and write performance than you would with a simple spanned volume. Like a spanned volume, you can create a striped volume by right-clicking one of the areas of unallocated space, and then clicking Create Volume. In the New Volume Wizard, choose to create a striped volume and follow the same steps that appeared in the previous section.

Another important point concerning striped volumes is that the areas of unallocated free space must be the same size. For example, you may want to use 500MB,

800MB, and 900MB areas of unallocated disk space to create a striped set. Because the areas have to be the same size, Disk Management configures 500MB from each disk, which means that you still have some unallocated space left over. This configuration enables data to be written evenly across the disks.

Finally, keep in mind that striped volumes are storage solutions that are designed to provide better performance. However, they do not provide any fault tolerance. If one disk in the stripe fails, then all of the data that is stored on the stripe will be lost. You should therefore have an effective backup plan.

To create a striped volume, right-click the desired area of free space, and then click New Volume. The New Volume Wizard appears, where you can choose the Striped volume option and then select the disks that you want to use.

Expert's Notebook: Fault Tolerance in Windows XP?

As you have been working with the Add Volume Wizard, you may have noticed some references to additional volume solutions that are fault-tolerant. These references refer to Microsoft's overall disk management solutions, even though the fault-tolerance options are not available on Windows XP. (Unlike Windows 2003 Server, Windows XP Professional does not support any kind of disk fault tolerance.)

The two types of fault tolerances available on Microsoft server software are disk mirroring and RAID 5. (RAID stands for Redundant Array of Inexpensive Disks.) Disk mirroring, which is supported on dynamic disks in Windows 2003 Server, is also called RAID 1, and requires two physical disks. When you configure a disk mirror, one disk volume maintains an exact copy of the first disk. In the event that one of the disks fails, you always have a redundant copy. However, the cost per megabyte for disk mirroring is high. Because you are maintaining an exact copy of a volume, everything that you save requires twice as much storage space as it normally would. Nonetheless, disk mirroring is a great choice for critical servers that must be up and running quickly.

The second type of fault tolerance supported under Windows 2003 server is RAID 5. It is a standard tolerance system that uses three or more dynamic disks in order to store data. Using a parity bit, which is a mathematical formula, data is written across the disks in a stripe fashion. If a single disk fails, then the data can be regenerated from the remaining disks. You can use up to 32 physical drives in a RAID 5 volume, but RAID-5 volumes cannot hold the system or boot partition. *Curt Simmons*

Taking Care of Windows XP and Automating Tasks

32

W indows XP includes a few helpful tools that solve common performance problems that you may experience. There is also a helpful task scheduler feature that enables you to automate the use of some of these tools. If you have used previous versions of Windows, then you won't see any dramatic surprises here. However, these tools are important for a healthy operating system, and so it is a good idea to get into the habit of running them regularly in order to help keep your computer in good shape.

Hard Disk Performance Tools

The hard disk is the storehouse for Windows XP, and so it should be no surprise that it may experience performance problems from time to time. Windows XP includes both an Error-checking tool and a Disk Defragmenter tool that enable you to resolve hard disk and fragmentation problems. There is also a Disk Cleanup tool that can help you to eliminate clutter. The following sections show you how to use these tools.

The Error-checking Tool

The Error-checking tool is on the Tools tab of the disk's Properties dialog box, as shown in Figure 32-1. When you click the Check Now button, you can use the check box options to find file system errors and recover bad sectors, as shown in Figure 32-2. In order for the Error-checking tool to work, it needs complete access to the disk, applications must be closed, and in some cases, Error-checking asks you to reboot before it starts, in order to gain complete access to the disk. If you use your computer a lot, it is good idea to run this tool every six weeks or so, just to make sure that your disk is in good working order.

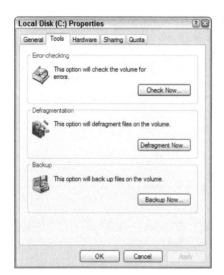

Figure 32-1: The Tools tab

Figure 32-2: The Check disk options

Note Anti-virus programs are notorious for causing problems with the Error-checking tool, and so you should make sure that you shut down any anti-virus programs before you try to use this tool. Also, you should make sure that you shut down any disk management tools.

The Disk Defragmenter Tool

The Disk Defragmenter helps to reduce fragmentation and is available on the Tools tab of the disk's Properties dialog box. This tool helps to repair file fragmentation, which occurs over time on any file system.

So what is fragmentation? Windows XP attempts to store files in a contiguous format. However, as you change a file and then resave it, the file system has to move data to different blocks of free space. As a result, a file may have "pieces" scattered over the disk. When you open the file, the system must work harder to retrieve all of the scattered pieces and assemble them. When this happens, the disk is said to be *fragmented*. You can use the Disk Defragmenter tool to defragment the drive and rearrange data so that the file system stores the data in a contiguous manner.

Fragmentation is a normal part of disk usage, however, the Disk Defragmenter tool does not completely cure fragmentation. Even though the tool cannot completely defragment a drive, you are likely to notice a performance improvement after you run the Disk Defragmenter tool if the drive is heavily fragmented. The following steps show you how to use this tool.

You may see better results when you run the Disk Defragmenter tool several times in a row, allowing it to further correct fragmentation. Give it a try!

Note If you are using Hibernation, the hibernate file can take up a considerable amount of space on your hard drive. Before defragmenting the drive, consider disabling hibernation. This allows the Windows defragmenter to access the space that the hibernation folder takes up. The Windows defragmenter or any of the other third party defragmenting applications cannot defragment an enabled hibernation file, neither can it defragment the page file. You can only defragment the page file offline — something the Windows defragmenter cannot do. If you want to defragment the page file, you need an alternative defragmentation application, such as Raxco Perfect Disk. www.raxco.com

1. **Open My Computer.** Right-click the disk that you want to defragment and click Properties. On the Tools tab, click the Defragment Now button. The Disk Defragmenter window appears, as shown in Figure 32-3.

2. **Click the Analyze button.** An analysis of the drive is performed, and a message appears telling you whether you should defragment the drive.

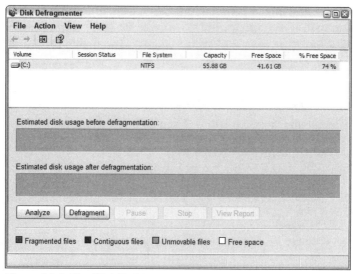

Figure 32-3: The Disk Defragmenter window

3. **You can also choose to view a report, as shown in Figure 32-4.**

4. **If the report shows that the disk needs to be defragmented, click the Defragment button.** The defragmentation process begins and may take some time, depending on how badly the drive is fragmented, as shown in Figure 32-5. Once the process is completed, you can view a report again.

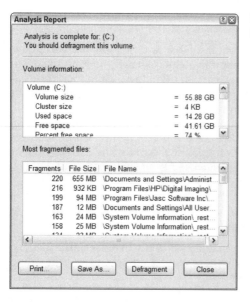

Figure 32-4: The Analysis Report dialog box

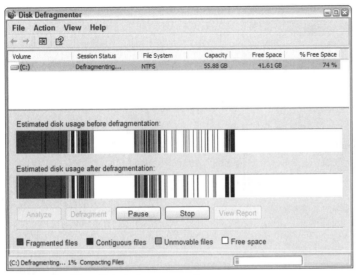

Figure 32-5: The disk defragmentation process

The Disk Cleanup Tool

Windows XP also has a Disk Cleanup tool, which basically examines your hard disk for temporary files and other file fragments that are no longer needed. You can access Disk Cleanup on the General tab of the disk's Properties dialog box. It is a good tool to use to remove unneeded files that have accumulated on your hard disk. The following steps show you how to use this tool.

1. **Open My Computer.** Right-click the disk that you want to clean up and click Properties.

2. **On the General tab, click the Disk Cleanup button, as shown in Figure 32-6.** Disk Cleanup runs a calculation check on your computer to see how much space it can free up, as shown in Figure 32-7. The check may take several minutes to complete.

3. **On the Disk Cleanup tab, shown in Figure 32-8, you can review the items that have been selected for cleanup.** You can select an item to read more about it, and you can also click the View Files button to see what files will be deleted. If there are any file categories that you do not want deleted, deselect the check box next to those items.

4. **Click the More Options tab, shown in Figure 32-9.** You can choose to remove optional Windows components, installed programs that you do not use, and data that was created after the most recent restore point.

5. **When you are ready, click OK. Your disk will be cleaned.**

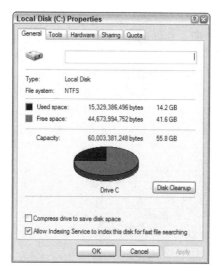

Figure 32-6: The General tab

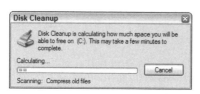

Figure 32-7: The Disk Cleanup dialog box

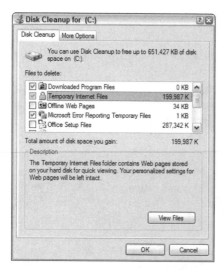

Figure 32-8: The Disk Cleanup tab

Figure 32-9: The More Options tab

Scheduling Tasks

You can use the Scheduled Task Wizard to schedule certain tools and utilities to run at specific times in order to automate the process of optimizing Windows XP performance. If you tried any of the tools in the previous section, you can immediately see how important this feature is because running those tools can be time-consuming. Consider using the Scheduled Task Wizard to run Disk Defragmenter or Error-checking tools during the night so that the tools do not interrupt your work. Also, make sure that the date and time on the computer's clock are accurate so that the wizard actually runs when you want it to. The Scheduled Task Wizard is easy to configure, and the following steps guide you through the process.

1. **Click Start ➪ All Programs ➪ Accessories ➪ System Tools ➪ Scheduled Tasks.**

2. **In the Scheduled Tasks folder, double-click the Add Scheduled Task Wizard.** The Welcome screen appears.

3. **Click Next.** The Schedule Task Wizard appears.

4. **Select the task that you want to schedule, as shown in Figure 32-10.** You can also browse for other programs, if necessary. Click Next.

5. **On the next page, shown in Figure 32-11, give the task a name and choose when you want to run the program**. For example, you can select daily, weekly, or monthly. Click Next. Depending on your selection, an additional page may appear where you can configure the time and day of the week, as shown in Figure 32-12.

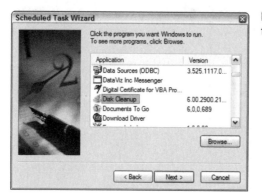

Figure 32-10: Choose a program that you want to run.

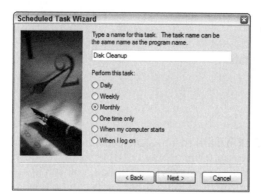

Figure 32-11: Type a name for the task, and choose a task option.

Figure 32-12: Choose a task schedule

6. **Make any necessary selections and then click Next.** Your username is listed in the next screen.

7. **If required, enter your password for your account.** Note that scheduled tasks are configured for a certain user—multiple users on the same computer can configure different scheduled tasks. Click Next.

8. **Review your settings and then click Finish.** If you want to see advanced properties for the scheduled task, click the check box before clicking Finish.

   If you chose to view advanced properties, the properties pages for the task appear. The Task and Schedule tabs allow you to make changes to the values that you configured when using the wizard. However, the Settings tab, shown in Figure 32-13, displays some additional configuration options, which are:

   - **Scheduled Task Completed:** You can choose to delete the task if it is not scheduled to run again. You can also choose to stop the task if it runs for *X* number of hours and *X* minutes. This is a safety feature that stops a task that is taking too long to complete.

   - **Idle Time:** You can choose to start the task only if the computer has been idle for *X* number of minutes, and you can stop the task if the computer ceases to be idle.

   - **Power Management:** You can choose not to start the task if the computer is running on batteries, and to stop the task if the computer begins battery mode.

Figure 32-13: The Settings tab

Once you create a scheduled task, it appears in the Scheduled Tasks folder. You can right-click the task and run it manually, delete it, or change the properties of the scheduled task. If you are having problems with scheduled tasks, or if you want to suspend all scheduled tasks, you can easily do so in the Scheduled Tasks folder.

Using Event Viewer and Performance Monitor

33

L ike previous versions of Windows, Windows XP provides two tools that can help you to manage your system, Event Viewer and the Performance Monitor (also called System Monitor). Both of these tools are designed to help you find out what is going on with your system. In other words, Event Viewer doesn't help you manage events, but it shows you what has occurred. Likewise, the Performance tool doesn't help your computer perform better, but it helps you locate potential problems and issues that could hinder system performance.

You may not use these two tools on a regular basis. However, when you suspect that things may be going wrong with your system, these two tools can be valuable resources.

Event Viewer

The Event Viewer is a tool that enables you to view events that occur on your system. Armed with the right information, you can troubleshoot and resolve any system problems that may be occurring.

The Event Viewer is available in the Administrative Tools folder in Control Panel, or you can also access it through the

Computer Management console. Either way, the Event Viewer is a standard Microsoft Management Console (MMC) interface that contains three different event logs — Application, Security, and System — as shown in Figure 33-1. Event Viewer uses these three categories to report information about hardware, software, and system problems, as well as security events. The following sections examine the three event logs that Windows XP records.

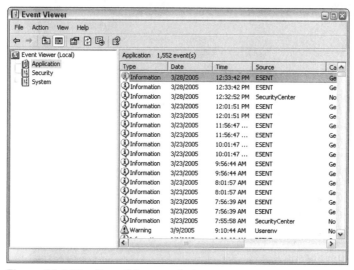

Figure 33-1: The Event Viewer window

The Event Viewer uses the data that is written to the event log to display a report of the information. The event log is helpful, but it takes up system resources. If you are conservative with system resources, and you want to turn off the event log, you can prevent it from starting by accessing MSCONFIG, and clearing the Event Log check box on the Services tab. Keep in mind that by stopping the event log, you essentially stop the Event Viewer from working because there will be nothing to report.

Application

The Application log contains events that are logged by applications or programs. Typically, you see errors concerning the operation of programs. If you click Application in the left console pane, you can see that events are primarily made up of information, warnings, and errors. If you double-click an event, you can read information about it, as shown in Figure 33-2.

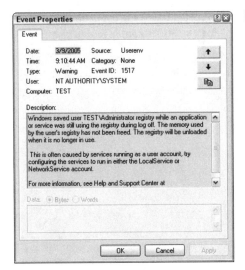

Figure 33-2: The Event tab

Security

The Security log displays information about security events on your system. These can include security audit events, logon or logoff events, and shared resource events. You can double-click any event to read more about it. Figure 33-3 shows you the Security log pane.

Type	Date	Time	Source
Failure Audit	3/23/2005	9:59:55 AM	Security
Failure Audit	3/23/2005	9:59:55 AM	Security
Failure Audit	3/23/2005	9:59:55 AM	Security
Failure Audit	3/23/2005	9:59:55 AM	Security
Failure Audit	3/23/2005	9:59:55 AM	Security
Failure Audit	3/23/2005	7:55:49 AM	Security
Failure Audit	3/23/2005	7:55:34 AM	Security
Success Audit	3/23/2005	7:55:34 AM	Security
Success Audit	3/9/2005	8:57:56 AM	Security
Success Audit	3/9/2005	8:57:56 AM	Security
Success Audit	3/9/2005	8:57:56 AM	Security
Success Audit	3/9/2005	8:57:56 AM	Security
Success Audit	3/9/2005	8:57:56 AM	Security
Success Audit	3/9/2005	8:57:56 AM	Security
Success Audit	3/9/2005	8:57:56 AM	Security
Success Audit	3/9/2005	8:57:56 AM	Security

Figure 33-3: The Security log pane

System

The System log displays information about Windows XP system components. You can view information about system-wide events, driver problems, or just about anything else that has to do with the system, including information events and error events. Figure 33-4 shows you an example of an error event.

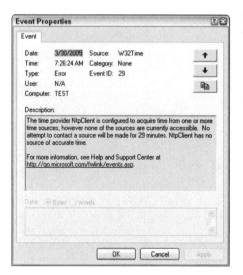

Figure 33-4: The Properties dialog box for an error event.

Helpful Usage Tips

Aside from viewing different events, there are a few other actions that you may find helpful as you use the Event Viewer. Keep the following tips in mind:

✦ **You can search for specific events by selecting a log and clicking View ➪ Find.** Under Types, choose the type of event for which you are looking, and specify additional information about the event.

✦ **You can clear an event log by clicking Action ➪ Clear All Events.**

✦ **You can archive an event log by clicking Action ➪ Save Log File As.**

Accessing More Information: Windows XP Log Files

Many services have detailed log files in addition to the information available with Windows XP Event Viewer. For example, the Windows XP FTP service tracks information, including the IP of connecting clients, the username used to connect, connection time, and what files were accessed. Most of the log files are stored in the C:\windows\system32\Logfiles folder. You can also configure Windows Firewall to generate a log. You can configure this log file to collect information about successful network connections (the default setting) and dropped connections. The firewall log contains a variety of information, including time, protocol, source and destination address, and source and destination port. The various log files kept by Windows XP can prove useful if you are trying to troubleshoot connectivity issues, such as for FTP/HTTP services. They can also be helpful when you are trying to track down a network issue, such as a worm infestation, that may be revealed by examining connectivity information. *David Dalan*

✦ **You can filter events in the event log using the Filter option on the View menu.**

✦ **You can set event logging options by clicking Action ⟹ Properties and clicking the General tab, as shown in Figure 33-5.**

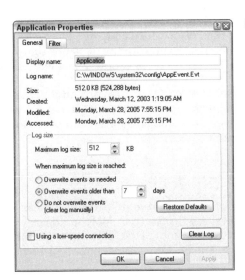

Figure 33-5: The General tab

Performance

If you have worked with previous versions of Windows, such as Windows 2000 Professional, you will notice that the Performance tool in Windows XP is essentially the same tool with almost no modification. Like the Event Viewer, the Performance tool doesn't do anything but monitor your system. In other words, you can't use the Performance tool to make your system perform better, but you can use the Performance tool to help you find performance problems with your Windows XP computer.

The Performance tool provides information on both hardware and software, and it can display data results in a chart, report, or histogram format. You can also log data and create administrative alerts that will help you determine when the per-formance of a component drops below a certain baseline. The tool functions by using counters, which are individual components. For example, you can configure Performance to monitor a "memory" counter, which then keeps tabs with the mem-ory on your system. Typically, performance monitoring is best used with a baseline of performance. This means that you use Performance over a period of time during peak and non-peak times in order to determine the baseline under which the compo-nent functions. By monitoring high and low peaks of performance, you can effectively determine what is "normal" and satisfactory operation for that component.

With the baseline, you can later use Performance monitor to see whether the component is functioning within normal parameters. If it is not, then you know that a problem exists with the component, or that the load placed on the component has increased. Either way, you can effectively identify the component that is not able to keep up with the demand placed on it; this component is referred to as a *bottleneck*. For example, you may monitor the memory counter and find that the results are high. You may then notice that your system seems to run slowly when you do a few things at the same time. Using the Performance counter, you would find that the memory is a bottleneck—it cannot keep up with the demands that you or the operating system is placing on it. The answer is, of course, a memory upgrade.

Running the Performance monitor also puts a strain on performance, just like any other application. Although the Performance tool is helpful when you have suspicions about a performance problem, you should not randomly use the tool unless you have a specific reason.

The Performance Tool Interface

Before you use the Performance tool, it is important to become familiar with the interface. Like most tools in Windows XP, it uses a basic MMC interface, but there are a few important things that you need to know. First, click Start ➪ Control Panel ➪ Administrative Tools ➪ Performance. The Performance Monitor tool opens, as shown in Figure 33-6.

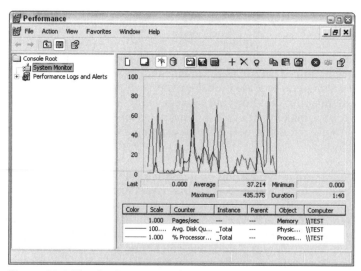

Figure 33-6: The Performance window

The left console pane contains the System Monitor node and the Performance Logs and Alerts node. However, you will generally be using the right console pane. There are three basic divisions in this pane, starting at the top:

✦ **Toolbar:** The toolbar contains icons that you use regularly to generate the types of charts and information that you want. The toolbar contains several standard button options, which identify themselves when you hover the cursor over them.

✦ **Information Area:** The information area contains the chart, histogram, or report that you want to view. Just click the desired button on the toolbar to view counter information in the specified format.

✦ **Counter List:** The bottom part of the window contains a counter list. All of the counters displayed in the list are currently being updated in the information area. You can easily remove or add counters from or to the list by using the toolbar. Each counter in the counter list is given a different color for charting and histogram purposes.

Using Counters

You primarily use Performance by accessing objects and choosing counters. You choose the counters that you want to monitor, and then view those counters in either a chart, histogram, or report format. The following steps show you how to add counters to the Performance monitor interface.

1. **Click Start ➪ Control Panel ➪ Administrative Tools ➪ Performance.**

2. **In the Performance MMC, click the New Counter Set button on the toolbar.** Then click the Add button on the toolbar.

FYI: How to Know When a Counter Displays a Performance Problem

When you work with the Performance tool, you need to know when a counter is showing a performance problem. Certain counters seem to vary widely, depending on what is happening on your system. As you monitor various counters, you can gain information about the performance of the system processes and components that you selected. Although high spikes are normal, consistently high readings on counters usually mean that a problem exists, indicating that the component or hardware is not able to meet the burden placed on it by the operating system's processes. This is, of course, where your baseline data is important. Using the baseline, you can tell if a component has higher-than-normal readings, and what those reading might mean for system performance. *Curt Simmons*

3. **In the Add Counters dialog box, shown in Figure 33-7, use the drop-down menu to choose a performance object.** This example chooses the "PhysicalDisk" counter.

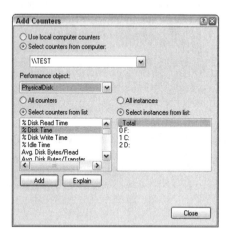

Figure 33-7: The Add Counters dialog box

4. **You can now choose to monitor all counters under the object that you selected, or you can choose individual counters.** To select individual counters, simply select the counter and click the Add button. Notice that the instances field of the dialog box may be active, depending on your selection. The instances field allows you to choose certain instances, if they are available. For example, as shown in Figure 33-8, there are three physical disks on the computer. You can either monitor all disks or selected ones.

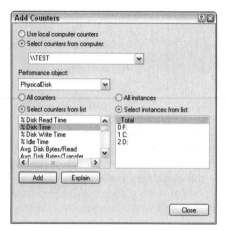

Figure 33-8: You can select instance options.

5. **Repeat the above steps until you have added all of the counters you want, and then click Close.** The counters that you have added are now being monitored.

6. **You can change the chart/histogram/report view by simply clicking a different option button on the toolbar.** As shown in Figure 33-9, the Report feature is currently being used.

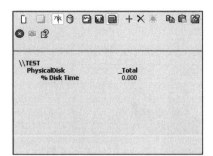

Figure 33-9: The Report feature in the Performance window

Logging Data

As you watch performance counters, you can take note of any counters that seem to run consistently high. But how can you gain that data without sitting in front of a screen all day? Also, if a particular object seems to be causing problems, how can you monitor that object during an entire day's operations without physically watching the screen? This is where the ability to log data is very important. Using Performance, you can log data over a period of time and then analyze that data. This feature enables you to sample data during a specific time period without you having to manually watch the data. The following steps show you how to configure a log file.

1. **In Performance Monitor, expand Performance Logs and Alerts in the left pane.** Right-click Counter Logs, and then click New Log Settings.

2. **In the New Log Settings dialog box that appears, give the log file a name and click OK.** The settings dialog box appears for the log.

3. **On the General tab, shown in the Figure 33-10, you can change the default log filename and storage location if you want.** Next, use the Add Objects and Add Counters buttons to add the objects and counters that you want to log. As shown in the example, two memory counters are being logged. Under the sample data section, choose how often you want the log file to sample data. In the example, Performance Monitor is sampling memory data every 15 seconds.

4. **On the Log Files tab, shown in Figure 33-11, you can choose the type of log file that you want to produce.** By default, this is a binary file. However, you can use the drop-down menu to configure a text file, binary circular file, or even an SQL database file. You can also adjust the file-naming scheme in the fields below.

Figure 33-10: The General tab

Figure 33-11: The Log Files tab

5. **The Schedule tab allows you to configure how the log file is started or stopped, as shown in Figure 33-12.** When you have finished specifying all of the settings for the log file, click OK.

Figure 33-12: The Schedule tab

Creating Alerts

Aside from logging data, another helpful feature that the Performance tool provides is administrative alerts. These alerts inform you when a certain counter that you are monitoring falls outside a certain baseline. For example, you may be monitoring the performance of memory. If the memory counter moves above the baseline that you have established, you will receive an alert in the form of a network message or an event in the Event log. To configure an alert for an existing counter, follow these steps:

1. **In Performance Monitor, expand Performance Logs and Alerts in the left pane.** Right-click Alerts and click New Alert Settings.

2. **Specify a name for the new alert setting in the dialog box that appears, and click OK.** The General tab of the dialog box appears by default, shown in Figure 33-13.

3. **You can add counters to the alert, just as you do for a log file.** Once the counters are added to the list, choose a baseline limit and a data sample rate.

Figure 33-13: The General tab

4. **On the Action tab, shown in Figure 33-14, choose an action that occurs when the event is triggered.**

Figure 33-14: The Action tab

5. **On the Schedule tab, you can configure a schedule for the alert.** This is the same Schedule tab that you see when configuring a log file.

Expert's Notebook: Accessing Quick Performance Information from Task Manager

Although the Performance tool allows you to identify and monitor specific counters, it can be a lot of work to monitor those counters and sift through the data that they provide. What if your computer is running sluggishly or experiencing another common performance problem and you want to quickly see what's going on? No problem. Windows XP's Task Manager can quickly provide a chart of common performance data. Just press Ctrl+Alt+Del to access Task Manager, and then click the Performance tab, as shown in the figure. You can get a quick look at CPU usage and Page File usage, along with some other information about memory. In this way, the Performance tab can quickly tell you whether the CPU or memory is the problem. Although you don't have any configuration options here, this feature is a great way to quickly view performance information.

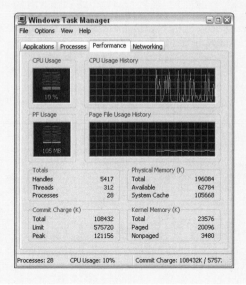

The Performance tab in Windows Task Manager.

System Information, System Restore, and Windows Help

34

Dealing with computer problems can be as enjoyable as dental surgery. You do it if you must, but you prefer to avoid it if at all possible. You have probably had the experience of spending a lot of time on the phone with technical support. Wouldn't it be great if your computer could simply fix itself?

Unfortunately, computers that can fix their own problems do not yet exist, but they have come a long way. Windows XP includes three important problem-solving tools—System Information, System Restore, and Windows Help—that can help you to fix problems quickly and easily, and to gain important information about your computer. The idea is to give you more tools so that you can recover from problems without having to call for help. In this chapter, you will learn about these tools and how to put them to work.

System Information

System Information is a powerful tool that provides all kinds of information about your computer system, and it includes some additional tools that can fix problems on your system, as shown in Figure 34-1. You can access System Information by clicking Start ➪ All Programs ➪ Accessories ➪ System Tools ➪ System Information. You can also access System Information by typing **msinfo32** at the Run line.

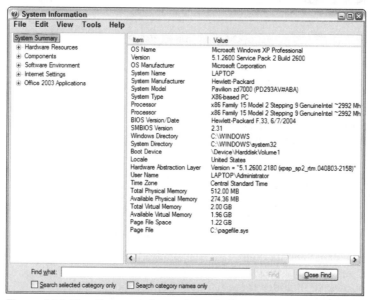

Figure 34-1: The System Information window

If you take a look at the left pane, you see a list of information categories. If you click the plus (+) sign next to each category, you can select specific topics for which you want to gather information. It is important to note here that you cannot configure or actually do anything with System Information, with the exception of the troubleshooting tools. However, the information that you gather can be helpful. This is because the more information that you can gather about your computer, the more likely you are to solve its problems. On a more practical note, System Information is very useful to telephone support personnel who you may need to call in the event of a problem that you cannot solve. Although having outside support is very helpful, it is always best if you can solve your own PC problems; the following sections tell you all about the information that you can gain in each major category, and I'll point out some tips for you along the way.

System Summary

When you first open System Information, the default view is the System Summary. This view simply gives you an overview of your computer. You see everything, from the operating system to the total amount of RAM installed on your computer. This page is very helpful if you want a quick report about the basics of your computer. You can easily print or export this page using the File menu.

Hardware Resources

The Hardware Resources category of System Information gives you a complete look at the hardware on your computer. This section is an excellent place to see exactly what is installed, what is working and what is not, and whether there are any conflicts, as shown in Figure 34-2. If there are any conflicts, then you will see warning messages in yellow, and conflict or error messages in red. This helps you to quickly identify problems if they exist. By expanding Hardware Resources in the left pane, you can display the following categories:

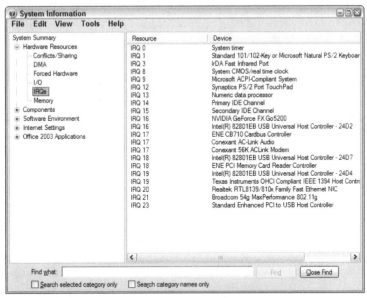

Figure 34-2: The Hardware Resources category in the System Information window

✦ **Conflicts/Sharing:** This option tells you whether there are any hardware conflicts between devices. In some cases, hardware devices share certain computer resources, and this section tells you about those, as well.

✦ **DMA (Direct Memory Access):** This option tells you which devices have direct access to memory resources.

✦ **Forced Hardware:** If you have problems installing a device and it has been "forced" onto your system using manual settings, the device will be listed here.

✦ **I/O (Input/Output System):** This option gives a report about input/output operation. Technical support personnel often find this information useful.

✦ **IRQs (Interrupt Request Lines):** Each device uses an IRQ to access your computer's processor. This option tells you which device is using which IRQ.

✦ **Memory:** This option provides a list of memory resource assignments for each device.

Components

The Components category provides a list of components that are installed and used on your system. Some of these have additional sub-menus as well, as shown in Figure 34-3. System Information displays problems in yellow-and-red lettering so that you can easily identify them. You can find information about the following:

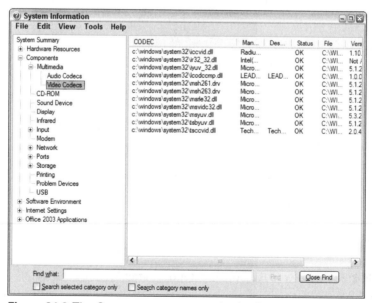

Figure 34-3: The Components category in the System Information window

✦ **Multimedia:** Gives you information about your audio and video configuration.

✦ **CD-ROM:** Information is listed here about your CD-ROM drive.

✦ **Sound Device:** Information about your sound card is listed here.

✦ **Display:** Information about your display appears here.

✦ **Infrared:** If you are using any infrared devices, they are listed here.

✦ **Input:** Any information about your keyboard and mouse or other pointing device is listed here.

✦ **Modem:** Modem information is listed here.

✦ **Network:** Network adapters, protocols, and WinSock information are provided here.

✦ **Ports:** Information is listed here about ports on your computer (such as serial and parallel ports).

✦ **Storage:** Information about the drives on your computer is listed here.

✦ **Printing:** Information about printers and print drivers is listed here.

✦ **Problem Devices:** If any devices are not working correctly, they are listed here. This is a very useful option to quickly find troublesome devices.

✦ **USB (Universal Serial Bus):** USB configuration and devices are listed here.

Software Environment

The Software Environment category, shown in Figure 34-4, displays information about the software configuration of Windows XP. If there are any problems or errors, they appear in red or yellow. This category is very helpful to technical support personnel who are helping you to solve a problem with Windows XP. You can find the following information in this category:

✦ **Drivers:** Lists the drivers that manage your computer's software environment.

✦ **Signed Drivers:** Lists of installed drivers that are certified by Microsoft.

✦ **Environment Variables:** Lists items such as your TEMP file, which is used for temporary files and other variables in the software environment.

✦ **Print Jobs:** Displays the information found in your print queue.

✦ **Network Connections:** Lists all network connections currently held by your computer are listed here.

✦ **Running Tasks:** Lists all of the tasks that are currently running on your computer.

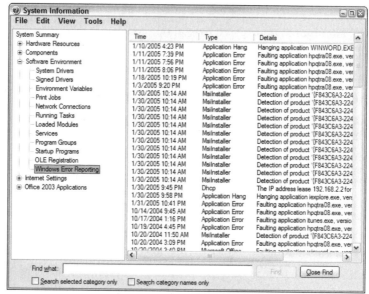

Figure 34-4: The Software Environment category

✦ **Loaded Modules:** Lists all software modules that are currently loaded.

✦ **Services:** Lists the services, such as automatic updates and fax, that are currently installed on your computer.

✦ **Program Groups:** Lists all program groups that are currently configured on your computer.

✦ **Startup Programs:** Lists all programs that are configured to run automatically when your computer starts up.

✦ **OLE Registration (Object Linking and Embedding):** Windows XP uses OLE to allow the various system components and programs to communicate with each other. OLE information is listed here.

✦ **Windows Error Reporting:** Provides a listing of software errors reported by the system.

The Windows Error Reporting option is a very helpful feature of System Information, as shown in Figure 34-4. You can find out here about errors that have occurred on your system.

Internet Explorer

This category, shown in Figure 34-5, provides information about the configuration of Internet Explorer. You can find the following information in this category:

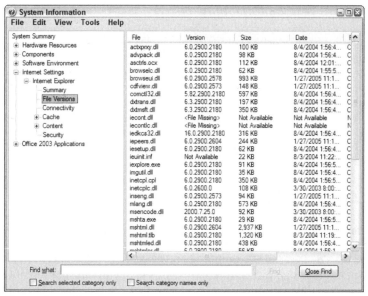

Figure 34-5: The Internet Explorer category

✦ **Summary:** Displays a quick summary of Internet Explorer's configuration.

✦ **File Versions:** Lists all files and file versions used by Internet Explorer.

✦ **Connectivity:** Displays a quick review of Internet Explorer's connectivity configuration. These are the settings that you configure in Internet Options in Internet Explorer.

✦ **Cache:** Internet Explorer uses a cache to store temporary Internet files. This option displays information about the cache size, as well as a list of objects in the cache.

✦ **Content:** Displays security and content settings.

✦ **Security:** Displays zone security configuration.

Note   You may have additional categories for some of your software, such as Microsoft Office.

System Information Tools

System Information also contains a Tools menu that allows you to easily access some features and tools in Windows XP. The Network Diagnostics tool and System Restore are explored elsewhere in this book. The other three tools — File Signature Verification Utility, DirectX Diagnostic Tool, and Dr. Watson — are explored in the following sections.

File Signature Verification Utility

In order to protect Windows XP, files that are in use by the operating system are *signed* by Microsoft to ensure compatibility and security. You can use the Signature Verification Utility to make certain that no unsigned files are in use on your system. By default, Windows XP gives you a warning message before you install unsigned files. You can use this tool to gather information about these files. When you open Signature Verification, click the Start button to run the verification scan. Once the scan is complete, a report displays all of the unsigned files on your system. Generally, you don't need to use this tool, but if you have installed some programs on your computer that are giving you problems, you can run this utility to check for signatures.

DirectX Diagnostic Tool

DirectX is a graphics technology that enables you to play really cool games. However, you can have problems with some versions of DirectX when it operates with your system hardware. The DirectX Diagnostic Tool provides an easy interface, as shown in Figure 34-6. The DirectX Files tab reports a variety of information to you; the Display, Sound, Music, Input, and Network tabs give you information about how DirectX is interacting with these system resources. Each of these tabs also contains a test button so that you can directly test how DirectX interacts with the hardware. This is a great tool to help you identify exactly which incompatibilities are occurring between DirectX and your hardware.

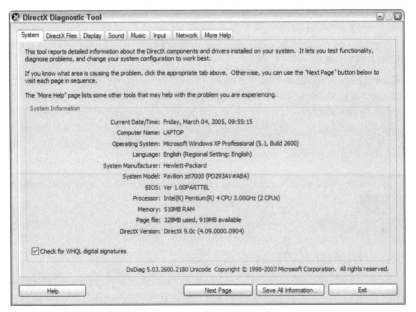

Figure 34-6: The DirectX Diagnostic Tool dialog box

Dr. Watson

Dr. Watson is a Windows tool that can inspect your system and then generate a report after a system fault has occurred. Dr. Watson can tell you what went wrong, and sometimes suggest what can be done to fix the problem, as shown in Figure 34-7. Should you ever need to contact technical support, they may request that you run Dr. Watson in order to take a "snap-shot" of your system; this report can then be used to solve the problem. The results are usually easy to understand. If you see a particular application or device listed, you may need to reinstall the application or device in question, or just remove it from Windows XP altogether.

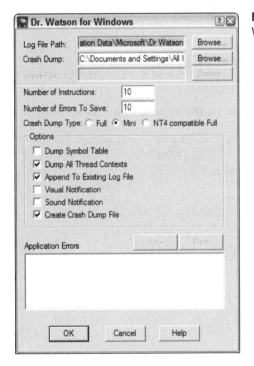

Figure 34-7: The Dr. Watson For Windows dialog box

Using System Restore

System Restore is a feature that enables you to essentially "roll back" your computer to an earlier time. For example, you may have installed a bad application, your computer may have problems starting, or your kids may have deleted some files from C:\Windows. When problems like this occur, System Restore offers an answer. I can emphatically say that System Restore is a great Windows XP feature that can get you out of all sorts of trouble. I have used System Restore numerous times, and without fail, it has worked flawlessly for me. System Restore is also easy to use, as the following sections demonstrate.

Enabling System Restore

By default, System Restore should be enabled on your computer. However, if you upgraded to Windows XP and originally did not have 200MB of free disk space, the feature will be turned off. To ensure that System Restore is enabled on your system, follow these steps:

1. **In the Control Panel, double-click System.** Alternatively, you can just right-click My Computer and then click Properties.

2. **Click the System Restore tab.**

3. **You can click the check box shown in Figure 34-8 to turn off System Restore for all drives on your computer.** If this check box is selected, just click to clear it so that System Restore is enabled.

4. **Click OK, and then click OK again on the System Properties dialog box.**

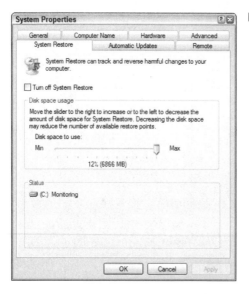

Figure 34-8: The System Restore tab

By default, the maximum setting of 12% of your disk is specified for System Restore. Although this may seem like a lot of space, it is best to leave this percentage configured in order to maximize the number of available restore points.

FYI: System Restore Requirements

System Restore functions by saving information about your system so that it can be restored in the event of a problem. System Restore is automatically installed and configured on Windows XP if your computer has at least 200MB of free disk space after Windows XP is installed. If your computer does not have 200MB of free disk space, System Restore is still installed, but it is not set up to run. In order for System Restore to function correctly, 200MB of free disk space are required, although System Restore may need more free space. Fortunately, if you are using a newer computer, you most likely have plenty of free disk space, and System Restore is already to use.

Creating Restore Points

System Restore functions by creating restore points. A restore point is a "snapshot" of your computer's configuration that is stored on your hard disk. If you need to use System Restore, you can access a restore point to reconfigure your computer and bring the computer back to a stable state. However, it is very important to note that System Restore only restores your operating system and applications — it does not save and restore any other files. For example, if you accidentally delete a Word document, then you cannot use System Restore to save that document. Also, System Restore does not affect other files, such as e-mail and Web pages. Performing a System Restore does not make you lose new e-mail or files — it only configures your system and application settings.

System Restore automatically creates restore points for you, so there is no need to manually create a restore point. However, what if you are about to try a configuration option, or to configure a software that you know may be risky or that has caused you problems in the past? Before trying the configuration or software, you can manually create a restore point so that you can later restore your system to its present state. To create a restore point, just follow these steps:

1. **Click Start ⇨ All Programs ⇨ Accessories ⇨ System Tools ⇨ System Restore.** The System window appears.

2. **Click the "Create a restore point" radio button, and then click Next, as shown in Figure 34-9.**

3. **In the window that appears, enter a description for the restore point.** You may want to include information that will help you to distinguish this restore point from others. The date and time of the restore point are added automatically.

4. **Click Create.** The restore point is created.

5. **Click OK to finish.**

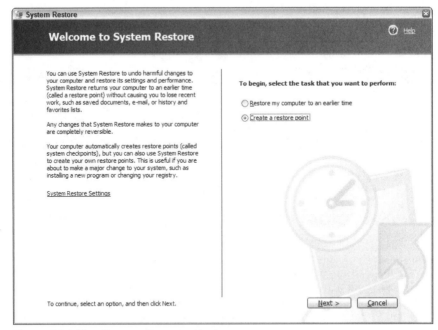

Figure 34-9: The System Restore window

Running System Restore

When you have problems with Windows XP, you can use System Restore to bring your computer back to its previous stable state. The following two sections show you how to use System Restore to do this.

Note   **Current documents, files, e-mail, and similar items are not affected during a restoration. However, if you installed an application after the last restore point was made, you must reinstall that application.**

If You Can Boot Windows...

If you can boot into Windows, follow these steps:

1. **Click Start ⇨ All Programs ⇨ Accessories ⇨ System Tools ⇨ System Restore.** The System window appears.

2. **Click the "Restore my computer to an earlier time" radio button, and then click Next.** A calendar and selection list appears, as shown in Figure 34-10.

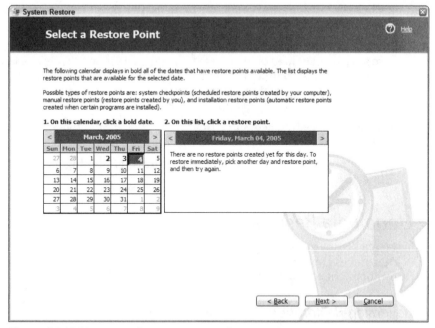

Figure 34-10: You can select a restore point.

3. **You can select different days to find a restore point.** If you did not create a restore point, you should choose to use the latest one that is available. The latest one is listed first in the current or previous day window. Select a restore point and then click Next. A message appears telling you to save all of your files and to close all open applications.

4. **When you are finished, click Next.** Restoration takes place on your computer, and then your computer automatically reboots once the restoration is complete.

5. **In the restoration dialog box that appears after you reboot, click OK.**

If You Cannot Boot Windows...

If you cannot boot Windows, follow these steps:

1. **Turn on your computer and hold down the Ctrl or the F8 key.** Do this until you see the Startup menu options.

2. **Choose Safe Mode, and then press Enter.** Once Windows boots, the Help screen appears with options to restore your computer.

3. **Click the System Restore link.**

4. **Click the "Restore my computer to an earlier time" radio button, and then click Next.** A calendar and selection list is presented to you.

5. **You can select different days to find a restore point.** If you did not create a restore point, you should choose to use the latest one that is available. The latest one is listed first in the current or previous day window. Select a restore point and then click Next. A message appears telling you to save all of your files and to close all open applications.

6. **When you are finished, click Next.** Your computer automatically reboots once the restoration is complete.

7. **In the restoration dialog box that appears after booting has taken place, click OK.**

Undoing a Restoration

In the unlikely event that a restoration causes more problems, you can always undo it. This process reverts the system to the condition that it was in before running the restoration. The following steps guide you through the process.

Reversing Restoration if You Can Boot Windows

To reverse a restoration if you can boot Windows, follow these steps:

1. **Click Start ⇨ All Programs ⇨ Accessories ⇨ System Tools ⇨ System Restore.** The System Restore window appears.

2. **Click the "Undo my last restoration" radio button, and then click Next.**

 Note

The "Undo my last restoration" option only appears when you have previously run a restoration.

3. **Close any open files or applications, click OK, and then click Next.** The previous restoration is removed, and your computer reboots.

4. **In the restoration dialog box that appears after rebooting, click OK.**

Undoing a Restoration if You Cannot Boot Windows

If you cannot boot into Windows and you need to undo a restoration, just follow these steps:

1. **Turn on your computer and hold down the Ctrl or the F8 key.** Do this until you see the Startup menu options.

2. **Choose Safe Mode and then press Enter.** Once Windows boots, the Help screen that appears gives you the option to restore your computer.

3. **Click the System Restore link.**

4. **Click the "Undo my last restoration" radio button, and then click Next.**
   A message appears telling you to save all of your files and to close all open applications.

5. **When you are finished, click the Next button.** Your computer is rebooted once the restoration has been removed.

Using Windows Help

Windows XP Help, shown in Figure 34-11 and available on the Start menu, gives you a streamlined way to search for help topics both within the help files and on the Internet at Microsoft.com. It contains a few important features that are described in the following sections.

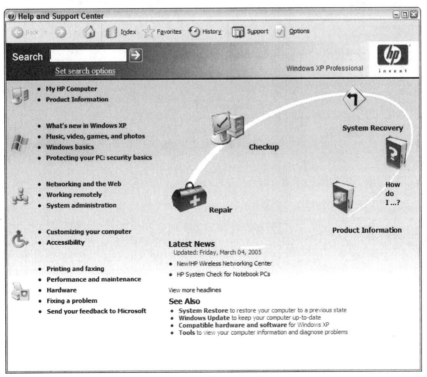

Figure 34-11: The Windows Help and Support Center

Index

An Index button is located in the Help and Support Center toolbar. As shown in Figure 34-12, this button accesses the information for you, instead of you having to look it up. To use the index, just click the Index button. In the left pane, an entire index displays in alphabetical order. You can use the scroll bar to locate a topic that you want, then select it, and then click the Display button. The information about that topic appears in the right pane. You can read the information, and then click the Print button to print a copy. You can also reorganize the window by clicking the Change View button.

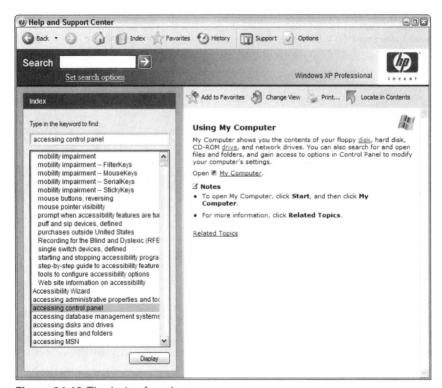

Figure 34-12: The Index function

Searching Windows Help

One way that you can use Windows Help is to search for topics. You can use the Search feature to find information about a certain topic or troubleshoot a problem. The Windows Help files support text searches, which simply means that you can type a keyword or keywords into a Search dialog box. Windows XP locates the topics that match your request. The Search dialog box appears in the upper-left corner of the Help window. Just type the subject that you want, and then click the Go button. Windows Help returns all of the possible matches for your request. For example, I have searched for the word "firewall" in Figure 34-13. The results are displayed in the left pane. I can double-click any of these results to read the information in the right pane.

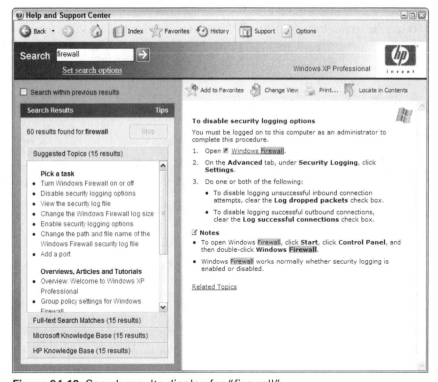

Figure 34-13: Search results display for "firewall"

Using Windows Troubleshooters

Within the Windows Help interface, you can access a very helpful component called a "troubleshooter." A troubleshooter is an HTML interface that appears on the Help window. The troubleshooter asks you a series of questions and tells you to try different actions in order to resolve your problem. There are many troubleshooters available in the Help files, and they are very easy to use. Just follow these steps:

1. **Click Start ➪ Help and Support.** The Help Search window appears.

2. **Type the kind of troubleshooter that you want.** For example, if you are having problems with a modem, you can type **modem troubleshooter**. To see a full list of the different troubleshooters, just type **troubleshooter**. Obviously, a troubleshooter does not exist for every possible problem that you may experience with Windows, but there are troubleshooters for most hardware devices.

3. **Begin the troubleshooter by clicking an appropriate link that comes back from your search.** Click Next to continue, as shown in Figure 34-14. Continue with the troubleshooter to find an answer to your problem.

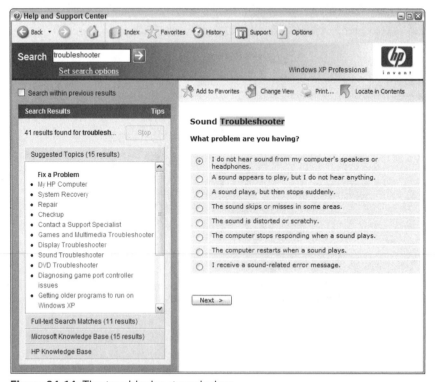

Figure 34-14: The troubleshooter window

Tips and Tricks for Speeding Up Windows XP 35

W indows XP is a complicated operating system, and as a result, it can lose optimization over time. This commonly occurs due to the myriad programs that we run, as well as the files that are left on our computers by other programs and the Internet. As a result, you may notice a general "slow-down" with your Windows XP computer over time. This is a common problem, and one that I have also experienced.

Windows XP may run slowly for many reasons. Although there is no way to solve every possible problem that is slowing down your system, this chapter contains some tips and tricks that may help you to increase the speed of your Windows XP computer.

Examining Virtual Memory

Windows XP uses Random Access Memory (RAM) to "remember" what is presently going on with your computer. Open applications and files are fed into RAM so that you can use them. However, RAM is a hardware component, and as such, it has limitations. Computer users often complain about not having enough RAM. This is because more RAM equals more power, and, as with all hardware, you are limited by your RAM as to how much you can do on your computer.

IN THIS CHAPTER

Working with Virtual Memory

Managing Registry Cleaning

Files, Startup, and More

Windows XP also uses *virtual memory* to give your system more "virtual" RAM. With virtual memory, some of the data in RAM can be written to the computer's hard disk and recalled as needed, thus freeing up more physical RAM. However, it is important to understand that there is no substitute for physical RAM. Virtual memory exists as an assistant for physical RAM, but not as a replacement.

Windows XP can generally manage its own virtual memory settings. However, you can manually specify a minimum and maximum size for the page file. The commonly recommended amount is 1.5 times the amount of physical RAM that is installed on the computer. For example, if you have 128MB or RAM, you may want to change the initial paging file size to 192MB. However, it is important to note here that Windows XP does a good job of managing its own memory settings, and as a general guideline, you should allow Windows XP to handle those settings on its own. Incorrectly specifying the virtual memory settings or choosing the "No paging file" option is likely to have adverse affects on system performance.

However, if you want to check your virtual memory settings and possibly tweak them, you can easily do so:

1. **Open Control Panel and then open the System Properties applet.**

2. **Click the Advanced tab and then click the Settings button under Performance.** The Performance Options dialog box appears.

3. **In the Performance Options dialog box, click the Advanced tab, and then click the Change button in the Virtual memory section, as shown in Figure 35-1.** The Virtual Memory dialog box appears.

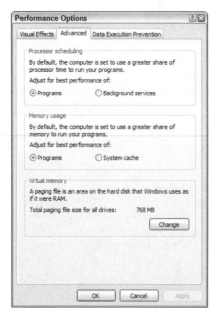

Figure 35-1: The Advanced tab of the Performance Options dialog box

4. **In the Virtual Memory dialog box, shown in Figure 35-2, you can configure a custom virtual memory size, or allow Windows XP to manage the size.** As a general rule, you should allow Windows XP to manage the virtual memory size, although, as you can see, you can also experiment with different settings here.

5. **When you are finished, click OK.**

Figure 35-2: The Virtual Memory dialog box

Expert's Notebook: Stop the Memory Caching of DLLs

Windows XP uses Dynamic Link Libraries (DLLs) files when you run programs. DLLs are loaded into memory, but they often do not leave memory right away, even after you close the application. You can free up memory by making sure that DLLs close when you close their related application. You need to edit the Registry to invoke this setting. Follow these steps:

1. **Click Start ⇨ Run. Type regedit, and then click OK.**

2. **In the Registry editor, navigate to HKEY_LOCAL_MACHINE\Software\Microsoft\ Windows\CurrentVersion\Explorer.**

3. **Right-click the Explorer folder and click New ⇨ Key.**

4. **Assign the name "AlwaysUnloadDLL" to the new key.**

5. **Set the default value for the new key to 1. This stops Windows XP from caching DLLs in memory.**

6. **Close the Registry Editor.**

If you have multiple hard disks, then you can probably relocate your virtual memory swap-file (pagefile.sys) location in order to improve performance. If you have Windows and application files on one disk (often C:) and the virtual memory swap file on another physical disk, then all of the files can be accessed simultaneously. Because most applications end up using virtual memory resources, this allows more timely access to the virtual memory swap file, application files, and data files that are used by the application. While the level of performance improvement may vary, there is really no downside to this configuration change if you have two physical hard disks.

Adjusting Visual Effects

Windows XP is the most "visual" operating system to date that has a nice interface with which to work. However, all of these graphics can put a drain on system resources, and so Windows XP allows you to adjust some of the visual effects. If you're having performance problems with Windows XP, you may try some of these settings to see if you can improve performance.

Expert's Notebook: Cheaper and Faster — Using the Right Hardware

I have generally found that a computer's operation is limited by (in order of greatest impact) processor, memory, and hard disk performance. Software tweaking is useful for getting the most out of your hardware, but if the hardware is inferior, you cannot expect miracles. The hard disk is often the most neglected of the three critical components. It is still relatively common to find otherwise high-end computers that are tragically hampered by 5400RPM ATA hard drives. With 7200RPM ATA and 10,000RPM SATA drives available at reasonable prices, there is really no reason to depend on older technology. Many software products depend on virtual memory (even if there is a lot of system memory), and hard disk performance has a huge impact on these applications. For example, many video- and audio-editing programs use both virtual memory and their own large temp files when processing large audio and video files.

But how big a difference can a faster drive make? One older benchmark found that a 500MHz computer with a 7400RPM drive scored a thirty-four percent increase in performance over the same system with a 5400RPM drive. By upgrading to a 1.3GHz processor, system performance only increased by six percent. What this tells you is that with a slower hard disk, you are wasting the potential of your other system components. The next time you buy, configure, or upgrade a computer, make sure to invest in a high-quality hard-disk configuration to maximize the output of your investment.
David Dalan

1. **Open System Properties in Control Panel.**

2. **Click the Advanced tab, and then click the Settings button under Performance.** The Performance Options dialog box contains a tab for Visual Effects (Figure 35-3). By default, Windows XP chooses which effects are best to use.

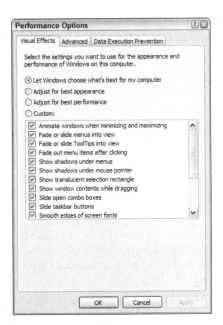

Figure 35-3: The Visual Effects tab

3. **You can customize the effects to improve performance.** You can also choose custom settings where you can disable different visual effects. Click OK when you're done.

Cleaning the Registry

The Registry is Windows XP's storehouse of data, and it holds an overwhelming amount of information. As a result, the Registry can easily fill up with files that slow down your computer's performance. Periodically, you should run a Registry cleanup tool on your Windows XP computer. There are several great Registry cleaning tools that are either free or inexpensive. Here's a quick look at my favorites.

✦ **RegClean:** This is a great tool that scans the Registry and deletes values that have been left behind by old programs that you have installed or uninstalled on your computer. The tool also creates an undo.reg file so that you can undo RegClean's work if something goes wrong. You can find RegClean at http://www.pcworld.com.

✦ **RegSeeker:** This is another great tool that scans the Registry, deleting old, left-behind items and duplicates. This software has been tested with Windows XP and appears to be completely safe. It also allows you to interact with the process to manually select items that you want to remove, and to create backup files as it works, in case something goes wrong. You can find RegSeeker at http://www.hoverdesk.net/freeware.htm.

✦ **Registry Mechanic:** This is a general-purpose tool that does a good job of cleaning up Windows XP's Registry as well as keeping the Registry in tip-top shape. This tool costs you $30 to download for a single computer. The interface and tools found in the Registry Mechanic are easy to use and understand. You can find out more about Registry Mechanic at http://www.winguides.com/regmech.

✦ **Registry tuneup:** This tool does a good job of searching through the Registry to remove files that have accumulated over time. It shows you which entries are invalid and creates backups in case something goes wrong. You can download a 30-day trial of this tool to check it out. Visit http://www.acelogix.com.

Speeding Up Boot Time

The boot process is another area of Windows XP that is likely to slow down over time. In most cases, this slowdown doesn't cause you major problems, but if you have noticed that your computer seems to be taking a little too long to boot, there are two primary issues that you need to consider:

✦ **Older device drivers can greatly slow down boot time.** If you have added hardware devices to your system since you purchased it, you should check the manufacturer's Web site for updated device drivers. Although many older device drivers will work with Windows XP, they simply do not work as well, and they can certainly slow down the boot time. See Chapter 3 to learn more about managing hardware.

Expert's Notebook: BOOTVis Is Not For You!

If you search the Internet for ways to reduce your computer's boot time, you may find information about a BOOTVis utility. BOOTVis is a Microsoft-developed utility for system architects who are designing systems for faster boot times. According to Microsoft, many published reports on the Internet state that you can download the BOOTVis utility and run it on your PC in order to speed up your boot time. However, Microsoft states that the utility was not developed for this purpose and that it will not reduce the boot time on a Windows XP PC. Windows XP already performs the routines that the BOOTVis utility performs. In short, it is an Internet myth that BOOTVis can help you. Don't waste your time running this utility. Visit `http://www.microsoft.com/whdc/system/sysperf/fastboot/bootvis.mspx` to learn more.

Expert's Notebook: Speed Up Dual-boot Timeout

If you dual-boot your computer with Windows XP and another operating system, you see an operating system selection menu on startup. This is fine, but if you typically boot into Windows XP and not the other operating system, then you can speed up the dual-boot timeout value so that you do not wait so long for the boot process to select your default operating system and continue with the boot process. The default timeout value is 30 seconds, but you can change this setting to 10. This gives you enough time to select the alternate operating system if you want, but it also speeds up the boot process if you do not need to select the alternate operating system. Follow these steps:

1. **Locate the boot.ini file on your computer. It is a hidden file by default, and is usually located in C:\boot.ini.**

2. **Open the file with Notepad (the default application).**

3. **Change the Timeout value to 10, as shown in the following figure. Click File ⇨ Save, and close Notepad.**

Tip

You can also set this value by opening System in Control Panel. Click the Advanced tab and click the Startup and Recovery button

You can change the boot timeout value.

✦ **Programs can slow down boot time.** The more programs that Windows XP has to start during boot-up, the longer boot-up will take. You have probably acquired utilities and other programs that start when Windows XP starts. If you take a look at the Notification Area, it will probably give you a good clue as to what these are.

Although you can reduce the programs that start up when Windows starts by removing old programs that you no longer use anyway, you can also stop other programs from starting by using MSCONFIG. Simply click Start ⇨ Run, and then type **msconfig**. You can access the Startup tab and see every program that starts when Windows XP starts, as shown in Figure 35-4. You can then review this list and clear the check box next to any program that you do not want to start.

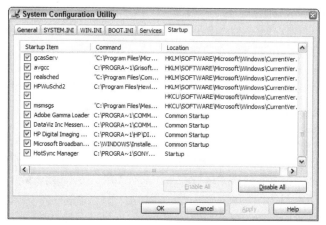

Figure 35-4: The Startup tab

Note

Be sure that you know what programs you are disabling before doing so. Some of the programs that you see here affect other programs, and so you should do a little homework.

Setting Application Priority

Windows XP enables you to set a priority for applications that are running on your computer. In a nutshell, if you have several applications and processes at work—which you always do, as Windows XP runs many internal processes—you can give a boost to a certain application that you are using by adjusting the priority of that application. When you change the priority of the application, you give that application first preference for processor cycles over other applications and processes. This feature can be helpful if you are using a program that needs to have priority over everything else, although it should not be used for general applications—let Windows XP take care of that.

If you want to give an application priority, follow these steps:

1. **Press Ctrl+Alt+Del.** The Windows Task Manager window appears, as shown in Figure 35-5.

2. **Click the Processes tab and locate the process for the application that you want to prioritize.**

3. **Right-click the application process, select Set Priority, and then choose the desired priority (shown in Figure 35-6).** Generally, a setting of Above Normal or High gives your application a boost. Be careful about using the Real Time setting. This setting prevents Windows from managing multiple processes, as it could bring your operating system to a standstill.

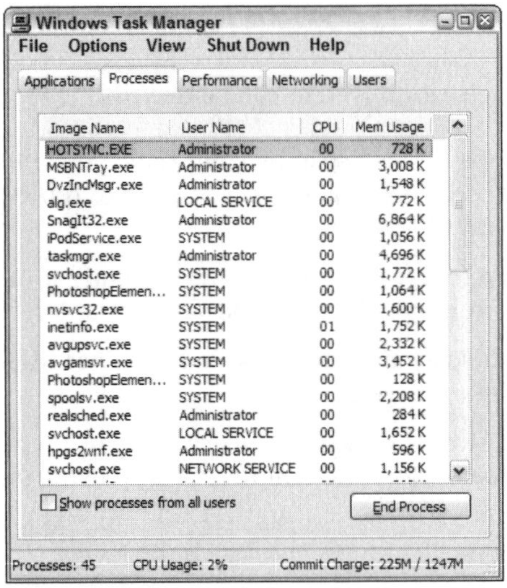

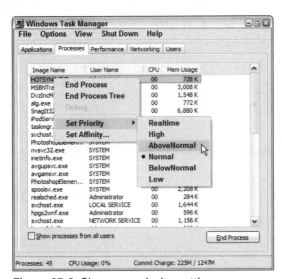

Figure 35-5: The Processes tab

Note

It is important to note that this procedure only changes the priority of the process while it continues running. When the process terminates, all effects of this procedure are discarded. Restarting the process will not retain the new priority setting.

Figure 35-6: Choose a priority setting

Other Tips and Tricks

Here are a few other tips and tricks to help your system run faster:

✦ **Keep old programs and utilities out of your system.** Over time, you will accumulate files that you don't really need, and so you should use the Add/Remove Programs utility periodically to remove old items.

✦ **Periodically run the Disk Cleanup tool, found on the General tab of the disk Properties dialog box.** This helps remove old Temp files and other junk files.

✦ **Set Internet Explorer to remove history and downloaded Internet files on a regular basis.** See Chapter 13 for more details.

✦ **Although anti-virus programs do slow your system down, they are a necessary evil in today's computing world.** Don't be tempted to stop using your anti-virus program for the sake of speed.

✦ **Run Disk Defragmenter periodically.**

✦ **Run the Disk-error Checking tool periodically.**

If you have a lot of zipped files (compressed files) on your computer, Windows XP's file-searching feature can become rather sluggish as it wades through all of those compressed files. You can easily stop the search function from looking through compressed files, which greatly speeds up search results. To enable this feature, click Start ⇨ Run. In the dialog box, type regsvr32 C:\winnt\ \ system32\zipfldr.dll /u. If the files are installed in the Windows directory, you can substitute "windows" for "winnt" in the previous command line. To turn searching back on for zipped files, type regsvr32 C:\winnt\ \system32\zipfldr.dll, or use "windows" for "winnt" if the files are located in the Windows directory.

Recovering from a Crash or Other Serious Problem

36

I n earlier versions of Windows, crashes and other serious problems were common. In fact, the *blue screen of death* was a well-known phenomenon that many veteran Window users will remember. Today, rather than the blue screen of death, you have probably experienced a "hard lock" where you cannot gain control of your computer, or a computer that cannot boot correctly.

Fortunately, Windows XP is the most stable operating system that Microsoft has ever produced. Although you can still experience problems, you are now less likely to, and if an application locks up, it is now easier to regain control of the application and your system. That being said, there is still a possibility that you will encounter a much more serious problem. This chapter provides valuable information that can help you to get out of a jam the next time you find yourself in one.

What to Do When Something Bad Happens...

Several years back, I worked in telephone support for Windows 98. Our job was to solve problems, and in many cases, I discovered that the problems were actually caused by the behavior of the users.

If you're an old pro with Windows, you may think that this section is not important. However, it can help to remind you of how to manage problems when they happen with your computer. When a problem occurs, you should keep the following points in mind:

✦ **Stop.** When a crash or other serious problem occurs, stop for a moment and think. All too often, users begin to randomly press keys, which usually creates more problems. Take a deep breath and take your time as you begin the troubleshooting process.

✦ **Take notes.** When a crash or other problem of this nature occurs, the first thing you should do is to get a piece of paper and write down what you were doing when the crash occurred. Were you working with several applications? Were you configuring a part of the system? What were you doing? Try to be as detailed as possible. The reason for this is simple: If you cannot untangle yourself from the problem and you have to call technical support, the support analyst is much more likely to solve your problem if you can tell them what you were doing when the crash occurred. This information gives the support analyst clues about where to start. Remember that troubleshooting is much like solving a jigsaw puzzle, and the more pieces of information that you have available, the better.

✦ **Try to isolate the most likely problem.** Think about what you were doing and what happened. What is the most likely cause of the problem? Although you may not be able to answer this question, ask yourself anyway. In many cases, your resulting train of thought will point you in the right direction as you begin to troubleshoot.

If you experience a crash or other serious problem, Windows XP has some tools and features that can help you to solve the problem. The rest of this chapter is devoted to using those tools and features.

Using Ctrl+Alt+Del

You can access the Windows Task Manager by pressing Ctrl+Alt+Del. If the computer seems to be hard locked, then you can usually reboot it by pressing Ctrl+Alt+Del twice.

In the case of an application lockup, you should use the Ctrl+Alt+Del feature to close the offending application. This should once again give you control of your system. Click the Applications tab, shown in Figure 36-1, to display any applications that are currently open. If an application is not working, its status will say Not Responding. You can select the name of the program and click the End Task button on the Applications tab. This action forces the application to quit so that you can regain control of your computer. However, unsaved data will be lost. If you need to reboot your computer, you can use the Shut Down menu on the Task Manager.

FYI: Using Windows Troubleshooters

Within the Windows Help interface, you can access a very helpful component called a *troubleshooter*. A troubleshooter is an HTML interface that appears in the Help window. Troubleshooters can often help you to solve hardware problems or different system problems within Windows XP. The troubleshooter asks you a series of questions and tells you to try different actions in order to resolve a problem that you are having. There are many troubleshooters available in the Help files, and they are very easy to use. Just follow these steps:

1. **Click Start ⇨ Help and Support.** The Help Search window appears.

2. **Type the kind of troubleshooter that you want.** For example, you can type **modem troubleshooter, ICS troubleshooter,** or **sound card troubleshooter.** To see a full list of troubleshooters, just type **troubleshooter.**

3. **Begin the troubleshooter by clicking an appropriate link that returns from your search, and then click Next to continue.**

4. **Continue the troubleshooter steps to try to solve the problem that you are experiencing.**

Figure 36-1: Use Task Manager to force failed applications to quit.

Tip

In the case of hard lock, where your computer does not respond to the keyboard or mouse, turn off the computer, wait ten seconds, and then turn it back on so that it can reboot.

Using Safe Mode

If you have used previous versions of Windows, then you will be familiar with Safe Mode in Windows XP. Safe Mode is a Windows feature that enables you to start Windows with a minimal number of drivers. It is used when you cannot start Windows normally. The idea is to get Windows up and running so that you can troubleshoot and fix whatever is preventing Windows XP from starting normally.

 Note

After you restart in Safe Mode, you can run System Restore, which can fix whatever problem is preventing Windows from booting normally. You should get to know System Restore because it can solve a number of problems for you. For more information, see Chapter 34.

There are several different Safe Mode options available to you so that you can boot Windows according your specific needs. They are:

✦ **Safe Mode.** If Windows XP does not start normally, then you can use this basic Safe Mode option, which attempts to load Windows XP with a minimal number of drivers.

✦ **Safe Mode with Networking.** This option boots into Safe Mode, but it also enables networking services and protocols so that you can access network resources within Safe Mode.

✦ **Safe Mode with Command Prompt.** This option boots into Safe Mode with the option to use the Command Prompt window for command line troubleshooting.

✦ **Enable Boot Logging.** This option logs the entire boot process. This feature can be helpful to support technicians or related personnel who can analyze the boot process and see where the boot process is failing.

Expert's Notebook: Having a Backup Plan

Even with the system recovery features that are available with Windows XP, it is still important to prepare for the worst. No matter what you do, there are some issues that cannot be effectively remedied with anything short of hard drive replacement or an operating system reinstall. By keeping your critical data files on removable media (such as tape, CDR, DVD-R, or USB key), you can make it through almost any system failure. A full backup that includes all relevant user data and the system's state is the best way to achieve a quick recovery. In addition to being comprehensive, you can also schedule backups so that there is no manual intervention required to keep backed-up information current. However, you can get by with less thorough procedures. For example, making copies of important files, such as any Outlook personal files (*.pst), and selecting folders within each user's profiles, such as My Documents, Desktop, and Favorites, is often enough. Once your system has been repaired and is operational, it is a simple matter to either copy files or restore your backup. *David Dalan*

Expert's Notebook: Your Service Contract and Spare Parts

Many times during a disastrous system failure, our first impulse is to get things back up and running. Therefore, as onsite technicians rush to find solutions, it is important to not overlook outside technical support. For example, in the organization where I work, we typically purchase multiyear support that includes onsite service. In fact, most servers, desktops, and laptops ship with (or have available) extensive service packages. You should resist the temptation to save a few bucks by getting a cheaper service contract and not buying a spare or redundant server. Most of the time it really is cheap insurance when you consider how much all of those employees are being paid to sit around and wait for you to fix the server.

On desktops and laptops, it is more of a cost issue because desktop and laptop failures tend to only affect one user, while server failures tend to affect large groups of users. To make these support packages more effective, you should have backup hardware available to temporarily restore operations. For example, a spare server can be brought online while the failed unit is serviced.

If you have onsite service, then use it. For example, one of our servers with redundant power supplies experienced a failure with the component that connects the two power units to the server. Suddenly, the spare was not so redundant! We called support, and a technician was dispatched to drive 250 miles and hand-deliver the part. Because we had a similar spare server available, we were able to cannibalize the failed component and get the server up and running until the spare part arrived. We used the spare part for about ten hours after the unit first failed. Between spare parts and a good service contract, we were only out of business for a few minutes the day of the "disaster," and for another few minutes during off hours while we put the new replacement part in the server. *David Dalan*

✦ **Enable VGA Mode.** This option boots Windows XP with a generic VGA driver for your display adapter. Incorrect display adapter drivers are a common reason for boot failure.

✦ **Last Known Good Configuration.** This option uses the last known good backup of the `CurrentControlSet` key in the Registry to boot Windows. Each time you successfully boot Windows, the `CurrentControlSet` key is backed up. The Last Known Good Configuration option allows you to boot using that saved registry key.

When you access Safe Mode, a menu appears, listing the options that you can select. You can access Safe Mode by holding down the Ctrl key on your keyboard, or by holding down the F8 key when you turn on your computer. A Startup menu allows you to choose Safe Mode, Safe Mode with Networking, and other options.

When your computer boots into Safe Mode, you can access the tools and Help files that you need to try to solve the problem. When you've finished, just reboot your computer, and it boots normally.

Using the Recovery Console

The Recovery Console is a powerful tool in Windows XP that can enable you to start your computer and fix problems when your computer will not boot normally. The Recovery Console is considered a power user or Administrator tool, and is not to be taken lightly. In fact, you can cause yourself a lot of problems and delete important data from your computer if you use the Recovery Console incorrectly. However, with the right knowledge, you can use it to get out of Windows XP jams when Safe Mode, System Restore, and other standard troubleshooting options have failed.

Using the Recovery Console, you can enable and disable services, format drives, view directories, copy files from a floppy disk or CD and place them in directories, read and write data on a local drive, and you can even fix the boot sector. There are also many administrative options that you may find helpful in order to fix Windows if you can't start the operating system.

It is important to note that the Recovery Console is not the Command Prompt (cmd.exe), and so you don't have the same number of options that you may find with a Command Prompt. For example, you can only access files in the root directory of any volume, in the %SystemRoot% folder and subfolders, in the Recovery Console folder and subfolders, and in files and folders on removable disks, such as floppy disks and CDs. Additionally, write access to removable disks is disabled, which prevents you from copying files from your system to a removable disk. Also, you cannot change the local Administrator password using the Recovery Console, and you cannot use any text-editing tools from within the Recovery Console.

If you are using dynamic disks on the installation, and you access them through the Recovery Console, you may not see the dynamic volumes displayed accurately in the Recovery Console. This is simply a technical limitation, and you can read more about it at Microsoft.com by accessing the Knowledge Base article Q227364.

Installing the Recovery Console

By default, the Recovery Console is not available in Windows XP, and you need to install it so that it appears as a boot menu option that you can select when you start Windows XP.

To install the Recovery Console as a startup option, follow these steps:

1. **Log on with the local Administrator account.**
2. **With Windows running, insert the Setup CD into your CD-ROM drive.**
3. **Click Start ⇨ Run.**
4. **Type the following, where *D*: is the CD-ROM drive letter:**

   D:\i386\winnt32.exe /cmdcons
5. **Follow the instructions on the screen.**

This option is fine if you have not installed Windows service pack 2 (SP2) as an upgrade. If SP2 is installed as an upgrade then recovery console will not install because the original Windows XP CD is older than the current version on your PC. A way around the problem is to either install the recovery console prior to installing SP2 or, alternatively, slipstream SP2 to your original Windows XP CD.

If, on the other hand, you have installed the latest version of Windows XP with SP2 already integrated then you should have no problem installing the recovery console. Further details are available in the Microsoft Knowledgebase Article number 898594.

Starting the Recovery Console from the Window XP setup CD-ROM

To start the Recovery Console from the Windows XP setup CD-ROM, follow these steps:

1. **Insert the Setup CD and restart the computer.** If prompted, select any options that are required to boot from the CD. The text-based part of the Setup begins.
2. **Follow the prompts; choose the repair or recover option by pressing the R key.**
3. **If you have a dual-boot or multiple-boot system, choose the installation that you need to access from the Recovery Console.**
4. **When prompted, type the Administrator password.**
5. **At the system prompt, type Recovery Console commands.** You can type **help** for a list of commands.
6. **To exit the Recovery Console and restart the computer, type exit.**

Starting the Recovery Console, if already installed

To start the Recovery Console if you have installed it as a startup option, follow these steps:

1. **During startup, select Recovery Console from the startup options menu.**

2. **If you have a dual-boot or multiple-boot system, choose the installation that you need to access from the Recovery Console.**

3. **When prompted, type the Administrator password.**

4. **At the system prompt, you can begin using the Recovery Console.**

5. **To exit the Recovery Console and restart the computer, type** exit.

Recovery Console Commands

Once you are in the Recovery Console, there are several commands that you can use to fix Windows XP. The following sections outline each command and its parameters. Use this section as a helpful reference when you are using the Recovery Console.

> **Note** Although experimentation is normally a good thing, remember that the Recovery Console gives you great power over system configuration, without all of the safety warnings that you normally see when you use the interface. Proceed with caution!

attrib

The attrib command changes file attributes for a single file or folder. This command sets or removes the read-only, system, hidden, and compressed attributes that are assigned to files or directories. You can use the following parameters:

```
attrib [+r|-r] [+s|-s] [+h|-h] [+c|-c] [[drive:][path]
filename]
```

- ✦ +r: Sets the read-only file attribute.

- ✦ -r: Clears the read-only file attribute.

- ✦ +s: Sets the system file attribute.

- ✦ -s: Clears the system file attribute.

- ✦ +h: Sets the hidden file attribute.

- ✦ -h: Clears the hidden file attribute.

- ✦ +c: Sets the compressed file attribute.

- ✦ -c: Clears the compressed file attribute.

- ✦ [[drive:][path] filename]: Specifies the location and name of the directory or file that you want to process.

batch

The `batch` command executes the commands specified in a text file. Use `batch input_file [output_file]` where *input_file* specifies the text file that contains the list of commands to be executed. The *input_file* can consist of a drive letter and a colon, a folder name, a filename, or a combination of these. The *output_file*, if specified, stores the output of the commands in the named file. If not specified, the output is displayed on the screen.

bootcfg

You can use the `bootcfg` command for boot configuration and recovery (Boot.ini for most computers). The `bootcfg` command, with different parameters, is available from the Command Prompt. Be sure to make a backup of your Boot.ini file before running any of these commands. A few examples are:

✦ `bootcfg /default`: Sets the default boot entry.

✦ `bootcfg /add`: Adds a Windows installation to the boot list.

✦ `bootcfg /rebuild`: Iterates through all Windows installations and allows the user to choose which installation to add.

✦ `bootcfg /scan`: Scans all disks for Windows installations and displays the results.

✦ `bootcfg /list`: Lists the entries already in the boot list.

✦ `bootcfg /disableredirect`: Disables redirection in the boot loader.

✦ `bootcfg /redirect [PortBaudRate] | [useBiosSettings]`: Enables redirection in the boot loader with the specified configuration.

chdir

The `chdir` command changes a directory; it displays the name of the current directory or changes the current folder. You have the following parameter options:

`chdir [drive:][path] [..] or cd [drive:][path] [..]`

✦ **none:** Used without parameters, `chdir` displays the names of the current drive and folder. Used with only a drive letter (for example, `cd C:`), `chdir` displays the current directory on the specified drive.

✦ `[drive:][path]`: Specifies the drive (if other than the current drive) and directory to which you want to change.

✦ `[..]`: Specifies that you want to change to the parent folder. Use a space between `chdir` and the two periods.

chkdsk

The chkdsk command creates and displays a status report for the disk, and it also lists and corrects errors on the disk. You have the following parameters available:

```
chkdsk [drive:] [/p] [/r]
```

✦ **none:** Used without parameters, chkdsk displays the status of the disk in the current drive.

✦ [drive:]: Specifies the drive that you want chkdsk to check.

✦ /p: Performs an exhaustive check, even if the drive is not marked for chkdsk to run. This parameter does not make any changes to the drive.

✦ /r: Locates bad sectors and recovers readable information. Implies the /p parameter.

cls

The cls command clears the screen. Once cleared, you only see the Command Prompt and insertion point.

copy

The copy command copies a single file to another location. The source of the copy can be any removable media disk, the current Windows installation, the root of any drive, or the Cmdcons directory. You have the following parameter options, but note that copy doesn't support wildcard characters.

```
copy source [destination]
```

✦ source: Specifies the location and name of the file to be copied. The source can consist of a drive letter and colon, a directory name, a filename, or a combination.

✦ [destination]: Specifies the location and name of a file or set of files to which you want to copy. Destination can consist of a drive letter and colon, a folder name, a filename, or a combination.

delete

The delete command deletes a single file. You have the following parameters:

```
delete [drive:][path] filename or del [drive:][path] filename
```

dir

The dir command displays a list of the files and subdirectories in a directory. You have the following parameters:

```
dir [drive:][path][filename]
```

✦ `[drive:][path]`: Specifies the drive and directory for which you want to see a listing.

✦ `filename`: Specifies a particular file or group of files for which you want to see a listing. Multiple filenames can be used, and spaces, commas, or semi-colons can separate filenames. You can use wildcard characters (? and *) in the filename parameter to display a group of files.

disable

The `disable` command disables a Windows XP, Windows 2000, or Windows NT 4.0 system service or device driver. You have the following parameters:

```
disable {[service_name] | [device_driver_name]}
```

✦ `[service_name]`: The name of the system service that you want to disable.

✦ `[device_driver_name]`: The name of the device driver that you want to disable.

diskpart

The `diskpart` command creates and deletes partitions on a hard drive. You have the following parameters:

```
diskpart [/add | /delete] [device_name | drive_name |
partition_name] [size]
```

✦ **none:** Used without parameters, the `diskpart` command starts the Windows character-mode version of `diskpart`.

✦ `/add`: Creates a new partition.

✦ `/delete`: Deletes an existing partition.

✦ `device_name`: Specifies the device on which you want to create or delete a partition. The name can be obtained from the output of the `map` command.

✦ `drive_name`: Specifies the partition that you want to delete, by drive letter. Used only with `/delete`.

✦ `partition_name`: The partition you want to delete, by partition name.

✦ `[size]`: The size, in megabytes (MB), of the partition you want to create. Used only with `/add`.

enable

The `enable` command enables a Windows XP, Windows 2000, or Windows NT 4.0 system service or driver. You have the following parameters:

```
enable {service_name | device_driver_name} [startup_type]
```

✦ `service_name`: The name of the system service that you want to enable.

✦ `device_driver_name`: The name of the device driver that you want to enable.

✦ `[startup_type]`: The startup type that you want to designate for the service or device driver. Valid startup types are `SERVICE_BOOT_START`, `SERVICE_SYSTEM_START`, `SERVICE_AUTO_START`, and `SERVICE_DEMAND_START`.

exit

The `exit` command closes the Recovery Console.

expand

The `expand` command extracts a file from a cabinet (.cab) file. You should not extract the entire cabinet file, as this process is time-consuming, but rather extract only the file that you need. You have the following parameters:

`expand source [/F:filespec] [destination] [/d] [/y]`

✦ `source`: Specifies the file to expand. Use this parameter if the source file contains a single file. The source can consist of a drive letter and a colon, a directory name, a filename, or a combination. You cannot use wildcard characters.

✦ `[/F:filespec]`: If the source contains more than one file, this specifies the name of the file that you want to extract. You can use wildcards for the files that you want to extract.

✦ `[destination]`: Specifies both the destination directory and the filename for the extracted file, or each individually.

✦ `[/d]`: Lists the files contained in the cabinet file without expanding it or extracting from it.

✦ `[/y]`: Suppresses the overwrite prompt when expanding or extracting files.

fixboot

The `fixboot` command writes a new boot sector to the system partition. The command is simply `fixboot [drive]`, where *drive* is the drive letter to which the new boot sector will be written.

fixmbr

The `fixmbr` command repairs the master boot record of the boot disk. The command for `fixmbr` is `fixmbr [device_name]`, where *device_name* is the device (drive) on which you want to write a new master boot record.

format

The `format` command formats the specified drive with the file system that you choose. You have the following parameters:

```
format [drive:] [/q] [/fs:file-system]
```

✦ `[drive:]`: Specifies the drive that you want to format. You cannot format a floppy disk from the Recovery Console.

✦ `[/q]`: Performs a quick format of the drive. The drive is not scanned for faulty sectors, and so you should use this parameter only on drives that you have previously formatted.

✦ `[/fs:file-system]`: Specifies the file system to use (FAT, FAT32, NTFS). If you don't specify a file system, the existing file system format is used.

help

The `help` command provides a listing of Recovery Console commands and parameters. See the Help section for listings and examples.

listsvc

The `listsvc` command lists all of the services and drivers on the computer.

logon

The `logon` command logs you onto the Windows XP installation that you want. You must have local Administrator privileges to log on to the Recovery Console.

map

The `map` command displays a mapping of drive letters to physical device names. This command is helpful when you want to use the `fixboot` and `fixmbr` commands, because you need to see the mappings in order to use those commands. The syntax is `map [arc]`, where *arc* instructs the `map` command to display Advanced RISC Computing (ARC) device names, such as multi(0)disk(0)rdisk(0)partition(1). See the Windows XP Help and Support Center to learn more about ARC paths.

mkdir (md)

The `mkdir` or `md` command creates a directory or subdirectory. You have the following parameters:

```
mkdir [drive:]path or md [drive:]path
```

✦ `[drive:]`: Specifies the drive on which you want to create the new directory.

✦ `path`: Specifies the name and location of the new directory. You cannot use wildcard characters.

more

The more command displays the contents of a text file. You have the following parameters:

```
more [drive:][path] filename or type [drive:][path] filename
```

✦ [drive:][path] filename: Specifies the location and name of the file that you want to view.

net use

The net use command connects a network share to a drive letter. You have the following parameters:

```
net use [\\ComputerName\ShareName [/user:[DomainName\UserName]
password] | [drive letter:] [/d]
```

✦ \\ComputerName\ShareName: Specifies the name of the server and the shared resource. If ComputerName contains blank characters, enclose the entire computer name, from the double backslash (\\) to the end of the computer name, in quotation marks. The computer name can be from 1 to 15 characters long.

✦ /user: Specifies the username with which the connection is made.

✦ DomainName: Specifies the domain name to use when validating the credentials for the user.

✦ UserName: Specifies the username with which to log on.

✦ password: Specifies the password needed to access the shared resource. Leave blank to produce a prompt for the password.

✦ [/d]: Indicates that this connection is to be disconnected.

rename (ren)

The rename command changes the name of a single file. You have the following parameters:

```
rename [drive:][path] filename1 filename2 or ren [drive:][path]
filename1 filename2
```

✦ [drive:][path] filename1: Specifies the location and name of the file that you want to rename. You cannot use wildcard characters.

✦ filename2: Specifies the new name for the file. You cannot specify a new drive or path when renaming files.

rmdir (rd)

The `rmdir` command deletes an empty directory. You have the following parameters:

> `rmdir [drive:]path` or `rd [drive:]path`

✦ `[drive:]path`: Specifies the location and name of the directory that you want to delete. You cannot use wildcard characters.

set

The `set` command displays and sets Recovery Console environment variables. You can use the command by itself to see a list of the current environment variables and their values. Also, you can only set environment variables if that capability has been enabled in the Security Analysis console. The `set` command is an optional command that must be used with Security Templates. The command is `set [variable=[string]]`, where *variable* specifies the variable that you want to set or modify.

systemroot

The `systemroot` command sets the current directory to the systemroot folder of the Windows installation on which you are logged.

type

The `type` command displays the contents of a text file. You can use the `type` or `more` command to view a text file without modifying it. You have the following parameters:

> `type [drive:][path] filename` or `more [drive:][path] filename`

✦ `[drive:][path] filename`: Specifies the location and name of the file that you want to view.

Removing the Recovery Console

If you installed the Recovery Console as a startup option, you can later choose to remove it. Simply follow these steps.

1. **Open My Computer.**

2. **Double-click the hard drive on which you installed the Recovery Console.**

3. **On the Tools menu, click Folder Options.**

4. **Click the View tab.**

5. **Click Show hidden files and folders, deselect the Hide protected operating system files check box.** Click OK.

6. **At the root directory, delete the \Cmdcons folder.**

7. **At the root directory, delete the Cmldr file.**

8. **At the root directory, right-click the Boot.ini file and then click Properties.**

9. **Deselect the Read-only check box, and then click OK.**

10. **Open Boot.ini in Notepad, and remove the entry for the Recovery Console.** It will look similar to this:

    ```
    C:\cmdcons\bootsect.dat="Microsoft Windows Recovery Console"
    /cmdcons
    ```

11. **Save the file and close it.**

A Primer on Registry Editing

T he mighty Windows Registry! The very name invokes fear in some, confusion and ambiguity in others. For some time, the Registry has been the heart of every Microsoft operating system. The Windows Registry controls a wide range of operating system behaviors, from desktop appearance to network configuration. In addition to holding a lot of practical information, the Registry is a tool for implementing customizations that are just not practical by any other means. Through Registry modification, Administrators can sometimes implement complex or obscure configuration changes to enhance functionality or enforce security policy. It is also through the Registry that you can change "default" settings that otherwise were thought to be immutable.

Windows Registry Basics

So what exactly is the Windows Registry? Under Windows XP, the Registry is a collection of individual files that store configuration information for both the computer system and individual users. These individual files are known as *hives*. Some of the hives are kept alongside user profile information in the Documents and Settings folder. Other machine-specific hives are located in the %system% folder; in most cases this is the C:\ WINDOWS\system32\config folder.

Think of these hives as a complex set of operating instructions. The Registry controls virtually all startup behavior, and in this way it is very similar to the .ini files (win.ini, system.ini) that were used extensively in Windows 3.1, 95, and 98.

Note | **Both the system.ini and win.ini files are still present in your Windows XP installation. However, they exist for the sole purpose of legacy application support. If you need to define some 16-bit system drivers for a legacy application to work, then these files may be useful. If not, then they are vestigial relics of earlier operating systems.**

In addition to startup information, the Registry controls settings such as which font to use in menus, which Web browser is the default, and which search engine to use when browsing the Internet. The amount of information stored in the Registry is truly staggering, and a lot of these features are accessible through various graphical interfaces. For example, many Control Panel settings actually modify Registry information. The various Control Panel applets simply provide a user-friendly method of changing specific settings.

However, there are more ways to change the Registry than through the Control Panels. With the regedit program (discussed in detail later), you can change any element of the Registry. This is a good and a bad thing, because working with the Registry can be hazardous to system stability. Standard disclaimers aside (make backups, don't practice on mission-critical systems), Registry editing is fairly risk-free if you plan what you want to do ahead of time, and double-check your work before saving changes to the Registry. Before delving into the tools for changing the Registry, let's look at how the Registry is organized in a bit more detail.

Understanding Registry Design

The Registry is a hierarchical database. At the root of this hierarchy is a series of five objects, called *keys*, which contain all of the other subordinate Registry entries. The design of the database is supposed to ensure that there is some kind of logical flow to how information is stored, but this is not always the case. For example, several of the registry keys contain information pulled from other registry keys during startup or logon. This process allows the Registry to store a variety of configuration packages that can vary, depending on the startup options selected or on the user who has logged on.

In general terms, the organization of the Registry makes it fairly accessible, but there always seems to be a key buried in some place that defies organizational logic. This is why the search function is so handy. You will examine the search function in just a bit, but for now, you'll explore the organization of the Registry in more detail. First, it is important to understand the keys that make up the Registry. If you find yourself in a situation where you need to solve a problem or figure out whether you can make a particular change, you need to understand the particular roles of the various registry keys. If you find a walkthrough on the Internet for implementing a particular feature, then you may not need to have such in-depth knowledge. However, not all of your plans turn out as described or expected, and so you may find it essential to understand the roles of various keys. Now let's look at the five Windows XP registry keys.

HKEY_CLASSES_ROOT

This key is primarily used to store file association information. For example, on a fresh installation of Windows XP, there is typically an association in this key that tells Windows to open .doc files with WordPad. There are many associations within this key, and it is probably not a good idea to come in here and begin changing them through the Registry Editor. This is one key that you are probably better off using the graphical tools in Windows XP to modify.

The second component of the CLASSES_ROOT key is Component Object Model (COM) object configuration information, Visual Basic, and assorted automation settings. A *COM object* is a piece of software that provides some kind of service. Typically this service is provided to other applications. An application may use a COM object to automate a process, kind of like a macro. In another situation, an application may invoke a COM object to perform a particular task. In this scenario, the object essentially becomes part of the application itself. Conceptually this is similar to a program plug-in (as in Adobe Photoshop) or module. To make use of COM services, the operating system and its applications need to know how to go about accessing COM, hence the configuration information in this registry key.

Information contained in this registry key is extracted from two locations: HKEY_LOCAL_MACHINE and HKEY_CURRENT_USER. Any relevant information (COM/Automation or file association information data) within either of these two keys is presented in the HKEY_CLASS_ROOT key. In fact, the HKEY_CLASSES_ROOT provides a shortcut (using pointers) to the stored data and does not actually store the association data within itself. There is some logic applied when generating the contents of this key. If the same information exists in both the LOCAL_MACHINE and the CURRENT_USER, then the information in the CURRENT_USER key takes precedence and is displayed and used for system operation. The net result is this: different users can have different COM and file association settings. This is handy if two users of the same system want to use different applications to access a common file type. It also prevents a configuration change on one user from affecting other users.

HKEY_CURRENT_USER

Within the CURRENT_USER key, the settings are stored for the user who is currently logged on. This key can also accurately be called the user's profile. This profile contains a wealth of user-specific configuration information. Items such as desktop settings, RAS connections, networked printers, and user-definable environment variables are kept here. On networks where roaming profiles are used, this key is the part of the Registry that is loaded and saved during logon and logoff.

Like the HKEY_CLASSES_ROOT, the HKEY_CURRENT_USER key contains information pulled from other registry keys. This key pulls information either from the remote Registry location (if using roaming profiles) or from the HKEY_USER key, where the currently logged-on user's information is stored. The first time a user logs on to the computer, the information for this key is pulled from the default user profile. Once the user logs off, the information from the default profile and any user-made changes to settings are then written to the user's profile in the HKEY_USER key. Because the information in this key is transitory (changing with each user's logon), making changes here affects only the currently logged-on user.

HKEY_LOCAL_MACHINE

Information stored in this key includes data about the configuration of hardware and operating system variables. Most notably, this key contains startup settings and drivers for the installed hardware. To organize the data in this key, there are five sub-keys.

- ✦ **HKEY_LOCAL_MACHINE\HARDWARE:** As the name implies, this key stores information about the installed hardware. Specifically, this key stores information about detected hardware, and the drivers that are needed to run that hardware. This key is re-created during system startup.

- ✦ **HKEY_LOCAL_MACHINE\SAM:** This key contains a copy of the Windows Security Accounts Manager (SAM) Registry entries. The SAM is the heart of Windows authentication services. The information in the SAM includes user account and group information. If the computer is part of a Windows domain, this information is pulled from a domain controller during startup. If the system is a stand-alone (Windows XP) computer, then the information is stored in a sub-key called HKEY_LOCAL_MACHINE\SECURITY\SECURITY and is not directly accessible through a Registry-editing program. To edit this key, you can use either the Local Users and Groups MMC snap-in (standalone system), or the Active Directory Users and Computers MMC for Domain-wide account management.

- ✦ **HKEY_LOCAL_MACHINE\SECURITY:** This key contains information about various computer policies. This is another key that is impractical to edit directly with a tool like regedit. By default, the contents of this key are not visible under Windows XP. Information manipulated by the Group Policy and Local Policy editors, as well Active Directory tools, is used to edit the data stored within the HKEY_LOCAL_MACHINE\SECURITY key.

- ✦ **HKEY_LOCAL_MACHINE\SOFTWARE:** This key is the clearing-house of information for installed software. When new software is installed, uninstalled and configured information in this key is often modified. While not all software has to use this key, most commercial applications do make use of it. Items listed in the "Add/Remove" programs Control Panel applet are contained in this registry key. The organization of information in this key is typically by vendor, with each vendor (such as Microsoft, IBM, Adobe, and Macromedia) creating a folder for their own applications. This is a voluntary arrangement, and not all software makers follow this organizational plan.

✦ **HKEY_LOCAL_MACHINE\SYSTEM:** Within this key, Windows XP stores a variety of startup information. For example, the information used to start a computer with the "Last Known Good" configuration option is stored in this key. Other important sub-keys are the ControlSet*number* and CurrentControlSet keys. Each numbered ControlSet entry (for example, ControlSet001) contains a set of startup hardware and software options. The CurrentControlSet sub-key contains the information used during the current Windows XP session. These multiple keys ensure that Windows can start in the event that a problem arises with some element in one of the ControlSets. Basically, this key, and its related sub-keys, is designed to help Windows start, even when there is a problem.

HKEY_USERS

Each of the computer's local profiles is stored in this registry key. Like the HKEY_CURRENT_USER key above, this key stores desktop, application, and other user-specific information. Individual user accounts are not listed by logon name, but rather by Security Identifier (SID). These are in the form of an alphanumeric string, such as S-1-5-21-346832259-4444469595-2291903390-1021. If you needed to directly edit configuration information for a particular user, you do so within this key. Changes here remain after logon and logoff, unlike the information stored in HKEY_CURRENT_USER, which is reloaded each time that Windows XP starts.

HKEY_CURRENT_CONFIG

The HKEY_CURRENT_CONFIG is another key that points to information in another location. The only data in this sub-key is a pointer to the neighboring sub-key HKEY_LOCAL_MACHINE\SYSTEM\CurrentControlSet\Hardware Profiles\Current. It is the two sub-keys (software and system) of the HKEY_LOCAL_MACHINE key that are visible in the HKEY_CURRENT_CONFIG key.

Note

If you have worked with previous Windows operating systems, you may recall that there was a configuration for controlling the size and growth rate of the Windows Registry. This feature was known as the Registry Size Limitation (RSL). It was removed in Windows XP in favor of a different strategy. The Registry is now able to grow as large as needed on the hard disk. It is also allowed to occupy as much paged memory as it needs. Although this may sound dire, the only real problem with RSL was when the Registry needed to grow larger than it was allowed. Data could not be either loaded to hives or to the paged memory file. This could make system operation slow and occasionally unstable. With the abundance of system memory and hard disk space on most computers, the relatively diminutive Registry is no longer a burden on system resources.

Each registry key contains a variety of entries (hundreds or thousands of them in some cases) that use one of five data types:

✦ **String Value (REG_SZ):** This is a simple text string of a fixed length.

✦ **Binary Value (REG_BINARY):** This is binary data that is used typically for hardware descriptor information. This data is displayed in hexadecimal form in the Registry Editor application.

✦ **DWORD (REG_DWORD):** This is a 4-byte number. This data type is often used to house parameters for system services and device drivers.

✦ **Multi-string Value (REG_MULTI_SZ):** This is a group of strings that is used for plain-English lists of entries.

✦ **Expandable String Value (REG_EXPAND_SZ):** This data type contains a string that is modified by a process when it accesses the key. This allows them to vary the size and content of the string as needed.

Making Registry Changes

So now you have an idea of what is in the Registry as well as some idea of how the keys relate to each other. The following sections of the Appendix focus on helping you become more comfortable with making changes to the Registry using the regedit application. They also tell you how to locate additional information about modifying the Registry. In this section, three popular types of Registry modifications, commonly called *Tweaks*, are examined: security, appearance, and Windows Explorer changes. In each example, you need to open the Registry Editor application. To do so, perform the following steps:

1. **Click the Start button and then select Run.**

2. **Type** regedt32 **in the box and click OK.** Figure A-1 shows the Registry Editor application.

Before you make any Registry changes, you need to ask yourself a couple of questions.

✦ Did you recently make a restore point?

✦ Will you be in deep trouble if this mission-critical system goes offline?

The answer to the first question should always be *yes.* For the second question, if the answer is *no* or *This system isn't mission critical,* then you should be safe to experiment. If the answer to the second question is *yes* in any form, then you need to make sure that you have a backup and backup plan in the event that you corrupt the Registry and make the system unusable. Always practice new Registry changes on non-mission-critical systems if at all possible.

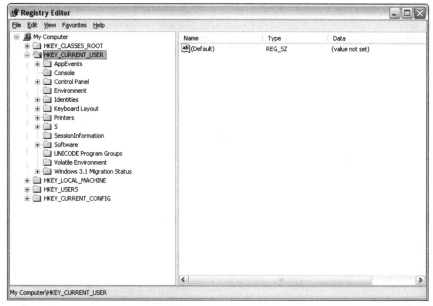

Figure A-1: The Registry Editor

Security Tweaks

Security tweaks are focused on either removing dangerous default system behaviors, or trying to rein in dangerous end-user behaviors. In this first tweak you remove the ability of Internet Explorer to cache passwords.

1. **Open the Registry Editor.**

2. **Disable cache passwords:**

   - **To only changes the currently logged-on user:** Browse to the HKEY_ CURRENT_USER\Software\Microsoft\Windows\CurrentVersion\ Internet Settings folder.

   - **To disable caching for all users:** Browse to the HKEY_USERS\.DEFAULT\ Software\Microsoft\Windows\CurrentVersion\Internet Settings folder.

3. **While the Internet Settings folder is highlighted, click Edit, and then click New and select the DWORD value.** You can give the new value a name, such as IE passwords.

4. **Double-click the entry that you have just created.**

5. **In the value box that opens, change the default value from 0 to 1.**

In a second (and last) security-related change, you learn how to clear the last logged-on username. When you've made this change, anyone logging on to the computer will not see the logon name of the last user to successfully access the computer. If you use the Welcome screen, then you do not see the last logged-on username anyway, and so you must disable the Welcome screen if you want to test this tweak.

1. **Open the Registry Editor.**

2. **In the Registry Editor, browse to the network configuration key called HKEY_LOCAL_MACHINE\SOFTWARE\Microsoft\Windows\CurrentVersion\ Policies\System.**

3. **Create a new DWORD entry called DontDisplayLastUserName and set the value to 1.**

4. **Log out and then log back on. The username field should now be blank.**

Appearance Tweaks

You can change many visualization options in Windows using the Registry. In the following example, you change the menu delay setting. By default, when you are browsing menus under Windows XP (for example, the Start menu), the delay is 400ms. Any value between 0ms and 999ms is valid.

1. **In the Registry Editor, browse to the network configuration key called HKEY_CURRENT_USER\Control Panel\Desktop.**

2. **Locate the MenuShowDelay DWORD entry, and set the value to one extreme or the other (0 or 999).**

3. **Close the Registry Editor, log off, and then log back on.** Begin browsing the menus to see the new menu settings. By setting the delay to an extreme value, the effect should be obvious.

Another interesting trick is to absolutely position your wallpaper. If you have a small background image and you want to position it in the upper right-hand corner, instead of tiling, stretching, or centering it, you can do so with the following steps.

1. **In the Registry Editor, browse to the network configuration key called HKEY_CURRENT_USER\Control Panel\Desktop.**

2. **Create two regular string values.** Use the name Wallpaperoriginx for one value and Wallpaperoriginy for the other. The values of each variable alter the related X/Y coordinate of the picture that you use for your wallpaper.

3. **Log out and then log back on to see your changes.**

Home (X=0, Y=0) is right around your start button. Increasing the X value moves the image to the right, and increasing the Y value moves the image up. You need to use a small image to see the effect of this modification. For example, the Zapotec wallpaper that comes with Windows XP works well.

Windows Explorer

Another element of Windows XP that can be customized with Registry changes is Windows Explorer. We begin with a relatively trivial change, but it is fun if you like to alter the appearance of Windows. You can change the color of encrypted files when they are seen in Windows Explorer.

1. **Open the Registry Editor and locate the key HKEY_CURRENT_USER\ Software\Microsoft\Windows\CurrentVersion\Explorer.**

2. **Within the above key, create a new binary value called AltEncryptionColor.** This value takes values in the form of RR GG BB OO. By assigning the RR GG BB elements numerical values of 01 to 99, you control the "mix" of the color that will be used to show encrypted files in Windows Explorer. For example, 90 90 90 would result in a black color, while 00 90 00 is almost pure blue.

3. **Open Windows Explorer and use the Folder options entry on the Tools menu to verify that encrypted files are going to be shown in color (under the View tab).**

4. **Log out and then log back in.** Right-click a folder, and select Properties from the contextual menu that appears. Click the Advanced button. Enable encryption. You should now see your custom color.

Because encryption is under discussion, we can look at another related Registry tweak. In this next series of steps, you enable encryption options from the contextual menu that appears when you right-click a file or folder.

1. **With regedt32 open, browse to the HKEY_LOCAL_MACHINE\SOFTWARE\ Microsoft\Windows\CurrentVersion\Explorer\Advanced key.**

2. **Create a DWORD entry called EncryptionContextMenu.**

3. **Double-click this entry and enable it by setting the value to 1.**

4. **Log out and then log back in. Right-click an unencrypted folder.** You can see an option in the contextual menu, called *encrypt*. If you right-click any encrypted file or folder, you will see an option called *decrypt*.

There are many changes that you can make by *hacking* the Registry. In the following section ("Additional Resources"), we look at some potential resources for additional walk-through examples, and ways to study the Registry in greater depth. Before we do that, let's look at some of the functions of the Registry Editor that you may find handy.

1. **Open up the regedt32 application and click any key within HKEY_LOCAL_ MACHINE.**

2. **Click File and then click Export.** A dialog box appears asking where you want to save the exported registry key.

3. **Save it to your desktop and name the file *sample*.** Minimize everything and then go to the file on your desktop called sample.reg.

4. **Right-click the file and then select Edit from the contextual menu that appears.** Figure A-2 shows what Registry information looks like when it appears as ASCII text.

You can use these .reg files to move Registry information from one computer to another. For example, if you copy this exported sample.reg file to another system and then execute it by double-clicking it, you are asked whether you want to merge the information in this file with your Registry. These Registry files are really scripts that tell Windows what changes to make to the Registry. One useful application for these exported files is in the support of logon scripts. The .reg file can be embedded in any .cmd, .bat, or Windows Scripting Host-compatible file, and invoked at logon to automate the distribution of Registry customizations.

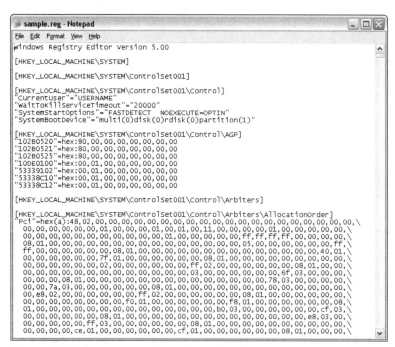

Figure A-2: Text representation of a registry key

There are two other features with which you should become familiar. First is the Registry search function. This works just like most text searches. You enter the string that you are looking for, and then specify what kinds of Registry objects you want to find, such as keys, values, or data. You can access the search option from the Edit menu, or the contextual menu that appears when you right-click any key or value.

The second feature is the Connect to Network Registry option under the File menu. If you are logged on as a user that has administrative rights to another computer on your network, then you can use this option to connect to the computer's Registry. However, you cannot access all of the same keys; for example, the HKEY_CURRENT_USER key is not viewable over a network connection.

Additional Resources

It is possible, at some point, that you will have a specific change that you want to make, or a problem that you want to solve. In these situations, you can benefit from guidance by those who have *been there, done that.* The Internet is filled with resources and technical information. Some resources are useful, while others are not. Below is a list of some sites that I have found useful.

✦ **WinGuides:** This is a Registry guide for Windows at http://www.winguides. com/registry/ that contains a wealth of configuration examples for many versions of Windows. In general, most of the examples for both Windows 2000 and Windows XP are usable with XP, but this is not always the case. Remember the note earlier in this chapter about making a restore point and not tweaking critical systems? If you plan on trying to use instructions for one operating system on another, then you must prepare for the worst, even though in most cases your changes simply do nothing at all.

✦ **Microsoft Registry Editor Overview:** This is a tidy little article authored by the folks at Microsoft, concerning the features of the Registry Editor. Check it out at http://www.microsoft.com/resources/documentation/windows/xp/all/ proddocs/en-us/regedit_overview.mspx.

✦ **Tech Net and the Microsoft Developers Network (MSDN):** These two sites contain information about what a particular key does. This is not always the easiest way to find information, but when you find what you are looking for, it is usually worth the effort. Tech Net is found at http://www.microsoft.com/ technet/default.mspx and MSDN is found at http://msdn.microsoft.com/ default.aspx.

Index

Continued

Continued

Continued

Microsoft®
Most Valuable
Professional

The Microsoft Most Valuable Professional (MVP) Program recognizes and thanks outstanding members of technical communities for their community participation and willingness to help others. The program celebrates the most active community members from around the world who provide invaluable online and offline expertise that enriches the community experience and makes a difference in technical communities featuring Microsoft products.

MVPs are credible, technology experts from around the world who inspire others to learn and grow through active technical community participation. MVPs represent a wide range of backgrounds, covering over 75 Microsoft technologies and 81 countries worldwide.

While MVPs come from many backgrounds and a wide range of technical communities, they share a passion for technology and a demonstrated willingness to help others. Microsoft MVPs are simply an amazing group of individuals who share a commitment to helping others in technical communities around the globe.

Microsoft MVPs are recognized throughout the industry as being outstanding experts in their communities, providing an independent voice in the community. The Microsoft MVP Program is how Microsoft formally acknowledges the accomplishments of these individuals and thanks them for their contributions to community.